D0882912

Biography Today

Profiles of People of Interest to Young Readers

Volume 15 — 2006
Annual Cumulation

Cherie D. Abbey
Managing Editor

615 Griswold Street
Detroit, Michigan 48226

Cherie D. Abbey, *Managing Editor*

Allison A. Beckett, Peggy Daniels, Sheila Fitzgerald, Margaret Haerens,
Laurie Hillstrom, Anne J. Johnson, Justin Karr, Eve Nagler, Sara Pendergast,
Tom Pendergast, Diane Telgen, and Rhoda Wilburn, *Sketch Writers*

Allison A. Beckett, Mary Butler, and Linda Strand, *Research Staff*

* * *

Peter E. Ruffner, *Publisher*
Frederick G. Ruffner, Jr., *Chairman*
Matthew P. Barbour, *Senior Vice President*
Kay Gill, *Vice President — Directories*

* * *

David P. Bianco, *Marketing Director*
Elizabeth Collins, *Research and Permissions Coordinator*
Kevin Hayes, *Operations Manager*
Barry Puckett, *Librarian*
Cherry Stockdale, *Permissions Assistant*

Shirley Amore, Martha Johns, Kirk Kauffman,
and Johnny Lawrence, *Administrative Staff*

Contents

Preface

Biography Today is a magazine designed and written for the young reader—ages 9 and above—and covers individuals that librarians and teachers tell us that young people want to know about most: entertainers, athletes, writers, illustrators, cartoonists, and political leaders.

The Plan of the Work

The publication was especially created to appeal to young readers in a format they can enjoy reading and readily understand. Each issue contains approximately 10 sketches arranged alphabetically. Each entry provides at least one picture of the individual profiled, and bold-faced rubrics lead the reader to information on birth, youth, early memories, education, first jobs, marriage and family, career highlights, memorable experiences, hobbies, and honors and awards. Each of the entries ends with a list of easily accessible sources designed to lead the student to further reading on the individual and a current address. Retrospective entries are also included, written to provide a perspective on the individual's entire career.

Biographies are prepared by Omnigraphics editors after extensive research, utilizing the most current materials available. Those sources that are generally available to students appear in the list of further reading at the end of the sketch.

Indexes

Cumulative indexes are an important component of *Biography Today*. Each issue of the *Biography Today* General Series Annual Cumulation includes a **Cumulative General Index**, which comprises all individuals profiled in *Biography Today* since the series began in 1992. The names appear in bold-faced type, followed by the issue in which they appeared. This index also contains the occupations, nationalities, and ethnic and minority origins of individuals profiled. The Cumulative General Index is followed by the **Places of Birth Index** and the **Birthday Index**. These three indexes, along with a **Names Index**, are featured on our web site, www.biographytoday.com. All *Biography Today* indexes are cumulative, including all individuals profiled in both the General Series and the Subject Series.

Our Advisors

This series was reviewed by an Advisory Board comprised of librarians, children's literature specialists, and reading instructors to ensure that the concept of this publication—to provide a readable and accessible biographical magazine for young readers—was on target. They evaluated the title as it developed, and their suggestions have proved invaluable. Any errors, however, are ours alone. We'd like to list the Advisory Board members, and to thank them for their efforts.

Gail Beaver
Adjunct Lecturer
University of Michigan
Ann Arbor, MI

Cindy Cares
Youth Services Librarian
Southfield Public Library
Southfield, MI

Carol A. Doll
School of Information Science and Policy
University of Albany, SUNY
Albany, NY

Kathleen Hayes-Parvin
Language Arts Teacher
Birney Middle School
Southfield, MI

Karen Imarisio
Assistant Head of Adult Services
Bloomfield Twp. Public Library
Bloomfield Hills, MI

Rosemary Orlando
Director
St. Clair Shores Public Library
St. Clair Shores, MI

Our Advisory Board stressed to us that we should not shy away from controversial or unconventional people in our profiles, and we have tried to follow their advice. The Advisory Board also mentioned that the sketches might be useful in reluctant reader and adult literacy programs, and we would value any comments librarians might have about the suitability of our magazine for those purposes.

Your Comments Are Welcome

Our goal is to be accurate and up-to-date, to give young readers information they can learn from and enjoy. Now we want to know what you think. Take a look at this issue of *Biography Today*, on approval. Write or call me with your comments. We want to provide an excellent source of biographical information for young people. Let us know how you think we're doing.

Cherie Abbey
Managing Editor, *Biography Today*
Omnigraphics, Inc.
615 Griswold Street
Detroit, MI 48226

editor@biographytoday.com
www.biographytoday.com

Congratulations!

Congratulations to the following individuals and libraries, who are receiving a free copy of *Biography Today* for suggesting people who appeared in 2006:

Kay Altland, West York Middle School Library, York, PA

Patricia Earl, Romeo High School Library, Romeo, MI

Lucille M. Koors, Manual High School Media Center, Indianapolis, IN

Mike Lajoie, Mansfield, MA

Renee Laune, New Haven, MO

Shatonna Lucius, Chicago, IL

Nicole Nava, Austin, TX

Howard Norris, Toledo, OH

Stephanie Nunez, North Heights, CA

Steven Ott, Oak Lawn, IL

Sarah Puckett, Northville, MI

Mary Beth Rapai, Frenchtown Township, MI

Marissa Rayford, Riverdale, MD

Rick Rill, Crystal Lake South High School Library, Crystal Lake, IL

Ashley Squires, Charlotte, NC

Theresa Velez-Balay, Rio Linda Junior High School Library, Rio Linda, CA

Tiffany Wood, Lehigh Acres, FL

Joyce Word, Watkins Middle School Library, Houston, TX

Carol Bellamy 1942-
American Lawyer, Politician, and Social Activist
Served as Executive Director of UNICEF and
Director of the Peace Corps

BIRTH

Carol Bellamy was born on January 14, 1942, in Plainfield,
New Jersey. She was the oldest of two children born to Lou
Bellamy, a telephone installer, and his wife Frances, a nurse.
She has one younger brother, Robert.

YOUTH AND EDUCATION

Bellamy grew up in Scotch Plains, New Jersey. She has described herself as "a pretty independent kid. . . . I never really

discussed things with anybody. I just made up my own mind." As a student at Scotch Plains-Fanwood High School, Bellamy acted in student plays, participated in sports, sang in the choir, and served as president of the debate club.

After graduating from high school around 1960, Bellamy enrolled at Gettysburg College in Pennsylvania, where she studied sociology and psychology. While studying in the college library one night, she came across a pamphlet describing a new service organization called the Peace Corps.

The Peace Corps was established by the U.S. government in 1961. It is a program that sends volunteers (usually college-aged students) to live and work in developing nations, where they support and train local communities in such skills as farming, technology, health, business practices, construction, and environmental preservation. Bellamy was inspired to join the Peace Corps after earning her bachelor's degree in 1963. "I was a bright-eyed, bushy-tailed liberal-arts graduate ready to save the world," she said of her decision. "I was absolutely unqualified to do anything."

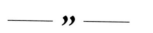

> *Bellamy was inspired to join the Peace Corps after finishing college. "I was a bright-eyed, bushy-tailed liberal-arts graduate ready to save the world," she said of her decision. "I was absolutely unqualified to do anything."*

Bellamy served for two years in the Central American nation of Guatemala. During this time, she worked on a chicken farm, ran a lunch program for schoolchildren, and hosted a radio show called "The Housewife's Hour" that promoted family health and nutrition. Bellamy learned a great deal from her experiences in the Peace Corps. "What I took out of the Peace Corps was that you need to be willing to try a lot of different things, and actually fail in some things," she related. "You get up and wipe your nose, and head forward." She also said that spending two years in Guatemala showed her that "there's a whole big world out there and you ought to give it a try."

Bellamy's time in the Peace Corps raised her interest in politics and international relations. Upon returning to the United States in 1965, she enrolled in the School of Law at New York University. She worked as a waitress in order to pay for her tuition and expenses, and she earned her law degree in 1968.

CAREER HIGHLIGHTS

Armed with her Peace Corps experience and law degree, Bellamy accepted a job as an associate attorney in a prestigious New York law firm in 1968. In addition to her work with the firm, she used her legal skills to help people in several other ways. For example, at that time organized demonstrations to oppose the Vietnam War were common, and many protesters were arrested. Bellamy helped create a group called the Lawyers Committee to End the War, which provided pro bono (free) legal services to people who were arrested for protesting against the war. She also joined the Council of New York Law Associates, which enabled her to support community organizations and antipoverty programs while learning about public policy issues. This experience provided her with a good foundation to enter politics.

Entering Public Service and Politics

Bellamy served for one year as the assistant commissioner for New York City's Department of Mental Health. Then, in 1972, she decided to run for the New York State Senate. She was elected and served two terms in office. One of the issues she supported during her campaign was passage of the Equal Rights Amendment (ERA), which would have changed the U.S. Constitution to specifically ensure legal equality between men and women. Although the New York State legislature voted to ratify (approve) the amendment, it was eventually defeated when it failed to be ratified by two-thirds of the states.

At the end of her second term as a state senator, Bellamy considered running for several higher offices, including the U.S. Congress and the New York State attorney general. She eventually set her sights on becoming the president of the New York City Council. As head of the group that works with the mayor and other officials to run the city's affairs, the council president is the second-most-powerful job in city government. Bellamy won the Democratic Party primary (a preliminary election to determine the final slate of candidates who compete in the general election). She beat four men, including the sitting council president, Paul O'Dwyer. In the general election she earned over 80 percent of the vote to beat her Republican opponent, John A. Esposito. Elected in 1978, Bellamy became the first female president of the New York City Council.

The liberal-minded Bellamy quickly gained notice for her outspokenness and activism. She made headlines because of her frequent clashes with the city's mayor, Ed Koch, on such issues as public safety, social services, taxes, and budgets. In her seven years in office, Bellamy led notable improvements in the areas of public transportation, mental health services, and gay

Bellamy in her office in 1981, as president of the New York City Council.

rights. "If you were a woman in the public arena, you were expected by your constituents to carry an additional burden, to automatically represent women's issues," she recalled of her career in politics. "I could say I'd rather talk about the city's pothole problems, but the reality was that if I didn't bring women's and children's issues up, no one else did."

In 1985 Bellamy decided to run against Koch in hopes of becoming the Democratic Party candidate for mayor of New York City. She was the first woman ever to run for mayor of the nation's largest city. In her campaign, Bellamy emphasized the need to improve the city's social services, infrastructure, housing, and transportation. When Koch defeated her and other opponents in the Democratic primary, Bellamy decided to run in the general election as the candidate of the Liberal Party. Koch won the general election as well, though, gaining almost 80 percent of the vote, while Bellamy earned only 10 percent.

In order to run for mayor, Bellamy had to step down from her position on the city council. When her term ended on January 1, 1986, she accepted a new job as an investment banker with Morgan Stanley & Co. Bellamy's work in finance continued to focus on community issues, such as providing funds for the improvement of schools and hospitals. "If it hadn't been about making people's lives better, I couldn't have done it," she said of her work in investment banking.

After four years out of the public eye, Bellamy decided to run for the office of state comptroller in New York. The comptroller is in charge of overseeing the state's finances and pension fund. The campaign against her Republican opponent, Edward V. Regan, was heated and controversial. Bellamy narrowly lost the election and returned to her work in investment banking, this time with Bear Stearns Companies. In 1993 Regan resigned, and she appealed to state lawmakers to appoint her to the position. As Bellamy saw it, her strong showing in the 1990 election indicated that voters supported her for the job. But the governor of New York, Mario Cuomo, promoted another candidate instead.

Becoming Director of the Peace Corps

Bellamy's many achievements in law, politics, and finance—as well as her reputation as an activist for liberal causes—caught the attention of President Bill Clinton. (For more information on Clinton, see *Biography Today General Series* July 1992 and Updates in the Annual Cumulations for 1994-2001.) Shortly after taking office in 1993, Clinton offered Bellamy the opportunity to serve in his administration as either deputy secretary of transportation or director of the Peace Corps. She chose the Peace Corps job, becoming the first volunteer ever to go on to run the organization. "I hoped that, at least as I visited volunteers in the field, I could bring kind of a sim-

Bellamy was the first Peace Corps volunteer ever to go on to run the organization. "I hoped that, at least as I visited volunteers in the field, I could bring kind of a simpatico for both the highs and the lows, the joys and the sorrows, the difficult moments, the lonely moments, and yet the wonderful exhilarating moments that volunteers experience," she stated.

patico for both the highs and the lows, the joys and the sorrows, the difficult moments, the lonely moments, and yet the wonderful exhilarating moments that volunteers experience," she stated.

In the years before Bellamy took over, the Peace Corps had suffered from funding cuts and poor leadership, so she found herself with many challenges to address. Bellamy decided that her priorities would be to increase the number of volunteers that joined the Peace Corps, improve their training, and ensure their safety. She also focused on publicizing the organization's activities more aggressively and finding ways for returning volun-

In her role as Executive Director of UNICEF, Bellamy visits a girls' school in Kabul, Afghanistan, in 2003, after the fall of the Taliban allowed girls to return to school.

teers to continue their service in the United States, by contributing their skills in schools or other social service agencies. Under her leadership, the Peace Corps increased the number of countries it served as well as the number of volunteers in its ranks.

Assuming Leadership of UNICEF

Bellamy's high-profile role as the head of the Peace Corps, along with her achievements in the areas of children's health and welfare, made her an excellent candidate to assume leadership of UNICEF. The United Nations International Children's Emergency Fund (UNICEF) was created in 1946 to provide food and health care to children in Europe after World War II. (Although the organization later changed its name to United Nations Children's Emergency Fund, it is still referred to as UNICEF.) Within a few years UNICEF expanded its activities to other parts of the world, wherever children's welfare was threatened by poverty and disease.

In 1995 United Nations Chairman Boutros Boutros-Ghali announced that he was seeking a female candidate to fill the position of executive director of UNICEF. (For more information on Boutros Boutros-Ghali, see *Biogra-*

phy Today General Series Apr. 1993 and Update in the 1998 Annual Cumulation.) After considering several European candidates, Boutros-Ghali selected Bellamy for the job. As was the case when she took over the Peace Corps, she immediately faced several problems as head of UNICEF, including a financial scandal. Critics of the organization's previous leadership charged that funds had been poorly managed and misused in some areas.

In addition to addressing these concerns, Bellamy focused on five key priorities for the organization: promoting immunization against disease; ensuring the availability of quality schooling for all boys and girls; limiting the spread of HIV/AIDS and reducing its effect on the lives of young people; protecting children from domestic violence and other forms of abuse and exploitation; and creating early childhood programs to ensure that very young children were healthy and ready for school. "I can think of no work that is more vital to humanity than working to ensure that children everywhere survive their early years and grow up with health, dignity, and peace," she said of her role in UNICEF.

"I can think of no work that is more vital to humanity than working to ensure that children everywhere survive their early years and grow up with health, dignity, and peace," Bellamy said of her role in UNICEF.

Bellamy encouraged world leaders to realize that investing in the health, education, and safety of children would help end poverty and instability in their countries. She also expanded UNICEF's focus to address the abuse and exploitation of children around the world who are forced to perform dangerous jobs, serve as soldiers, or work as slaves. As part of her job, Bellamy often visited 20 or more countries a year. She went to the war-torn nation of Afghanistan, for instance, to address the Taliban, the strict Islamic government that ruled the country from 1996 until 2001. Bellamy challenged the Taliban to change its policy forbidding girls to attend school. She also met with leaders of African countries where HIV/AIDS affects the lives of millions of children.

In 2002 the United Nations General Assembly on Children held a special session in New York City. This international conference about the issues facing children worldwide was attended by over 7,000 people, including heads of state and other government officials, as well as leaders in the fields of business, academics, and religion. At Bellamy's invitation, hun-

Bellamy speaking to Sri Lankan children forced into a relief camp by the devastating tsunami.

dreds of children from around the world also appeared at the conference to make presentations to the "grown-ups" in attendance. In a speech before the assembled dignitaries, Bellamy asked: "Are you getting all your children into the classroom? Are you protecting all your children against disease? Are they safe from abuse, exploitation, and violence? Unfortunately, we already know the answers. We know we have work to do." The conference resulted in a document titled "A World Fit for Children," which established 21 goals toward promoting the health and welfare of children worldwide. It was adopted by 180 nations.

Another focus of Bellamy's tenure at UNICEF was the importance of meeting the needs of women and mothers in order to build stability for children everywhere. In many countries around the world, women face limited opportunities for education and jobs, physical abuse by husbands and family members, poor health care, and other threats to their well-being. "As women are the primary caretakers of children around the world, the better off women are, the better off their children are," Bellamy explained. "When women are educated, when they are moderately empowered to earn an income, and are generally healthy, their children are more likely to survive, go to school, and grow into productive citizens themselves. That is why educating girls and ensuring the rights of women is central to the vision of UNICEF." Charles MacCormack, president of Save the Children, an international organization dedicated to children's health, praised Bellamy's efforts. "There's no way that children will survive and thrive if their mothers are not healthy and literate," he noted. "Carol was a pioneer in drawing attention to this very crucial reality."

While Bellamy expanded the scope of UNICEF's work, some people expressed concerns that she had lost sight of the organization's original mission: ensuring children's survival by tending to their most basic and immediate health needs. Pointing out that 10.5 million children died each year before reaching the age of five, critics charged that UNICEF could do more good if it returned its focus to countries with high child mortality rates. Yet Bellamy oversaw a number of impressive achievements as head of UNICEF. During her ten years with the organization, child mortality dropped worldwide, incidents of preventable diseases declined, many countries adopted laws protecting and serving children's needs, and the number of children who did not attend school reached an all-time low. In recognition of her accomplishments, *Forbes* magazine named Bellamy as one of the 100 Most Powerful Women in the World in 2004.

"As women are the primary caretakers of children around the world, the better off women are, the better off their children are," Bellamy explained. "When women are educated, when they are moderately empowered to earn an income, and are generally healthy, their children are more likely to survive, go to school, and grow into productive citizens themselves. That is why educating girls and ensuring the rights of women is central to the vision of UNICEF."

Becoming CEO and President of World Learning

Education has always been a major priority for Bellamy throughout her career. In 2005, after serving two five-year terms as the head of UNICEF, Bellamy resigned to accept a new position as chief executive officer and president of World Learning. World Learning is a private organization based in Vermont that provides education, training, and other programs to promote understanding, social justice, and economic development among nations and cultures. One of World Learning's programs sends high-school students to live in other countries to study new languages, cultures, and environments. "It's great to follow on from my years at UNICEF, during which I saw very clearly how important education is for both individuals and nations," Bellamy explained. Also in 2005, Bellamy was appointed to the New York State Board of Regents, a panel that sets education policy statewide.

HOME AND FAMILY

Bellamy, who describes herself as a "workaholic," is unmarried and has no children.

HOBBIES AND OTHER INTERESTS

Bellamy is a fan of baseball's New York Mets. She also enjoys gardening and hiking. In 1986 she went on an all-women hiking trek through the Himalayas, a mountain range in Tibet.

HONORS AND AWARDS

Award for Innovation in Public Health (*Discover* magazine): 2004

FURTHER READING

Books

Encyclopedia of World Biography Supplement, Vol. 25, 2005

Periodicals

Boston Globe, Dec. 9, 2004
Chicago Tribune, Mar. 27, 1994, p.4
Christian Science Monitor, Nov. 30, 1983, p.3; Nov. 29, 1995, p.13; Dec. 24, 1996, p.12; Apr. 29, 2005, p.7
Current Biography Yearbook, 1999
Los Angeles Times, Apr. 30, 1995, p.M3
New York Times, Oct. 3, 1990, p.B1; Apr. 22, 2002, p.A25; Jan. 14, 2005, p.B2
People, Nov. 27, 2000, p.203
Philadelphia Inquirer, May 25, 1995, p.G8
Washington Post, Sep. 29, 1993, p.A21; Mar. 2, 1994, p.B1

Online Articles

http://ourworld.worldlearning.org
  (*OurWorld*, "UNICEF Director Tapped as New President of World
  Learning," Jan. 18, 2005)
http://www.unicef.org/specialsession
  (UNICEF, "World Leaders Say Yes for Children," May 2005)

Online Database

Biography Resource Center Online, 2005, articles from *Biography Resource
  Center*, 2001; *Encyclopedia of World Biography Supplement*, 2005

ADDRESS

Carol Bellamy
World Learning
P.O. Box 676
Kipling Road
Brattleboro, VT 05302-0676

WORLD WIDE WEB SITES

http://www.peacecorps.gov
http://www.unicef.org
http://www.worldlearning.org

Miri Ben-Ari 1972?-
Israeli-Born American Violinist and Composer
Known as the Hip-Hop Violinist

BIRTH

Miri Ben-Ari was born around 1972 (some sources say 1978)
in Ramat-Gan, Israel, a middle-class suburb of Tel Aviv. Her
father was a violinist. She has described her Jewish family as
"culturally aware" but not religious.

YOUTH

Ben-Ari, known today as the "hip-hop violinist," never heard
hip-hop music as a child in Israel. "I grew up in a classical

bubble," she laughed. "We never had any other type of music in our home—at least not any type with words." She began taking classical violin lessons when she was six years old. "It was very difficult," she remembered, "and that's why I liked it."

Although Ben-Ari quickly demonstrated great promise as a musician, her violin lessons soon became too expensive for her family. Fortunately, she came to the attention of renowned violinist Isaac Stern, who took a special interest in helping promising young artists. (For more information on Stern, see *Biography Today Performing Artists*, Vol. 1.) Recognizing her gift, Stern gave the young musician a violin of her own and arranged for her to receive a scholarship from the America-Israel Cultural Foundation so that she could continue her lessons. Ben-Ari also took private lessons from Stern and from famed violinist Yehudi Menuhin. Despite her training, however, Ben-Ari felt little connection to classical music. "Growing up, I was always looking for something else, but never heard it," she explained.

At the age of 18, Ben-Ari started her mandatory military service (Israel requires all of its citizens to serve two years in the Israeli army). "It directly influenced me and put my life in perspective," she recalled of the experi-

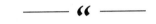

"I grew up in a classical bubble," Ben-Ari laughed. "We never had any other type of music in our home—at least not any type with words."

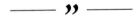

ence. "When you go to basic training, every soldier is a soldier. They treat us the same. And I love that because I seriously believe that every individual is just as good as another individual. Nobody's better than anybody else."

During this time, Ben-Ari auditioned for and was chosen to play in the highly selective Israeli Army String Quartet. She felt grateful for this opportunity to continue her musical training. "If you have a bad audition, you might have to say goodbye to your instrument for two years," she noted. "But I had a good audition." Ben-Ari also served during the 1991 Persian Gulf War. Although she never saw combat, she did see Iraqi missiles sailing through the air above Tel Aviv.

It was also during her military stint that Ben-Ari began to branch out from classical music. The first time she heard an album by the acclaimed jazz saxophonist Charlie Parker, she was hooked. "That was the beginning and end. My soul was sold. He's a genius—the way he plays, he's talking to you," she explained. "I just loved it. It's all coming out of love. When you love something, you'll do anything to pursue, develop, evolve, and go with it."

EDUCATION

Ben-Ari received her early education in Tel Aviv. After completing her military service, she moved from Israel to New York City to study jazz at the Mannes School of Music, and she also continued taking private violin lessons. Further musical education came from the clubs where she performed and the studios where she worked as a background musician. "For the most part I learn on stage and from listening to records, which is real school," she said. "Every time I listen to music I learn. I never stop playing and I will always learn."

> "For the most part I learn on stage and from listening to records, which is real school," Ben-Ari said. "Every time I listen to music I learn. I never stop playing and I will always learn."

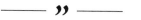

CAREER HIGHLIGHTS

Miri Ben-Ari has brought a new sound to the music world through her crisp, percussive violin and keen ear for melody. From classical to jazz to hip-hop — with forays into pop, blues, Latin, Middle Eastern, klezmer, and Celtic — Ben-Ari has explored multiple musical forms with her violin. Rather than moving progressively through the genres, abandoning one when she picks up another, she has incorporated elements from each into her music. "Music is music," she said simply. "You're always developing, just taking a journey of music. You don't leave one thing. You move on, but you don't leave things behind. You take things with you."

Joining the Jazz Scene

After hearing the music of Charlie Parker, Ben-Ari began playing jazz herself. In the late 1990s she moved from Israel to the United States, determined to make a name for herself as a jazz musician. Although she studied for a time at the Mannes School of Music in New York City, she soon devoted herself to professional work. She played in orchestra pits for such Broadway productions as *Miss Saigon* and *Les Miserables* and in such jazz clubs as New York's legendary Blue Note. Ben-Ari also performed as a

Ben-Ari with Kanye West performing at the American Music Awards, 2004.

background musician with R&B singer Luther Vandross, guitarist Les Paul, and the singing group Manhattan Transfer. During this formative period of her career, she also found jazz mentors like trumpet player Wynton Marsalis. "When you're on the stage with a person like Wynton Marsalis," she said, "you just humble yourself, listen, and learn."

A chance encounter brought Ben-Ari together with the jazz vocalist Betty Carter, and soon the violinist joined the late singer's jazz education program, Jazz Ahead. "The whole idea behind Jazz Ahead," Ben-Ari explained, was "being yourself and not sounding like someone else." In 1998 they performed together at the Kennedy Center in Washington, DC. Ben-Ari credits Carter for teaching her "the importance of being original and the importance of not being afraid to be original. To stick to your guns with pride," she said. "You are who you are and that's it."

With her entry into jazz, Ben-Ari's reputation as a passionate, no-holds-barred performer grew. "Miri Ben-Ari plays the violin like her life depended on it," the *Village Voice* raved. She also completed three albums in short order. Her first, *Sahara,* was released in 1999 and featured all her own compositions. "The songs have clearly pronounced melodies," Jason Koransky wrote in *Down Beat,* "combining a decisively contemporary, funky sound with a jazz fiddle sensibility emerging from early swing and hot jazz."

Her next CD, *The Song of the Promised Land,* released in 2000, featured Marsalis on trumpet on two selections. Mike Joyce in the *Washington Post* praised the call-and-response between Marsalis and Ben-Ari on the album's title track. "Her impressive horn-like agility betrays her bop influences, and her Middle East background sometimes colors her tone and writing," the reviewer said of Ben-Ari. "Yet swing she does." Ben-Ari dedicated the album to the cause of peace in the Middle East. "Music is the biggest proof that you can take people from different backgrounds, and they can communicate with each other on a high level," she noted. "I wish that the Middle East would come up with some other kind of communication that can transcend this fighting." In 2003 Ben-Ari released a live album, *Temple of the Beautiful,* which was recorded at the Blue Note jazz club.

> "
>
> *"Nobody likes you the way a hip-hop audience likes you," Ben-Ari said. "It's so true and raw, the attitudes and emotions of hip-hop. This music is about soul, it's about truth, it's about honesty."*
>
> "

Busting into Hip-Hop

During the period when Ben-Ari was recording her three jazz albums, she also worked as a studio musician and helped arrange songs for rap and R&B artists like Alicia Keys, Jay-Z, and Wyclef Jean. She soon found herself drawn to hip-hop. "Right away, I knew hip-hop was for me. It was all about being who you are and not being who you're not," she noted. "Sometimes when I play the violin, I feel like I'm spittin' a verse. I feel like I'm a rapper because I don't hold back."

Before long, Ben-Ari's unique "urban classical" sound helped her move from the studio background into the spotlight. She began writing, producing, and performing for such diverse artists as Allure, Dallas Austin, Brandy, Janet Jackson, Jay-Z, Joe, Patti LaBelle, Jennifer Lopez, Mya, Rahzal, Britney Spears, Thalia, 3LW, and The X-ecutioners. Over time, she built a solid rep-

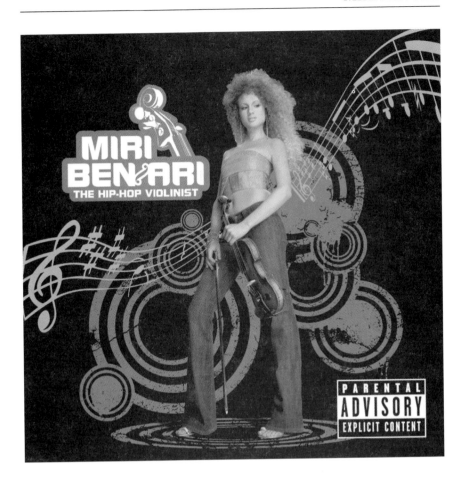

utation as a skilled and versatile collaborator. The challenge of blending her classical/jazz sound with the heavy percussion and strong vocals of hip-hop music appealed to Ben-Ari. "There are challenges in all types of music," she noted. "Hip-hop is hip-hop. It's not classical. It's not jazz. It's not pop music or bubblegum music. Hip-hop is its own unique genre."

Soon Ben-Ari began performing with popular rappers Biggie and Puff Daddy at venues like Carnegie Hall and the Apollo Theater. Her break-through performance on NBC's "Showtime at the Apollo" drew a standing ovation, and she followed up with appearances on BET's music shows "106 and Park" and "Rap City." Each appearance on the cable network drew unprecedented amounts of viewer correspondence, with fans demanding to know more about the "hip-hop violinist." Ben-Ari's subsequent appearance on Twista's hit single and music video "Overnight Celebrity" brought the musician even further into the limelight.

Among those impressed with the hip-hop virtuoso was Kanye West, who asked Ben-Ari to write, produce, arrange, and perform the strings on his blockbuster 2004 debut album, *The College Dropout*. The CD received both popular and critical acclaim, and its breakout smash "Jesus Walks" won the 2005 Grammy for Best Rap Song. Ben-Ari went on tour with West for sold-out performances throughout the country and appeared with the rapper on major television shows, including "The Late Show with David Letterman" and "The Tonight Show with Jay Leno."

———— **"** ————

"I don't hold anything back," Ben-Ari stated. "And that's my advice to young players. You might play classical. You can play jazz. You can play hip-hop. But whatever you do, let the world hear everything you have. Don't you dare hold anything back. That's the attitude that will help you succeed."

———— **"** ————

Ben-Ari's energetic live performances have been described as legendary. "The way that I play," she said, "I don't hold back. When I get on stage, I give my hundred percent. There's something about hip-hop that allows me to do that. Nobody likes you the way a hip-hop audience likes you. It's so true and raw, the attitudes and emotions of hip-hop. This music is about soul, it's about truth, it's about honesty."

Earning a Place in the Spotlight

How a classically trained Israeli violinist could be so naturally gifted in rap music is a mystery even to Ben-Ari. "Whenever I play, it just comes out like R&B and hip-hop," she related. "I said to my mom that I must have been black in a past life; it just comes to me. I don't even try. It's just sick, you know what I'm sayin'? It's like going to a foreign country for the first time and being able to speak the language." Ben-Ari claimed that growing up in the conflict-ridden Middle East provided her with a unique connection to rap music. "It's not easy living in Israel," she explained. "It's very rough, and there's constant struggle. And that struggle makes you stronger. That's part of what attracted me to hip-hop — it's raw, and the independent spirituality and philosophy behind it is part of who I am."

In 2005 Ben-Ari released her fourth album, *The Hip-Hop Violinist*. It blends her strings with vocals from singers like Fabolous, Anthony Hamilton, Lil' Mo, Musiq, Mya, Pharoahe Monch, Scarface, and Twista. The project is "hard to explain," Ben-Ari noted. "There's nothing like it. The only thing I could compare it to would be Carlos Santana's projects, because he's an instrumentalist who mixes different elements like pop, rock, and Latin music. And I'm doing the same with classical and hip-hop."

Ben-Ari described the album's first single, "We Gonna Win," recorded with lyricist Styles P, as "a song of triumph. It represents my personal belief that with hard work, talent, and dedication, everything is possible. It's a one-of-a-kind marriage between rap and classical music, where the music doesn't accompany the vocalist, but rather stands on its own."

"One of a kind" is a term that has often been applied to Ben-Ari, as well. "When you create something totally brand new," she said, "there's no history. It's a lot of work, belief, and letting people know there's room for it." Reflecting on her eclectic "urban music" fusion of hip-hop, rhythm and blues, jazz, and classical forms, Ben-Ari noted that "Whatever kind of musician you are, you take everything you know, and you bring it to the music you are making. I don't limit myself to one style or form. It's just music. It's all good. It's all beautiful."

With concert tours and more collaborations in the works, the Israeli-born, classically trained, hip-hop violinist has shown the world she can stand on her own. "I don't hold anything back," Ben-Ari stated. "And that's my advice to young players. You might play classical. You can play jazz. You can play hip-hop. But whatever you do, let the world hear everything you have. Don't you dare hold anything back. That's the attitude that will help you succeed."

HOME AND FAMILY

Ben-Ari, who became a U.S. citizen in 2003, lives in New York City.

SELECTED RECORDINGS

Sahara, 1999
The Song of the Promised Land, 2000
Temple of the Beautiful: Live at the Blue Note, 2003
The Hip-Hop Violinist, 2005

HONORS AND AWARDS

Grammy Award: 2005, Rap Song of the Year, for "Jesus Walks" (with C. Smith and Kanye West)

FURTHER READING

Books

Contemporary Musicians, Vol. 49, 2004

Periodicals

Billboard, Nov. 20, 2004, p.67
Down Beat, Dec. 1999, p.56
Interview, Apr. 2005, p.70
Jerusalem Post, Feb. 24, 2005, p.24
Jewish Week, Sep. 21, 2001, p.45
Miami Herald, Oct. 21, 2004, p.E2
San Luis Obispo Tribune, July 13, 2001, p.3
Strings, Feb. 2005, p.43
Syracuse Post-Standard, Feb. 6, 2001, p.D4
Vibe, July 2004, p.82
Washington Post, Nov. 17, 2000, p.N9

Online Databases

Biography Resource Center Online, 2005, article from *Contemporary Musicians,* 2004

ADDRESS

Miri Ben-Ari
Universal Music Group
2220 Colorado Ave.
Santa Monica, CA 90404

WORLD WIDE WEB SITE

http://www.miriben-ari.com

BLACK EYED PEAS

William Adams (will.i.am) 1975-
Alan Pineda Lindo (apl.de.ap) 1974-
Jamie Gomez (Taboo) 1975-
Stacy Ferguson (Fergie) 1975-
American Hip-Hop Group
Creators of the Hit Records *Elephunk* and *Monkey Business*

EARLY YEARS

The funky hip-hop group the Black Eyed Peas includes four members: will.i.am (William Adams), apl.de.ap (Alan Pineda

Lindo), Taboo (Jamie Gomez), and Fergie (Stacy Ferguson). While each of the Black Eyed Peas comes from a different cultural background, they all had similar experiences growing up. Each was raised by a single parent and grew up in a poor, working-class area in which they were in the minority. For each, their ethnic origins became an important part of their lives. These shared experiences made them more alike than different, which helped them form a strong bond as a group.

―――― " ――――

"The black people hung out by the lunch tables, the Mexicans hung out by the bathrooms, the white people hung out by their cars, the Asian people stood next to their lockers," will recalled. "I would always wander between the different sections. If I didn't go to that school, Black Eyed Peas wouldn't be what it is."

―――― " ――――

will.i.am

will.i.am was born William Adams on March 15, 1975. His mother raised six children by herself, two of whom were adopted. will is African-American and grew up in a Mexican neighborhood in east Los Angeles. His mother set strict rules for will. She wouldn't allow him to wear any clothing with sports logos on it, and he wasn't allowed to wear sneakers either. She made him wear suits most of the time, especially for church every week. He has said that her strictness is the reason that he stayed out of trouble when he was growing up. He attended a mixed-race high school that was a 45-minute bus ride from his home. It was tough at the time, but today he credits his experiences there with helping him define his approach to music. "The black people hung out by the lunch tables, the Mexicans hung out by the bathrooms, the white people hung out by their cars, the Asian people stood next to their lockers," he recalled. "I would always wander between the different sections. If I didn't go to that school, Black Eyed Peas wouldn't be what it is."

apl.de.ap

apl.de.ap (pronounced "apple") was born Alan Pineda Lindo on November 28, 1974, in Sapang Bato, a small town north of Manila in Pampanga, Philippines. His mother, Christina Pineda, is Filipino, and his father was an African-American U.S. Air Force serviceman. His father left the Philippines before he was born, and apl never knew him. He lived with his mother and four brothers and two sisters in the Philippines, and the family struggled financially. apl was adopted by Joe Ben Hudgens, an American attorney who met apl's family through an organization that supports poor children in the Philippines. When he was a teenager, apl moved to Los Angeles, California, to live with his adoptive father. "I left in the afternoon," he recalled about the move, "and it was the saddest sunset ever. I didn't know where I was going. I was 14, and I'm getting on a plane by myself, and I could see the sun set." He struggled as a teenage immigrant. "I would get chased from junior high school to my house every day," he said. "You know, I could have easily joined the gangs that were surrounding me. I was exposed to that. But I chose dancing instead. That led me in a good direction."

—— " ——

Taboo

Taboo was born Jamie Gomez on July 14, 1975. He is Mexican-American and was raised by a single mother. Growing up in Rosemead, California, Taboo was taunted by the neighborhood kids, who made fun of him for being Latino but "dancing black." He didn't care too much what the other kids thought of him, and he continued to develop his break dancing talent. "I grew up in a predominantly Asian and Mexican community," Taboo recalled, "and because I did break dance and poplock and all that, I did get a lot of criticism: 'You're Mexican,

"I would get chased from junior high school to my house every day," apl.de.ap said. "You know, I could have easily joined the gangs that were surrounding me. I was exposed to that. But I chose dancing instead. That led me in a good direction."

—— " ——

why are you doing that?' I would say, 'It don't matter if you're Mexican, white, or black, I just like to dance.' It made me a stronger person. 'Oh yeah? Check this out.' It didn't matter, because I had that skill."

Fergie

Fergie was born Stacy Ferguson on March 27, 1975. She is part white and part Native American. She grew up in Hacienda Heights, California, in a mostly Mexican and Asian neighborhood. Her parents, who were both teachers, separated when she was very young, and afterwards she and her mother had very little money. Growing up, Fergie wore mostly hand-me-down clothes that were given to her family by a local church. She began working in entertainment when she was eight years old, doing voice-overs for commercials and "Peanuts" television specials. She was a cast member on the Disney Channel's Saturday-morning television show "Kids Incorporated" for five years. After that, Fergie was part of Wild Orchid, an all-girl trio that produced two moderately successful albums in the late 1990s. Wild Orchid's pop music style included a lot of harmonizing, which led to comparisons with En Vogue, another female singing group that became popular in the 1990s. Despite the modest success of Wild Orchid, Fergie grew dissatisfied with the group and eventually quit. As a teenager, Fergie said, "I had my white girlfriends and my Mexican friends. . . . I'd go to the beach and to rock concerts, like Metallica, with my white girlfriends. Then I'd go dancing and to house parties with my Mexican girlfriends, and we'd listen to hip-hop and Lisa Lisa and Cult Jam and all that kind of stuff."

> ———— " ————
>
> *As a teenager, Fergie said, "I had my white girlfriends and my Mexican friends. . . . I'd go to the beach and to rock concerts, like Metallica, with my white girlfriends. Then I'd go dancing and to house parties with my Mexican girlfriends, and we'd listen to hip-hop and Lisa Lisa and Cult Jam and all that kind of stuff."*
>
> ———— " ————

FORMING THE BAND

The group that eventually became the Black Eyed Peas was first formed when the boys were just teenagers. will and apl were both living in California when they met in the eighth grade in 1989. They shared the same intense interest in the emerging hip-hop scene and quickly became close friends. They joined a break dancing group called Tribal Nation and began performing around Los Angeles. They also spent a lot of time hanging out at the mall, practicing their dance moves. In fact, the two were routinely kicked out of the Glendale Galleria for break dancing.

"We were the only black family in a bad Mexican neighborhood," will recalled, "and apl was the only person my mum allowed me to hang out with because he was a foreigner. I went to good schools. apl was a good influence on my life. I wouldn't be here if he hadn't been sent to America; I would have had nobody to dream with. We would lie awake at night imagining the first time we'd go on stage in New York, and who we would thank if we got an MTV award."

After they graduated from high school, will and apl left the dance group Tribal Nation and created their own group, Atban Klann, which combined break dancing and rap. Atban was an acronym for A Tribe Beyond A Nation, their way of acknowledging their beginnings with Tribal Nation. By 1992, rapper Eazy-E signed Atban Klann to a contract with Ruthless Records. Atban Klann recorded an album, but it was never released. The album didn't fit in with the other Ruthless Records releases, or in any other music category either. Atban Klann's album featured dance tracks and positive raps while all of the other Ruthless artists were doing gangster rap, and the label simply didn't know what to do with will and apl. Eazy-E had been their only supporter at the label, but he was unable to get their record out. After Eazy-E died on March 26, 1995, Atban Klann ended their contract with Ruthless.

While searching for a new direction, will and apl met Taboo at a Los Angeles break dancing club. Taboo was a talented dancer and rapper who had been working odd jobs, most notably cleaning up horse manure at Disneyland and serving lunches in a high school cafeteria. will, apl, and Taboo soon became friends, and the three formed the Black Eyed Peas. The group reportedly had to come up with a new name because the name Atban Klann was owned by Ruthless Records as a term of their old contract. They chose the name Black Eyed Peas because it seemed to represent a humble connection to the soul community. (Black-eyed peas are a simple, popular soul food dish.)

CAREER HIGHLIGHTS

The Black Eyed Peas signed their first record contract with Interscope in 1997. Although their style had caused problems at Ruthless Records, the Peas were hopeful that their new record label would be more supportive. The trio of will, apl, and Taboo forged a new sound together, blending different musical styles and adding creative raps with positive themes. At that time, most other rap and hip-hop acts were focused on violent imagery and darker messages of urban ghetto life. The Peas were reaching back to the earliest days of hip-hop, when party music and dance tracks were the norm. They wanted to bring back some of those themes. "We like to have a good time, but we are positive, conscious people," will said. "Since rapping is what we do, people call us conscious rappers, and that's cool. That's who I am, a conscious person. If I were a plumber, I'd be a conscious plumber."

Early Releases

The Peas released their first record, *Behind the Front*, in 1998. The group had recorded about 50 songs between July 1997 and January 1998. They chose 16 tracks for the record, which music critics described as "food for the hip-

The Black Eyed Peas in performance on the Warped Tour in 1999.

hop soul." *Behind the Front* created a splash because it used live musicians at a time when most other hip-hop performers were using recorded backup sounds. The "relentlessly positive" raps also distinguished the Peas from other hip-hop groups. Their unique style could not be easily categorized. But instead of being a problem for them as it once was, it now allowed them to reach out and connect with many different audiences.

The Peas toured extensively to promote their new record. They were included in a few different multi-band traveling shows, such as the Smokin' Grooves hip-hop tour, the Sno-Core snowboard tour, the Lyricist Lounge hip-hop tour, and the Vans Warped tour featuring punk pop bands. The Peas also opened for OutKast on their tour. (For more information on OutKast, see *Biography Today*, Sep. 2004.) These live performances gave the Peas an opportunity to introduce themselves, and they quickly developed a national fan base. The tours also helped the Peas earn praise from the music industry. *Vibe* credited the Peas with "pushing the culture forward by incorporating funky-fresh dance steps and break dancing moves into their routines." And *Rolling Stone* said that *"Behind the Front* offers an organic mixture of sampled melodies and live instruments aimed at those of us seeking a little enlightenment with our well-oiled boogie."

The Peas released their second album, *Bridging the Gap,* in 2000. Will described the title as a reflection of American culture becoming more and more unified. "The suburbs are becoming urbanized, and urban doesn't mean black anymore, it means Latino, it means poor white folks, it means some Asian people. . . . The music is a bridge," will said. The title *Bridging the Gap* "means we're bridging the gap between rock and hip-hop." The record continued the Peas' tradition of mixing different musical styles to create a unique sound. Several other artists made guest appearances on the record, including rapper Mos Def, singer Macy Gray, and De La Soul, a group that has been an inspiration for the Peas. *Bridging the Gap* was critically acclaimed and received numerous award nominations, particularly for music video awards.

Fergie Joins the Group

The Black Eyed Peas had used back-up singers, notably singer Kim Hill, on their early releases. Hill decided to leave the Peas while the group was working on *Elephunk* in 2001. The group needed to find a singer for the female part in "Shut Up," a male/female duet about the end of a relationship. Fergie was introduced to the group by a mutual friend who thought she might do well with the Peas' freewheeling musical style. The Peas originally planned to have Fergie perform on just that one song, but she meshed so well with the others that they brought her in as a full-fledged Pea. Fergie jumped at the opportunity to join the dynamic group, seeing it as the creative outlet she needed and hadn't yet been able to find in her own music career.

With her performing history, previous experience singing with a band, multicultural background, and open-minded approach to making music, the other Peas thought that Fergie would fit right in. And, in fact, she did. "She's like a sister to us," said will. She soon put her talents to work on many of the album's hit songs, enabling the Peas to attract yet more fans. Despite the fun she has with the Peas, Fergie takes her job very seriously. She says, "I couldn't feel more blessed about the guys taking a chance and putting me in the band. I give 110 percent. This isn't some little cool cute thing I decided to do."

Elephunk

The Peas' third record, *Elephunk,* was released in 2003. "We liked the idea of an elephant meaning something which is strong and can be aggressive, although that isn't its nature," will said. "We wanted to bring in the idea of funk that isn't typical." And *Elephunk* was anything but typical, especially

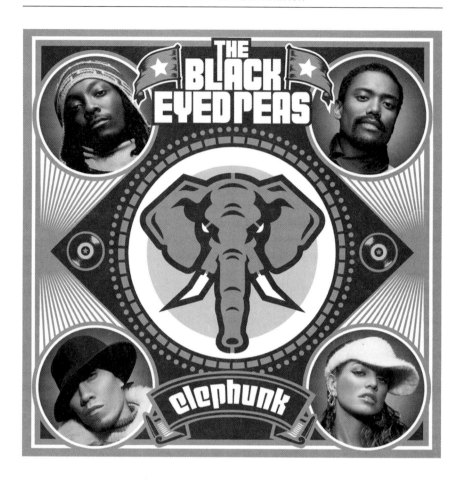

for hip-hop. It blended musical elements of Motown, heavy metal rock, Brazilian samba beats, Jamaican reggae, Middle Eastern sounds, and jazz. It quickly became a gold record, rising to No. 1 on the *Billboard* Top 40 chart and achieving platinum-plus sales.

"Where Is the Love," the Peas' first No. 1 hit song, was written, recorded, and produced with Justin Timberlake. The song is a response to the tragedies of September 11, 2001. As will explained, "9-11 opened our minds up and opened our eyes up. With 'Where Is the Love,' I think we're asking questions the whole world is asking. . . . The song is connecting [with people] because everyone can relate to it." After this successful collaboration, the Peas were invited to tour with Justin Timberlake and pop diva Christina Aguilera. That opportunity helped the Peas expand their fan base even more, and sales of *Elephunk* soared.

Several more songs from the record became hits and were recognized with industry awards. "Let's Get It Started" was awarded the 2004 Grammy for Best Rap Performance by a Duo or Group. "Hey Mama" won a 2004 MTV Video Music Award for Best Choreography. MTV also nominated the song for Best Hip-Hop Video and Best Dance Video that year.

Responding to Criticism

In the midst of the success of *Elephunk*, the Peas were also being harshly criticized by some of their long-time fans. The Peas were accused of "selling out" because they recorded and toured with Justin Timberlake and especially because they added Fergie to the group. Because Timberlake had been part of N'Sync, an all-male group that recorded pop tunes, he was dismissed by some Peas fans as being "too pop." Fergie had also recorded pop songs with Wild Orchid, but beyond that, some Peas fans saw her as lacking in hip-hop credibility and unworthy of being part of the Black Eyed Peas. *Vibe* reports that some fans were complaining that the Peas had become "too commercial" in their quest for hit records.

"They call it a sell-out for what reason? Because we have a white girl in our group now? I don't think that just because one day you do a jazzy record and then you do a funky record, [doesn't] mean you sold out. It just means you like music and you're trying to dabble in every ray of color in the music world."

Fans posting on web site discussion boards were writing things like, "The Black Eyed Peas were dope before when they were underground, and before they got that girl." Fergie was very hurt by such comments. She felt that these fans weren't even giving her a chance. "I've had to prove myself show by show. . . . I cried a lot in the beginning," she admitted. "It was a big change for them. Certain fans from the underground scene didn't want to see their Black Eyed Peas change, and to a lot of people, it was my fault."

But will responded to these comments with surprise, saying, "And they call it a sell-out for what reason? Because we have a white girl in our group now? I don't think that just because one day you do a jazzy record and then you do a funky record, [doesn't] mean you sold out. It just means you like music and you're trying to dabble in every ray of color in the music

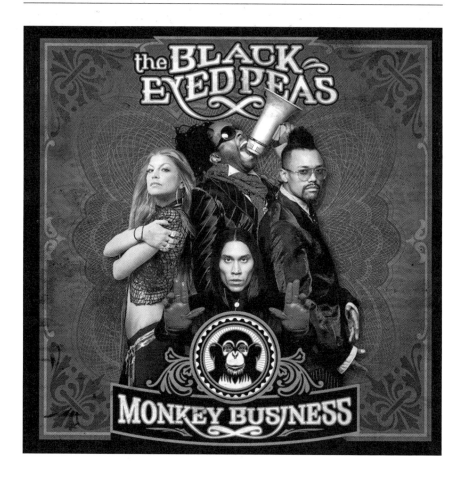

world." The Peas insisted that adding Fergie to the group was not a calculated move to increase record sales. After Kim Hill left the group, they simply needed another female singer. "We had been hanging out with her a lot in 2002, and we just realized that Fergie had the same spirit as us," will explained. "What's more important—appeasing somebody else, or surrounding ourselves with talented [people]? We all knew the answer to that one." The phenomenal success of *Elephunk* proved that most fans agreed.

Monkey Business

After the release of *Elephunk*, the Peas went on tour for 18 months straight. will brought along a mobile recording studio, and *Monkey Business* was recorded all over the world—in airplanes, trains, hotel rooms, and anywhere else the group found themselves with some time to fill. Fergie recalled "It was hard for me to get used to writing and recording on the road, because usually I'm doing studio time all at once, and then touring all at once," Fergie recalled. "This way was a big challenge, but it turned out to be this creative waterfall which just fell down into the huge ocean of *Monkey Business*."

Monkey Business was the first album to be co-written by all four Peas. This produced a record that is musically diverse in the usual Peas way, but also includes some surprises. For example, on the track "Bebot," apl raps the entire song in Tagalog, the language of his home province in the Philippines. "I'm proud of who I am, where I came from, what I was born into, and I would represent that till I die. As much as I could put into this business, I want to involve who I am and my culture." There are also guest spots by Justin Timberlake, British pop singer Sting, and godfather of soul James Brown. "*Monkey Business* is very much about the types of songs we play live. It's about a party," will said. "It's very much about us and the crowd on this record."

> **"**
>
> *Their widespread appeal, according to will, is because the Peas love what they do. "I think the fact that we just have fun with music is the reason why it works for us. . . . It's really that simple."*
>
> **"**

By 2004, *Monkey Business* had triple-platinum sales in Switzerland, Sweden, Germany, the United Kingdom, Australia, New Zealand, Canada and Singapore. The band has performed all over the world, including a tour stop in Vietnam, where they were the first American group to perform since 1972. "Don't Phunk With My Heart" was nominated for Best Group Video in the 2005 MTV Video Music Awards, and the Peas received two American Music Awards in 2005, for Favorite Group in both the Pop/Rock and Rap/Hip-Hop categories.

Living with Fame

The runaway success of their last two records has resulted in lots of new opportunities for the Peas. Their music has been used in ads for Dr. Pepper, iPod, and Best Buy. "Let's Get It Started" has become a sports anthem for NBA basketball, and the Peas performed at the 2005 Super Bowl. "Everybody loves the Black Eyed Peas. The group is a social connector whose music bridges generations," said Tracy Perlman, director of entertainment marketing for the NFL. The Peas even appeared as characters in the computer game "Urbz: Sims in the City," for which they re-recorded some of their hits in Simlish, the language of the Sims world. They have continued to tour with diverse musicians, including the Dave Matthews Band, Cold Play, No Doubt, Metallica, Everclear, Blink-182, and the Rolling Stones. Their widespread appeal, according to will, is because the Peas love what they do. "I think the fact that we just have fun with music is the reason why it works for us. . . . It's really that simple." Taboo agreed, saying that "We make songs that can be understood by the normal listener. You don't have to be a part of the scene to understand what we're talking about."

Fame means that the Peas lead a busy public life on the road. They travel all over the world to perform in concerts and at other events. They participate in charity benefits and fundraisers, and are heavily involved in Rock the Vote, a political awareness group for young people. In between, they field media requests, appear at promotional events, and somehow find time to write and record new music. Taboo describes a typical day in the life of a Pea: "This is how my day goes. We perform at exactly 9:30 at night, get off the stage at about 10:40 p.m., then there's the after party at every city. We're at the after party until like 2 a.m. Then we get on the tour bus, drive for about six hours until we get to the next city, get to the hotel, lay down for a couple of hours, do phoners [phone interviews], and my whole day starts all over again."

> ——— " ———
>
> *Taboo describes a typical day in the life of a Pea: "This is how my day goes. We perform at exactly 9:30 at night, get off the stage at about 10:40 p.m., then there's the after party at every city. We're at the after party until like 2 a.m. Then we get on the tour bus, drive for about six hours until we get to the next city, get to the hotel, lay down for a couple of hours, do phoners [phone interviews], and my whole day starts all over again."*
>
> ——— " ———

But the Peas aren't complaining. All their hard work has begun to pay off, and they have big plans for the future. "We've all worked so long and hard for this," Fergie declared. "And we understand that it can go away, beause we've all tried things that have been less successful. We're definitely all still hungry."

The members of the Black Eyed Peas. From left: apl.de.ap, will.i.am, Taboo, and Fergie.

HOME AND FAMILY

Little has been reported about the home lives of the group members. Perhaps because she is a favorite target of paparazzi and reporters, Fergie keeps quiet about her personal life. Taboo is a single father, raising his son Joshua, who was born in 1993. will admits to working all the time, while apl is planning to bring his family from the Philippines to the U.S.

HOBBIES AND OTHER INTERESTS

Although their busy schedule leaves little time for outside interests, the Peas still manage to pursue their own musical projects. Taboo, apl, and Fergie all plan to release solo albums. Taboo plans a Spanish-language record, apl wants to make a record of Filipino music, and Fergie is preparing an R&B record. will founded his own record label, the will.i.am music group, and has already signed a contract with Fergie for her solo album. will has also teamed up with Justin Timberlake to form JAW Breakers, a record production company. will's entire life is music, and he has a reputation for being a workaholic. "When I go to sleep at 7 in the morning," he revealed, "there is still music playing in my head."

Movie projects are also in the works for some of the Peas. Taboo has a part in *Dirty*, an upcoming movie starring Cuba Gooding Jr. Meanwhile, Fergie is appearing in her first major movie with a part in *Poseidon*, a remake of the 1972 shipwreck disaster film *The Poseidon Adventure*. She will play a singer and perform two songs in the movie, one of which she co-wrote with will specifically for the film. And although apl doesn't have any plans to appear in a movie himself, a Filipino television station has produced a movie based loosely on his life.

The Peas are also involved in projects outside the entertainment industry. A former student at the Los Angeles Fashion Institute of Design and Merchandising, will established his i.am Clothing company and recently premiered his line of women's and men's wear. Meanwhile, Taboo described himself as a dedicated shoe lover and confessed to owning more than 700 pairs. He buys them wherever the Peas travel on tour and jokes about opening his own shoe store someday. Taboo has also been active in philanthropic work; he is funding the development of a community center in his hometown of Rosemead, California.

SELECTED RECORDINGS

Behind the Front, 1998
Bridging the Gap, 2000
Elephunk, 2003
Monkey Business, 2005

HONORS AND AWARDS

Grammy Award: 2004, Best Rap Performance by a Duo or Group, for "Let's Get It Started"; 2006, Best Rap Performance By a Duo Or Group, for "Don't Phunk With My Heart"
American Music Awards: 2005, Favorite Pop/Rock Band, Duo or Group and Favorite Rap/Hip-Hop Band, Duo or Group
Patrick Lippert Award (Rock the Vote): 2005

FURTHER READING

Books

Contemporary Musicians, Vol. 45, 2004

Periodicals

Billboard, July 31, 2004, p.15
Cosmo Girl, Nov. 2004, p.138
Entertainment Weekly, May 27, 2005, p.44

Los Angeles Times, Feb. 4, 2001, p.8
Mix, June 1, 2004, p.7
Newsweek, May 16, 2005, p.66
San Francisco Chronicle, Aug. 8, 2005, p.C1
Seventeen, Sep. 2005, p.222
USA Today, June 9, 2005, p.D7
Vibe, July 2005, p.104

Online Articles

http://www.mtv.com/bands/b/black_eyed_peas/news_feature_053005
(*MTV.com*, "Black Eyed Peas: Mad All Over the Place," May 27, 2005)
http://www.mtv.com/music/#/music/artist/black_eyed_peas/bio.jhtml
(*MTV.com*, "Black Eyed Peas: Bio," undated)
http://www.rollingstone.com/artists/4522/biography
(*RollingStone.com*, "Black Eyed Peas Biography," undated)

Online Databases

Biography Resource Center Online, 2006, article from *Contemporary Musicians*, 2004

ADDRESS

Black Eyed Peas
A&M Records
2220 Colorado Avenue
Santa Monica, CA 90404

WORLD WIDE WEB SITE

http://www.blackeyedpeas.com

Bono 1960-

Irish Musician and Political Activist
Lead Singer and Songwriter for the Rock Group U2
Influential Advocate for Africa, AIDS Victims, and
Debt Relief for Third-World Countries

BIRTH

Bono was born Paul David Hewson on May 10, 1960, in Dublin, Ireland. His father, Robert Hewson, was a postal worker, and his mother, Iris (Rankin) Hewson, was a secretary in a dairy. His only brother, Norman, is seven years older. Norman runs a café in Dublin and has been involved in business ventures with Bono.

YOUTH

Bono was the child of a "mixed marriage": his mother was a Protestant and his father was a Roman Catholic in a strongly Catholic country. When Bono was a boy, children of so-called "mixed marriages" in Ireland were expected to be brought up as Catholics. But his mother raised her sons as Protestants. On Sundays, his father would drop the two boys and their mother off at a Protestant chapel, then wait outside during the service.

This small divide in his family reflected the serious and brutal split that existed in nearby Northern Ireland. The United Kingdom (UK) is made up of four countries: Northern Ireland, plus England, Scotland, and Wales (these three together make up Great Britain). Bono grew up in the Republic of Ireland (usually called just Ireland), which is a separate country. Fierce religious divisions have affected this region. The predominant religion in the United Kingdom is Protestantism, while the predominant religion in Ireland is Catholicism. Northern Ireland included both of these groups: Protestants were the majority and were aligned with the ruling United Kingdom, while Catholics were the minority and wanted the nation to break off from the UK to become part of the inde-

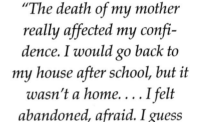

"The death of my mother really affected my confidence. I would go back to my house after school, but it wasn't a home. . . . I felt abandoned, afraid. I guess fear converts to anger pretty quickly. It's still with me."

pendent Republic of Ireland to the south. Brutal violence between the two groups, known as "the troubles," became a regular occurrence through much of the later 20th century.

Throughout his childhood, Bono was aware of the violence that played out almost daily in the struggle between the two factions in Northern Ireland. Although he is an avowed Christian, Bono came away with distaste for organized religion. As he explained to radio host Larry King: "I learned that religion is often the enemy of God. . . . Religion is the artifice — you know, the building — after God has left it."

Bono has very little memory of his childhood. "The little pieces that I can put back together are, if not violent, then aggressive," he said. His relationship with his father was difficult, because his father was often critical and distant. His relationship with his mother was warmer, but she died suddenly after suffering a stroke at her own father's funeral. Bono was only 14 at the time, and the loss was difficult for him: "The death of my mother really affected my confidence. I would go back to my house after school, but it wasn't a home. . . . I felt abandoned, afraid. I guess fear converts to anger pretty quickly. It's still with me."

Bono began to channel his emotions into creative activities, including painting, acting, and ultimately music. In spite of the difficulties at home, music had always filled the Hewson household—anything from Frank Sinatra to classical to opera, which Bono's father loved. "His dad had an incredible voice," a childhood friend said. Bono's older brother taught him to play the guitar and exposed him to the Beatles and other rock groups. John Lennon, with his superb song writing and idealistic vision of world peace, was a major influence on Bono. "I was 13, I suppose, and I became enthralled with his dream," he said. The English new-wave group The Clash was another influence. After he heard them, "a band was what he wanted to do," said his friend Bob Geldof, the singer and leader of the Boomtown Rats, an Irish rock band.

EDUCATION

Bono attended Glasnevin National Primary School in Dublin, where he was a successful and popular student. At age 11, he moved to the next stage of Irish education at a Catholic all-boys' school called St. Patrick's. But things changed there. He lost his motivation, began to skip classes, and developed a reputation as a troublemaker.

His parents decided to move him to the co-educational Mount Temple High School, one of Ireland's first non-religious schools. Though he was still academically restless, he thrived socially and found stimulation among a group of creative and rebellious friends. Together they invented an "alternative community" that they called Lypton Village. "[We] used to put on arts installations, when we were 16, 17, with manic drills and step ladders," Bono said. "We invented our own language, gave each other names, and we'd dress differently." It was from a Lypton Village friend that Bono got his distinctive nickname, which is short for "Bono Vox." The friend lifted the name from a hearing-aid store in Dublin. At the time, Bono didn't realize that the phrase is an approximation of "good voice" in Latin, the language of the ancient Romans—a fitting name for a future singer.

After he graduated from Mount Temple, Bono enrolled briefly at the National University of Ireland to study English and history. But he was thrown out. "I had falsely matriculated [graduated], they told me. In National University, you are supposed to speak the national language, and I didn't," he recalled. "I had flunked Irish [language classes], and they found that out."

CAREER HIGHLIGHTS

Bono gained fame and respect as the lead singer and lyricist for U2, one of the world's most popular rock bands. He is known for his impassioned singing style and for the spiritual foundation of many of his lyrics. Though not openly Christian, many of his songs center on messages of peace, harmony, and fellowship—foundations of the Christian faith. In addition, in the late 1990s, Bono began to promote humanitarian causes. His political work on behalf of developing nations and the poor has won him praise and awards.

Forming a Band

Bono has been part of the band that became U2 since he was just a teenager. When he was 16, he responded to a notice on the school bulletin board posted by Larry Mullen Jr., a fellow student and drummer looking for musicians to form a rock band. Only he and three others turned up at the first meeting: Adam Clayton, who brought a bass guitar, an amp, and a sense of self-confidence that was much bigger than his musical ability; Dave Evans, an experienced guitarist who later adopted the name the Edge; and Evans's brother, Dick, who dropped out of the group in 1978.

"We walked up on stage; I was playing guitar, and when I heard that D chord, I got some kick," Bono said about the band's first gig. "It was like four blind kids blustering away and there was evidence of just a little light in the corner and we started to work towards that. We built ourselves around that spark."

Later, Mullen described the group's initial meeting to *Time* magazine music critic Jay Cocks: "The Edge could play. Adam just looked great. Big, bushy hair, long caftan coat, bass guitar, and amp. He talked like he could play, used all the right words, like gig. I thought, this guy must know how to play," he recalled. "Then Bono arrived, and he meant to play the guitar, but he couldn't play very well, so he started to sing. He couldn't do that either. But he was such a charismatic character that he was in the band anyway, as soon as he arrived. I was in charge for the first five minutes, but as soon as Bono got there, I was out of a job."

U2 performing at the US festival in California in 1983. Bono is in the center at the microphone, with the Edge on guitar on the left.

In spite of his show of confidence at the audition, Bono didn't think he could sing or play well enough to be in a band. But his doubts about his musical ability vanished in the thrill of performing. He told journalist Niall Stokes about the band's first gig: "We walked up on stage; I was playing guitar, and when I heard that D chord, I got some kick," he said. "It was like four blind kids blustering away and there was evidence of just a little light in the corner and we started to work towards that. We built ourselves around that spark."

In its early days, the band went by the names Feedback and The Hype before settling on U2, after an American military aircraft.

U2 Develops Its Songs and Style

Originally, the band members could barely play well enough to imitate other people's songs. So they began to compose their own. They developed an unusual process that has continued throughout their successful career: Bono or the Edge bring an idea to the group — a riff, a fragment of melody, or a phrase. Then Clayton and Mullen participate in actually building the song. In the process, the band tries to pinpoint a powerful, honest emotion or truth in the melody. Only then does Bono begin to work on composing lyrics.

According to Bono, he relies heavily on the emotion he first hears when experiencing the music. Bono told Richard Hilburn of the *Los Angeles Times* that he learned to be truthful from listening to John Lennon's solo albums. "He showed that the best way to unlock yourself as a writer was simply to tell the truth," Bono said. "When you've got a song to write or a blank page, just describe what is on your mind—not what you'd like to be on your mind. If you feel you have nothing to say, your first line then is, 'I have nothing to say.'"

Soon the band was composing songs that Hilburn described as "pop music at its most ambitious—personal and independent enough to satisfy discerning listeners, yet open and accessible enough to pack stadiums." The band also nurtured a distinctive sound driven by the Edge's signature guitar line, with a ringing sound played on the instrument's upper strings; Hilburn called it "the bright clarion cry of his guitar." Mullen and Clayton laid down an often-driving rhythm on bass and drums. Over it all, soared Bono's singing, which over time became powerful, passionate, and expressive. It soon became clear that Bono was the charismatic focus of the group. As *Time* magazine put it, "It is on Bono . . . that all eyes stay fixed. U2 carries the day, but he carries the show."

First Records

U2 had its first big break in a talent contest run by CBS Ireland. The company signed U2 and released a three-song EP (extended-play vinyl record) called *U2-3*. The disk topped the Irish charts and drew bigger crowds than ever to their live show. But CBS refused to issue the record outside of Ireland. Dissatisfied, Bono sent tapes to radio stations and journalists. In 1980 the band won a contract with Island Records, an independent English label known for backing new-wave groups.

U2 released it first album, *Boy*, in 1980, with songs that expressed the anger and energy of punk music. But instead of punk's nihilism, the songs hinted at hope and idealism. As the band's lyricist, Bono struck out at social and political injustice. "I Will Follow" had the anthem-like, almost religious quality that would mark much of U2's output. The critic Sean O'Hagan likened such songs to "rock hymns, their clarion calls riding on huge rolling guitar signatures." After the song was featured on the soundtrack of a movie called *The Last American Virgin*, U2 gained a key fan base in the United States.

A second album, *October* (1981), reflected conflict within the band. At the time, Bono had joined a Christian group and was struggling to reconcile his new rock-star role with a commitment to becoming a Christian.

Mullen and the Edge had similar conflicts. Meanwhile, Clayton just wanted to get on with rock, where his heart lay. The band members became somewhat estranged. "We were, during *October*, interested in other things, really," Bono said. "We were getting involved in reading books, the Big Book [the Bible], meeting people who were far more interested in things spiritual."

War

The band members managed to overcome their personal differences and produced their breakthrough album, *War*, in 1983. Riding on the success of *October*, it entered the sales charts at No. 1 in the United Kingdom. On the strength of several memorable songs, it also made the Top 10 in the United States. The surging emotional power of "I Will Follow" returned in "New Year's Day," a stinging anti-war piece. Politics took center stage in the hard-hitting "Sunday Bloody Sunday." The song centers on a 1972 incident in Northern Ireland when British paratroopers fired on unruly protest marchers, killing 13 people. Critics noted that U2 managed to oppose the violence of modern Ireland in the song without taking sides.

"More than any other record, *War* is right for its time," Bono said at the time. "It is a slap in the face against the snap, crackle, and pop. Everyone else is getting more and more style-orientated, more and more slick. John Lennon was right about that kind of music; he called it 'wallpaper music.' Very pretty, very well designed, music to eat your breakfast to. Music can be more. Its possibilities are great. Music has changed me. It has the ability to change a generation. Look at what happened with Vietnam. Music changed a whole generation's attitude towards war."

With the release of *War*, U2 began to get noticed for its strong political message as well as its distinctive, dense, layered sound. In a time of superficial pop music, U2 was welcomed as a throwback to the 1960s, when politics and social change were key elements of rock music. Also fueling the band's success was the airplay it received on MTV, which was just getting started at that time as a music video network. Bono's energy and magnetism in the video single for "New Year's Day" attracted many fans. The band soon sealed its status as a global phenomenon with the release of a live album and concert video, both called *Under a Blood-Red Sky* (1983).

>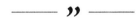
>
> *"More than any other record,* War *is right for its time,"* Bono said. *"It is a slap in the face against the snap, crackle, and pop. Everyone else is getting more and more style-orientated, more and more slick. John Lennon was right about that kind of music; he called it 'wallpaper music.' Very pretty, very well designed, music to eat your breakfast to."*

With the release of its fourth album, *The Unforgettable Fire* (1984), U2 switched producers, from Steve Lilywhite to the more experimental Brian Eno and Daniel Lanois. New elements came into their music, including jazz-influenced instrumental sections. *The Unforgettable Fire* drew the most negative reviews of the band's career to date. But it also enjoyed huge success with the single "Pride (In the Name of Love)," a tribute to the American civil rights leader Martin Luther King Jr. In 1985, rock magazine *Rolling Stone* named U2 "the band of the 1980s."

Becoming an Activist

Following the popularity of *War,* U2 had been invited to perform in Live Aid, the pioneering rock concerts organized by Bob Geldof. The effort raised $200 million for famine victims in Africa. His involvement with African issues inspired Bono to spend six weeks with his wife Alison in Ethiopia in 1985, working at a refugee camp. This initial involvement would later grow into his high-profile lobbying for African and third-world causes. Years later, Bono told a church congregation that his activism started with his trip to Ethiopia. "It's a journey that changed my life forever," he said.

> ———— **"** ————
>
> **"The Joshua Tree** *finally confirms on record what this band has been slowly asserting for three years now on stage: U2 is what the Rolling Stones ceased being years ago — the greatest rock 'n' roll band in the world. In this album, the band wears that mantle securely."*
> **—Robert Hilburn,**
> *the* **Los Angeles Times**
>
> ———— **"** ————

In the meantime, Bono and the band got involved in other political crusades. U2 contributed to a Sun City album with other musicians to raise money to fight racist policies in South Africa. They also headlined a tour with other artists in 1986 to benefit Amnesty International, a group that fights human-rights abuses worldwide. In interviews and even onstage, Bono began to comment on these issues and other political matters, including the violence in Northern Ireland and America. Reactions to his activism were mixed: some disliked what they regarded as his air of pompousness and self-importance, while others appreciated his passion and commitment.

The Joshua Tree

In *The Joshua Tree,* released in 1987, Bono and the band focused on American politics. The critic Niall Stokes noted that the album expresses the "sense of outrage that America's unique combination of arrogance and apathy inspires from an Irish perspective." Bono and the band used as their central image the Joshua Tree, a species that thrives in the southwestern American desert. Critics saw the plant as representing the human idealism and compassion that can blossom even in the barren desert of contemporary American power politics. "A lot of the songs were ones that were recorded in Larry's spare bedroom or Adam's living room. When the red

U 2
T H E
J O S H U A
T R E E

light's on we often don't respond to it. When we're just left to be, left to make music our own way, well some of the tracks are almost like demos. We had to fight to make them work and there were a lot of songs left over. It could have gone off in a number of different directions. We wanted the idea of a one-piece record, not a side-one, side-two thing."

The Joshua Tree became the album that catapulted the group to super-stardom. Two of the album's singles, "With or Without You" and "I Still Haven't Found What I'm Looking For," became No. 1 hits in the United States — U2's first U.S. top hits. *Time* magazine put the band on its cover and proclaimed it "Rock's Hottest Ticket." At the 1988 Grammy Awards, *The Joshua Tree* earned U2 the award for best performance by a rock group and album of the year award. The band was at this time acknowledged as the most popular and powerful rock band in the world. "This is the album that will catapult U2 from cult status to worldwide superstardom," Daniel Brogan wrote in the *Chicago Tribune.* "The only question is how they will deal with it. My guess is that U2 will be remembered as the most influential band of the late '80s and early '90s."

"[The album is] a masterpiece, a work of profound elegance and mystery and faith," wrote Robert Hilburn of the *Los Angeles Times.* "In *The Joshua Tree,* U2 fills in the sketches with sometimes breathtaking signs of growth. The music . . . is more tailored and assured as it expands on the moody textures of songs like "Bad" and reaches out with great effect for new, bluesy touches. . . . In a time when the rock 'n' roll world feasts on the banality of such acts as Bon Jovi, *The Joshua Tree* is asking more of mainstream audiences than any pop-rock album since Bruce Springsteen's *Nebraska.* [And] the band presents its case in such majestic, heartfelt and accessible terms. . . . *The Joshua Tree* finally confirms on record what this band has been slowly asserting for three years now on stage: U2 is what the Rolling Stones ceased being years ago — the greatest rock 'n' roll band in the world. In this album, the band wears that mantle securely."

After the great success of *The Joshua Tree,* Bono and U2 set out on a journey of musical discovery across America. They visited the American South to find the roots of rock and roll in such styles as Appalachian folk music, African-American gospel, the blues of artists like Robert Johnson, and the jazz of singers like Billie Holiday and others. They also explored country music, from early artists like Hank Williams to more recent stars like Johnny Cash. The tour included a stop at Sun Studios in Memphis, Tennessee, where Elvis Presley and Johnny Cash got their start. The group also collaborated with music legends like B.B. King and Bob Dylan, who co-wrote "Love Rescue Me."

These experiences were presented in a black-and-white documentary film called *Rattle and Hum,* which was released in 1988 along with an album of the same name. The record was a success with such hits as "Desire," and some critics praised the disk's energy and daring. But some reviewers and fans thought the Irish rockers were presumptuous to suggest they could reveal insights about American music.

Achtung Baby

Between 1988 and 1990, Bono and the band took a break from recording. They came back in 1991 with *Achtung Baby,* recorded over several months in Berlin, Germany. The Edge said that with this album, the band was "smashing U2 and starting all over again." Instead of politics, the album explored the darker themes of disappointed love and sexual jealousy. The band experimented with electronic elements that added a new edge to their music—for example, Bono used devices like distortion pedals to make his tenor voice sound lower. The ballad, "One," is a signature song from the record.

"At their best, these Irishmen have proven—just as Springsteen and the Who did—that the same penchant for epic musical and verbal gestures that leads many artists to self-parody can, in more inspired hands, fuel the unforgettable fire that defines great rock & roll," Elyse Gardner wrote in *Rolling Stone*. "In the past, U2's frontman has turned out fiercely pointed social and political diatribes, but his more confessional and romantic songs, however felt, have been evasive. On *Achtung*, though, Bono deals more directly with his private feelings. . . . That's not to say that U2 has forsaken its faith or that Bono has abandoned his quest to find what he's looking for. On the radiant ballad 'One,' the band invests an unexceptional message—'We're one/But we're not the same/We get to carry each other'—with such urgency that it sounds like a revelation. Few bands can marshal such sublime power."

> *Daniel Brogan wrote in the* **Chicago Tribune**, *"My guess is that U2 will be remembered as the most influential band of the late '80s and early '90s."*

The Zoo TV tour that the band launched with the album also showed a new side to U2. Instead of their usual stripped-down stages, they devised a concert set where cars hung from the ceiling and gigantic TV screens displayed messages and video. Bono himself also began to adopt extreme stage personas during this period, including Fly, a leather-clad hoodlum; the Mirrorball man, a take-off on TV evangelists; and Mister MacPhisto (a play on the devil's name, Mephisto), who wore a gold-lame suit and was a combination of middle-aged Elvis and Lucifer himself. Offstage, Bono began to wear the wrap-around sunglasses that have become his trademark.

Between the close of the Zoo TV tour in late 1992 and the start of the European tour in May 1993, U2 paused to put together a "mini-album," *Zooropa*. But it soon grew into a full-length recording, with songs that often ventured into techno-dance music. Critics generally approved of the experimental and spontaneous results. But some reviewers agreed with a *People* magazine commentator, who wrote that "some of these songs needed more planning and polishing."

The members of U2 (left to right): the Edge, Bono,
Adam Clayton, and Larry Mullens.

In 1997, U2 re-emerged as a dance-rock band in the album *Pop*. Howie B.,
a techno producer and performer, brought convincing credentials to the
project. It received mixed reviews. But when the band took the show on
the road for the Pop tour, it met with a lukewarm reception. With elaborate
props, including a 35-foot-tall mirror ball, the tour cost about $250,000 a
day, and with tickets selling poorly, the band barely broke even.

All That You Can't Leave Behind

Fans responded more warmly when Bono and U2 greeted the new millennium with *All That You Can't Leave Behind* (2000), a nod to their 1980s
roots. "Pop music often tells you everything is OK, while rock music tells
you that it's not OK, but you can change it," Bono said about the record.

"There's a defiance in rock music that gives you a reason to get out of bed in the morning. Most pop music doesn't make you want to get out of bed, I'm sorry to say. It puts you to sleep."

Songs like the hit "Beautiful Day" returned to the guitar-propelled simpler sound of the band's earliest hits. After the terrorist attacks on New York and Washington DC on September 11, 2001, many fans adopted the album's song "Walk On" as an anthem of hope and perseverance. Although the song was released before the attacks occurred, many found that its lyrics spoke directly to the moment. During their 2001 Elevation tour after September 11, the band paid tribute to the victims and heroes of the attacks by projecting their names on large screens during their performances. U2 was chosen to perform at the 2002 NFL Super Bowl before a huge live crowd and an appreciative TV audience. That year the band earned four Grammy awards.

"On *All That You Can't Leave Behind*, U2 distills two decades of music-making into the illusion of effortlessness usually only possible from veterans," wrote *Rolling Stone*. "The album represents the most uninterrupted collection of strong melodies U2 [has] ever mounted. . . . *All That You Can't Leave Behind* flexes with an interior fire. Every track—whether reflective but swinging, like 'Wild Honey,' or poised, then pouncing, like 'Beautiful Day'—honors a tune so refined that each seems like some durable old number. Because this is U2, there's a quick impact to these melodies, yet each song has a resonance that doesn't fade with repeated listening. . . . Bono's singing has lost some of the extra flamboyance it's had in the past, but it's as passionate as ever—by reining himself in, he has invested his voice with a new urgency."

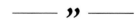

"Pop music often tells you everything is OK, while rock music tells you that it's not OK, but you can change it," Bono said. *"There's a defiance in rock music that gives you a reason to get out of bed in the morning. Most pop music doesn't make you want to get out of bed, I'm sorry to say. It puts you to sleep."*

A Leading Humanitarian Activist

During the 1990s, Bono and U2 continued to support political causes. They contributed songs to albums released to fund education about AIDS. Their 1992 tour ended with a benefit concert for the ecology-minded charity

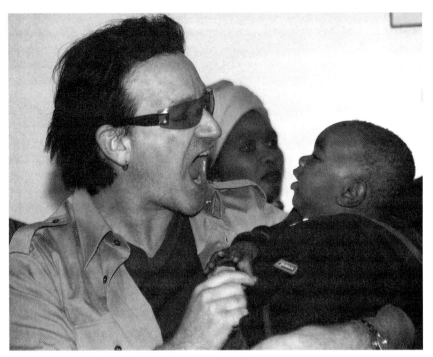

Bono's work as an activist has included several trips to Africa. On this visit to South Africa in 2002, he visited an HIV clinic at a hospital in Soweto.

Greenpeace, which incorporated a protest about nuclear power in the United Kingdom.

While Bono was interested in a variety of political causes, activism remained in the background of his life. That changed in 1997 when an advocate for African development, Jamie Drummond, contacted Bono with a stark statistic: Live Aid raised $200 million to help Africa. But that was a drop in the bucket compared to the loan payments that burdened most African countries. Countries would borrow money to pay for crucial expenses, but many African nations were too poor to pay back those loans. For example, Ethiopia was obliged to pay $500 million every year to banks to repay its debts. Drummond wanted Bono to get involved with Jubilee 2000, a campaign that asked governments to mark the new millennium by canceling debt for third-world countries. Bono soon agreed to become a spokesman for the cause.

But Bono wasn't satisfied to become a mere figurehead. He began to fly to Washington DC to learn everything he could about the economics of Africa. He discovered that Congress, not the president, had the power to erase African debt. So he began to lobby members of Congress—Democrats, Republicans, across the board. It took a while for him to be taken seriously, but it only took one meeting for even the biggest skeptics to see that Bono knew his stuff. According to Bill O'Reilly, a conservative American news commentator, "I think Bono should win the Nobel Peace Prize. He's not a phony." That view was echoed by Paul Wolfowitz, president of the World Bank: "Pomposity and arrogance are the enemies of getting things done. And Bono knows how to get things done."

Bono quickly developed a reputation as a knowledgeable humanitarian. He was soon welcomed by the world's most prominent politicians and world leaders, from Presidents Bill Clinton and George W. Bush, to South African former President Nelson Mandela, to Pope John Paul II (who reportedly tried on Bono's sunglasses). Often his meetings got results—for example, the Jubilee 2000 campaign was a success. And partly due to Bono's influence, Bush launched programs to give drugs to poor Africans suffering from HIV. The president also released funds to developing governments, on the condition that they agreed to accountability standards.

"They really are a group, the only real group I've ever met," Brian Eno, the noted composer, musician, and producer, said about U2. "They realize that intuitively, and there is a great loyalty, perhaps because they realize that none of them would have been a musician without the others."

In 2002, Bono co-founded DATA—Debts, AIDS, Trade in Africa—a nonprofit organization devoted to his favorite causes. Bono didn't want people to think it was a "vanity" project, so he found grants to fund it instead of paying for it himself. Bono emphasized that the group is not just for fund-raising, but also for organizing a real movement to create political change. "Each generation has to ask itself what it wants to be remembered for. Previous generations have ushered in civil rights in America, gotten rid of apartheid in South Africa, and brought down the iron curtain," he said. "I think this generation can bring that kind of energy and conviction to the problems in Africa."

In July 2005, Bono helped to organize Live 8, a series of free international concerts designed to raise the profile of the issues of debt forgiveness, fair trade, and financial aid to Africa. The concerts took place at the same time as the G-8 summit—a forum where leaders representing the world's wealthiest countries were meeting to discuss common issues. Bono and DATA reps met with five of the eight leaders and helped influence the group to approve $50 billion in aid. The leaders also promised antiretroviral drugs for millions of poor people with HIV. They cancelled the debt of 18 of the poorest African countries. Bono didn't do it on his own, said Paul Martin, prime minister of Canada. "But it's hard to imagine much of it would have been done without him," he said.

In 2005, Bono was nominated for the Nobel Peace Prize and was named Person of the Year by *Time* magazine (along with Microsoft billionaires and fellow activists Bill Gates and Melinda Gates) for his work on behalf of Africa. Also in 2005, Bono helped launch the Red label in partnership with such companies as Gap, Converse, American Express, and Giorgio Armani. Red products are made in Africa from African resources. One percent of the profits from their sales go to the Global Fund to Fight AIDS, Tuberculosis, and Malaria.

—————— **"** ——————

"How to Dismantle an Atomic Bomb is quintessential U2, taken to the next level. The sound is bigger, the playing better, the lyrics sharper, and the spirituality more compelling than anything the act has done in many years. . . . Songwriting may be the most impressive part of a record on which U2 scales new peaks: . . . the album is full of great songs, performed with the vitality of a band that keeps surprising us by simply being itself."
— *Wayne Robins,* **Billboard** *magazine*

—————— **"** ——————

A Rock-Solid Band

In addition to his work as an activist, Bono remains committed to U2. The band displayed its extraordinary staying power, nearly 30 years after forming, with the 2004 release of *How to Dismantle an Atomic Bomb*. The best-selling album yielded such major hits as "Vertigo" and "Sometimes You Can't Make It on Your Own," a tribute to the singer's father, who died in 2001. It also spawned the highly successful Vertigo tour, where fans of many ages confirmed their devotion to the group.

Critics, too, were quick to express their appreciation for the new work. *"How to Dismantle an Atomic Bomb is the catchiest album U2 has ever made. Mostly it's perfectly rendered grandiose pop, enormous in sound and

theme," Josh Tyrangiel wrote in *Time*. Reviewer Chuck Arnold agreed, writing in *People* magazine, "After a mid-career slump (*Pop*, anyone?), U2 reclaimed its title as the World's Greatest Rock Band with 2000's smashing comeback *All That You Can't Leave Behind*, which found Bono, the Edge, and company going back to what they do best: anthemic rock that elevates you to a higher place. Having reignited their unforgettable fire, they keep the fuse burning brightly on *How to Dismantle an Atomic Bomb*, another vintage U2 album." Writing in *Billboard* magazine, critic Wayne Robins had this to say: "*How to Dismantle an Atomic Bomb* is quintessential U2, taken to the next level," Robins wrote. "The sound is bigger, the playing better, the lyrics sharper, and the spirituality more compelling than anything the act has done in many years. . . . The Edge has never played with greater confidence, . . . and Bono's mature phrasing puts his well-crafted words across with conviction. Songwriting may be the most impressive part of a record on which U2 scales new peaks: . . . the album is full of great songs, performed with the vitality of a band that keeps surprising us by simply being itself."

Indeed, the commitment of the members of U2—to their music and to each other—is remarkable in the fast-changing music world. According to Brian Eno, the noted composer, musician, and producer, "They really are a group, the only real group I've ever met. They realize that intuitively, and there is a great loyalty, perhaps because they realize that none of them would have been a musician without the others."

> "Rock music can change things. I know that it changed our lives," Bono declared. "Rock is really about the transcendent feeling. There's life in the form. I still think that rock music is the only music that can still get you to that eternal place where you want to start a revolution, call your mother, change your job, or change your mind. I think that's what rock music can do."

Bono's commitment to rock music hasn't changed either after all these years. "Rock music can change things. I know that it changed our lives," he declared. "Rock is really about the transcendent feeling. There's life in the form. I still think that rock music is the only music that can still get you to that eternal place where you want to start a revolution, call your mother, change your job, or change your mind. I think that's what rock music can do."

MARRIAGE AND FAMILY

Bono married his high-school sweetheart, Alison Stewart, in 1982. "It's almost impossible to be married and be in a band on the road, but Ali is able to make it work," Bono said. The couple has four children, Jordan, Eve, Elijah, and John. Bono told Oprah Winfrey in 2003, "I don't know why I have the life I have. I don't deserve it. I think the family is as strong as it is because of my wife, Ali. She is just really so cool."

The family lives outside Dublin, Ireland, where Bono says he can exist "below the celebrity radar." He is never away from his family for more than a few weeks. "You may get the impression I'm always out there, but I'm usually home driving my kids to school," he said. Bono and his family also spend time at their homes in New York City and the south of France.

HOBBIES AND OTHER INTERESTS

Bono is an avid reader. He has found inspiration for his songs in everything from biblical scriptures to the works of the American writers Flannery O'Connor and Charles Bukowski.

SELECTED RECORDINGS (with U2)

Boy, 1980
October, 1981
War, 1983
Under a Blood-Red Sky, 1983
The Unforgettable Fire, 1984
Wide Awake in America, 1985
The Joshua Tree, 1987
Rattle and Hum, 1988
Achtung Baby, 1991
Zooropa, 1993
Pop, 1997
Best of U2 1980-1990, 1998
All That You Can't Leave Behind, 2000
Best of U2 1990-2000, 2002
How to Dismantle an Atomic Bomb, 2004

SELECTED HONORS AND AWARDS (with U2)

Grammy Awards, with U2: 1987 (two awards), for album of the year and best rock vocal performance by a duo or group, both for *The Joshua Tree*; 1988 (two awards), for best rock vocal performance by a duo or group, for *"Desire"* and best performance in a music video, for "Where the Streets Have No Name"; 1992, for best rock vocal performance by a duo or group, for *Achtung Baby*; 1993, for best alternative music album, for *Zooropa*; 1994, for best music video, long form, for *Zoo TV: Live from Sydney*; 2000 (three awards), for record of the year, song of the year, and best rock vocal performance by a duo or group, all for "Beautiful Day"; 2001 (four awards), for best pop vocal performance by a duo or group for "Stuck in a Moment That You Can't Get Out Of," best rock vocal performance by a duo or group for "Elevation," record of the year for "Walk On," and best rock album, for *All That You Can't Leave Behind*; 2004 (three awards), for best rock vocal performance by a duo or group, best rock song, and best short-form music video, all for "Vertigo"; 2005 (five awards), for album of the year and best rock album, both for *How to Dismantle an Atomic Bomb*, song of the year and best rock vocal performance by a duo or group, both for "Sometimes You Can't Make It on Your Own," and best rock song, for "City of Blinding Lights"

British Record Industry Awards, with U2: Best International Group: 1988, 1989, 1990, 1998, 2001; Outstanding Contribution to the Record Industry, 2001; Most Successful Live Act, 1993

Humanitarian Laureate Award (Simon Wiesenthal Center): 2002

Humanitarian Award (Martin Luther King Jr. Center): 2003

Salute to Greatness Award (Martin Luther King Jr. Center): 2004

Ambassador of Conscience (Amnesty International): 2005

Inducted into the Rock and Roll Hall of Fame: 2005 (with U2)

Order of Liberty (President of Portugal): 2005 (with U2)

Person of the Year (*Time* magazine): 2005 (with Bill and Melinda Gates)

Pablo Neruda Arts Award (President of Chile): 2006

FURTHER READING

Books

Assayas, Michka. *Bono: Conversations with Michka Assayas*, 2005
Dunphy, Eamon. *Unforgettable Fire*, 1988
Encyclopedia of World Biography Supplement, Vol. 24, 2005
Jackson, Laura. *Bono: His Life, Music, and Passions*, 2001
Parkyn, Geoff. *Touch the Flame*, 1988
Who's Who in America, 2006

Periodicals

Christian Century, Mar. 21, 2006, pp.20 and 23
Christianity Today, Mar. 2003, p.38
Current Biography Yearbook, 1993
Los Angeles Times, June 6, 2002, p.14; Aug. 8, 2004, p.1
Newsweek, Jan. 24, 2000, p.58
O: The Oprah Magazine, Apr. 2004, p.195
Rolling Stone, Oct. 8, 1987, p.43; Nov. 3, 2005, p.48
Time, Mar. 4, 2002, p.62; Apr. 27, 1987, p.72; Sep. 15, 2001, p.52; Dec. 26, 2005, pp.38, 46, and 65; May 8, 2006, p.116
Vogue, Mar. 2005, p.524
Washington Post, Sep. 20, 1987, p.1

Online Databases

Biography Resource Center Online, 2006, article from *Encyclopedia of World Biography Supplement*, 2005

Wilson Web, 2006, article from *Current Biography: World Musicians*, 1993, updated 1998

ADDRESS

Bono
Universal Music Group
1755 Broadway
New York, NY 10019

WORLD WIDE WEB SITES

http://www.u2.com
http://www.data.org

BRIEF ENTRY

Kelsie Buckley 1995-

American Student
Fundraiser for Hurricane-Damaged Libraries and
Large-Print Books

EARLY YEARS

Kelsie Buckley was born on March 11, 1995, in Houston,
Texas, to Kelly and Thomas Buckley. Her father is a self-em-
ployed welder. In the first years of her life, the family traveled
through Texas and California as her father worked at different
jobs.

When she was four Kelsie could read at a second-grade level, according to her mother. At that same young age, she became interested in the political process. "She wanted to know everything about elections and how the government works," explained her mother.

Kelsie attended kindergarten at O.M. Roberts Elementary School in Lake Jackson, Texas. One day, when recess was cut back 15 minutes for an assembly, she staged a sit-in at school. "She just wrapped her arms around a pole and refused to come inside because it was too early," her mother recalled. "It was kind of funny! But after that, we talked to her about it being all right to ask questions, but you have to be polite and respectful. She learned that lesson real quick."

The Buckleys moved to Benicia, California, when Kelsie was in first grade, and then settled in Morton, Mississippi, about a year later. She became a home-schooled student, with her mother as her teacher. Kelsie was an avid reader, getting through two or three chapter books a week. She loved adventure books as well as history books. One of her favorite subjects was Benjamin Franklin.

When Kelsie was nine years old, she began to notice that the words in books looked fuzzy. In a few short weeks, she could not see the print at all and her eyes became very sensitive to light. Her eyes burned "like when you touch a heater that's been on a long time," she said.

Onset of Vision Problems

In June 2004, when Kelsie was nine years old, she began to notice that the words in books looked fuzzy. In a few short weeks, she could not see the print at all and her eyes became very sensitive to light. Her eyes burned "like when you touch a heater that's been on a long time," she said.

Her parents took Kelsie to many eye doctors, but they could not agree on what was wrong. Finally, a pediatric eye specialist from Los Angeles diagnosed her problem as ocular histoplasmosis syndrome. It is a disease caused by a fungus that scars and inflames the retina and can, in some cases, lead to permanent blindness. In October 2005, the specialist operated on Kelsie. The operation made her eyes less sensitive to light. She has no vision in her left eye and has limited vision in her right eye. She was fitted with special glasses that help her get around by herself and watch television. But she could not read books unless the letters were printed in type about twice the normal size.

The size of the letters in books, magazines and newspapers is measured in points. The typical print size is about 10 or 12 points (like the size of the print in this book). By the time she turned nine, Kelsie could no longer read 12-point type. She went to the Morton Public Library, near her home, to take out large print books. The Morton library, like most libraries in the United States, has a small collection of large print books. But the print in those books is usually 16-point type, which is still too small for Kelsie. She could read them with a magnifying glass, but her arm got tired after a few pages. She needed books that were printed in 20-point type or larger. But the only way to get them was for her parents to buy them for her, and they were very expensive.

"My first goal was to raise enough money for 200 books, [and] that would come to around $4,000," Kelsie said. "After I reached my goal, I donated 12 inches of my hair to a child that had gone through chemotherapy. I had never gotten a haircut before, but I was excited about helping others."

MAJOR ACCOMPLISHMENTS

First Fund-Raising Campaign

Determined to help children with vision problems, Kelsie decided to take action. She began a fund-raising effort, asking people to donate money so the Morton Public Library could buy books with 20-point type. "My first goal was to raise enough money for 200 books, [and] that would come to around $4,000," Kelsie said on her web site, http://www.kelsiesbooks.net. "After I reached my goal, I donated 12 inches of my hair to a child that had gone through chemotherapy. I had never gotten a haircut before, but I was excited about helping others."

Kelsie also began writing letters to elected officials in Mississippi, as well as President George W. Bush. She knew that in 2001 the U.S. Congress had passed the Elementary and Secondary Education Act (often called the "No Child Left Behind" Act). President George W. Bush had supported the bill, which set high standards for the learning of all children, regardless of their background or ability. Kelsie wrote to the president, telling him, "You said no child left behind. I am telling you that I feel left behind. . . . Please write back so I can tell you my plan, but not after 8:30 because that is my bedtime."

In February 2005, nine-year-old Kelsie spoke at a hearing of the House Public Health Committee at the Mississippi House of Representatives. "I

Hurricane Katrina wreaked devastation on schools and libraries,
as shown in this 2005 photo of the Gorenflo Elementary School library
in Gulfport, Mississippi.

think that it is sad that I am an American child and I can't go to my local library and check out a book to read," she said.

Kelsie received telephone calls of support from a staff member of the office of First Lady Laura Bush, as well as staffers in the offices of U.S. Sen. Thad Cochran of Mississippi and Mississippi Governor Haley Barbour. U.S. Rep. Chip Pickering called Kelsie himself. She asked them all to back her plan: to make funds available so all low-vision children can get any book they want at the type-size they need. "They all promised to help," said her mother, Kelly Buckley. "And Kelsie made sure to keep calling them back, just to check up on them and keep them to their word!"

Hurricane Katrina

In August 2005, Hurricane Katrina slammed into the coasts of Louisiana and Mississippi. One of the tornadoes spawned by the storm hit Kelsie's hometown of Morton. She and her parents huddled in the bathtub as the tornado approached because the bathroom was the central room in the house and there were no windows. "I was really scared," she recalled. "It felt like our house was a small rowboat and a big wave was coming over us."

71

Fortunately, the family was not hurt, but their house was wrecked. There were no hotel rooms available, so the family camped out, sharing food and supplies with their neighbors. They later moved in with friends in Jackson, Mississippi. They went to Florida next, but were soon hit by Hurricane Wilma in October 2005. "After Hurricane Wilma hit Florida, we'd had enough," Kelly Buckley said. "We called FEMA." The Federal Emergency Management Agency (FEMA) is an agency of the federal government that manages the government's response to natural disasters. FEMA offers assistance, including temporary housing, to victims of national disasters. Because so many people were left homeless in the wake of Hurricane Katrina and the other Atlantic storms of 2005, FEMA commissioned cruise ships to provide shelter to some victims. The Buckleys lived for eight weeks on a ship docked in Pascagoula, Mississippi.

> ——— " ———
>
> *During Hurricane Katrina, one of the tornadoes spawned by the storm hit Kelsie's hometown. She and her parents huddled in the bathtub as the tornado approached because the bathroom was the central room in the house and there were no windows. "I was really scared," she recalled. "It felt like our house was a small rowboat and a big wave was coming over us."*
>
> ——— " ———

Kelsie's Book Trail Ride

Despite the upheaval in her life, Kelsie did not forget about her book campaign. "Kelsie begged from the time we got on the ship to go see the libraries," her mother recalled. As it turned out, there were no libraries near her home to see. Seven libraries in Mississippi, including the Morton library, were destroyed by Hurricane Katrina.

A week before Christmas 2005, the Buckleys moved into a house trailer provided by FEMA. Kelsie began planning a new fund-raising campaign. Her goal was not just raising money for large-print books anymore. Now she also wanted to help fix the seven damaged libraries for the sake of all the area's children, according to her mother. "Kelsie realized that you need a building before you need books," Kelly Buckley said.

For Christmas that year, Kelsie had gotten a horse she named Chester. On March 2, 2006, she climbed onto Chester to begin Kelsie's Book Trail Ride. She and her parents led supporters on horseback and in buggies on a 10-day journey from Morton to Gulfport, Mississippi. Kelsie wanted to raise

Buckley and First Lady Laura Bush being interviewed by reporter
Steve Hartman for CBS News.

$10,000 for each of the seven damaged libraries. The caravan stopped in towns along the way to collect money from local residents. The ride, which ended on her 11th birthday, raised $9,000 and generated a lot of publicity.

On March 31, 2006, Kelsie appeared on national TV on the "CBS Evening News." The reporter, Steve Hartman, asked her what it was about books that motivated her to act. "Books are to help you get your mind off the bad things that are going on," she said. Hartman also asked if she would feel mad if she went completely blind from her eye disease and couldn't see any books. "No sir, I wouldn't be mad," Kelsie replied. "Actually, I'd just — I might cry, but I would still keep on going."

After Kelsie appeared on television, thousands of people from across the United States and around the world logged on to her web site and made donations. In less than a month, she raised almost $80,000, which she gave to state library officials. She also passed along the numerous autographed books that authors sent her. Kelsie said that she planned to "start all over again" and raise another $70,000 for Mississippi libraries.

Soon after the CBS report aired, First Lady Laura Bush, who is a former librarian, called Kelsie. The first lady invited Kelsie to be her guest when she traveled to Biloxi, Mississippi, to award grants from the Laura Bush Foundation to help school libraries restock their books. During a speech in

>
>
> *Asked why she became interested in Kelsie, First Lady Laura Bush replied, "Well, of course it was because she loves books. And she wanted schools to have books and libraries to have books. That's what I like to do. And when I was Kelsie's age, that was my favorite thing to do — read."*

Biloxi on May 3, 2006, Bush thanked Kelsie for all her efforts. One of the dignitaries attending the speech was Ann Moore, the chairman and CEO of Time Inc., who donated $20,000 to Kelsie's library campaign. The first lady and Kelsie were later interviewed together by Steve Hartman of CBS. Asked why she became interested in Kelsie, Laura Bush replied, "Well, of course it was because she loves books. And she wanted schools to have books and libraries to have books. That's what I like to do. And when I was Kelsie's age, that was my favorite thing to do — read."

By spring 2006, the Buckley family had moved out of the FEMA trailer, which had a leaky roof, and into their own travel trailer, which can be pulled by a truck. In late May 2006, Kelsie and her parents traveled to Johns Hopkins Hospital in Baltimore, Maryland, for an examination by eye specialists there. After her examination, Kelsie and her parents went to the White House, at the invitation of First Lady Laura Bush. The Buckleys also met with President George W. Bush. "It was cool to meet the president," Kelsie said. "He told me that I was doing a great job and that I was an inspiration for all kids in America."

HOBBIES AND OTHER INTERESTS

When she isn't working on her library campaign, Kelsie likes to spend her time reading, collecting rocks, riding her horse, riding her bicycle, and swimming. She also likes to paint pictures, using oils or pastel chalks. When asked if she has difficulty seeing what she's drawing, Kelsie replied, "You see with your heart."

FURTHER READING

Periodicals

Biloxi (MS) Sun Herald, Feb. 18, 2005, p.A4; Mar. 7, 2006, p.B1; May 2, 2006, p.A4; May 4, 2006, p.A1
Hattiesburg (MS) American, Mar. 5, 2005, p.C1

Online Articles

http://www.cbsnews.com/stories/2006/03/31/eveningnews/main1461732.s
html
(CBS News, "Seeing Life Clearly: 11-Year-Old with Vision Trouble
Raises Money to Rebuild Katrina-Ravaged Libraries," Mar. 31, 2006)
http://www.cbsnews.com/stories/2006/05/04/eveningnews/main1584977.s
html
(CBS News, "First Lady Meets First Bookworm: Laura Bush Goes to
Mississippi to Thank Extraordinary 11-Year-Old," May 4, 2006)

ADDRESS

Kelsie Buckley
Kelsie's Books
P.O. Box 506
Morton, MS 39117

WORLD WIDE WEB SITE

http://www.kelsiesbooks.net

Dale Chihuly 1941-

American Glass Artist
Creator of Such Series of Works as "Baskets," "Sea
Forms," "Venetians," "Floats," and "Chandeliers"

BIRTH

Dale Patrick Chihuly (pronounced chuh-HOO-lee) was born
on September 20, 1941, in Tacoma, Washington. His father,
George Chihuly, worked as a meatcutter and trade union or-
ganizer. His mother, Viola (Magnuson) Chihuly, was a homemaker and later became a waitress. Dale had one older brother, George Jr.

YOUTH

Chihuly grew up in a working-class neighborhood of Tacoma. He developed an early love for nature by playing in his mother's garden and climbing a nearby hill to watch the sunset over Puget Sound. On weekends, his family would go to the Pacific Ocean and take long walks on the beach. Chihuly always searched the shoreline for small pieces of sea-polished glass. "Pieces of glass on the beach looked like gems to me when I was a kid," he remembered. "I was always fascinated with color and light."

Tragedy struck Chihuly's family during his teen years. In 1957 his older brother was killed in a Navy Air Force training accident. The following year, his father died of a heart attack. Chihuly's mother was forced to take a job as a waitress to support the family. Chihuly grew rebellious and became involved with a group of juvenile delinquents. At one point, he was arrested for throwing a brick through the windshield of a police car. He credited his mother—whom he once described as "industrious, encouraging, progressive in her child-rearing"—with keeping him out of more serious trouble. "If it hadn't been for my mother, I'd have probably been a bum," he acknowledged.

"Pieces of glass on the beach looked like gems to me when I was a kid," Chihuly remembered. "I was always fascinated with color and light."

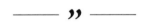

EDUCATION

Chihuly graduated from Stadium High School in Tacoma in 1959. Despite a lack of interest in continuing his studies, he then enrolled at the College of Puget Sound. "I was never a good student," he admitted. "I only went to college because my mother told me I should." Chihuly did not originally intend to study art in college, but two events inspired him to turn in that direction. First, he wrote a term paper on the famous artist Vincent van Gogh. Second, his mother allowed him to remodel a small den in the basement of their home. Writing the term paper increased his interest in art, while remodeling the den taught him that he enjoyed creating and decorating space.

Once he decided to focus on art, Chihuly transferred to the University of Washington, where he majored in interior design and architecture. His academic career soon went off track, however, when he joined the Delta Kappa Epsilon fraternity and spent more time partying than studying. In 1962 Chihuly decided to take a year off and conduct his own art education.

After selling the car his brother had left him, he traveled to Europe. He spent time in Italy and France, then lived on a kibbutz (collective farm) in the Negev Desert in Israel.

The year overseas helped Chihuly become more mature. "I went from being a boy to a man," he noted. Upon his return to the University of Washington, he recalled turning into "a great student, kind of a workaholic." Chihuly created his first artistic works involving glass during this time, by incorporating pieces of glass into woven tapestries. "I found I had to fire my own glass so I could embed wire into the glass to make it possible to weave it," he remembered. "The more I worked, the more the pieces became more glass than fiber."

After graduating with a bachelor's degree in interior design in 1965, Chihuly went to work for a Seattle architecture firm. Around this time, he began experimenting with glassblowing in his basement art studio. "One night I melted some glass between four bricks until it was liquid, then took a steel pipe and blew a bubble," he recalled. "It was kind of a miracle, because you have to get it at exactly the right moment. But it happened! Then I was hooked completely." Chihuly soon quit his job in order to explore his growing interest in glass art.

In 1966 Chihuly enrolled in the country's only hot glass program, at the University of Wisconsin at Madison. He studied under Harvey Littleton, who was widely considered the founder of the studio glass movement in American art. In 1962 Littleton had invented a small furnace that allowed independent artists to blow glass in small studios. Previously, glass work had required people to use huge furnaces in factory settings. Littleton thus helped transform glassblowing from an industry into an art form.

Chihuly earned a master's degree in sculpture from Wisconsin in 1967, then continued his education at the prestigious Rhode Island School of Design. While there, he worked with fellow student James Carpenter to create large installations involving glass, steel, and neon. Their most famous collaboration was "20,000 Pounds of Neon and Ice," which Chihuly reproduced at several exhibitions over the years. He earned a second master of fine arts degree in 1968.

CAREER HIGHLIGHTS

Dale Chihuly is widely credited with turning glassblowing into a respected art form. The bold and innovative artist is largely responsible for expanding the basic concept of blown glass from small, decorative pieces to large, colorful sculptures. Chihuly creates glass objects in brilliant colors and unique

Glassmaking

The main ingredient of glass is sand, like that found on a beach. When sand is combined with soda and lime and heated to extreme temperatures (between 2000 and 2500 degrees Fahrenheit), it melts and forms glass. Glass exists in a natural form around volcanoes, and it may also be created naturally when lightning or fire occurs on a beach.

Humans first began making glass about 5,000 years ago in Mesopotamia, an ancient civilization in the area of the Middle East that is now Iraq. About 3,000 years ago, the ancient Egyptians learned how to wrap hot glass around a core of clay in order to make containers. The process of glassblowing originated in the Roman Empire more than 2,000 years ago. Like modern craftsmen, the Romans used a long tube to blow air into hot glass, creating a thin bubble that could be formed into many shapes and sizes.

Throughout its early history, glass was considered precious because it was so difficult and time-consuming to make. During the modern era, glassmaking evolved into a craft for the creation of functional objects, like ashtrays and candy dishes. This view changed during the 1960s, with the launch of the studio glass movement. The movement began when an artist and teacher named Henry Littleton developed a small furnace for melting glass. His invention allowed individual artists to create "art glass" in a studio environment. Before this time, most glassmaking had been done by industrial designers in large factories.

The process of creating blown-glass art begins when a blob of hot, molten glass is placed on the end of a five-foot-long blowpipe. The glassblower, called a "gaffer," blows gently through the tube to make a bubble in the hot glass. This bubble can be stretched and twisted into various shapes. The gaffer must reheat it every minute or two in order to keep it soft enough for molding. Once it attains the desired shape, the glass is cooled with fans or in special ovens until it hardens into its final form. Color can be added at various stages of the process.

Chihuly at work in his studio with a member of his glass-blowing team.

shapes that "dazzle the eye," "tantalize the mind," and "push the edges of art glass beyond anything made anywhere in the world," according to Marilynne S. Mason in the *Christian Science Monitor*. His work is held in the permanent collections of nearly 200 museums around the world, and major exhibitions of his work often attract record crowds. "I call myself an artist for lack of a better word," Chihuly once said. "I'm an artist, a designer, a craftsman, interior designer, half-architect. There's no one name that fits me very well."

Learning and Teaching

After completing his education, Chilhuly traveled to Venice, Italy, which has been a center of European glassmaking since the 13th century. He learned ancient Venetian techniques of glassblowing while serving as an apprentice to master craftsmen on the island of Murano. Upon his return to the United States, Chihuly joined the faculty of the sculpture department at the Rhode Island School of Design. He taught there for ten years and founded the school's glassmaking program.

In 1971 a couple of Seattle art patrons offered Chihuly 64 acres of wooded property overlooking a lake to build a glassmaking school. With the help of a number of fellow artists, he built the Pilchuck School of Glass on the site. Chihuly served as the first artistic director for the school, which attracted students and artists from around the world. "The impact of Pilchuck on the studio-glass movement, not just in the U.S. but around the world, is immeasurable, and Dale's contribution to that success is almost beyond description," explained fellow glass artist Benjamin Moore. "He has personally pushed glassblowing farther than anyone ever imagined it could be pushed, and his whole impulse is to share his knowledge with anyone and everyone he can bring together."

Losing Sight but Gaining Focus

In 1976 Chihuly accompanied a friend on a lecture tour of England. While there, he was involved in a terrible automobile accident. Chihuly was thrown through the windshield of the vehicle and suffered critical injuries. Doctors told him later that it took more than 250 stitches to repair his face. He ended up losing the sight in his left eye and sustaining permanent damage to his right foot and leg. It took nearly a year of recovery before he was able to work again. "You don't realize how much you depend on two eyes working together," he noted. "It's your depth perception that throws you. I couldn't pour water into a cup. Heck, I couldn't even walk properly. At first it was very disturbing."

Chihuly was determined to overcome his disabilities and continue his career as an artist. He began wearing a black eye patch and custom-made orthopedic boots. Since he wore the boots all the time—even when he worked—they became splattered with paint. "My shoes seem to soak up every spill and splash," he acknowledged. "I paint with a squirt gun, a mop, anything but a brush. Consequently, my shoes become more colorful every day." The eye patch and paint-splattered boots, along with a wild mane of curly hair, became his signature look.

—— **"** ——

"Chihuly's practice of using teams has led to the development of complex, multipart sculptures of dramatic beauty that place him in the leadership role of moving blown glass out of the confines of the small, precious object and into the realm of large-scale contemporary sculpture," wrote biographer Davira S. Taragin.

—— **"** ——

Chihuly also had to change the way he worked after his accident. His loss of depth perception made it difficult or even dangerous for him to continue blowing glass. So instead of handling the blowpipe himself, he developed a team approach. Chihuly starts every new project by making a large, rough drawing of the object he wants to create, then discussing it with a hand-picked team of glassblowers. The team performs the physically demanding work of blowing and shaping the glass, while Chihuly presides over the operation, shouting directions and encouragement. "I had been blowing glass for a decade and when I had to give it up, I didn't really miss it. I had wonderful people on a team, and it was easy for them to work from my drawings," he noted. "In glass, there are lots of things you can't do by yourself anyway. It makes life richer to work with someone."

Chihuly was the first major artist to apply a collaborative team approach to glassmaking. Many people in the art world consider this to be one of his most important contributions. Working with a team allowed him to produce a large and diverse body of work, including many pieces that were significantly larger and more complex than he could have achieved working alone. "Chihuly's practice of using teams has led to the development of complex, multipart sculptures of dramatic beauty that place him in the leadership role of moving blown glass out of the confines of the small, precious object and into the realm of large-scale contemporary sculpture," Davira S. Taragin wrote in a biography for Chihuly's web site.

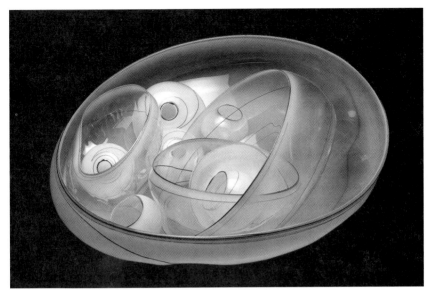

*Vessels inside of vessels are characteristic of the pieces
in Chihuly's "Baskets" series.*

Gaining Fame with Series

Chihuly is best known for creating series of works that center around a
general theme. Each series eventually grows to include hundreds or even
thousands of pieces, which evolve and change over time. "Chihuly and his
teams have created a wide vocabulary of blown forms, revisiting and refin-
ing earlier shapes while at the same time creating exciting new elements,"
Taragin explained. In addition to their distinctive forms, his works are also
known for their vibrant colors. Bold reds, blues, yellows, and greens, as
well as more subtle shades, infuse each piece so that they seem to glow
with internal light.

Chihuly first came to public attention in 1977, when he launched his
"Baskets" series. This series was inspired by the traditional baskets produced by Native American tribes of the Pacific Northwest. "I was struck by
the grace of their slumped, sagging forms," the artist recalled. "I wanted to
capture this grace in glass." Chihuly created about 100 pieces that were
shown in successful exhibits at the Seattle Art Museum and the Smith-
sonian Institution.

Around this time, New York City's Metropolitan Museum of Art acquired
one of Chihuly's works for its permanent collection. A number of other
prominent museums and art collectors began commissioning works as

well, and by 1980 he was earning enough money to quit teaching and focus all of his time and energy on his art. Over the next few years, his fame continued to grow and the prices he received for his works continued to rise.

Chihuly launched one of his most popular series, "Sea Forms," in 1980. These pieces were made using ribbed molds, which gave them a rippled appearance, and were adorned with long spirals of colored glass. "The 'Sea Forms' seemed to come about by accident, as much of my work does," he stated. "We were experimenting with some ribbed molds when I was doing the 'Basket' series. . . . Then the 'Baskets' started looking like sea forms, so I changed the name of the series to 'Sea Forms,' which suited me just fine in that I love to walk along the beach and go to the ocean."

> ———— " ————
>
> *"The 'Sea Forms' seemed to come about by accident, as much of my work does," Chihuly stated. "We were experimenting with some ribbed molds when I was doing the 'Basket' series. . . . Then the 'Baskets' started looking like sea forms, so I changed the name of the series to 'Sea Forms,' which suited me just fine in that I love to walk along the beach and go to the ocean."*
>
> ———— " ————

Chihuly's next series, "Macchias" (the Italian word for "spotted"), began in 1981. It grew out of his interest in using all 300 colors available to glassmakers. He typically used one color on the inside of the vessel and another on the outside, separated by a cloudy white layer in the middle. He also applied a ribbon of glass in a contrasting color, called a "lip wrap," around the edge. "Each piece was another experiment. When we unloaded the ovens in the morning, there was the rush of seeing something I had never seen before," he recalled. "The unbelievable combinations of color — that was the driving force."

As an indication of his growing international stature, in 1986 Chihuly became only the fourth American artist ever honored with a solo exhibition at the Louvre museum in Paris, France. Two years later he launched his "Venetians" series. Inspired by the decorative vases produced by Venetian artisans of the early 20th century, the series consisted of vase-shaped vessels covered with brightly colored strands of glass in the shape of stems, leaves, and flowers.

In 1991 Chihuly started one of his most ambitious series, "Floats." Its large, brightly colored glass spheres were inspired by the floats that Japanese fishermen once used to mark their lines. Some of the spheres reached 40 inches in diameter and weighed up to 80 pounds, making them some of the largest glass objects ever blown manually. "Even though a sphere or ball is about the easiest form you can make in glass, when you get up to this scale . . . it becomes extremely difficult," Chihuly noted.

In 1992 Chihuly expanded his vision even further with the "Chandeliers" series. These huge installations, which were usually hung from a ceiling or wall, included hundreds of individual pieces. In 1995 he displayed 14 of his "Chandeliers" over the canals and

Chihuly's "Sea Form" pieces, with their characteristic ripples and spirals, grew out of his "Baskets" series.

historic sites of Venice. "Chihuly Over Venice" also included more than 1,000 pieces by other glass artists. The million-dollar exhibition became the subject of a 1998 PBS documentary.

Another ambitious exhibition in 2000, "Chihuly in the Light of Jerusalem," involved 17 installations at the Tower of David Museum in Israel. First Lady Hillary Rodham Clinton invited the artist to design a millennium installation for the White House that year, and his work was also featured in a retrospective exhibition at the Victoria and Albert Museum in London.

After the turn of the century, Chihuly began focusing his attention on the interaction between nature and art. In 2002 he displayed many of his organically shaped sculptures at the Garfield Park Conservatory in Chicago, in an exhibition titled "Chihuly in the Park: A Garden of Glass." In 2003 he launched his "Fiori" series (from the Italian word for "flowers"). The "Fiori" are cylinders of glass ornamented with brightly colored petals, leaves, and other organic forms. Large installations can include hundreds of pieces arranged in a garden- or forest-like grouping.

Creating Controversy

As his works gained worldwide attention, Chihuly built his glassmaking studio into a major business enterprise. The center of this enterprise is the Boathouse, a former factory on Lake Union in Seattle that serves as his home, studio, and office. He employs 200 people in various roles, including glassmaking, packing and shipping, and marketing and sales. Chihuly travels often for lectures and exhibitions, but he stays connected to his employees through a voice-mail system that allows him to leave messages for all of them at once. The marketing arm of Chihuly's business arranges exhibitions around the world, produces videos about his life and work, and sells prints and coffee-table books.

Over the years, Chihuly has provoked controversy within the art world. Some critics complain about his tireless self-promotion. Others dismiss his work as "craft," which is generally considered a less intellectual pursuit than "art." Chihuly's glass pieces and installations are very accessible to average viewers, and thus his work enjoys widespread popular appeal. In fact, it has been commissioned for the lobby of a Las Vegas hotel-casino and the dining room of a Disney cruise ship. But some people in the art world believe that works of art should be more challenging. "Chihuly's glass figures are pretty close to Everyman's notion of what art should be," Christine Biederman wrote in the *Dallas Observer.* "But by advocating a diet of nothing but eye candy, Chihuly compromises art's standards ever so slightly—a process that, in the end, leads us into temptation, into a betrayal of art's possibilities. He denies us the pleasure of being puzzled, of being intrigued or curious enough to sally forth into the books and learn."

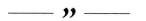

> "Each piece [in the 'Macchias' series] was another experiment. When we unloaded the ovens in the morning, there was the rush of seeing something I had never seen before," Chihuly recalled. "The unbelievable combinations of color—that was the driving force."

Such criticism does not bother Chihuly. He considers himself a populist when it comes to art, meaning that he wants ordinary people to like his work and is less concerned about what art critics think. "What I like to do is work on my work more than anything else," he stated. "It's varied in such a way that I can work on a chandelier, do a drawing . . . design a book, make some phone calls about an exhibition. That means a lot to me, being able to put it up in a nice way, and have a lot of people look at it, and really like it."

On a typical day, Chihuly gets up at four in the morning to begin producing sketches for his team of glassblowers. Although he maintains artistic control, he still tries to allow his assistants to exercise some creativity. "I

Chihuly's "Macchias" are often displayed in groups that showcase the stunning use of form, light, and color.

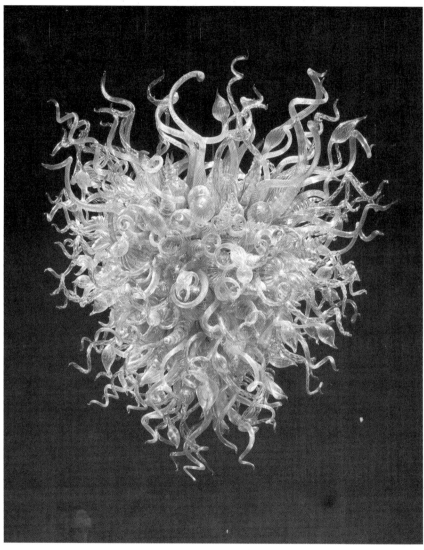

A chandelier by Chihuly includes many interlocking pieces. No two are the same.

rely heavily on the intuition of my craftsmen," he explained. "My job is to be a catalyst—to set the wheels in motion, keep the energy level high, and let things happen." They make all the individual elements of large installations in the studio and put them together. Then the sculpture is taken apart, packed into cardboard boxes, and shipped to the exhibition site, where it is reassembled. This complicated process means that no two exhibitions of Chihuly's work are ever exactly alike.

Throughout his 40-year career as a glass artist, Chihuly has maintained his love for the material. "I think glass is just a magical material that people appreciate universally," he stated. "You can't help but be interested in glass: Everybody is fascinated by the translucence and the colors. These are qualities that you cannot get in any other material—there are very few materials that are transparent. That means light can go through it, and it means it's possible to light it in ways that you can't light an opaque material. Also, I think glass is generally a mysterious material to people. The fact that it breaks makes it unique."

"You can't help but be interested in glass: Everybody is fascinated by the translucence and the colors. These are qualities that you cannot get in any other material—there are very few materials that are transparent. That means . . . it's possible to light it in ways that you can't light an opaque material. Also, I think glass is generally a mysterious material to people. The fact that it breaks makes it unique."

MARRIAGE AND FAMILY

Chihuly married his first wife, playwright Sylvia Peto, in 1987. The marriage ended in divorce in 1991. He married his second wife, Leslie Jackson, in 2005. The couple was introduced by a mutual friend and dated for ten years before getting married. They have a son, Jackson, who was born in 1998.

Chihuly and his family maintain a residence in the Boathouse, the former factory on Lake Union in Seattle that also serves as his studio. Their home has several unique features, including a lap pool with a bottom made out of dozens of colorful glass pieces, and an 87-foot-long dining table carved from a single tree.

HOBBIES AND OTHER INTERESTS

Chihuly collects vintage cars and motorcycles, Native American blankets and baskets, and handmade canoes. He also spends a great deal of time giving talks and demonstrations of his artistic techniques at schools across the country. In 1994 Chihuly and a friend, Kathy Kaperick, created the Hilltop Artists-in-Residence Program. This program takes at-risk kids off the streets of Tacoma and allows them to express themselves through art. "How could you not want to help young people?" he asked. "It gives me joy."

SELECTED WRITINGS

Chihuly: Color, Glass, and Form, 1986
Chihuly: Form from Fire, 1993
Chihuly: Projects, 2000

HONORS AND AWARDS

Louis Comfort Tiffany Foundation Award: 1967
Visual Artist's Award (American Council for the Arts): 1984
Golden Plate Award (American Academy of Achievement): 1994
Jerusalem Prize for Arts and Letters (Friends of Bezalel Academy of Arts
    and Design, Israel): 1998
Phoenix Award: 1998
Gold Medal Award (National Arts Club): 2002
Lifetime Achievement Award (Glass Art Society): 2003

FURTHER READING

Books

Authors and Artists for Young Adults, Vol. 46, 2002
Chihuly, Dale. *Chihuly: Color, Glass, and Form,* 1986
Chihuly, Dale. *Chihuly: Form from Fire,* 1993
Chihuly, Dale. *Chihuly: Projects,* 2000
Vignelli, Massimo. *Chihuly,* 1997
Warmus, William. *The Essential Dale Chihuly,* 2000

Periodicals

Christian Science Monitor, Nov. 30, 2001, p.20
Current Biography Yearbook, 1995
Dallas Observer, Dec. 20, 2001
Forbes, June 19, 1995, p.268; May 14, 2001, p.212
Los Angeles Times, July 20, 1994, p.A5; July 7, 2002, Sunday Calendar, p.6
National Geographic World, Mar. 1999, p.6
Newsday, Nov. 16, 1997, p.D28
Norfolk Virginian-Pilot, Mar. 28, 1999, p.E1
People, Dec. 13, 1999, p.117
School Arts, Mar. 1992, p.27
Seattle Times, Nov. 18, 1990, p.L1; Aug. 27, 1995, p.M1; Dec. 3, 1995, Pacific
    section, p.12
Washington Post, Nov. 26, 1978, p.K1

Online Articles

http://www.chihuly.com/essays
  (*Garden Design Journal*, "A Glass Act," Feb.-Mar. 2002)

Online Databases

Biography Resource Center Online, 2005, article from *Authors and Artists for Young Adults*, 2002
Wilson Web, 2005, article from *Current Biography*, 1995

ADDRESS

Dale Chihuly
1111 Northwest 50th Street
Seattle, WA 98107-5120

WORLD WIDE WEB SITE

http://www.chihuly.com

Neda DeMayo 1960-

American Wildlife Conservationist
Founder of Return to Freedom — The American Wild
Horse Sanctuary

BIRTH

Neda DeMayo was born on January 20, 1960, in New Haven,
Connecticut. She is the daughter of William S. DeMayo, a fi-
nancial consultant and professor at the University of New
Haven, and his wife, Stella DeMayo. Neda has a sister, Diana.

YOUTH AND EDUCATION

DeMayo started taking riding lessons at the age of five in Ham-
den Connecticut. "I cannot remember a time when I did not

love horses," she recalled. "One of my first words was 'horse.'" A defining moment in her life occurred at age six, when she first became aware of the U.S. Bureau of Land Management (BLM) policy of rounding up and capturing wild horses. "I can remember seeing wild horses on television being chased by everything from cowboys to hovering helicopters and wanting to help them escape and have a place for them to remain free, together, and safe," she said. "As I grew up, my relationship with horses deepened and I began to think about somehow, some way to start a sanctuary for wild horses."

When DeMayo was eight years old, her family moved to a home on four acres in the woods in Cheshire, Connecticut. She got a horse of her own — a black Morgan named Sam — and practically lived on his back. She and her friends rode their horses to the local Dairy Queen for ice cream, and to a nearby pond to go swimming. They even went camping by horseback on full moon nights.

After graduating from Hammonassett High School, DeMayo left Connecticut and headed west with her best friend and her dog. For the next few years, she traveled all over the world studying traditional healing methods and holistic medicine. In the mid 1980s she studied fashion design in San Francisco and eventually joined her sister in Los Angeles, where she also worked in the theater and film industry.

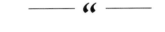

"I can remember seeing wild horses on television being chased by everything from cowboys to hovering helicopters and wanting to help them escape and have a place for them to remain free, together, and safe," DeMayo said.

CAREER HIGHLIGHTS

Pursuing Her Childhood Dream

Living in California in the late 1980s, DeMayo worked as a holistic healing practitioner and also as a costume designer for theatrical productions. Within a few years she was serving as a fashion stylist for Hollywood stars, including Sandra Bullock, Antonio Banderas, and David Duchovny. In 1994, however, she was involved in two serious car accidents that made her reconsider her career path. "I realized that I was focused on a career and was always running to survive while holding the dream that one day I would buy a ranch and have a sanctuary for animals and humans. I needed to get clear about how I wanted to spend my time because you don't know how long your life is going to last."

Creating a sanctuary to protect wild horses was a long-time dream for DeMayo.

Remembering her childhood passion for horses—and especially her concern for wild horses—DeMayo began pursuing her lifelong dream of creating a horse sanctuary. Over the next few years, she visited existing wild-horse sanctuaries in North America. During this period she also learned about habitat conservation programs, worked with several nonprofit groups, and traveled around California and New Mexico searching for suitable land.

In the mid 1990s, DeMayo purchased an Arabian mare and re-entered the world of horses to study horse behavior and communication. She visited wild horses in a few locations and frequently brought friends to a sanctuary in Northern California. Her quest for knowledge also led her to trainer Carolyn Resnick. A famous "horse whisperer" who used leadership dynamics predicated on daily behavior and relationships in wild horse herds, Resnick followed an approach that was based on respect for the complex inner nature of horses. Upon visiting Resnick's ranch, DeMayo noticed that "There was an awakeness in the animals there, a spirit you don't find in most domesticated horses. . . . Her horses were free when they were with her."

Saving the Mustang

During her preparations for the launch of her wild-horse sanctuary, De-Mayo learned a great deal about the history of horses in America. The modern horse evolved in North America about 1.6 million years ago. Early humans hunted the species to extinction on the continent, but horses were reintroduced by Spanish explorers in the late 1500s. Native Americans, early European farmers and settlers, and the U.S. Cavalry all domesticated horses for different uses over the next three centuries. Some of these horses escaped or were set free, and they adapted to the land and established wild herds. By 1900 around two million wild horses, or mustangs, roamed free in the United States. Due to habitat loss and government-sponsored capture and removal programs, however, the wild horse population has declined to only about 35,000 today. The remaining mustangs live in ten U.S. states, with the largest number in Nevada, followed by Wyoming, California, Oregon, Utah, and Arizona.

American wild horses received federal government protection in 1971 with the passage of the Wild Free-Roaming Horse and Burro Act, which gave the Bureau of Land Management responsibility for managing the herds. Calling mustangs "living symbols of the historic pioneer spirit of the west," the legislation said that the BLM could only remove wild horses and burros from public lands if the animals were overpopulating or causing habitat destruction. But the BLM faced a great deal of pressure from powerful ranchers and beef producers who wanted the horse herds removed so that they would have more public grazing land for their livestock. Over the years, the ranching interests succeeded in grad-

"The ancestors of these horses helped us build this country. They carried us across the land from east to west. They took us forward into battle; they pulled our plows; they drove our cattle. The horse holds a mythical status for Americans; he touches us deeply, symbolically, archetypically. He touches our hearts."

ually weakening the protections—and reducing the amount of land— granted to mustangs. In order to keep wild horse numbers in check and ensure adequate grazing areas for cattle, the BLM held annual roundups and offered "excess" horses for adoption to private individuals.

DeMayo argued that wild horses deserve protection because of their important role in American history and culture, as well as their unique genetic and behavioral characteristics. The mustang "has earned special status by having woven himself into everything that is American," she stated. "The ancestors of these horses helped us build this country. They carried us across the land from east to west. They took us forward into battle; they pulled our plows; they drove our cattle. The horse holds a mythical status for

Americans; he touches us deeply, symbolically, archetypically. He touches our hearts."

Preserving Horse Communities

In 1997, with the help of her parents and sister, DeMayo purchased a 300-acre ranch in the rolling hills of Lompoc, California, about 30 miles from Santa Barbara. She turned this property into Return to Freedom — The American Wild Horse Sanctuary. As she prepared to bring the first horses to the sanctuary, DeMayo decided to take a unique approach aimed at preserving entire herds of mustangs. In their natural environment, wild horses live in groups that work together like human families or communities. A mustang herd is typically led by a dominant male horse (called a stallion) with a lead mare. A herd also includes a number of adult female horses (mares), as well as younger horses of both sexes. BLM roundup and adoption programs often isolated individuals from their herds, causing deep trauma in captured horses and disrupted herds alike. DeMayo wanted to prevent that.

Beginning in 1998, Return to Freedom (RTF) became the new home of almost 200 wild horses in six herd groups. Some of the horses had been captured on the open range, like those DeMayo had seen on television as a child. Some had been rescued from horse auctions, where they might otherwise have been purchased by slaughterhouses. Others had been removed from adoptive homes after the owners decided that the animals could not be trained. "We have been able to relocate entire herds to RTF, where they are thriving because they are together in their natural family and social groups," DeMayo explained. "We have also been working with various experts on natural and non-intrusive population management programs so we don't have to separate the stallions from the herds. Return to Freedom has garnered support and interest as a model program because of our innovative approach to natural herd management."

DeMayo also decided to include an educational component to RTF. "I knew I had to educate because I knew I couldn't save every horse," she noted. "We recognize that, just as the earth has much to teach us about life, animals have much to teach us about living, communication, and instinct." RTF operates as a "living museum" that offers clinics, tours, and guided "wild horse walks" to the public in exchange for a small donation. The facility also invites groups of at-risk children — many of them from the inner city. At RTF, these kids get the opportunity to experience nature and learn compassion, trust, and confidence. No one is allowed to ride the mustangs that live at RTF. Instead, the horses roam freely with their herds, and

DeMayo helps visitors observe and interact with the animals in their natural environment. "You don't have to ride a horse to have a relationship with it," she explained. "Horse people—riders, breeders, trainers—who know far more about horses than I do, leave here in tears when they see wild horses living as they're meant to. They say, 'Oh my God, I never knew.'"

Providing a Home for Spirit

In 2002 RTF gained a famous resident when it was selected to be the permanent home of Spirit, the Kiger mustang stallion that served as the model for the main character in the animated film *Spirit: Stallion of the Cimarron.* The movie, which took four years to complete, was one of the most technically complex animated films of its time. It tells the story of Spirit's struggle to maintain his freedom during a period of rapid change and development in the Old West.

Once the movie was completed, the production company DreamWorks SKG searched the country for an appropriate home for the real-life mustang. "We were looking for two things: a place that had a philosophy we were comfortable with, and a location appropriate to the personality of Spirit," said Ann Daly, head of the feature animation department. "We felt we found it with the American Wild Horse Sanctuary. It allowed us to make a choice that's best for Spirit's personality and to extend the message of what the movie is about."

"You don't have to ride a horse to have a relationship with it," DeMayo explained. "Horse people—riders, breeders, trainers—who know far more about horses than I do, leave here in tears when they see wild horses living as they're meant to."

DeMayo praised the message of the film and expressed gratitude for the gift of the well-known horse. "Horses are a symbol of freedom and the American spirit, just like the bald eagle," she said. "In the animated movie *Spirit,* both animals travel across the plains side-by-side. That's why it was particularly thrilling that RTF was chosen . . . to be the home of the horse that the movie's drawings, animation, and spirit were based on." Spirit has served as a sort of ambassador, bringing media attention, visitors, and donations to RTF. "They couldn't have picked a more perfect horse," DeMayo noted. "He's fun to be with. He has a wonderful temperament. He's beautiful. He's a great representation of the Kiger [breed]."

*DeMayo with Spirit, the Kiger mustang that served as
the model for the animated movie hero.*

Fighting Political Battles

In addition to operating RTF, DeMayo has also been involved in political actions aimed at preserving the remaining mustangs in the United States. In the summer of 2004, RTF spearheaded the American Wild Horse Preservation Campaign (AWHPC) after she and a few colleagues rented a plane in Nevada and investigated a few herd management areas. These are areas where captured animals are kept. What they saw was disappointing and confirmed their suspicions. The AWHPC was created as a campaign supported by a coalition of organizations.

Then in November 2004, U.S. Senator Conrad Burns of Montana quietly added an amendment to a major Congressional spending bill that overturned many of the protections that wild horses had enjoyed for 34 years. The Burns Amendment allowed captured wild horses to be sold for commercial purposes, including slaughter. Previously, the BLM was required to place these animals in adoptive homes, and the private owners were required to keep them for at least one year before transferring ownership. Senator Burns argued that his amendment was necessary because it cost the government $19 million per year to keep thousands of mustangs in long-term holding facilities. He claimed that the new rule only applied to horses that were not considered adoptable because they were over ten years old or had already been offered for adoption three times.

Immediately after passage of the Burns Amendment, the coalition of wildlife conservation and environmental organizations supporting the American Wild Horse Preservation Campaign numbered 25 groups and represented over 10 million Americans nationwide. This coalition tried to raise public awareness of the need to preserve wild horses and their habitat and fought for new laws to protect the remaining mustangs. DeMayo and others in the campaign claimed that the Burns Amendment was a poorly disguised attempt to dispose of wild horses that should have been allowed to remain in the wild. The urgency of the situation became clear in the spring of 2005, when 41 wild horses that had been purchased under the Burns Amendment were slaughtered and turned into meat products for sale in Europe. Horse meat is a standard food in some European countries.

In November 2005 DeMayo and other mustang supporters won passage of an amendment that prevented the slaughter of American horses—both wild and domestic—for one year. The legislation prohibited meat inspectors from the U.S. Department of Agriculture (USDA) from working at horse slaughterhouses. Since all meat must be inspected by the USDA before it can be exported to foreign countries (and horse meat is not consumed in the United States), the bill effectively shut down all horse-slaughtering operations in America.

Wild mustangs deserve our protection, according to DeMayo.

DeMayo has also worked toward finding a solution that will allow wild mustangs to remain on public lands. She and other experts dismiss claims from ranching interests that wild mustangs are too hard on the land. In fact, they argue that horses provide valuable ecological benefits to the land by improving the soil and reseeding native plants with their manure. DeMayo also asserts that the four million privately owned cattle that range across public lands do far more environmental damage than 35,000 wild horses. "They're not asking for much," she said of the last mustangs. "You can't look at their numbers and say they're a nuisance out there. They're just not making anyone any money. I think they belong to the American people, because they represent us out there. They are the American spirit."

Planning for the Future

Today, DeMayo is nationally recognized as an expert in wild horse behavior and non-invasive horse-handling methods. RTF serves as home to 220 animals, and the operation includes six full-time staff members in addition to DeMayo and her family. It costs about $35,000 per month to run the sanctuary, and much of this funding comes from grants, private donations, and free services from veterinarians and other professionals. DeMayo hopes to acquire more land to expand the sanctuary in the near future. "I didn't want to run a little rescue operation," she noted. "I wanted to create a way of preserving these horses over the long term."

Toward this end, DeMayo is working hard to establish The American Wild Horse Conservancy—the next step for Return to Freedom. A historical land trust, the conservancy would be a large scale wildlife preserve that would integrate wild horses as a wildlife species and maintain them in genetically viable herd groups.

DeMayo and RTF have attracted the support of a number of prominent horse lovers, including actress and singer Hilary Duff, star of the TV series "Lizzie McGuire," and actor Viggo Mortensen, star of the hit films *Hidalgo* and *The Lord of the Rings* trilogy. Another supporter was John Fusco, the mustang preservationist and screenwriter (*Spirit: Stallion of the Cimarron, Hidalgo*), who aligned with Return to Freedom's efforts to establish the conservancy. Actor Robert Redford also lent his powerful name to the cause, drafting a letter to members of Congress in support of legislation that would ban the slaughter of wild horses.

—— " ——

"Human beings have a tendency to see the natural world as a threat, as something they need to conquer, enhance, or profit from," DeMayo said. *"In the process, we often destroy the things we love and the things we need. As stewards of this world, I believe we have a responsibility to maintain a healthy balance between our desires and the needs of other creatures and the environment."*

—— " ——

Through her work with wild horses, DeMayo tries to help people understand the importance of preserving wildness in the world. "Human beings have a tendency to see the natural world as a threat, as something they need to conquer, enhance, or profit from," she said. "In the process, we often destroy the things we love and the things we need. As stewards of this world, I believe we have a responsibility to maintain a healthy balance between our desires and the needs of other creatures and the environment."

MARRIAGE AND FAMILY

While traveling in Europe in the early 1980s, DeMayo met a Dutch man with whom she was involved for 11 years. The couple traveled between Europe and America for a few years and settled in California. They were married for five years, but have since divorced. DeMayo lives in a house on the Return to Freedom sanctuary in Lompoc, California. Her parents moved to another house on the ranch and her sister lives with her family in Van Nuys, California. They are all actively involved in the project.

FURTHER READING

Books

Rappaport, Jill, and Wendy Wilkinson. *People We Know, Horses They Love,* 2004
Resnick, Carolyn. *Naked Liberty,* 2005

Periodicals

California Riding, May 2005, p.56
Lifetime Magazine, Sep. 2004, p.111
Los Angeles Times, July 20, 2001, Southern California Living, p.1
People, May 9, 2005, p.219
Santa Barbara (CA) News-Press, June 12, 2002, p.B1
Santa Maria (CA) Times, June 22, 2002, p.C5
Teen Newsweek, Feb. 15, 2005, p.7
Young Rider, May/June 2004

Online Articles

http://www.californiaheartland.org/archive/hl_641/horsesanctuary.htm
(*California Heartland,* "Program 641: Horse Sanctuary," undated)
http://news.nationalgeographic.com/news/2001/10/1024_TVmustangs.html
(*National Geographic News,* "U.S. Wild Horses: Too Many Survivors on Too Little Land?" Oct. 26, 2001)

ADDRESS

Neda DeMayo
Return to Freedom
P.O. Box 926
Lompoc, CA 93438

WORLD WIDE WEB SITES

http://www.returntofreedom.org
http://www.wildhorsepreservation.com
http://www.dreamworks.com/spirit

Dakota Fanning 1994-

American Actress
Star of the Films *The Cat in the Hat, Uptown Girls,
Dreamer,* and *Charlotte's Web*

BIRTH

Hannah Dakota Fanning was born on February 23, 1994, in
Conyers, Georgia. She was the first of two daughters born to
Steve Fanning, an electrician and salesman, and Joy (Arrington)
Fanning, a homemaker. Her mother liked the name "Hannah,"
while her father preferred "Dakota." They compromised by giv-
ing their daughter both names, and she eventually went with
her father's choice. Dakota has a sister, Mary Elle (known as
"Elle"), who was born in 1998.

103

YOUTH

Dakota comes from a very athletic family. Her father played minor-league baseball, while her mother earned a college tennis scholarship. From a very early age, however, it was clear that acting — rather than sports — was Dakota's first love. At the age of four, for instance, she often pretended to be pregnant by stuffing a blanket inside her dress. Then she would stage a dramatic play for her parents in which she gave birth to her baby sister.

When Dakota was five, her parents encouraged her interest in acting by enrolling her in a one-week drama class at the Village Playhouse in Atlanta. "My mom saw that [I liked to act,] and she got me with a playhouse where you study for the play and then do the play at the end of the week," she remembered. Amazed by her talent, the director told her parents to take her to a talent agency. Representatives from the local Hot Shot Kids agency were also impressed with Dakota's physical attractiveness and natural acting abilities. "I knew immediately she was a little prodigy and a child star," said talent agent Joy Pervis. "She has such a sparkle about her — she's a one-in-a-million kid."

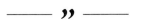

> *One of Fanning's first acting jobs was in a Tide laundry detergent commercial. "I didn't have any lines," she recalled. "I was just eating pudding, and then I spilled some on my dress. I had to do that about 20 times! But the pudding was really good."*

Hot Shot Kids sent videotapes of Dakota to their affiliate agency in Los Angeles, the Osbrink Agency. The owner immediately asked her parents to bring her to Los Angeles, where Dakota filmed three commercials in two weeks. The most prominent was a national Tide laundry detergent commercial. "I didn't have any lines," she recalled. "I was just eating pudding, and then I spilled some on my dress. I had to do that about 20 times! But the pudding was really good."

EDUCATION

By all accounts, Fanning is intelligent and mature beyond her years. By the time she launched her acting career at the age of six, she could already read at a fifth-grade level. Her busy movie schedule prevents her from attending a traditional school. Instead, Fanning has a private tutor who travels with her to movie locations and teaches her at home when she is between projects. She has said that she'd like to go to a "normal, well, not 'normal,' but regular" high school one day.

CAREER HIGHLIGHTS

Breaking Through to Stardom

As soon as Fanning's commercials began airing on television, her acting career took off. Within a few months she was cast in small roles on several television series, including "ER," "Ally McBeal," "The Practice," "CSI," "Spin City," and "Malcolm in the Middle." Realizing that their six-year-old daughter had real potential as an actress, her parents then decided to move the family to Hollywood. Fanning made her film debut in 2001, at the age of seven, with a minor role in the movie *Tomcats,* starring Jerry O'Connell. Later that year, she received a larger role in the movie *Father Xmas,* which explored the true meaning of Christmas through the experiences of a family in wartime.

Fanning's breakthrough to stardom came in the 2001 film *I Am Sam.* Sean Penn starred as Sam Dawson, a mentally disabled single father struggling to raise a precocious young daughter (played by Fanning). Sam named his little girl Lucy Diamond, after the Beatles song "Lucy in the Sky with Diamonds." Since Sam's mental capacity is limited to that of a seven-year-old, young Lucy is forced to become the primary decision-maker in the family. As a team of social workers and attorneys tries to decide what is best for Sam and Lucy, Lucy is mainly concerned about protecting her father's feelings.

Both Penn and Fanning received a great deal of critical attention for their sensitive portrayals of the father and daughter. In fact, Penn received an Academy Award nomination for the role, and many critics felt that Fanning deserved an Oscar nod as well. In a review for the *Hollywood Reporter,* Kirk Honeycutt described Fanning as "an absolute angel with smarts — she delivers her lines like a seasoned pro." Fanning explained that the role came naturally to her because she has an aunt who is mentally challenged.

Fanning's performance in *I Am Sam* also received notice from several professional organizations. For instance, she received a nomination as Best Supporting Actress from the Screen Actors Guild. Only eight years old at the time, she became the youngest person ever nominated for an award in the organization's history. Although Fanning did not claim that honor, she did win the Best Young Actor Award from the Broadcast Film Critics Association (commonly known as a "Critics' Choice" award), beating out

Fanning with Sean Penn in a scene from I Am Sam.

Daniel Radcliffe (*Harry Potter*) and Haley Joel Osment (*AI: Artificial Intelligence*). When Fanning went on stage to accept her award, she found that she was not tall enough to reach the podium. Presenter Orlando Bloom had to pick her up and hold her near the microphone while she gave a surprisingly long acceptance speech.

In 2002 Fanning appeared in the movie *Trapped,* with Kevin Bacon and Charlize Theron. She played Abby Jennings, a young girl who is kidnapped. Fanning also appeared in the 2002 romantic comedy *Sweet Home Alabama,* playing a younger version of the movie's star, Reese Witherspoon. Fanning returned to television that year to narrate and star in "Taken," a 10-part, 20-hour science-fiction miniseries produced by Steven Spielberg for the Sci Fi Channel. The story covers more than 50 years in the lives of three families that are changed through their contact with extraterrestrials. "Ultimately all plot lines lead to Allie, a human-alien girl played with remarkable poise and intelligence by eight-year-old Dakota Fanning," Terry Kelleher wrote in *People.*

Appearing Alongside Major Stars

In 2003 Fanning appeared in a live-action version of *The Cat in the Hat,* based on the classic 1957 children's book by Dr. Seuss. She played Sally Walden, one of the two children who receive a visit from a mischievous cat (played by Mike Myers) while their mother is not home. Although *The Cat in the Hat* received generally poor reviews, Fanning enjoyed making the film. She especially liked learning and performing all of the physical stunts.

In her next film, *Uptown Girls* (2003), Fanning played a spoiled rich girl, Ray, who gets a new nanny, Molly (played by Brittany Murphy). Molly is the kooky, party-girl daughter of a late rock star. Her carefree personality clashes with that of uptight Ray, but they eventually come to an understanding. The nanny learns to be more responsible, while Fanning's character becomes more playful. "Ray belongs to a long line of precocious Hollywood brats, but Fanning . . . displays the stellar presence and originality that made her so appealing" in earlier roles, Kevin Thomas wrote in the *Los Angeles Times*.

In 2004 Fanning starred opposite Denzel Washington in *Man on Fire.* She played the daughter of a wealthy American businessman living in Mexico, and Washington played a former CIA operative who is hired to act as her bodyguard. The outgoing little girl helps the troubled agent open up, and when she is kidnapped he risks his life to save her. Washington—a highly regarded actor with an Academy Award to his credit—had high praise for his young co-star's performance. "Twice in my career I can remember doing a scene and finding myself just watching the other actor," he stated. "Once was with Gene Hackman, and once with Dakota." The role earned Fanning a Critics' Choice Award nomination for Best Performance in a Feature Film.

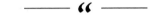

"Twice in my career I can remember doing a scene and finding myself just watching the other actor," Denzel Washington said. "Once was with Gene Hackman, and once with Dakota."

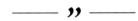

Fanning appeared in several films in 2005. She joined an all-star female cast—including Glenn Close, Holly Hunter, Sissy Spacek, and Robin Wright Penn—in the film *Nine Lives.* She played one of nine central characters whose lives intertwine in a series of vignettes. Next, Fanning decided to challenge herself by taking on a darker role. She played Emily, the troubled daughter of a psychologist (Robert DeNiro), in the thriller *Hide and Seek.* After witnessing her mother's suicide, Emily develops an imaginary friend named Charlie who begins threatening her father. Fanning wore a brown wig and dark makeup under her eyes to give her a spooky appearance in the film. "I had a really exciting time developing such a different character than myself," she noted.

Also in 2005, Fanning played the role of Tom Cruise's daughter in the highly anticipated action film *War of the Worlds*. Based on the classic 1953 story by H.G. Wells, the big-budget movie about an alien invasion received mixed reviews. Despite the early anticipation, many critics were unimpressed by the move. For example, critic Roger Ebert called it "a big, clunky movie containing some sensational sights but lacking the zest and joyous energy we expect from [director] Steven Spielberg." Others disagreed, as in this comment from Leah Rozen: "Fanning again proves herself remarkably gifted. . . . *War* is a sizzling summer popcorn movie offering two hours of solid story and gee-whiz, special effects-driven scares, all viewed from the comfortable safety of one's seat in a theater."

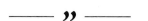

> *Fanning complains that the hardest part of acting is saying good-bye to the cast and crew at the end of filming. "You get to know everybody for so long, for two months, and then you have to say good-bye and then you're like, NO!"*

In *Dreamer*, released later in 2005, Fanning played the daughter of a horse trainer (Kurt Russell) who nurses a broken horse back to health and helps it win the Breeder's Cup. The movie was inspired by the true story of a horse with a broken bone that returned to racing: Mariah's Storm, winner of the 1995 Breeder's Cup. Fanning's role originally called for a boy, but producers eagerly made a change when they found out she was available. Fanning said that she "never really had any experience with horses" before the movie, but she learned how to ride for the part. In fact actor Kurt Russell, who plays her father in *Dreamer*, bought a special gift for her after they finished filming: he gave her a horse. "He's a palomino, and I keep him near where I live in California and ride him every weekend," she said.

Fanning has recently completed filming a live-action version of the beloved E.B. White book *Charlotte's Web*, scheduled to be released in June 2006. She plays Fern, with a stellar list of actors providing voices for the barnyard characters, including Julia Roberts, Oprah Winfrey, Steve Buscemi, John Cleese, Robert Redford, Cedric the Entertainer, Jennifer Garner, and André Benjamin, to name a few. "*Charlotte's Web* is one of my favorite books," Fanning says. "It's a dream part." After that, she will play the title character in two movie adaptations of the "Alice in Wonderland" books by Lewis Carroll.

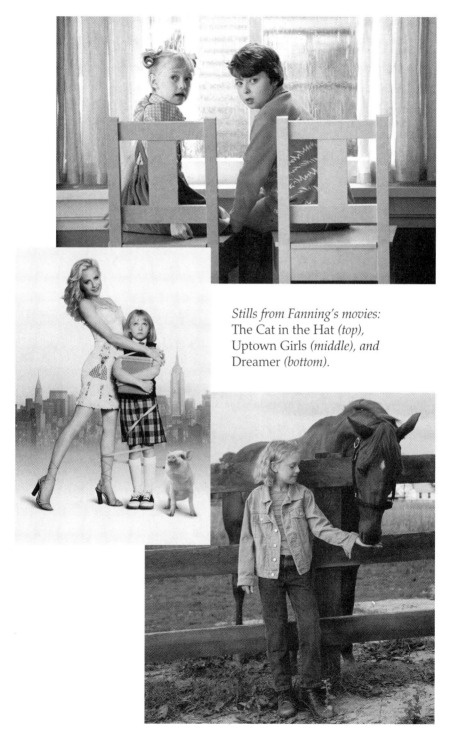

Stills from Fanning's movies:
The Cat in the Hat *(top),*
Uptown Girls *(middle), and*
Dreamer *(bottom).*

Trying to Stay Grounded

Before even reaching her teen years, Fanning has become a force to be reckoned with in the entertainment industry. Since she made her film debut in 2001, her movies have outperformed those of most major actresses in Hollywood, according to *Entertainment Weekly*. Her movies have earned more than $600 million at the box office, which exceeds the draw of such stars as Julia Roberts ($586 million), Nicole Kidman ($497 million), and Reese Witherspoon ($338 million).

Despite her youth, Fanning has consistently received high praise for her acting skills. "She's incredibly talented and she has a wisdom in her expressions that belies her age," said Elizabeth Gabler, president of the movie company Fox 2000. "She comes into your office, and after a minute you forget her age," added Adam Goodman, president of production at Dreamworks. "It's like being in a meeting with a really savvy, experienced film vet."

> "I can't even picture myself doing anything but acting. Acting is a real positive experience. We joke around, do some takes, and then have fun talking about it. Nothing is ever really hard. But it's always a challenge to take on a new character and stay in character."

Fanning earns over $3 million per picture, and she receives more than 200 fan letters each day. Despite her wealth and popularity, insiders claim that she remains humble, polite, and remarkably normal. While she is often described as having an "old soul," she is also frequently called "sunny" and "fun." When a script calls for her to cry, she says that she remembers the night when her goldfish, Flounder, flopped out of his bowl and died. She also complains that the hardest part of acting is saying good-bye to the cast and crew at the end of filming. "You get to know everybody for so long, for two months, and then you have to say good-bye and then you're like, NO!" she explained.

To keep things interesting and challenge her acting ability, Fanning tries to alternate between "fun" movies and "serious" ones. She insists that she acts not for money or fame, but because she loves it. "From the day that I did the Tide commercial, I knew that I wanted to do this forever," she stated. "I can't even picture myself doing anything but acting. Acting is a real positive experience. We joke around, do some takes, and then have fun talking about it. Nothing is ever really hard. But it's always a challenge to take on a new character and stay in character."

HOME AND FAMILY

Fanning lives in Los Angeles with her parents and younger sister, Elle, who is also a talented actress. She has appeared in *Daddy Day Care* with Eddie Murphy (2003) and in *The Door in the Floor* with Jeff Bridges and Kim Basinger (2005).

HOBBIES AND OTHER INTERESTS

In her spare time, Fanning likes to knit, read, play piano, and ride horses. She also speaks Spanish and is an avid swimmer. Despite her adult career, Fanning insists that she has a "kid side" and still enjoys playing with toys. "When I go home, I play with my baby dolls and strollers and stuffed animals," she said.

Fanning also enjoys watching movies. Among her favorites are *My Best Friend's Wedding, Gone with the Wind, Titanic,* and *Steel Magnolias.* Her favorite actresses include Cameron Diaz, Julia Roberts, Meryl Streep, and Hilary Swank — "not just because they're great actresses, but because they are amazing people," she noted.

SELECTED CREDITS

Films

Tomcats, 2001
Father Xmas, 2001
I Am Sam, 2001
Trapped, 2002
Sweet Home Alabama, 2002
The Cat in the Hat, 2003
Uptown Girls, 2003
Man on Fire, 2004
Nine Lives, 2005
The War of the Worlds, 2005
Dreamer, 2005

Television

"Taken," 2002

HONORS AND AWARDS

Golden Satellite Award: 2002, for *I Am Sam*
Best Younger Actress Award (Broadcast Film Critics Association): 2002, for
    I Am Sam
Young Artist Award: 2002, for *I Am Sam*
Emmy Award: 2003, for "Taken"

FURTHER READING

Books

Newsmakers, Issue 2, 2005

Periodicals

Bergen (NJ) County Record, Feb. 4, 2005, p.G8
Entertainment Weekly, July 29, 2005, p.10
Orange County (CA) Register, Jan. 29, 2005
Orlando Sentinel, Dec. 1, 2002, p.4
People, Aug. 25, 2003, p.75
Time, Mar. 7, 2005, p.76
Times (London), Jan. 29, 2005, p.22
USA Today, Mar. 6, 2002, p.D2
Variety, Jan. 31, 2005, p.48

Online Databases

Biography Resource Center Online, 2005, article from *Newsmakers,* 2005

Additional information for this profile came from interviews with Dakota
    Fanning for "CNN Live Today" (conducted on January 30, 2002, and
    August 20, 2003) and for "The Today Show" (conducted August 7, 2003).

ADDRESS

Dakota Fanning
Osbrink Talent Agency
4343 Lankershim Blvd., Suite 100
Universal City, CA 91602

GREEN DAY

William (Billie Joe) Armstrong 1972-
Michael Pritchard (Mike Dirnt) 1972-
Frank Edwin Wright III (Tré Cool) 1972-

American Punk Rock Band
Creators of the Hit Records *Dookie* and *American Idiot*

EARLY YEARS

Green Day is a three-man punk rock group whose members include Billie Joe Armstrong (lead singer and guitarist), Mike Dirnt (bassist), and Tré Cool (drummer).

113

Billie Joe Armstrong

William (Billie Joe) Armstrong was born on February 17, 1972, in Rodeo, California. He is the youngest of six children. His father, Andy, was a truck driver and jazz drummer in his spare time. His mother, Ollie, was a waitress at Rod's Hickory Pit, a local roadside diner.

Even as a young child, Armstrong enjoyed singing and performing. When he was only five years old, he would perform for patients in children's hospitals and for residents of nursing homes. "Music has always been in my household," he remembered, "whether it was my dad playing jazz or my sister playing clarinet or something like that." During an interview with MTV, Armstrong said that he watched the Ramones' film called *Rock 'n' Roll High School* when he was nine years old. "To me, what I saw was the perfect rock band," he recalled. "They had songs that just stuck in your head. Just like a hammer, they banged right into your brain." By the time he was 15, Armstrong could play the guitar, piano, drums, harmonica, mandolin, and saxophone.

"Music has always been in my household," Armstrong remembered, "whether it was my dad playing jazz or my sister playing clarinet or something like that."

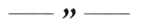

When Billie Joe was just ten years old, Andy Armstrong died of cancer of the upper digestive tract, which had spread through the rest of his body. Billie Joe and his father had a very close relationship. He recalls, "Only a few days before he drew his last breath, he gave me my first guitar. I gave it a name—Blue—because it was a blue Fender Stratocaster copy. It ended up battered, covered in duct tape and stickers, because I played it so much. It's become my trademark, and I still use replicas on stage and in videos."

After Andy died, Ollie had to struggle to make ends meet. She continued to work at the diner, but other things changed for the worse. Billie Joe's sister, Anna, confided in an interview, "Our family changed a lot because my parents had been very kid oriented. And all of a sudden, my mother withdrew and threw herself into waitressing. The family structure broke up. Then my mom remarried about a year or two afterward, and that was a big change for the negative." One positive in all this was his friendship with Mike Dirnt, who became his best friend.

On the day before his 18th birthday, Armstrong dropped out of high school. He decided that the demanding schedule of his music career should take precedence over his education.

Green Day in New York City in 1994.

Mike Dirnt

Mike Dirnt was born Michael Pritchard on May 4, 1972, in Rodeo, California. His birth mother was a heroine addict at the time of his birth. She gave Dirnt up for adoption when he was a baby. His adoptive father was white, and his adoptive mother was Native American. They divorced when he was seven years old. For a while, Dirnt divided his time between both parents' homes. After several confrontations with his father, he finally settled in with his mother. They lived in conditions barely above poverty level. "When I was in fourth or fifth grade, my mom stayed out all night, came home the next day with a guy, and he moved in," Dirnt said. "I'd never met the guy before, and all of a sudden he's my stepdad." Initially he did not get along with his new stepfather. But the two eventually developed a very close relationship and remained close until his stepfather passed away when Dirnt was 17.

Dirnt used to play guitar, playing with his friend Billie Joe Armstrong. But then one day his friend's brother told him that no matter how many guitar players there are in a band, there would be only one bass player. That's when Dirnt said, "Bingo!" His mom bought him an old bass from a pawn shop. It was not in good condition, but it worked. According to Dirnt, "It had buttons all over it and two flat-wound strings: E and A. But the bass made the right sounds, so I could have band practice. Billie and I would just plug into the same amp and play all night."

When Dirnt was 15 years old, his mother moved out of the area. He didn't want to move with her, so he moved out on his own. After living out of his truck for a while, he rented a room in Armstrong's house. Dirnt worked as a busboy and a cook to earn money to support himself.

> "It had buttons all over it and two flat-wound strings: E and A," Dirnt said about his first bass guitar. "But the bass made the right sounds, so I could have band practice. Billie and I would just plug into the same amp and play all night."

Although Armstrong dropped out of high school, Dirnt continued and graduated. He is the only one of the three band members to graduate from high school. He did take a few college courses but never received his college degree.

Tré Cool

Tré Cool was born Frank Edwin Wright III in Germany on December 9, 1972. His father had been a helicopter pilot in Vietnam. When he returned to the United States, the family moved to Willits, California, which is in a very remote area in the Mendocino Mountains. Cool's father, Frank Wright II, worked as a builder, bus driver, and trucking company owner. His mother, Linda, was a bookkeeper.

When Cool was in second grade, he learned to play the violin. He later switched to drums, which Linda said was "pretty noisy, but a definite improvement on the violin." Luckily the noise didn't bother the Wrights' closest neighbor, who lived a mile away. That neighbor, Lawrence Livermore, was the leader of a band called The Lookouts. Livermore was also a writer for *MaximumRockNRoll*, a San Francisco punk rock publication, and he later founded Lookout! Records. As there wasn't much to do in Willits, Cool started to hang out with Livermore, who eventually asked him to join The Lookouts as their drummer. Cool was just 12 years old.

Cool was class president in high school, but he eventually dropped out to pursue his music career. For a time after Cool joined Green Day, his dad drove the band around. His mother, Linda, recalled that "We always fretted when they went far from home. Frank wanted to be sure they had a good driver."

FORMING THE BAND

Both Armstrong and Dirnt grew up in Rodeo, California, which is approximately 15 miles north of Berkeley. The community in which they lived was mostly blue-collar. They were surrounded by large chemical refineries and oil refineries. Their hometown was "the most unscenic place on the planet," Armstrong once said. "We went to this elementary school, and they used to always send kids home with headaches. They figured it was because of the toxins that the refineries were throwing in the air."

Armstrong and Dirnt met when they were 11 years old and became fast friends. They shared an interest in music. They listened to and played music together, Armstrong on vocals and guitar and Dirnt on bass. There were no record stores in their town, so new music was hard to come by. "If you wanted to hear music, you had to play it [yourself]," Dirnt said. The two performed for other people any chance they had, in nearby cafes, at parties, and at friends' homes. They were not paid for these performances.

The two best friends began to hang out at the Gilman Street Project in Berkeley, a weekend underground punk club. The business was actually a caning and wicker shop by day, but it was a very well known destination for punk rockers on weekends. The club was started by a group of volunteers to encourage creativity in a violence-free environment. The nonprofit club was open to the public of all ages. They did not sell alcohol, but it was not uncommon to see people drinking outside the club. According to Armstrong, "That place and that culture saved my life. It was like a gathering of outcasts and freaks."

In 1987, Armstrong and Dirnt formed a band called Sweet Children. They recruited drummer John Kiffmeyer to join their band. Kiffmeyer used the stage name Al Sobrante, a play on the name of his hometown, El Sobrante. The group made their debut performance at Rod's Hickory Pit, where Armstrong's mother worked as a waitress and Dirnt worked as a bus boy. Owner Richard Cotton said, "Billie Joe was a good kid. He used to sing and dance for our old folk in the banquet room. I remember telling Ollie, 'I'm going to see this kid in lights one day.'"

One other very significant performance, although they didn't know it at the time, was at a high school party where they played with another local band,

The Lookouts. The leader of the other band was Lawrence Livermore, and the drummer was Tré Cool. The performance itself was not a major event—there were only about five people there—but they played their hearts out. Livermore recalled that Sweet Children "played to those five kids as if they were the Beatles at Shea Stadium. It was only their third or fourth show ever, but I said right then that I was going to make a record with these guys."

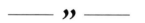

> "The first time I ever saw Tré was when I went to see The Lookouts and I was outside . . . with these girls," Armstrong recalled. "And Tré was walking by wearing a weird, old man's plaid suit—none of which was color-coordinated whatsoever—and an old bathing cap. These girls were like, 'Oh, The Lookouts!' And Tré just kind of turned to them and bowed. I remember thinking that was pretty cool."

BECOMING GREEN DAY

Sweet Children started to perform at the Gilman Street Project in 1988. They played a handful of shows through the end of March 1989 and began to develop a following in the local punk scene. They played their last Gilman Project show as Sweet Children on April 1, 1989. Later that month, they changed their name to Green Day. By that time, they were working with Lawrence Livermore and Lookout! Records to release their first EP.

Green Day released a four-song EP entitled *1,000 Hours* under the Lookout! label. They continued to play as many gigs as they could get. They played at the Gilman Project under their new name for the first time on May 28, 1989. They became regulars there, performing on a monthly basis. They played with The Lookouts again in June 1989 for an audience of 1,300 at Veterans Hall in Garberville, California. In July 1990, Livermore and the rest of The Lookouts disbanded. Meanwhile, the members of Green Day—Armstrong, Dirnt, and Sobrante—worked odd jobs and played as stand-ins for other bands in order to earn money for their emerging band.

CAREER HIGHLIGHTS

Toward the end of 1989, Green Day and Lookout! Records decided that it was time to record a full-length album. For 22 hours, starting on December 29, 1989, the band recorded a 10-track album and called it *39/Smooth*. It cost them a total of $600 to record the album, which was released in 1990.

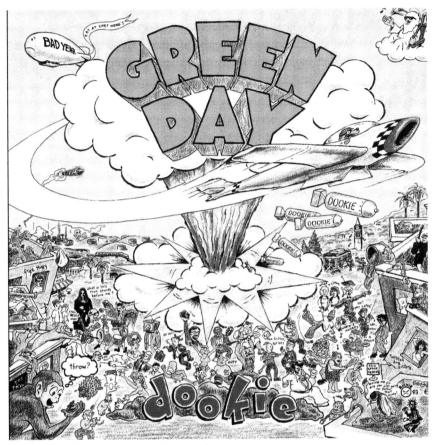

The cover of the CD Dookie, Green Day's first big success.

In April 1990, Green Day recorded a four-song EP titled *Slappy*. The band decided it was time to tour the United States, so they toured through the end of summer. At the end of the tour, Sobrante decided to quit the band and go to college. That left Green Day without a drummer, so Armstrong and Dirnt asked Tré Cool to join the group. As Armstrong recalled, "The first time I ever saw Tré was when I went to see The Lookouts and I was outside . . . with these girls. And Tré was walking by wearing a weird, old man's plaid suit—none of which was color-coordinated whatsoever—and an old bathing cap. These girls were like, 'Oh, The Lookouts!' And Tré just kind of turned to them and bowed. I remember thinking that was pretty cool."

In November 1990, the new Green Day set off for a 64-day European tour. They were one of five bands touring together. The band was still struggling

119

financially at that time; they didn't even have their own equipment, so they borrowed where they could. "It made us a really good band," Armstrong said, "playing on different equipment and in different situations. I think it made us better because obviously there's a language difference and it meant we had to be more animated and project a bit more physically. We seemed to get a good response because we were so different from most of the bands playing."

When they returned from their European tour, they were ready to get serious. Cool's dad, Frank Wright II, fixed up an old bookmobile to serve as the band's tour bus. He built equipment racks and sleeping quarters on the bus. Also in 1991, Lookout! put the *39/Smooth* album together with *Slappy* on one album and released it as *1039/Smoothed Out Slappy Hours*.

> *Critic Michael Baker described* Dookie *as "a hot slice of straight-ahead snarl-pop, each of the 14 songs created according to Billie's maxim—'short, catchy, and in your face, so you'll want to hear it again.'"*

Kerplunk

In 1992, with Cool as their new drummer, Green Day released the album *Kerplunk* under the Lookout! label. The album was an immediate success, breaking sales records for Lookout! The band toured extensively in North America and Europe, stopping in the United Kingdom, Germany, Czechoslovakia, Holland, Italy, and Poland. Through the tours, the band got their name out, and their popularity continued to grow. Several major record labels started to pay attention to this three-man punk band from California.

In 1993, Green Day and Lookout! parted on friendly terms. The band signed on with Reprise Records, a subsidiary of Warner Brothers. In their contract with Reprise, however, they did make sure that Lookout! Records retained all rights to their early recordings, including *Kerplunk*.

Dookie

In 1994, Green Day released *Dookie*. The music continued the punk sound from the group's earlier releases, what critic Michael Baker described as "a hot slice of straight-ahead snarl-pop, each of the 14 songs created according to Billie's maxim—'short, catchy, and in your face, so you'll want to hear it again.'" That view was echoed by music reviewer Christopher John Farley. "Bad attitudes often make for good rock 'n' roll," Farley wrote.

Green Day performing in 2004.

"Green Day takes its adolescent snottiness and channels it into music. The result is a cathartic punk explosion and the best rock CD of the year so far. This is music for people with raging hormones and short attention spans. . . . Every song on *Dookie* is brief and hard—the entire 14-track album is just 39 minutes long. Most of the songs are built around seductive guitar riffs, and each one is performed with controlled frenzy. The lyrics are about being young and screwed-up, about having your hopes and dreams dipped in disillusionment and then swallowed whole like so many Chicken McNuggets. . . . Green Day's punk nihilism works because it's delivered with self-deprecating humor, not with narcissistic rock angst."

Dookie was a huge smash for the young group. The album debuted on the *Billboard* album charts at No. 127 and eventually reached No. 2 on the charts. They recorded a video for the first single on the album, "Longview," which fueled its popularity. *Dookie* reached platinum status ten times over by selling over 10 million copies.

On August 13 and 14, 1994, a two-day concert event called Woodstock II was held in Saugerties, New York, to commemorate the 25th anniversary of the original 1969 Woodstock event. Approximately 250,000 tickets were sold to the show in Saugerties, and Green Day was scheduled to perform on the afternoon of August 14. As the day went on, Green Day fans started to become impatient to see them. They booed other artists as they performed and chanted for Green Day. The event organizers finally started to announce, "Green Day will be on when their turn comes; please give these musicians their turn." By the time it was Green Day's turn to perform, things had started to get out of control. Fans threw mud everywhere, including on stage, and a huge mud fight broke out. The band tried to play, but their instruments were covered in mud, and the fans were wild. They finally had to be air lifted off the stage. By that time, Dirnt's front teeth had been shattered by security guards because he was so covered in mud that they couldn't tell him from the wild fans that had hopped on stage. "It was the closest thing to anarchy I've ever seen in my life, and I didn't like it," Armstrong admitted.

> *"Bad attitudes often make for good rock 'n' roll," wrote music reviewer Christopher John Farley. "Green Day takes its adolescent snottiness and channels it into music. The result is a cathartic punk explosion and the best rock CD of the year so far. This is music for people with raging hormones and short attention spans."*

Making It in the Big Time

It was clear that Green Day's fan base was growing—and growing fast. Their songs appealed to people of all ages. Parents and kids could listen to their music together, although some of their songs contain rather graphic language and the subject matter may not be appropriate for young kids. However, their songs were being played on radio stations with a variety of formats, including top 40, adult pop, modern rock, and hard rock. Their picture appeared on the covers of several music magazines. Part of Green Day's appeal has been that they are polite, articulate, and all-around good guys. They have even made every effort to keep ticket and merchandise prices low for their fans.

However, while the crossover appeal and the move to a big record label were great news for the band, many of their hardcore punk fans accused them of selling out. Few other punk bands ever made it big enough to move up as Green Day was doing. Dirnt responded to this accusation by saying, "Selling out is compromising your musical intentions, and we don't know how to do that." However, they found that they were no longer welcome at the Gilman Street Project, where their careers had begun.

Trying to Stay on Top

Green Day continued to tour. In October 1995, they released their next album, titled *Insomniac*. It debuted at No. 2 on Billboard's album charts and reached double platinum status. *Spin* magazine voted it No. 15 out of 20 of the best albums of 1995. Still, some critics were not as impressed with this album as they had been with the group's previous release.

The band had scheduled a European tour for 1996, but they unexpectedly cancelled, saying that they were too exhausted. They spent the next year resting and writing new material for their next album, *Nimrod*, which was released in 1997. *Nimrod* reached only No. 10 on the charts.

For the next three years, Green Day took more time off. They released their next album, *Warning*, in 2000. This album did not hit the charts like their earlier albums. Some critics started to think that Green Day's popularity was coming to an end. Shortly thereafter, in 2001, they released a compilation album titled *International Superhits!* It included many of their previously released songs. The album topped out at No. 40 on the charts and went gold. The following year, Green Day released *Shenanigans*, another compilation album that included some of their less popular previously recorded songs.

Working Out Their Differences

Perhaps one reason for Green Day's declining popularity was the tension that had been building among the members. For three years after the release of *Warning*, the group did not talk about things for fear of "rocking the boat." By 2001, Dirnt admitted, "breaking up was an option. We were arguing a lot and we were miserable. We needed to shift directions." Things had gotten so bad that Armstrong was afraid to show the other two his new songs. He was afraid that they would immediately criticize him.

Armstrong finally realized that "to be the greatest band in the world, we would have to work on the small stuff." In 2003, the band got together to make a new record. At Armstrong's suggestion, the band agreed that once a week, they would start their daily band practice with conversation. Dirnt said, "We bared our souls to one another." Cool added, "Admitting we cared for each other was a big thing. We didn't hold anything back." At 31, Armstrong realized that it was time to grow up. "I felt like I was too old to be angry anymore," he said. "I didn't want to come across as the angry older guy. It's sexy to be an angry young man, but to be a bitter old [man] is another thing altogether."

This seemed to work for the band. Within five months, the band had recorded 20 new songs. Then one day the band came in to find that the master for these 20 tracks had been stolen. The master has not yet been recovered. While the band was furious at this discovery, it forced them to

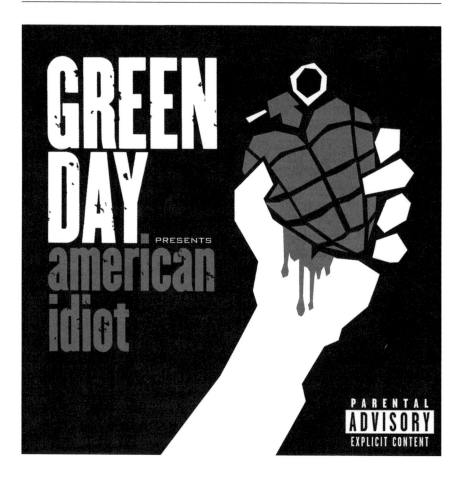

start from scratch. Armstrong headed to New York, leaving his family and the other band members for a month. He told *Rolling Stone*, "I was searching for something. I'm not sure it was the most successful trip." He spent a lot of time thinking and questioning himself.

American Idiot

After Armstrong returned from New York, the group found the theme for their next album while watching television footage of U.S. troops invading Iraq. "We were in the studio watching the journalists embedded with the troops, and it was the worst version of reality television," Armstrong recalled. "Switch the channel, and it's Nick and Jessica. Switch, and it's 'Fear Factor.' Switch, and people are having surgery to look like Brad Pitt. . . . It's a sign of the times." After this experience, the group decided that the album would have a political theme.

Armstrong came up with the idea of writing a rock opera. The other two loved the idea, and they decided to call it *American Idiot*. Together, they worked on the story line, pushing to make it both a more personal and a more political album than their earlier releases. On *American Idiot*, the group was very critical of President George W. Bush and his political decisions. "The atmosphere can be anti-Bush, and I definitely had that in mind, but when you get down to it, it's a human story," Armstrong explained. "This album is about feelings. I didn't want to make a Rage against the Machine record. I wanted to make an album of heartfelt songs."

"The statement that we're making is that this is a pretty serious time," Armstrong said. "There are a lot of people living in fear, and people need something to relate to. This album is a reflection of what's going on." The song "Holiday" has very strong anti-war sentiments, while "Boulevard of Broken Dreams" talks about loneliness and disillusionment. Another popular song on the album was "Wake Me Up When September Comes." While the video for the song depicts a young man going off to war to provide for his lover, the song was really written by Armstrong about his father's death. "It's a song about how I watched my dad die," he admitted. "I had no problem letting the director turn my song into an anti-war statement. But the truth is, it's about my dad." According to reviewer Doug Small, "The album explores the confusion in an America split right down the middle politically, and the need to find one's individuality once again in the midst of too much information."

> *"We were in the studio watching the journalists embedded with the troops, and it was the worst version of reality television,"* Armstrong recalled. *"Switch the channel, and it's Nick and Jessica. Switch, and it's 'Fear Factor.' Switch, and people are having surgery to look like Brad Pitt. . . . It's a sign of the times."*

But *American Idiot* was not just a political statement—it was a record, too, that showed a variety of musical inspirations. "I used everything I knew about music," Armstrong revealed. "Show tunes, musicals like *Grease*, and the struggle between right and wrong, *The Joshua Tree* [by U2]—I tried to soak in everything and make it Green Day." That mix of musical sounds was a big advantage to reviewer Matt Hendrickson, who wrote that "The sound of *American Idiot* careens from old-school punk to Motown soul and Who-style anthems."

*The members of Green Day. From left: Mike Dirnt,
Billie Joe Armstrong, and Tré Cool.*

And ultimately, it was the music that captured its many fans, according to reviewer Tom Sinclair. "What most fans — Democrats, Republicans, and anarchists alike — seem to be connecting with is the irresistible passion, intensity, and hookiness of the music, all of which had been in short supply on the band's last two albums," wrote Sinclair. "And *Idiot's* brash sound has done more than just connect with the public. It's also struck a decisive blow for rock music — make that loud, butt-kickin' rock music, the kind that shakes your nerves and rattles your brain."

Green Day debuted *American Idiot* in its entirety on September 16, 2004, in a live concert at Hollywood's Henry Fonda Music Box Theatre. It was an immediate success. *American Idiot* debuted at No. 1 on Billboard's album chart and remained in the top 10 for over a year. In 2005, the album was nominated for seven Grammy Awards, including Best Rock Album of the Year and Record of the Year. It won the award for Best Rock Album of the Year. Also in 2005, Green Day won four MTV Video Music Awards — Video of the Year, Best Group Video, Viewers' Choice Award, and Best Rock Video — for "Boulevard of Broken Dreams." This video has also won awards for best cinematography, best direction, and best editing. Then, in 2006, Green Day won another Grammy Award for another song from *American Idiot*, "Boulevard of Broken Dreams," which won the award for Record of the Year.

With the success of *American Idiot*, Green Day proved to the world that they still had it. As Dirnt declared, "Ten years ago, a lot of people [wrote us off]. 'That's just a snotty little band from the Bay Area.' But we're a career band. And this album is a testament to what we perceive to be a great career." Cool added, "We've been together for 15 years. For a marriage to last that long is an achievement. And that's only two people. This is three!"

MARRIAGE AND FAMILY

Armstrong met his wife, Adrienne Nesser, during Green Day's first tour. They lost touch for about a year but eventually met up again and were married in 1994. They have two sons, Joseph Marciano, born in 1995, and Jakob Danger, born in 1998. Billie Joe and Adrienne are co-owners of Adeline Records, a small independent label.

Mike married his longtime girlfriend, Anastasia, in 1996. They have a daughter, Estelle Desiree, born in 1997. Mike and Anastasia divorced but remain on friendly terms. Dirnt remarried in 2004. He is currently a co-owner of Rudy's Can't Fail Café in Emeryville, California.

— " —

"[What most fans] seem to be connecting with is the irresistible passion, intensity, and hookiness of the music," said reviewer Tom Sinclair. "And Idiot's *brash sound has done more than just connect with the public. It's also struck a decisive blow for rock music — make that loud, butt-kickin' rock music, the kind that shakes your nerves and rattles your brain."*

— " —

Tré Cool married Lisa Lyons in 1995. They have a daughter, Ramona, who was born earlier that year. The two divorced, and Cool remarried in 2000. He and his second wife, Claudia, had a son named Frankito in 2001. Tré and Claudia divorced in 2003.

RECORDINGS

1039 / Smoothed Out Slappy Hours, 1991
Kerplunk, 1992
Dookie, 1994
Insomniac, 1995
Nimrod, 1997
Warning, 2000
American Idiot, 2004

HONORS AND AWARDS

Grammy Award: 1994, for Best Alternative Music Performance, for *Dookie;* 2005, for Best Rock Album, for *American Idiot;* 2006, for Record of the Year, for "Boulevard of Broken Dreams"
MTV Video Music Awards: 2005 (four awards), Video of the Year, Best Group Video, Viewers' Choice Award, and Best Rock Video, for "Boulevard of Broken Dreams"

FURTHER READING

Books

Contemporary Musicians, Vol. 40, 2003
Small, Doug. *Omnibus Press Presents the Story of Green Day*, 2005

Periodicals

Current Biography Yearbook, 2005
Entertainment Weekly, Feb. 11, 2005, p.26
Minneapolis Star Tribune, Sep. 16, 2005, p.E1
Rolling Stone, Feb. 24, 2005, p.40

Online Articles

http://www.freep.com
   (*Detroit Free Press*, "Green Day's Story: 14 years, 7 discs," Sep. 9, 2005)

Online Databases

Biography Resource Center Online, 2006, *Contemporary Musicians*, 2003

ADDRESS

Green Day
Reprise Records
3300 Warner Boulevard
Burbank, CA 91505

WORLD WIDE WEB SITES

http://www.greenday.com
http://www.mtv.com/bands/az/green_day/bio.jhtml

Freddie Highmore 1992-

English Actor
Star of the Movies *Charlie and the Chocolate Factory*
and *Finding Neverland*

BIRTH

Freddie Highmore was born on February 14, 1992, in London,
England. His father, Edward Highmore, is an actor. His mother is a prominent film talent agent. Her job is to find work and
negotiate good pay and conditions for her actor clients.
Highmore has a younger brother, Bertie.

YOUTH AND EDUCATION

Highmore's acting career began at about the same time that he began school, so he has had a lot of unusual childhood experiences. But he stresses that when he's not on the set of a movie, his daily life is much the same as that of other kids his age. "I try to stay a normal boy as much as possible," he said. "My friends think it's pretty cool that I've done one or two films. They don't treat me any differently."

In the fall of 2005 Highmore entered the equivalent of U.S. eighth grade. "When I am not filming, I go to a normal, local school [in north London]," he said. "While working I have a tutor, but I still follow the same curriculum as my school." Highmore is particularly good at foreign language classes. He is most fluent in Latin, but he also enjoys French and Spanish.

CAREER HIGHLIGHTS

With two parents in show business, acting was a natural choice for Highmore. "I started doing little parts on television," he said. "People thought I wasn't too bad, and so I got offered bigger roles." He made his first film appearance at age six, playing the son of a woman played by English actress Helena Bonham Carter, in *Women Talking Dirty* (1999).

———— **"** ————

"I try to stay a normal boy as much as possible," Highmore said. "My friends think it's pretty cool that I've done one or two films. They don't treat me any differently."

———— **"** ————

Highmore took minor roles in several other movies over the next few years. Then, in 2004, he appeared with the noted English actor Kenneth Branagh in *Five Children and It.* In this film, Highmore and several other children befriend an ancient, cranky sand fairy. The fairy grants them a wish each day. But the children learn that magic can be a messy and dangerous force.

Growing Acclaim

That same year, Highmore secured his first major film role, sharing the screen with twin tiger cubs in the movie *Two Brothers*. He played Raoul, the son of a French administrator in Southeast Asia in the 1920s. After the cubs are cruelly separated, Raoul receives one as a gift. He is certain that he can domesticate the wild animal. But he is forced to give up his beloved pet after it ravages his parents' house and attacks the family dog. Later, the grown cubs are pitted against each other by their human owners in a con-

A scene from Finding Neverland.

test in which they are expected to fight to the death. But the brothers recognize each other despite their long separation and refuse to fight. Eventually, the brothers escape the clutches of their human captors and disappear into the wild together.

The movie was made by Jean-Jacques Annaud, who had a hit in 1988 with *The Bear.* Filmed in Cambodia and Thailand, *Two Brothers* won praise for its vibrant wildlife photography. But a number of reviewers dismissed the story line as predictable and superficial, and Highmore and the other human actors did not attract much notice.

Finding Neverland

Highmore received much more acclaim for his next role, in *Finding Neverland* (2004). His breakthrough performance won him wide recognition and the highest critical praise. The film is loosely based on the life of the famous author J.M Barrie, who was played by Johnny Depp. It explores how Barrie's friendship with four fatherless brothers inspired his best-known work, *Peter Pan.* Highmore plays Peter Llewelen Davies, the boy most affected by his father's death. Things only get worse for Peter when his mother (played by Kate Winslet) becomes seriously ill. But his evolving relationship with Barrie helps him deal with his deep sorrow.

In a typical rave review, Todd McCarthy of *Variety* wrote: "Highmore is crucially emotive and heartrending as the boy whose name Barrie took for his fictional creation." His performance is "defiantly uncute," wrote Jonathan Dee in the *New York Times.* He noted that it is Highmore's "guardedness, that instinct not to show us everything so rare in a child actor that makes Highmore's performance so startlingly free of artifice." According to *Back Stage,* "As excellent as his costars Johnny Depp and Kate Winslet are in *Finding Neverland,* Highmore steals the film."

The film's director, Marc Forster, chose to shoot one of Highmore's key scenes early in the filming. He wanted both Johnny Depp and Kate Winslet to see the caliber of young actor with whom they would be working. Forster chose a scene in which Peter becomes enraged, tears up a book, and destroys a playhouse. "I wanted [them] to be aware that this is the tone and level of acting I expected from everyone and that [Highmore] was the standard, because there was not a false moment in this little kid," Forster said. After the scene, according to Forster, "Johnny just looked at me and said: 'Oh my God, this gift is scary.'" Winslet later confirmed Depp's impression, declaring that Highmore "is the most breathtaking child actor I have ever worked with, seen, or experienced in my life."

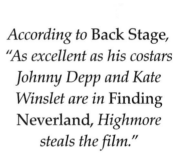

According to **Back Stage,** *"As excellent as his costars* **Johnny Depp and Kate Winslet are in** Finding Neverland, *Highmore steals the film."*

One of the hardest days of filming for Highmore was a crucial funeral scene. The challenge did not stem from the emotional intensity that the scene demanded, but rather from the fact that the scene was filmed beneath the busy flight path of a London airport. "[Every] half-minute we'd have to stop and wait for the planes," he recalled. The sickly appearance of his on-screen mother proved to be another distraction in several scenes. "When Kate [Winslet] didn't look well because of the makeup, we were all so worried," Highmore recalled. "We kept asking and checking to make sure she was OK. She had to keep telling us she was fine, it was only makeup."

Although his character was based on a real-life boy, Highmore did no research to prepare for the role. Instead, he read and re-read the script. "He's

A scene from Charlie and the Chocolate Factory, *with Johnny Depp.*

a very sad child," he said of Peter. "He's always thinking about his father. His father, even though he's dead, is still the most important person in Peter's life. And when Barrie tries to take over that role, Peter doesn't like it, so he tries to force him out." Getting into Peter's troubled mind was "quite easy," Highmore explained. "When you think about it, your dad's dead and your mum's dying, so, yes, it is quite sad."

Developing a Friendship with Johnny Depp

Despite the seriousness of his character, Highmore had a great time on the film set. He played football with his on-screen brothers, for example. Depp also helped him and the other young actors to keep loose. In one scene, for example, the children were expected to engage in silly behavior that disrupts a stodgy dinner gathering. Depp assisted by installing a whoopee cushion beneath the table without telling anyone. As the cameras started to roll, he let it rip. "I just let loose on the thing," Depp said. "The boys went crazy. I mean, they lost their minds."

Depp and Highmore became fast friends as the filming progressed. Depp called him "an amazing kid. Beyond that, he's an amazing guy. Very pure. Very honest. Very normal. That's very refreshing." Highmore returned Depp's compliments. "He's fantastic. Every scene you do with him is a special scene," he said. Both said that the hardest part of *Finding Neverland* was saying good bye to each other at the end of filming.

The separation turned out to be brief, however, because Depp recommended Highmore for a starring role in *Charlie and the Chocolate Factory*, another film in which Depp had a lead role. "It's neat, because, in the film, Charlie has a dream to visit the chocolate factory, and it comes true," Highmore said. "My dream was to work with Johnny again, and it also came true."

Charlie and the Chocolate Factory

Charlie and the Chocolate Factory was a new film version of the popular children's novel by Roald Dahl. In 1971 Dahl's book was made into a musical movie, *Willy Wonka and the Chocolate Factory*. The movie became a cult classic, in large part due to the performance of Gene Wilder as Willy Wonka. For the remake, director Tim Burton wanted to create a film that would be truer to the darkly humorous spirit of the original story. It features a poor boy, Charlie Bucket, who wins a golden ticket to tour the mysterious chocolate empire of Willy Wonka. He makes his once-in-a-lifetime visit with four other gold-ticket winners who turn out to represent a checklist of obnoxious kid behavior: a glutton, a gum-chomper, a spoiled rich girl, and a boy addicted to all things video. Highmore was cast to play humble, polite Charlie opposite Depp's Willy Wonka.

> *"I liked my character, Charlie," Highmore said. "On the outside, it doesn't look like he's got much. He's poor. He eats cabbage soup. But he's kind and he has a family who loves him. So actually, he's got quite a lot."*

As the film begins, Charlie lives in a ramshackle, drab dump with his four bed-ridden grandparents and his downtrodden but loving parents. "I liked my character, Charlie. On the outside, it doesn't look like he's got much," Highmore said. "He's poor. He eats cabbage soup. But he's kind and he has a family who loves him. So actually, he's got quite a lot."

When Charlie enters Willie Wonka's factory, he finds a glistening candy wonderland. "Tim actually built the entire chocolate factory, from the grass on the ground to the real trees where the Oompa Loompas hide," Highmore marveled. It wasn't hard for him and the four other children to "act" awed and delighted. "All Tim Burton had to do was shoot our real thoughts," he said.

Charlie finds the golden ticket.

Charlie and the Chocolate Factory was generally a hit with audiences. But many critics gave it mixed reviews. A number of them questioned Johnny Depp's unusual portrayal of Wonka as a bobbed-haired, high-voiced character who was openly rude to the children. Todd McCarthy voiced a typical reaction in *Variety* when he described Depp's performance as ranging from "bizarrely riveting to one-note and vaguely creepy."

Nevertheless, many reviewers agreed with McCarthy that, in spite of its flaws, the film was inventive and well made. They reserved special praise for the performances given by Highmore and the other supporting players. *New Yorker* reviewer Anthony Lane noted that *Charlie and the Chocolate Factory* author Roald Dahl knew how to tap into the wishes and fears of the young. "[That] is why Freddie Highmore, as Charlie, is the nerve center of the film," Lane wrote. "[Highmore] is up for high jinks, but he sees through low tricks. You catch a straightforwardness in him, a sanity in his gaze, that Dahl would have trusted."

For Highmore, the film was a great experience, in part because of the presence of other children on the set. "It's great because other kids are around. Sometimes you can feel a bit lonely, you know, when you're just on your own, when you're the only kid," he said. "I've just been very lucky to have been able to have the chance [to play Charlie]. I'm similar to Charlie, I guess, in that way. He's been very lucky to have been able to go to the factory."

The filming also deepened Highmore's friendship with Depp, with whom he stays in touch by e-mail. "He's fantastic," Highmore said. "I also say chocolate's fantastic, but I think Johnny's better than chocolate, so I need another word for Johnny. Something better than fantastic."

Looking to the Future

Highmore seems poised for even greater screen success in the years to come. He is set to appear with Russell Crowe in *A Good Year*, which is scheduled to be released in 2006. He also will star as Arthur in *Arthur and the Minimoys*, based on the book by Luc Besson. The film will blend animation with live action. "Minimoys are small people about the size of a tooth," explained Highmore. "There's a treasure in the garden and they help me find it." He is also taking a leading role in *Awful End*, a film based on the children's book trilogy by Philip Ardagh.

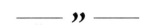

"I'm not sure what I'd like to do when I'm older," Highmore said. "I'm still quite young. I don't think I have to decide quite yet."

Despite his acting success, though, Highmore refuses to commit to a lifelong career in acting. "I'm not sure what I'd like to do when I'm older," he said. "I might want to travel and see the world. That would be quite fun. . . . I'm still quite young. I don't think I have to decide quite yet."

HOME AND FAMILY

Highmore lives in north London with his parents and brother.

HOBBIES AND OTHER INTERESTS

Highmore likes music and plays clarinet and guitar. He is a huge fan of his local London soccer team, or "football" team, as the British call the sport. He loves to play football himself, too. He also likes computers. "I play video games," he said, "but not as much as Mike Teavee," the boy addicted to video games in *Charlie and the Chocolate Factory*.

SELECTED FILMS

Women Talking Dirty, 1999
Jack and the Beanstalk: The Real Story, 2001
I Saw You, 2002
Two Brothers, 2004
Five Children and It, 2004
Finding Neverland, 2004
Charlie and the Chocolate Factory, 2005

HONORS AND AWARDS

Best Young Actor (Critic's Choice Awards): 2004, for *Finding Neverland;*
    2005, for *Charlie and the Chocolate Factory*
Best Supporting Actor (Broadcast Film Critics Award): 2005, for *Finding
    Neverland*

FURTHER READING

Periodicals

Backstage West, Jan. 6, 2005, p.12
Boys' Life, July 2005, p.7
Chicago Sun-Times, July 10, 2005, p.1
New York Times, Nov. 14, 2004, sec. 6, p.71
Time, Nov. 29, 2004, p.155
USA Today, Nov. 12, 2004, p.E3; July 13, 2005, p.D3

ADDRESS

Freddie Highmore
Artists Rights Group Ltd.
4 Great Portland Street
London W1W 8PA
England

WORLD WIDE WEB SITES

http://chocolatefactorymovie.warnerbros.com
http://www.miramax.com/findingneverland

Russel Honoré 1947-
American Lieutenant General in the U.S. Army
Leader of the Military Response to Hurricane Katrina

BIRTH

Russel L. Honoré (pronounced ON-er-ay) was born in 1947 in
Lakeland, Louisiana. Lakeland is a rural community in Pointe
Coupee Parish, located northwest of Baton Rouge and about
two hours from New Orleans. His father was a subsistence
farmer, meaning that he grew crops and raised animals to feed
the family. Honoré has described his father as a "master of
provisions, of providing for the family."

Honoré was the youngest boy in a family of 12 children, which included nine boys and three girls. According to family legend, he was born during a hurricane: a 1947 storm that ripped across the Gulf of Mexico, killing 51 people in its path.

YOUTH

Like many people from Louisiana, Honoré boasts a rich ethnic heritage. He has described himself as a "Louisiana Creole African-American." Creoles are descended from the original European settlers of the Gulf Coast region and share a distinctive dialect.

Honoré was raised in a close-knit family where everyone helped out on the farm. "I grew up poor, but we had a good family," he noted. They grew sugar cane, corn, squash, and cotton, and they also raised pigs and chickens. Honoré once won a 4-H contest with their only cow, Weasel. As a boy, he spent two summers living with relatives in New Orleans. He recalled playing in the streets of the historic city and listening to its famous blues and jazz music.

EDUCATION

Honoré attended Southern University and A&M College, a historically African-American school in Baton Rouge. He worked on a dairy farm during his college years, and he also served in the Reserve Officer Training Corps (ROTC). ROTC is a leadership course offered in some high schools and colleges by branches of the U.S. military. A student completing ROTC in college can earn an officer's rank. College scholarships are available for ROTC participants, who pay back the scholarship by agreeing to serve in the military. Honoré earned a Bachelor of Science (BS) degree in agriculture in 1971 at Southern University and A&M College. Later, during his military career, he added a Master of Arts (MA) degree in human resource management from Troy State University in Alabama.

CAREER HIGHLIGHTS

Building a Military Career

After completing his undergraduate education, Honoré joined the United States Army. Thanks to his ROTC training, he entered the military as an officer, receiving his commission as a second lieutenant of infantry (ground troops). Honoré originally planned to serve in the military for a few years and then quit to become a farmer. But he soon found that he enjoyed the military and decided to make it his career. "The Army gave me open sky," he explained. "I got in the military and I liked what I was doing and the opportunity to be judged by your performance as opposed to other measures."

Honoré has held a variety of command and staff positions during his nearly 35 years in the Army. He served overseas in Korea and Germany, for instance, and was posted to Saudi Arabia during the 1991 Persian Gulf War. He also worked in Washington, DC, as vice director of operations for the Joint Staff (a group consisting of representatives from all branches of the U.S. military). He helped the Department of Defense organize its response to Hurricane Hugo in 1989, and in 2001 he commanded rescue efforts during catastrophic flooding in the African nation of Mozambique.

Honoré welcomed the challenge of preparing these part-time soldiers — reservists and guardsmen — for the conditions they would face overseas. "I take this personal that we prepare every son and daughter to go fight," he stated. "We will have them ready. Failure is not an option."

In 2002 Honoré was appointed commander of the Standing Joint Force Headquarters in the Department of Homeland Security, which was created in the wake of the terrorist attacks of September 11, 2001. In this role, he devised plans for the military response to terrorist attacks and natural disasters.

In 2004 Honoré was promoted to lieutenant general and given command of the First U.S. Army, one of two continental armies in the United States. He was assigned to Fort Gillem, Georgia, where all U.S. Army Reserve troops and National Guard units east of the Mississippi River received training before serving in Iraq and Afghanistan. As opposed to active-duty forces, whose main job is military service, reservists and guardsmen hold civilian (non-military) jobs, but they can be called up for active duty as needed.

Honoré welcomed the challenge of preparing these part-time soldiers for the conditions they would face overseas. "I take this personal that we prepare every son and daughter to go fight," he stated. "We will have them ready. Failure is not an option." Honoré employed a system called "theater immersion training" to expose the troops to realistic battle conditions. He built imitation Iraqi markets and mosques and hired Iraqi-Americans to play the roles of villagers, religious leaders, and terrorists. He set up exercises in which the soldiers would face such dangerous situations as roadside bombs and rioting crowds. Honoré wanted to ensure that the training took place "in a tough, realistic environment" because "we're a nation fighting a war."

Hurricane Katrina Hits New Orleans

Honoré soon faced a new challenge. In August 2005 a large tropical storm formed in the Atlantic Ocean. It reached hurricane force and received the name Hurricane Katrina. Katrina struck southern Florida on August 25, killing 11 people. It weakened over land but quickly regained strength as it moved across the warm waters of the Gulf of Mexico. On August 27 it increased in strength to become a Category 3 hurricane, with 115 mile per hour winds, and the National Weather Service issued a hurricane warning for the southern coast of Louisiana. By August 28 Katrina had grown into a Category 5 monster, with 160 mph winds. The National Weather Service predicted that it would cause catastrophic damage to the coastal city of New Orleans, and Mayor Ray Nagin issued a mandatory evacuation order for residents.

> "[Katrina] was coming to New Orleans, then took a diversionary turn toward Mississippi," Honoré noted. "Then it hit the city anyway, knocked out all of our communications, our television. We were blind. It did everything an effective enemy is supposed to do. It was classic."

At that time, New Orleans was a city of about 500,000 people located at the mouth of the Mississippi River, where it flows into the Gulf of Mexico. Its location made it one of the most important shipping ports in the United States. Yet it also left New Orleans particularly vulnerable to hurricanes. Known as the "Big Easy," the city was mostly built below sea level. It was protected by a complicated system of levees (walls made of concrete and earth) that held back the waters of the Mississippi River to the south and Lake Pontchartrain to the north. This low-lying city is nestled in between the Mississippi River, Lake Pontchartrain, and the Gulf of Mexico. Some disaster experts have compared it to a bowl waiting to be filled with water.

On August 29, Hurricane Katrina made landfall just east of New Orleans, near Buras, Louisiana. By this time it had weakened slightly to a Category

4 storm with 145 mph winds. A storm of that size packs the energy of a 10-megaton nuclear bomb exploding every 20 minutes. Katrina also produced a 29-foot storm surge on the Gulf of Mexico — the highest ever recorded in the United States. The high winds and rising water in the Gulf caused severe damage along the Gulf Coast of Louisiana and Mississippi, knocking down trees and power lines, tearing off the roofs of houses, blowing out the windows of buildings, and tossing ships onto the shore. Honoré compared the storm to a military attack. "It was coming to New Orleans, then took a diversionary turn toward Mississippi," he noted. "Then it hit the city anyway, knocked out all of our communications, our television. We were blind. It did everything an effective enemy is supposed to do. It was classic."

Honoré speaking during a news conference, with New Orleans Mayor Ray Nagin looking on.

The Levees Break

Destruction from the hurricane was severe, but initially it seemed that New Orleans had escaped the worst of the damage from Katrina. But the destruction was still severe, and it soon became catastrophic. On August 30, a major levee broke and sent the high waters of Lake Pontchartrain coursing into the streets. It flooded 80 percent of the city with a toxic soup of water, chemicals, sewage, and corpses.

An estimated 60 percent of New Orleans residents had followed the evacuation order and left the city before the hurricane hit. But more than 100,000 people had remained behind. Some of these people ignored the order and stayed in their homes and businesses by choice, but most of them were unable to leave. About 20 percent of New Orleans residents live in poverty, and the same percentage do not own cars. The city and state governments did not provide an organized system of transportation to help the poor, ill, and elderly evacuate before the hurricane struck. Many people who wanted to evacuate were trapped, with no way to get out of

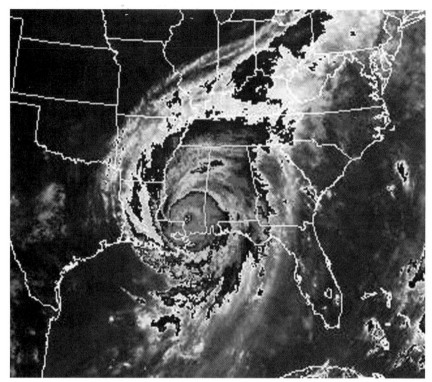

A satellite image of Hurricane Katrina on August 29, 2005, at 1:45 p.m. It made landfall earlier that day, at about 6:00 a.m., near New Orleans.

the city. Some of the survivors climbed into trees or onto rooftops to escape the flooding. Thousands of others made their way to designated shelters at the New Orleans Superdome and Convention Center.

Government—at the federal, state, and local levels—was slow to respond to the disaster in New Orleans. Much-needed rescue and relief operations were delayed for several days as various government agencies tried to decide who was in charge. The Federal Emergency Management Agency (FEMA) usually directed the response to natural disasters, but it had become part of the Department of Homeland Security following the September 11 terrorist attacks. Critics claimed that Homeland Security focused all of its time and money on reducing the threat of terrorist attacks rather than preparing for natural disasters.

As frustrated New Orleans residents waited for help, conditions in the city deteriorated rapidly. Desperate people broke into stores to find food, water, and emergency supplies, while lawbreakers took advantage of the chaos to steal non-emergency goods. The Superdome and Convention Center sustained damage during the storm and lacked electricity, water, or working toilets. The thousands of people stuck in these emergency shelters endured extreme heat, hunger, dehydration, overflowing toilets, and occasional violence.

Leading the Military Relief Effort

On September 2, five days after the hurricane hit New Orleans, President George W. Bush toured the area and acknowledged that the government relief effort was failing to meet the needs of the city and its people. Shortly afterward, he appointed Honoré commander of Joint Task Force Katrina. In this position, the three-star general took responsibility for coordinating the largest humanitarian relief effort in U.S. history. He led all military relief operations in the city of New Orleans and throughout the Gulf Coast region devastated by the hurricane. Honoré brought several important advantages to the job: he had extensive training in disaster management; he was a Louisiana native who could connect with the mostly poor, black victims of the hurricane; and he was a tough, no-nonsense officer who knew how to get things done.

> **"**
>
> *"He came off the doggone chopper, and he started cussing, and people started moving," recalled New Orleans Mayor Ray Nagin. "I give the president some credit on this, he sent one John Wayne dude down here that can get some stuff done."*
>
> **"**

Honoré arrived in New Orleans on September 3. After surveying the damage from a helicopter, he realized that the city had suffered "a disaster of biblical proportions." He immediately took charge of the situation on the ground, moving aggressively where many government agencies had hesitated. His strong leadership helped restore order to New Orleans and gave new hope and confidence to victims of the disaster. "He came off the doggone chopper, and he started cussing, and people started moving," recalled Mayor Ray Nagin, who had sharply criticized earlier government relief efforts. "I give the president some credit on this, he sent one John Wayne dude down here that can get some stuff done."

By the time Honoré arrived, a number of news reports had created the impression that the city streets were unsafe, filled with marauding bands of looters and violent criminals. As a result, some of the Army troops entering

Honoré hit the ground running upon arriving at the Louisiana Emergency Operations Center.

the city were fearful. Honoré immediately began working to change this impression. A CNN camera crew followed him as he stood on a New Orleans street corner and barked out orders to the troops. He continually told the soldiers to lower their weapons, reminding them that they were involved in a humanitarian relief effort. "Imagine being rescued and having a fellow American point a gun at you," he stated. "These are Americans. This is not Iraq." Honoré felt that the media had exaggerated reports of the violence and frightened people unnecessarily. He challenged journalists to assess the situation personally. "You need to get on the streets of New Orleans, you can't sit back here and say what you hear from someone else," he declared. "It is secure. We walk around without any issues."

After securing the downtown area, Honoré led the evacuation of survivors from the crowded Superdome and Convention Center. He acknowledged the frustration of people who had been stuck in the shelters for nearly a week. "By and large, these are families that are just waiting to get out of here," he noted. "They are frustrated. I would be, too." He also admitted that it was difficult for the Army to provide food and water to everyone in the shelters. "If you ever have 20,000 people come to supper, you'll know what I'm talking about," he said. "If it was easy, it would have been done already."

While his tough leadership was impressive, Honoré also demonstrated compassion for the suffering of New Orleans residents. "These were mostly poor people who didn't have much other than their homes," he explained. "We didn't pull anybody off those rooftops that said, 'Damn, I left my Lexus!'" Having grown up poor himself, Honoré said he could identify with the plight of the evacuees. "When it's hot, they're hotter," he stated. "When it's cold, they're colder. When the wind blows, they go over farther. And when a plague hits, they die faster." At one point, the general personally stepped in to help an exhausted young mother struggling to carry infant twins down the street in terrible heat and humidity. He ordered a soldier to carry the babies for her, and he helped her reach a military hospital ship for medical treatment.

Under Honoré's leadership, "the character of the relief effort [changed] from a mad scramble to an increasingly orderly and effective rescue and restoration," Patrik Jonsson wrote in the *Christian Science Monitor.* By September 19, 2005, the Army had delivered 13.6 million meals, handed out 24.2 million liters of water, and sent out more search-and-rescue helicopters than currently flying in Iraq and Afghanistan combined.

> *Having grown up poor himself, Honoré said he could identify with the plight of the evacuees. "When it's hot, they're hotter," he stated. "When it's cold, they're colder. When the wind blows, they go over farther. And when a plague hits, they die faster."*

Becoming a National Hero

For the duration of Joint Task Force Katrina, Honoré was based at Camp Shelby, Louisiana, about 100 miles north of New Orleans. He gave a press briefing there every morning and then traveled by helicopter to the disaster zone. He spent most of each day riding around New Orleans in the back of an army truck, assessing the relief efforts and assigning more manpower wherever it was needed. He returned to Camp Shelby late at night for another press briefing. Despite the hectic schedule, Honoré was glad that the military was able to help victims of the disaster. "We're usually in the business of breaking things," he said. "Now we're trying to fix things."

Honoré quickly organized U.S. troops to help with disaster response at the New Orleans Convention Center.

Honoré won over the media and the American people with his colorful press briefings, which were full of interesting metaphors and peppered with profanity. In one of his most famous metaphors, Honoré compared the hurricane and the relief efforts to a football game in which the home team must fight to overcome a big first-quarter deficit. "By definition, you're going to lose the first quarter in a disaster," he explained. "[But] what does the coach do when his team is losing 25-0 after the first quarter? Does he call the quarterback over and tell him how stupid he is because he didn't play right, or does he get out the white board and start making adjustments? Now we can stay talking about the first quarter. All of you are talking about the first quarter. But there's still three quarters left to this thing."

Before long, Honoré emerged as the face of the disaster response. The gruff, cigar-chomping general known to troops as the "Ragin' Cajun" became an overnight celebrity. He received countless interview requests, and he appeared on several television news programs, including "Larry King Live," "Meet the Press," and "Face the Nation." "I can't swing a stick and not hit a reporter," he complained. "I didn't know there were so many of them." Honoré's aide, Lieutenant Colonel Richard Steele, noted that "The general is getting tired of all of these profiles. He's a humble guy. He didn't want to become a celebrity from all this. He wants the focus to be on the mission and not on himself."

By late 2005, the death toll stood at 972 in Louisiana and 221 in Mississippi at the end of house-to-house searches, and the insurance industry placed losses at $34.4 billion, making Katrina the costliest natural disaster in U.S. history. In the weeks after Hurricane Katrina, as the death toll mounted and the extent of the damage became clear, military and civilian sources alike praised Honoré's contribution to the relief effort. Some observers claimed that his performance as commander of Joint Task Force Katrina was likely to earn him a fourth general's star from President Bush, giving him the highest rank in the Army. "He's less a man than a force of nature," said one of his officers, Major John Rogers. "He knows the way and that's why he's leading."

> "He's less a man than a force of nature," said one of his officers, Major John Rogers. "He knows the way and that's why he's leading."

MARRIAGE AND FAMILY

Honoré has been married to his wife, Beverly, since he started his military career. They have two daughters, Stephanie and Kimberly, and two sons, Michael and Stephen. Honoré and his wife live in Atlanta with their youngest, Stephen, who is still in high school. Stephanie lives in Florida and recently gave birth to Honoré's first grandchild. Michael is a sergeant in the Louisiana National Guard and recently completed a year of service in Iraq.

Kimberly lives in New Orleans, but she was out of town when Hurricane Katrina hit the city. When her father took charge of the military relief effort, she asked him to go to her apartment and rescue her cat. "I've got 80 helicopters in the air and we're trying to evacuate 20,000 people from the Convention Center, and she's e-mailing me every day about her cat," Honoré recalled. He eventually did make it to the apartment, where he found the cat healthy after ten days on its own. "The cat was living large in that place," he joked.

HOBBIES AND OTHER INTERESTS

Honoré is an avid gardener, calling it his favorite form of relaxation and exercise. He grows pumpkins, tomatoes, beans, peas, potatoes, and peppers, and he shares his fresh produce with the Fort Gillem troops at barbeques. Honoré also enjoys the music of Tina Turner and B.B. King, and he wants to learn to play the guitar someday.

HONORS AND AWARDS

Honoré has received numerous military awards, including the Defense Distinguished Service Medal, the Distinguished Service Medal, the Legion of Merit with Four Oak Leaf Clusters, the Bronze Star, the Defense Meritorious Service Medal, the Meritorious Service Medal with Three Oak Leaf Clusters, the Army Commendation Medal with Three Oak Leaf Clusters, and the Army Achievement Medal.

FURTHER READING

Periodicals

Atlanta Journal-Constitution, July 16, 2004, p.B4; Dec. 3, 2004, p.A14; Sep. 4, 2005, p.A13
Chicago Tribune, Sep. 9, 2005, p.A5
Christian Science Monitor, Sep. 9, 2005, p.1
Inside the Army, Sep. 5, 2005, p.1
Newsweek, Sep. 12, 2005, p.42
Time, Sep. 19, 2005, p.56
Washington Post, Sep. 12, 2005, p.C1

Online Articles

http://www4.army.mil
   (*Army News Service,* "Troops Ready to Assist with Hurricane Katrina," Aug. 29, 2005)
http://cnn.com
   (CNN, "Lt. Gen. Honoré a 'John Wayne Dude,'" Sep. 3, 2005)
http://www.insightnews.com
   (*Insight News,* "Honoré's Peace," Sep. 20, 2005)
http://www.nola.com
   (*New Orleans Times-Picayune,* "Three-Star Celebrity," Sep. 19, 2005)
http://usinfo.state.gov
   (USinfo.state.gov, "Louisiana Native General in Charge of New Orleans Relief," Sep. 4, 2005)
http://www.washingtonpost.com
   (*Washington Post,* "Ragin' Cajun General Spurs Katrina Aid," Sep. 11, 2005)

ADDRESS

Lt. General Russel Honoré
Fort Gillem
Headquarters, First U.S. Army
4705 North Wheeler Drive
Forest Park, GA 30297

WORLD WIDE WEB SITES

http://www.army.mil
http://www.nationalveteransday.org/speakers/honore.htm

Tim Howard 1979-

American Professional Soccer Player
Goalkeeper for England's Manchester United
Soccer Team

BIRTH

Tim Howard was born on March 6, 1979, in North Brunswick,
New Jersey. Howard was the product of a mixed-race and
mixed-nationality marriage: his father, Matthew Howard, is
African-American, and his mother, Esther Howard, is a Hungarian-born white woman. Howard has one older brother,
Chris.

YOUTH

Howard's early years were shaped by the divorce of his parents when he was three years old. He and his brother lived with their mother in a cramped apartment in North Brunswick, in a heavily industrialized part of northeastern New Jersey. "It was a one-bedroom apartment she made into a three-bedroom apartment," remembered Howard. "I don't know how she did it." His mother worked several jobs to help provide for the family. Though Howard's father, a long-distance truck driver, did not live with the family, he was a regular presence in the lives of his two sons.

The Howard boys developed a love of sports from an early age. Their father bought the boys a variety of sports equipment before they even learned to walk, and he watched closely to see which sports they gravitated toward. From early on, Tim took to both soccer and basketball. He maintained these interests throughout his youth, and as he entered middle school and high school he began to stand out as an athlete. In high school, for example, Howard averaged 15 points a game in basketball. During his senior year, he helped lift his team all the way to the state finals.

Where Howard really shined, however, was on the soccer field. He spent a lot of time in youth leagues as a midfielder, considered the most physical-

Tim Mulqueen, who coached Howard as a youth and later as a professional, described his abilities as a 12-year-old player like this: "[Howard] was probably the best player on the field. He could do anything he wanted. . . . He was a natural."

ly demanding of all the soccer positions. Midfielders have to be able to cover the entire field and demonstrate both offensive and defensive skills. But over time, he showed even more potential as a goalkeeper. By the time he reached middle school, his coaches were actively encouraging him to attend soccer camps to improve his goalkeeping skills. One coach who attested to his early skill was Tim Mulqueen, who coached Howard as a youth and later as a professional. Mulqueen later said that as a 12-year-old, "[Howard] was probably the best player on the field. He could do anything he wanted. . . . He was a natural." At age 15, he was selected to play in goal for a U.S. national team in tournaments against teams from other countries. He played on a U-17 team, a team consisting of players under the age of 17.

Diagnosed with Tourette's Syndrome

Howard's athletic skill helped him cope with a major challenge that he faced during his childhood. When Howard was around ten years old, he and his parents began to notice that he was developing strange mannerisms. He cleared his throat repeatedly and compulsively; he felt the need to touch objects in a specific order before he could move on to a different task; he recited certain numbers; and before he could talk to his mother, he felt a nearly uncontrollable impulse to touch her on the shoulders in a certain pattern.

As Howard's family struggled to understand what was happening, the youngster also felt embarrassed by his growing inability to conceal his odd habits from his schoolmates. "In the beginning, I wasn't very bothered about [TS] myself. I was just a kid, having fun, playing sports," Howard explained. But as he entered middle school and high school and became interested in girls, it became a bigger problem. "It hurt, especially coming into adolescence and high school," he continued. He knew that some classmates made fun of him behind his back, yet he never let the syndrome keep him from having a good high school experience. "Thankfully," he joked, "I was a popular guy—and I was big."

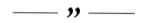

> "In the beginning, I wasn't very bothered about [Tourette's Syndrome] myself. I was just a kid, having fun, playing sports," Howard explained.

Around 1990, the mystery surrounding Howard's behavioral ticks was solved. He was diagnosed with a mild case of Tourette's Syndrome, a neurological disorder that is characterized by involuntary physical movements and vocal expressions. In its most severe forms, Tourette's Syndrome (or TS) causes some sufferers to involuntarily blurt out obscene words. This form of TS is called coprolalia. It is the source of most public misunderstandings of the disorder, since numerous television shows and movies have used this type of TS as a source of humor. Fortunately for Howard and his family, his case of TS was relatively mild.

EDUCATION

Howard attended public schools in North Brunswick, New Jersey. As he neared completion of his education at North Brunswick High School, Howard weighted whether to go on to college on an athletic scholarship or become a professional soccer player. College offered the opportunity to get an education and gain experience as a soccer player, but Howard knew that the opportunities to develop his soccer skills would be greater in the pro ranks.

Howard agonized about this choice until a month before his high school graduation. At that time he received an invitation from his old mentor Tim Mulqueen that he decided he could not turn down. Mulqueen had become the coach for the North Jersey Imperials, a professional team in the Premier Development Soccer League (PDSL). This league was part of the MLS Project 40 program developed by Major League Soccer (MLS), the top professional soccer league in the United States. This program gave top young players a chance to learn from top soccer pros by including them on the rosters of various MLS teams.

Howard jumped at Mulqueen's invitation, and before he knew it he was training as a backup goalkeeper for the New Jersey MetroStars of the MLS. "I thought I would have taken a step back athletically [by going to college]," he explained. By the time he graduated from North Brunswick High School in 1997, he was already earning a paycheck from the PDSL.

CAREER HIGHLIGHTS

Learning with the Imperials

After joining the Imperials in 1997, Howard impressed his coaches with his confidence and athleticism. At 6' 3" and 210 pounds he was an imposing physical presence, with quick reflexes and strong hands. He was an aggressive keeper, moving forward to close off scoring attempts, yet he also played under control. Mulqueen acknowledged that Howard, like most young goalkeepers, needed to improve his decision making on the field. But he praised the netminder as someone who "never gets rattled. He's very composed."

Howard's maturity served him well during his second year in the pros. During the 1998 season, the MetroStars' starting goalkeeper, Tony Meola — who had led the U.S. squad in the 1994 World Cup — was benched after receiving a yellow-card suspension. Howard suddenly found himself slated as the team's starting goalkeeper for its next game, an August 18 tilt against the Colorado Rapids. He was nervous and flustered at the outset of the game, but he soon settled down and helped his team register a 4-1 victory. This triumph put the 19-year-old Howard in the MLS record book as the youngest goalkeeper ever to post a win in league history.

Howard played for five seasons with the New York-New Jersey MetroStars.

Balancing Pro and International Competition

During his first few years with the MetroStars Howard served as the back-up keeper, first to Meola, then to Mike Ammann. During this apprentice-ship Howard had the opportunity to represent his country in several inter-national games and tournaments. He played on the U.S. U-20 (under 20) national squad, which made a strong showing in the 1999 World Youth Championship. Later that same year he got three starts (and allowed just two goals) for the U.S. U-23 (under 23) team at the Pan American Games.

His strong performance helped the squad earn a bronze medal in that competition. In 2000 Howard served as a backup to goalkeeper Brad Friedel in the Summer Olympics, in which the U.S. team finished fourth.

Howard then returned to the MetroStars, where he trained furiously for an opportunity to be the team's starting goalkeeper. He got that chance at the start of the 2001 season, after Ammann was traded. Howard expressed excitement about the upcoming season, but he also knew that it would be a big challenge. He was still young for a goalkeeper, a position that often takes years to learn. Many top keepers don't reach their best form until they are in their early thirties. "It is somewhat unprecedented for a 21-year-old goalkeeper to get the full-time nod," he acknowledged.

As it turned out, Howard sparkled in his first season as a full-time starter. He played every minute of all 26 games played by the MetroStars, and although the team had only a marginally successful record of 13 wins, 10 losses, and 3 ties, he won accolades for his performance in goal. He allowed an average of just 1.33 goals per game, recorded four shutouts, and led the league with 146 saves. By the end of the season Howard had collected a stunning string of awards: he was named to the MLS All-Star Team and honored as MLS Goalkeeper of the Year, among several other awards.

> *"[Tourette's Syndrome is] a hurdle, but it's certainly not a brick wall," said Howard. "A speed bump, but not a stop sign."*

The year 2001 was a milestone for Howard in another way as well, for it was the year that he acknowledged publicly that he had Tourette's Syndrome. Previously, he had worked hard to keep his symptoms in check, but he finally decided it was time to divulge his secret. He was pleasantly surprised to find that both his teammates and the press were quite supportive.

Before the year was out Howard had agreed to become a spokesman for the Tourette's Syndrome Association of New Jersey, a sure sign that he was growing more comfortable with talking about his illness. It also indicated his growing awareness that he could be a role model for others who suffered from TS. In fact, he made a point of talking to young people with TS and emphasizing that "[Tourette's Syndrome is] a hurdle, but it's certainly not a brick wall. A speed bump, but not a stop sign." MLS acknowledged Howard's community work by naming him the league's Humanitarian of the Year in 2001.

In 2003 Howard joined Manchester United, the most famous soccer team in the world.

Stardom Brings Opportunity

Howard's second year as the starting keeper for the Metro-Stars was a bit of a disappointment, both for himself and his team. After finishing second in their division in 2001 the Metro-Stars fell to fourth in 2002. Howard's goals-against average rose to 1.66 per game, placing him tenth among goalkeepers in the league. Observers felt that the falloff was not due to his play, however. The MetroStars defense was weak throughout the season, and Howard faced more shots and made more saves than anyone in the league. In fact, his efforts earned him a spot on the MLS All-Star Team for a second straight year.

Howard's steady play with the MetroStars caught the attention of Tony Coton, who coached goalkeepers for Manchester United, a team in the English Premier League (EPL). Manchester United is considered by many to be the most famous and perhaps the best professional soccer team in the world. Midway through the 2003 season, Coton and team manager Sir Alex Ferguson cut a deal with the MetroStars to bring Howard to Manchester United (often known by the nicknames Man United or just Man U).

Though he had been enjoying a terrific season with the first-place MetroStars, Howard was delighted to make the leap from the American league to the glamorous EPL. His salary soared from less than $30,000 a year to $1.4 million a year, with the promise of a $1.5-million bonus if he became the team's starting keeper. To the surprise of soccer fans across Europe, Howard was made starting keeper for Manchester United in an exhibition game played against Italian team Juventus at Giants Stadium in New Jersey. Just days after his mid-July acquisition, he shone in goal, leading Man United to a 4-1 victory.

Life with Man United

Though he wowed Man United coaches and American fans during the summer exhibition season, fans and the press in England were not so eager to embrace the young American keeper. Some of the English newspapers, in fact, were downright vicious. They referred to Howard as "disabled" and described him as "United's Zombie" because of his TS. The "zombie" reference reflected a belief that he took medication to control his Tourette's Syndrome; in reality, though, he has never taken any drugs to treat his TS because of concerns that the medication might dull his reflexes. But Howard shrugged off all the cruel remarks. "All sorts of dumb, silly things were written about me," he admitted. "I was not bothered. It could have impeded my career if I'd listened to the tabloids. But I don't read my own press, good or bad. I was quite comfortable with who I am and left it at that."

Instead, Howard focused on his soccer. He leapfrogged over famed French goalkeeper Fabien Barthez to win the opening-day start for Man United, then recorded a shutout as his team romped to a 4-0 victory. His run continued from there, as Howard became the regular starting keeper. He recorded 14 shutouts for the 2003-04 season, and Man United lost just three of its first 20 games. Howard suddenly found himself a celebrity in football-mad Manchester, unable to walk down the street or go out to a movie without being recognized and hounded by autograph seekers. As in the United States, fans embraced the handsome, soft-spoken American keeper and set aside their concerns that his Tourette's Syndrome might somehow cost their team a match. Even the notoriously hostile English press warmed to him. "He has the aura of a brick wall," declared the *Daily Telegraph*. "A lot of goalkeepers want to look good . . . [but Howard] doesn't mind making ugly saves. It's the sign of a great goalkeeper."

> "All sorts of dumb, silly things were written about me," Howard admitted. "I was not bothered. It could have impeded my career if I'd listened to the tabloids. But I don't read my own press, good or bad. I was quite comfortable with who I am and left it at that."

Howard's honeymoon ended in March 2004, when a brief stretch of inconsistent play led Ferguson to bench him in favor of backup keeper Roy Carroll. Instead of complaining about being benched, Howard praised Ferguson for recognizing that he needed a break and set his sights on re-

Howard in goal for Manchester United, 2004.

gaining his competitive edge. He returned to goal in late April, in time to close out the remaining games of the EPL season. He then prepared to face Milwall in the FA Cup, an annual competition between the top professional teams in England. Howard was spectacular in helping Manchester United cruise to a 3-0 victory. This triumph made him the first American player to play for a team winning the FA Cup.

Reflecting on his strong finish to the 2003-04 season, Howard stated that he was "certainly a much better goalkeeper now than when I came to the club. Before, I was more of an athlete wearing goalkeeper gloves. But in my time here . . . I've become more than just an athlete; I feel I've become a goalkeeper." Premier League players agreed, naming him Keeper of the Year.

Struggles Lead to Demotion

Howard began Man United's 2004-05 campaign as the number one keeper, but early mistakes diminished Ferguson's confidence in his young player and he was soon demoted to second string behind Roy Carroll. Over the course of the year Howard played in some 30 games, but he never displayed the consistency that he had shown in his first year.

At season's end, Manchester management shuffled its goalkeeping corps with a series of moves that sent mixed signals about Howard's future. On the one hand, he was signed to a lucrative four-year contract that would keep him with the team through 2009. But the team also signed Dutch goalkeeping sensation Edwin Van Der Sar to a two-year contract and named him their number one keeper. The Man United coaches explained that in Van Der Sar, they had signed not only the best goalkeeper of the present, but someone who could serve as a mentor to Howard, who they still saw as the team's goalkeeper of the future.

British fans and newspapers speculated that Howard was unhappy about taking a back seat to Van Der Sar, but he denied these reports. "It's not easy in Europe," he said, "and it never was going to be easy. Do I just pack up and leave and go somewhere where it's easier? I could, a lot of people would and do. I chose not to do that. I choose to fight it out."

As the 2005-06 season kicked off, Howard found himself in the familiar if somewhat frustrating position of being a back-up goal keeper for both Manchester United and the United States national team. By 21 games into Man United's 2005-06 season, Howard had been given the starting nod only three times. Meanwhile, head coach Bruce Arena of the U.S. national team continued to refer to Howard as the "keeper of the future." Many viewed this as a sign that veterans Kasey Keller or Brad Friedel are more likely to be the starting netminder for the Americans in the 2006 World Cup, the world championship of international soccer.

"It's not easy in Europe," Howatd said, "and it never was going to be easy. Do I just pack up and leave and go somewhere where it's easier? I could, a lot of people would and do. I chose not to do that. I choose to fight it out."

Nonetheless, many soccer analysts believe that Howard is destined for greater stardom in the future. They point out that he is only now reaching the age at which most goalkeepers are considered to reach their prime. And they note that he has already proven himself as a legitimate goalkeeper in the most competitive league in Europe. For his part, Howard has expressed continued determination to be recognized someday as one of the best goalkeepers in the world.

MARRIAGE AND FAMILY

Howard became engaged to his wife, Laura, early in 2003. The couple planned to be married in the fall of that year in a big wedding. Howard's

July 2003 signing with England's Manchester United disrupted those plans, however. Eager to move to England together, the couple arranged a hasty marriage ceremony in New York's Central Park with a handful of friends and family. They had their first child late in 2005.

The Howards live most of the year in a country house outside of Manchester, England, but they also keep a home in Germantown, Tennessee, a suburb of Laura's hometown of Memphis.

HOBBIES AND OTHER INTERESTS

A quiet man of strong Christian faith, Howard does not drive fancy cars or spend money on expensive hobbies. He enjoys spending the offseason in Tennessee, where he is not hounded by soccer fans as he is in England. "[I like doing] all the stuff I can't do in England," he said. "Just hanging out, enjoying time with my family."

HONORS AND AWARDS

Major League Soccer (MLS) Keeper of the Year: 2001
Major League Soccer (MLS) Humanitarian of the Year: 2001
Major League Soccer (MLS) All-Star: 2001, 2002
English Premier League Keeper of the Year (Professional Footballers Association): 2004

FURTHER READING

Periodicals

Current Biography Yearbook, 2005
Daily Telegraph (London), May 13, 2005, p.17
Esquire, June 2004, p.70
Manchester Evening News, Sep. 9, 2003, p. SPT8; May 21, 2004, p.SPT2; Apr. 5, 2005, p.SPT2
Observer (London), Aug. 1, 2004, p.61
Philadelphia Inquirer, July 26, 2004, p.D1
Soccer Digest, Dec. 2002, p.36
Sports Illustrated, Aug. 11, 2003, p.60; Mar. 22, 2004, p.90
USA Today, July 31, 2003, p.C11; Jan. 23, 2004, p.A1

Online Articles

http://www.ussoccer.com/bio/index.jsp_1728.html
    (*U.S. Soccer,* "Biographies: Tim Howard," undated)

Online Databases

Biography Resource Center Online, 2004

ADDRESS

Tim Howard
Manchester United
Sir Matt Busby Way
Manchester M16 0RA
England

WORLD WIDE WEB SITES

http://www.manutd.com
http://www.tsa-usa.org

Cynthia Kadohata 1956-
American Young Adult Novelist
Winner of the 2005 Newbery Medal for *Kira-Kira*

BIRTH

Cynthia Kadohata was born on July 2, 1956, in Chicago, Illinois. Her mother, Jane Akiko Kaita, was born in California and grew up in Hawaii. Her father, Toshiro Kadohata, grew up in California, where his parents were tenant farmers. Cynthia has an older sister and a younger brother.

During World War II, Toshiro Kadohata was interned along with his family and thousands of other Japanese-Americans in the Poston internment camp in Arizona. It was located on the Colorado River Indian Reservation in the Sonoran desert. At that time, the United States was at war with Japan. Some Americans worried that Japanese and Japanese-American people living and working in the U.S. might be traitors who would sabotage the American war effort — even though most thought of themselves as loyal Americans. President Franklin Delano Roosevelt ordered that people of Japanese descent should be evacuated from their homes and imprisoned in internment camps. Approximately 120,000 people, including Toshiro Kadohata, were confined to these internment camps. Later, he was drafted out of the camp and served with the U.S. Military Intelligence Service in Japan.

YOUTH

At the time of Kadohata's birth, her mother and father owned a small grocery store in Chicago. Her father decided to find a job in chicken sexing, which is the painstaking process of separating male chicks from female chicks. Chicken sexing was developed in Japan, and the men who practiced it were overwhelmingly Japanese and Japanese-American. After training, he was offered a job at a hatchery in Tifton, Georgia, where the family moved when Cynthia was two years old. Like the other chicken sexers, he often worked 100 hours a week, taking amphetamines to stay awake through the night.

When the hatchery closed, the family moved to Springdale, Arkansas, where they were the only nonwhite members of the local Presbyterian church. Kadohata recalls that she did not have many friends during this time. "We fit in by not fitting into it, by being part of a very small community," she said in an interview. "When we went to a party, it was almost always with a group of other Japanese or Japanese Americans who worked as chicken sexers, separating male and female chicks in the hatchery. I remember a little girl asking me something like, 'Are you black or white?' I really stumbled for an answer. I said, 'I don't know.'" After her brother was born, the entire hospital staff gathered to see him because no one in town had seen a Japanese baby before.

When Kadohata was young, her parents began to grow apart. "When my mother began taking us to the library, she discovered a love of reading at the same time we did," Kadohata said in her Newbery acceptance speech. "Someone once said to me, 'The problems between your parents began when your mother started reading.'" Despite the difficult times, there were also good times too. "One of my favorite childhood memories is of when my mother became obsessed with the stars. She made charts of the constellations and lay with us in the back yard at night to look at the clear skies of our small Arkansas town. One of the family activities I remember most vividly is burning our garbage together in the incinerator in back at night, the ashes sparkling through the air as the fire warmed our faces."

Kadohata's parents divorced when she was nine years old. Her father remained in Arkansas, but her mother moved with Cynthia and her siblings back to Chicago. The 1960s were an exciting time in the city, and Kadohata made the most of her time there. "I loved Chicago and the Sixties!" she remembered. "I loved Twiggy, the Beatles, the clothes. I loved Bobby Kennedy, and the night he died I slept on a concrete floor in our apartment and prayed and cried myself to sleep. Later . . . I loved secretly staying at the beach overnight with my friends." She had a lot of freedom as a teenager. "My mother worked full-time and went to school nights, taking the subway home and returning late to find us still awake," she wrote. "We were all three good students, and we were never punished, for anything."

EDUCATION

In 1972, when she was 16, Kadohata moved with her family to Los Angeles. She enrolled at Hollywood High School, but she ran into trouble right away. "I had gone to an alternative high school in Chicago, and Hollywood High wouldn't accept a lot of my credits," she stated. "But I also didn't fit in. I became intensely shy. It got to the point that going to the grocery store and talking to the cashier really made me nervous." A year later, at the beginning of her senior year, she dropped out of Hollywood High School. "Previously I had been a straight-A student," she asserted. "But for some reason I could no longer understand what my teachers were talking about. I could not understand algebra, and I did not understand what 'theme' meant when applied to a novel. History was so boring I could not bear to open my book. I would sit for two hours at the table with my books in front of me, but I could not open them."

Kadohata dropped out of high school in 1973. She got a job as a waitress, clerked at a department store, and worked at a fast-food restaurant. She also sought out her local library. "Seeking it out was more of an instinct, really, not a conscious thought," she said in her Newbery acceptance speech. "I didn't think to myself, 'I need to start reading again.' I felt it. I rediscovered reading—the way I'd read as a child, when there was constantly a book I was just finishing or just beginning or in the middle of. I rediscovered myself." Today libraries hold a special place in her heart. "I look back on 1973, the year I dropped out of school, with the belief that libraries can not just change your life but save it," she acknowledged. "Not the same way a Coast Guardsman or a police officer might save a life, not all at once. It happens more slowly, but just as surely."

She also wrote her first short story. "When I was 17, I wrote the most idiotic story in the world," she recalled in an interview. "It was about all these ducks that had only one leg. They lived on another planet and were a metaphor for humans. I actually sent that story to the *Atlantic Monthly* and, of course, immediately got a rejection. I don't think I wrote anything again until I was in college, when I wrote for the school newspaper." When she was 18, she was admitted to Los Angeles City College. She eventually transferred to University of Southern California, where she graduated with a Bachelor of Arts (BA) degree in journalism in 1977.

"Previously I had been a straight-A student," Kadohata said about changing high schools. "But for some reason I could no longer understand what my teachers were talking about. I could not understand algebra, and I did not understand what 'theme' meant when applied to a novel. History was so boring I could not bear to open my book. I would sit for two hours at the table with my books in front of me, but I could not open them."

That same year Kadohata was injured in a freak auto accident. While she was walking down the street in Los Angeles, a car jumped the curb and hit her. She broke her collarbone and severely mangled her right arm. A doctor told her that if she had come to the hospital any later, she might have had her arm amputated. After several weeks of recovery, she took a month-long trip through parts of America on a Greyhound bus, hoping to find creative inspiration. "I think I felt I needed to conjure up some spirits," she recalled. During that trip, she

met several fascinating people and began to rediscover her appreciation of America. It also awakened in her a sense of what it meant to be an American writer. "It did not mean shared history or even shared values with other Americans, but a shared landscape," she contended. "What all of us shared were the factories, the deserts, the cities, the wheat fields. That sharing was an immense responsibility we had to one another. I understood then that I could write about my section of that shared landscape."

Shortly after her travels, Kadohata moved to Boston to live with her sister. She frequented the city's bookstores and began to realize the potential of

Kadohata with her dog, a Doberman named Shika Kojika.

good fiction. "I started looking at short stories," she recalls. "I had always thought that nonfiction represented the 'truth.' Fiction seemed like something that people had done a long time ago, and wasn't very profound. But in these short stories I saw that people were writing now, and that the work was very alive. I realized that you could say things with fiction that you couldn't say any other way."

Becoming a Writer

Determined to become a writer, Kadohata started sending stories to the *Atlantic Monthly* and the *New Yorker* at the rate of one a month. "I wrote 20 to 40 stories, and I got rejections for all of them," she recounts. "But I got letters back that were encouraging, so I kept writing. I remember in 1986, right before I sold my first story to the *New Yorker*, I told a friend that I didn't think I was ever going to sell a story; I wondered if I should stop writing. About three weeks later, I got a phone call from an editor at the *New Yorker*." After 25 rejections, the magazine had accepted one of her stories, entitled "Charlie O," for publication, and in the coming months they published two more of her stories. Her fiction also appeared in *Grand Street* and the *Pennsylvania Review*.

Kadohata was accepted into the graduate writing program at the University of Pittsburgh. But she felt torn between formal university classes and the education offered through traveling and everyday life. "It's always a battle in my head: 'Oh, I've got to be reading. I feel so guilty,'" she noted. "On the other hand, I feel if I don't go out there and do wacky things, like traveling, it will make my writing dry. Besides, you can't help admiring people who never went to school, travel around, and are incredible writers. There's something romantic about it."

Although she enjoyed her short stint at the University of Pittsburgh, Kadohata wanted to live in New York City. In 1987 she transferred to the graduate writing program at Columbia University. After several months, however, she realized that Columbia's writing program was not helping her. "I went there and I still didn't feel I was getting better, faster," she stated, "so I said, 'Forget it. In the old days they used to say that a young writer has to live in New York to establish a career, but you don't have to anymore.' I had read that somewhere and I said, 'I'm leaving.'" She dropped out of Columbia University in 1988 and committed to becoming a full-time writer.

CAREER HIGHLIGHTS

In late 1987, while on a plane, Kadohata read a profile about successful literary agent Andrew Wylie. When she arrived home to New York, she found two letters from him in her mailbox. He had read her story "Jack's Girl" in the *New Yorker* and was inter-

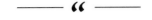

Kadohata felt torn between formal university classes and the education offered through traveling and everyday life. "It's always a battle in my head: 'Oh, I've got to be reading. I feel so guilty,'" she noted. "On the other hand, I feel if I don't go out there and do wacky things, like traveling, it will make my writing dry. Besides, you can't help admiring people who never went to school, travel around, and are incredible writers. There's something romantic about it."

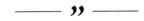

ested in representing her. She was thrilled, and after signing with him she worked to convert the stories she had written into a novel. When she was finished, Wylie took the manuscript, entitled *The Floating World,* and showed it to publishing companies. In the spring of 1988, Viking informed her that they were going to publish her novel.

Even after her first book was accepted for publication, Kadohata did not really think of herself as a writer. "I would go into bookstores and browse through all those how-to-write books," she admitted in an interview. "It still doesn't feel totally natural to say that I'm a writer. I'm still really drawn to that section in a bookstore, and it's still discouraging. It's sort of like picking at a scab." Despite her doubts about herself, however, she did not want to stop writing. "It seems like I had a hunger inside and the only way to feed it was to write," she said.

Writing Novels for Adults

Kadohata's first novel, *The Floating World* (1989), is a coming-of-age tale narrated by 12-year-old Olivia, a young Japanese-American girl growing up in the 1950s. Her father is constantly searching for a job, so Olivia's family moves from town to town, living in what her grandmother Obasan calls "the floating world." Olivia is torn between her Japanese heritage, represented by Obasan, and her American identity, which is encouraged by her parents, who are eager to assimilate into modern America. *The Floating World* received glowing reviews from critics, and Kadohata was praised as a noteworthy new voice in Japanese-American fiction. She had mixed feelings about that. "For the first time in my life, I saw that there could be expectations of me not only as a writer but as an Asian-American writer," she said in *Publishers Weekly*. "On the one hand, I felt like, 'leave me alone.' On the other hand, I thought, 'This is a way I can assert my Asianness.' I wrote the book, and I'm Asian, and I'm the only person who could have written it."

Around the time that *The Floating World* was published, Kadohata moved back to Los Angeles. She quickly fell in love with the city. "At its best, L.A. has a bizarre serenity," she asserted. "When I first moved out here, I remember feeling really disappointed over things, and yet now when I look at the city, I just think it's beautiful. I'm enamored of the city now."

Kadohata's second novel, *In the Heart of the Valley* (1992), did not fare as well with critics or readers. Set in Los Angeles in 2052, it tells the story of a 19-year-old woman named Francie as she struggles to survive in a world that has fallen into lawlessness and chaos. Kadohata had always wanted to write science fiction. "There is something in futuristic fiction that warns, and yet something in it that's very hopeful," she said. "And you can express paranoia in a way that you can't quite do in the present. I like the idea that the author is creating a world that doesn't exist, rather than documenting one that does." Critics, however, found the novel to be unconvincing and ultimately disappointing.

Kadohata's third novel, *The Glass Mountains* (1995), did not receive any significant critical attention. In the story, a young girl's fairy-tale life is torn apart by violence, and she is forced to take drastic action to save her par-

Kadohata's first book for young adults, Kira-Kira, *won the Newbery Medal.*

ents and her village. With the failure of *The Glass Mountains*, Kadohata explored other ways to express herself. In the late 1990s she tried her hand at writing screenplays and worked as a secretary in a food-processing plant.

Becoming a Young Adult Writer

With the advice of a friend, Kadohata soon changed her approach to writing. Caitlyn Dlouhy, an old friend and an editor at Atheneum Books for Young Readers, encouraged her to write a book for young adults. Preoccupied with other projects, Kadohata resisted at first. But when Dlouhy sent boxes of young adult books for her to read, Kadohata began to realize the potential and challenge of young adult fiction. "My previous novels were from the POV [point of view] of young narrators, so the jump from adult books to children's books wasn't extreme," she explained. She was also inspired to write about her childhood. "I guess my childhood is something that has inspired me to do a lot of my writing," she continued. "It's funny, because while I was living my childhood I never dreamed that any of it was future writing material. But I think all of us, no matter what we do and where we live, have fascinating childhoods. So there is always something to write about."

> "I guess my childhood is something that has inspired me to do a lot of my writing," Kadohata said. "It's funny, because while I was living my childhood I never dreamed that any of it was future writing material. But I think all of us, no matter what we do and where we live, have fascinating childhoods. So there is always something to write about."

Kadohata's first young adult book, *Kira-Kira,* tells the story of two young Japanese-American sisters, Lynn and Katie, growing up in Georgia in the 1950s. Katie, the novel's narrator, idolizes her strong older sister, who taught her the meaning of "kira-kira," which is the Japanese word for "glittering." The family faces prejudice and discrimination as well as economic and emotional hardships, which are compounded when Lynn becomes ill. During this difficult time, Katie comes to appreciate small moments with her sister and her family and struggles to keep her joy of life despite her sister's illness. According to Kadohata, "the message behind *Kira-Kira* is that life is complicated, but wonderful, and you should never lose the ability to feel wonder over even the smallest thing."

Kira-Kira was a huge success with critics and readers. Reviewers praised Kadohata's lyrical prose and insightful descriptions of people in the book. They believed that the novel really expressed the challenges of growing up as a Japanese-American in the 1950s as well as the experience of illness and loss. Kadohata was awarded the prestigious Newbery Medal for *Kira-Kira,* which is an impressive achievement for a first-time young adult author. Receiving the award was an amazing experience for her. "It was shocking and purely joyful," she exulted. "I've never experienced a feeling like it. The joy was just so incredibly intense. One analogy I can think of is that it was like in Chicago when we would go to Lake Michigan on windy days and the waves would hit us so hard we would fall over and even get bruised. And yet it was so much fun. The feeling when the waves hit you was thrilling and yet also a strong physical feeling."

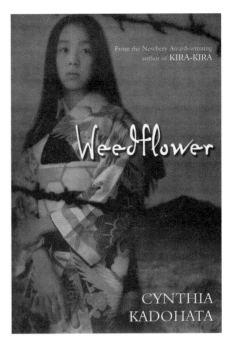

In her next book, *Weedflower* (2006), Kadohata focused on the experiences of Japanese-Americans uprooted from their lives and moved to internment camps during World War II. In the book, a young Japanese girl, Sumiko, forms an unlikely friendship with a Mohave boy. Reviewers praised her vivid descriptions of life in the camp and the compelling character portrayals in the novel, as in this comment from *Publishers Weekly:* "Kadohata clearly and eloquently conveys her heroine's mixture of shame, anger, and courage. Readers will be inspired."

Kadohata was moved to write about this dark time in American history by her father's experiences. "My father was interned in that camp," she revealed. "The other reason has to do with my belief that it is not just the sharing of values but the sharing of this amazing land that makes us Americans. So I wanted to write about how two groups of people sharing a land can change the world."

ADVICE TO YOUNG WRITERS

Kadohata has advised young writers to keep at it, because writing is a difficult profession. "Persevere," she cautioned. "If your parents are smart they will tell you not to be a writer. You have to be 100 percent certain that you want to do it." She has described her own creative process as writing everything and then going back and editing later. "I had read a long time ago that the best way to write is make a mess and then clean it up. I've read that some writers write each sentence over and over until it's perfect and then move on to the next sentence. [But] I try to get everything down as quickly as possible. Then I have a tremendous mess and I clean it up and think it's wonderful. Then my editor tells me to rewrite it!"

MARRIAGE AND FAMILY

Kadohata has been married once. She and her husband divorced in 2000, but she doesn't talk much about it. Today she has a serious boyfriend whom she describes as a great supporter of her writing. She lives in Long Beach, California, with her son, Samuel Bahytzhan Kadohata, whom she adopted in 2004 from Kazakhstan (part of the former Soviet Union). She also has a dog, a Doberman named Shika Kojika that she adoped from a dog rescue service.

HOBBIES AND OTHER INTERESTS

Traveling is one of Kadohata's favorite hobbies. "I'm a road hog!" she claimed. "I love to travel around this amazing country. The beautiful landscape, the highways — I love it. Traveling, seeing the country, is one of the things from which I derive my 'writing energy.' Just thinking about the American landscape and focusing on it puts me in touch with what I think of as the real, essential me. I have to be in touch with this real, essential me whenever I sit down to write."

WRITINGS

Novels for Young Adults

Kira-Kira, 2004
Weedflower, 2006

Novels for Adults

The Floating World, 1989
In the Heart of the Valley of Love, 1992
The Glass Mountains, 1995

HONORS AND AWARDS

National Endowment for the Arts Fellowship: 1991
Whiting Writers Award (Whiting Foundation): 1991
Newbery Medal (American Library Association): 2005, for *Kira-Kira*

FURTHER READING

Periodicals

Horn Book Magazine, Mar.-Apr. 2004, p.183; July-Aug. 2005, p.419
Los Angeles Times, Apr. 30, 2006, p.10
Publishers Weekly, Aug. 3, 1992, p.48
School Library Journal, May 2005, p.38
Washington Post, Jan. 31, 2005, p.C12

Online Articles

http://cynthialeitichsmith.blogspot.com/2006/02/author-feature-cynthia-kadohata.html
(Cynastations, "Author Feature: Cynthia Kadohata," Feb. 20, 2006)
http://www.lili.org/read/letstalk/themes-books/otherrev.htm#kadohata
(Other Americas Author Information and Book Reviews, Idaho Commission for Libraries, "Cynthia Kadohata," June 6, 2006)
http://www.timeforkids.com/TFK/kidscoops/story/0,14989,1028042,00.html
(Time for Kids, "TFK Talks with Cynthia Kadohata," Feb. 28, 2005)

Online Databases

Biography Resource Center Online, 2006, articles from *Contemporary Authors Online,* 2006, and *Notable Asian Americans,* 2006

ADDRESS

Cynthia Kadohata
Simon & Schuster
1230 Avenue of the Americas
New York, NY 10020

WORLD WIDE WEB SITE

http://www.kira-kira.us

Coretta Scott King 1927-2006
American Civil Rights Activist, Writer, and Speaker
Widow of Slain Civil Rights Leader Dr. Martin Luther
King Jr. and Founder of The King Center

BIRTH

Coretta Scott King was born Coretta Scott on April 27, 1927,
in Heiberger, Alabama. She was the second of three children
born to Obadiah "Obie" Scott, a truck driver and grocery store
owner, and Bernice (McMurry) Scott, a homemaker. She had
an older sister, Edythe, and a younger brother, Obie.

YOUTH

Although they were not rich, Coretta Scott King's family was considered fairly well off by standards of the time for African Americans. They lived in a two-room house in Perry County near Marion, Alabama, on land that had been owned by the Scott family for three generations, since slavery was abolished at the end of the Civil War. African-American landowners were rare in the southern United States at that time.

King's father, Obie Scott, worked a variety of jobs to provide for the family. He was the first African American in the area to own a truck, and he used it to haul logs and pulp wood for the local timber companies and saw mills. At various times he was also a barber, a taxi driver, and a farmer, and he briefly owned his own sawmill. He made enough of an income that Coretta's mother did not have to work. This was unusual at the time. The United States was in the midst of the Great Depression, and poverty was widespread. Most people — black and white — struggled just to get by.

To earn spending money for movies and other treats, King sometimes picked cotton on neighbors' farms. She wrote in her autobiography, "If you made four or five dollars in the course of a season, that was pretty good money in those Depression days. I remember one special year when I made seven dollars picking cotton. I was always very strong, and I made a very good cotton picker." She enjoyed being outdoors, running and playing games. She was also a tomboy who often got into fights with her brother.

In 1937, when Coretta was ten years old, the Scott family left their farmhouse and moved to a larger house. They rented the new house to be closer to town and the children's school. Her father continued to operate his trucking business and he also opened a small grocery store in town.

Experiencing Segregation and Racism

King grew up in a time of widespread legal discrimination against African Americans. Racial segregation was enforced throughout the southern United States by "Jim Crow" laws. This meant that African Americans and whites had "separate but equal" public facilities — housing, schools, bathrooms, drinking fountains, seating in movie theaters and on buses, and more. Although these separate facilities were called equal, in reality the facilities provided for whites were far superior to those provided for African Americans.

Segregation was such a part of everyday life that African Americans were not allowed to sit in an ice cream parlor or drink from a glass in a restau-

King grew up at a time when segregation was widespread in the American south, as in this 1938 photo of a "colored" drinking fountain at a county courthouse.

rant. They could not vote or serve on a courtroom jury. They were treated as inferior, and they were expected to act subservient to whites. In many places, blacks were required to step aside to allow whites to pass by on the sidewalks. "As an African American growing up in the segregated south, I was told, one way or another, almost every day of my life, that I wasn't as good as a white child," King recalled. "When I went to the movies with other black children, we had to sit in the balcony while the white kids got to sit in the better seats below. We had to walk to school while the white children rode in school buses paid for by our parents' taxes. Such messages, saying we were inferior, were a daily part of our lives."

The "Jim Crow" laws made it very dangerous for African Americans to disobey the rules of segregation. Punishments ranged from harassment to being put in jail, and sometime even lynching — murder by a mob without a trial or legal protection. Because her father's business ventures were in direct competition with white men doing the same type of work, he was often subjected to threats and intimidation. The family's rented house burned down, as did his sawmill after being in business for only two weeks. There were rumors that the fires had been purposely set by local white supremacists who wanted to scare King's father so that he would stop taking away their business. Nothing came of these suspicions and the fires remained a mystery that was never investigated.

Obie Scott responded to the destruction of his family's rented home by building a much larger, nicer three-bedroom house in town. The new house was located next to the grocery store he owned and near the African Methodist Episcopal Zion Church attended by the family. Coretta's parents encouraged their children to rise above their circumstances and not to give in to those who wanted to see them fail. Coretta explained, "I had wonderful parents who inspired me to be the best person that I could be, and my mother always told me that I was going to go to college, even if she didn't have but one dress to put on. So I grew up knowing that I was going to somehow find a way out of the situation I grew up in."

EDUCATION

King began her education at the Crossroads School in Marion, Alabama. She walked five miles every day to get to the one-room school for African-American children. Every day she was passed by a school bus carrying white children to their school. The white school was closer than Crossroads, but segregation laws prevented her from enrolling there. She thought about this every day as the school bus passed her by. Later in her life, she remembered this as the very beginning of her realization that society needed to change.

After graduating from Crossroads at the top of her class, King attended the private Lincoln High School in Marion. The school was ten miles away, so students normally had to stay in town for the school week, only going home on the weekends. Her mother, Bernice Scott, thought that the children should not have to be away from home for that long, so she decided to find a way to allow them to come home every day. She located a bus and she drove the children back and forth to school every day herself. During that time, this was an extremely unusual thing for a woman to do. Most women didn't drive at all, and if they did, they certainly didn't drive buses.

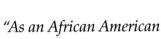

"As an African American growing up in the segregated south, I was told, one way or another, almost every day of my life, that I wasn't as good as a white child," Coretta recalled. *"When I went to the movies with other black children, we had to sit in the balcony while the white kids got to sit in the better seats below. We had to walk to school while the white children rode in school buses paid for by our parents' taxes. Such messages, saying we were inferior, were a daily part of our lives."*

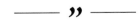

Lincoln High was an unusual school for that time and place. It was a high school for African-American students, and all of the students were black. But the teaching staff was integrated, with both black and white teachers. Perhaps most shocking at the time, teachers of both races lived together in dormitories. Despite this unconventional arrangement, there were no reported racial incidents directed at the school. The school was progressive, encouraging independent thinking as well as academic excellence. It was the first time King had known any college-educated people, and she quickly began to thrive as a student. She was interested in philosophy and began to form her own ideas about the social changes that she thought were needed. She also developed a keen interest in music, learning to play the trumpet and the piano and discovering a talent for singing. She graduated as valedictorian of her class in 1945.

> "I had wonderful parents who inspired me to be the best person that I could be, and my mother always told me that I was going to go to college, even if she didn't have but one dress to put on. So I grew up knowing that I was going to somehow find a way out of the situation I grew up in."

Going to College

After high school, King enrolled in Antioch College, a progressive, integrated school in Yellow Springs, Ohio. Although she was awarded a scholarship, she was initially hesitant about studying at Antioch. She knew that northern schools were generally better than schools in the south, and also that at that time there weren't any colleges in Alabama that would accept African-American students. Antioch College was her best opportunity to continue her education. Even so, she was worried about having to compete with white students who were much better prepared for higher education, having attended better elementary and high schools than those available to African Americans. She went to Antioch in spite of her worries, and later said that it was there that she learned how to live in a white community.

Antioch was known for its emphasis on training students to create social change. King credits the college with preparing her for the role she would play later in life. She became very politically aware at Antioch and began her career as an activist. She joined the local chapter of the National Association for the Advancement of Colored People (NAACP) in its very early days and was also a member of the college's Race Relations and Civil

An enlarged secton of a class photo from Antioch College, November 1945. King is marked #355.

Liberties Committees. In 1948, she was named a delegate to the founding convention of the Young Progressives organization.

The college's mandatory work-study program was another unique aspect of the Antioch educational approach. As one of the students who pioneered the new program, King was required to alternate semesters of study with time spent working at a job. She felt that her classes were more meaningful because of this, as working helped her apply what she was learning in the classroom to a real situation. During her working semesters, she had jobs as a waitress, a camp counselor, a library assistant, and a nursery school attendant. Sometimes she worked in her father's store as a bookkeeper, and she also ordered the store's supplies and waited on customers. These seemingly odd jobs were all credited as part of the college's work-study program.

Planning a Career in Music

King also continued her music studies at Antioch. She sang in the choir and was a soloist with the Second Baptist Church in Springfield, Ohio. In 1948 she gave her first singing concert. She decided to pursue a degree in music and elementary education, thinking that she would have a career teaching and singing in concerts. But when it came time to perform her student teaching, she discovered that none of the schools in the area would accept an African-American teacher. She had no option other than to take a student teaching position at the Antioch Demonstration School, which was operated by the College.

This was a great disappointment to King and caused her to rethink her plan to work as a teacher. She was angry and frustrated, and thought about how she had come to Ohio from Alabama specifically to escape segregation. She later recalled telling herself, "I have to face these problems. So I'm not going to let this one get me down. I'll have to accept a compromise now, but I don't have to accept it as being right. I'm going to do something about this situation. I don't want those who come after me to have to experience the same fate I did." She graduated from Antioch in 1951 with a Bachelor of Arts (BA) degree in music and education, a new plan to continue her music studies, and a resolve to work for social change.

King applied for and received a scholarship to the New England Conservatory of Music in Boston, Massachusetts. The scholarship paid for her tuition, but she was responsible for all her other expenses. She worked part-time as a mail order clerk and also cleaned house for a Boston family in exchange for a room and breakfast each day. With hardly any money left over to buy food, she existed as best she could on a diet consisting mainly of crackers, peanut butter, and fruit. After her first year at the Conservatory, King began to receive financial aid from the State of Alabama, under a program that assisted African-American students who were not allowed to enroll in the state's colleges. Things were a little better for her with the increased financial support, and she was able to focus more fully on her studies.

A Fateful Meeting

While she was studying at the New England Conservatory, a mutual friend introduced Coretta to Martin Luther King Jr. After a short telephone conversation, she agreed to meet him for lunch. When they met for the first time in person, she remembered being very unimpressed. She thought he was too short, and she was put off by his plans to become a Baptist minister. However, as they got to know each other over lunch, she began to change her mind. She realized that he was not the stereotyped preacher that she had imagined. "In those few minutes I had forgotten about Martin being short and had completely revised my first impression. He radiated charm. When he talked, he grew in stature. . . . I knew immediately that he was special," she recalled. But when he told her at the end of that first date that he wanted to marry her, she replied, "That's absurd. You don't even know me." She later reflected that he seemed very certain of what he was proposing. "It was as if he had no time for mistakes, as if he had to make up his mind quickly and correctly, and then move on with his life."

After they had dated for awhile, Martin again asked her to marry him. Coretta took six months to think it over before she said yes. Although she felt that marrying him would mean giving up her wish for a career as a singer, she realized that they shared similar goals in life. They both wanted very much to bring about social changes for the benefit of African Americans. Writing in her autobiography, Coretta recalled, "I had a strong faith. I always believed that there was a purpose for my life, and that I had to seek that purpose, and that if I discovered that purpose, then I believed that I would be successful in what I was doing. And I thought I had found that purpose when I decided that music was going to be my career—concert singing. . . . After I met Martin and prayed about whether or not I should open myself to that relationship, I had a dream, and in that dream, I was made to feel that I should allow myself to be open and stop fighting the relationship. And that's what I did, and of course the rest is history."

> "I had a strong faith. I always believed that there was a purpose for my life, and that I had to seek that purpose. . . . After I met Martin and prayed about whether or not I should open myself to that relationship, I had a dream, and in that dream, I was made to feel that I should allow myself to be open and stop fighting the relationship. And that's what I did, and of course the rest is history."

Getting Married

Coretta Scott married Martin Luther King Jr. on June 18, 1953, in the garden of her parents' home in Marion, Alabama. The wedding ceremony was performed by Martin Luther King Sr., who reluctantly agreed to Coretta's unconventional refusal to include the bride's traditional vows to obey her husband. The wedding was the largest event the town had ever seen, with 350 guests representing a combination of big city visitors from Atlanta and local residents and farmers. Because all the hotels near Marion were whites-only and would not rent rooms to African Americans, the newlyweds spent their wedding night at the home of the local undertaker.

*King and her husband, Martin Luther King, with three of their four children at
their home in Atlanta, Georgia, March 1963. From left: Martin Luther III, age
five; Dexter Scott, age two, and Yolanda Denise, age seven. Their youngest
daughter, Bernice Albertine, was not yet born at the time of this photo.*

After the wedding, the couple returned to Boston and lived there while
Coretta finished her studies. She earned her second Bachelor of Arts (BA)
degree in voice and violin from the New England Conservatory in 1954.
They moved to Montgomery, Alabama, in September 1954. They eventual-
ly had four children: Yolanda Denise King, Martin Luther King III, Dexter
Scott King, and Rev. Bernice Albertine King.

CAREER HIGHLIGHTS

Challenging Segregation

During the mid-1950s, people all over the south were beginning to challenge segregation. African Americans had already been organizing in groups to protest segregation in transportation and schools. Then on December 1, 1955, in Montgomery, Alabama, Rosa Parks refused to give up her seat on a city bus to a white passenger. (For more information on Parks, see *Biography Today*, April 2006.) Parks was arrested and put on trial for causing a public disturbance and violating segregation laws, sparking a call for a city-wide boycott of the transportation system. When Martin was chosen to lead the Montgomery Bus Boycott, Coretta's life changed forever. She was no longer simply the wife of a southern Baptist preacher — she was becoming the wife of a civil rights pioneer.

The Montgomery Bus Boycott and the ensuing legal battles lasted just over a year. The boycott still stands as one of the largest and most successful nonviolent protests against racial segregation ever held. Martin's role in leading and organizing the boycott resulted in hundreds of death threats and threats of violence against his family. In January 1956, just a month after the Montgomery bus system was integrated, several anonymous telephone calls came to the King family home. Callers threatened to bomb the house if Martin didn't leave town within three days. He ignored the threats. Three days later, on January 30, 1956, Coretta was at home with her infant daughter and a friend. A bomb thrown at the house blew up the front porch, with Coretta, her friend, and the baby barely escaping harm. Coretta said that from that day on, she knew that her family would always be in danger.

> **"**
>
> *"My wife was always stronger than I was through the struggle," Martin Luther King wrote. "I am convinced that if I had not had a wife with the fortitude, strength, and calmness of Coretta, I could not have stood up amid the ordeals and tensions surrounding the Montgomery movement. . . . In the darkest moments she always brought the light of hope."*
>
> **"**

Despite the ongoing threats and her deepening involvement in civil rights activism, Coretta remained committed to her husband's mission. Martin wrote in his autobiography, "My wife was always stronger than I was through the struggle. I am convinced that if I had not had a wife with the fortitude, strength, and calmness of Coretta, I could not have stood up amid the ordeals and tensions surrounding the Montgomery movement. I came to see the real meaning of that rather trite statement: 'A wife can either make or break a husband.' Coretta proved to be that type of wife with qualities to make a husband when he could have been so easily broken. In the darkest moments she always brought the light of hope."

As her husband began to travel extensively to organize and support protests across the country, Coretta stayed home to handle administrative duties of the civil rights movement while raising four children. She sometimes traveled with him, most notably on a 1957 trip to Ghana and a month-long tour of India in 1959. By 1960, the family had moved to Atlanta, Georgia. Martin was one of the most recognized leaders in the civil rights movement, and Coretta was gaining a reputation as an activist in her own right.

Working as an Activist

Coretta was a dedicated assistant in her husband's civil rights work, but she also made her own contributions to the movement. In 1962 she served as a Women's Strike for Peace delegate to the Disarmament Conference held in Geneva, Switzerland, and attended by representatives of 17 nations. Coretta taught voice in the music department of the Morris Brown College in Atlanta, and also used her musical talents to advance civil rights. She created and performed several critically acclaimed Freedom Concerts, blending music, spoken word narration, and poetry to portray important events in the civil rights movement. She used these performances to raise money for her husband's Southern Christian Leadership Conference (SCLC), an organization he helped to found to promote non-violent social activism. In 1965, Coretta accompanied her husband on the famous march from Selma, Alabama, to Montgomery, Alabama.

The march had started as a peaceful event. But when protesters tried to cross the Edmund Pettus Bridge, which led into Selma, they were met by Alabama state troopers. The troopers began a violent assault on the protestors, which was documented by reporters. The attack in Selma quickly came to be known as "Bloody Sunday." The police response was so terrible and vicious that it horrified the nation. Within the next few days, demonstrations in support of the marchers were held in 80 cities. Thousands of religious and lay leaders, including Coretta and Martin Luther King, flew to Selma. Outraged citizens flooded the White House and Congress with letters and phone calls. Bloody Sunday convinced President Lyndon B.

Coretta and Martin lead the final lap of the Selma to Montgomery march demanding voter registration rights for blacks, March 1965.

Johnson to send new voting-rights legislation to Congress. On August 6, 1965, Johnson signed the Voting Rights Act into law. It ended literacy tests and poll taxes and ordered the appointment of federal voting registrars who would ensure the rights of black voters, resulting in a dramatic increase in the number of African Americans who were able to vote. It has been called the single most effective piece of civil rights legislation ever passed by the United States Congress.

Meanwhile, amidst impressive progress towards real social change, Martin continued to receive death threats. When the threatening anonymous telephone calls came, Coretta sometimes responded by informing the caller that her husband was busy and did not wish to be disturbed. She would say, "He told me to write the name and number of anyone who called to threaten his life so that he could return the call later." Not surprisingly, no one ever provided her with that information. But responding in this way projected the attitude of quiet confidence that came to characterize Coretta's personality.

The Assassination

On April 4, 1968, Coretta went on a shopping trip with her youngest daughter Yolanda. They were buying new dresses to wear for Easter. When they returned home, Coretta received a telephone call from Rev. Jesse Jackson, telling her that her husband had been shot. Martin Luther

187

King Jr. had been assassinated in Memphis, Tennessee, where he had gone to lead a protest march. "It hit me hard," Coretta said, "that the call I seemed subconsciously to have been waiting for all our lives had come." She recalled that when President John F. Kennedy had been shot and killed in 1963, Martin told her, "That's exactly what's going to happen to me."

In the days immediately following the assassination, race riots erupted in cities across the country. Coretta spoke out to ask for a restoration of peace, and is credited with helping to subdue the violence before it became too severe. The day before her husband's funeral, Coretta stepped in to lead the march that he had planned in Memphis. Speaking to the 50,000 marchers, she said, "I would challenge you today to see that his spirit never dies. We are going to continue his work to make all people truly free." She would say later that it never crossed her mind not to continue his work. In her grief, she took over the speaking engagements that had been arranged before Martin's death. At first she spoke from the notes that he left or relied on extensive quotes from his previous speeches. She eventually found her own voice and spoke compellingly in her own words.

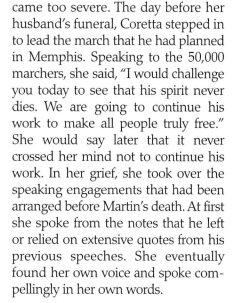

> ——— " ———
>
> *The day before her husband's funeral, Coretta stepped in to lead the march that he had planned in Memphis. Speaking to the 50,000 marchers, she said, "I would challenge you today to see that his spirit never dies. We are going to continue his work to make all people truly free."*
>
> ——— " ———

On June 26, 1968, just a few months after her husband's death, Coretta founded the nonprofit Martin Luther King Jr. Center for Nonviolent Social Change, later known as the King Center. Originally, she ran the group from of her home in Atlanta, Georgia. Her goal was to carry on Martin's philosophy of nonviolent resistance. The Center was intended to establish a living memorial to Dr. King, to preserve his papers, and to promote his teachings. At the same time, Coretta also formed a committee to work towards the establishment of a national holiday in his honor. Determined to make both the Center and the holiday a reality, she would spend the next 15 years in pursuit of that goal.

In 1969 Coretta published her autobiography, titled *My Life with Martin Luther King, Jr.* The book is a personal account of the unfolding civil rights movement as she witnessed it, including glimpses of their private life.

Although the book has been criticized for providing an incomplete, uncritical picture of the civil rights leader, it has also been praised as a warm and human recounting of events. Ultimately, it is seen as a personal portrait of Martin as only his wife could provide.

Fighting Racial Discrimination

In the years after the assassination of her husband, Coretta Scott King dedicated herself to continuing his unfinished work. She made it her life's mission to promote his philosophy of nonviolent social action and to continue to speak about his ideals. She became a talented, respected speaker who was widely admired and much in demand. She brought attention to human rights issues and began to speak out against racial discrimination—not only in the United States, but all over the world. King visited many countries to bring her husband's message of using nonviolence and peaceful resistance to create social changes. On March 17, 1969, she became the first woman to ever make a speech in the historic St. Paul's Cathedral in London, England.

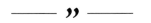

"I had a commitment even before I met Martin. If I didn't believe in this, I wouldn't be working 18-hour days. I don't have another life. This is my life. . . . I didn't learn my commitment from Martin. We just converged at a certain time."

King was soon recognized as an influential civil rights leader. She received several awards from international organizations honoring her humanitarian efforts and dedication to civil rights for all people. In 1968 she was named Woman of the Year by the National Association of Television and Radio Announcers. And in 1969, the American Library Association gave its first annual Coretta Scott King Award to honor authors and illustrators who have promoted the vision of Martin Luther King Jr. The award, which is still given today, focuses specifically on works that may have been overlooked because of conscious or unconscious racism.

Throughout the 1970s King used her speaking engagements to tirelessly promote the dream of creating what her husband called a "beloved community," a world in which all people were treated with equal dignity and given equal opportunities to succeed. In January 1975, a Good Housekeeping magazine poll named Coretta Scott King as one of the 40 most respected women in the United States. She also received several honorary doctorate degrees from colleges and universities all over the country. But it was in the 1980s that her dedication and hard work was rewarded as she achieved two of her most important goals.

President Reagan at the signing ceremony in the White House Rose Garden for Martin Luther King Day holiday legislation, November 1983.

Two Victories

In 1981, King relocated the operation of the King Center from her home to a brand new facility that opened in Atlanta. The expansive new complex houses several exhibit areas documenting the civil rights movement, a 250-seat auditorium for presentations and speeches, an extensive library and archive Martin Luther King's papers and writings, and his gravesite. Millions of people visit the Center each year to pay their respects to his memory, learn about the civil rights movement, study his work, and be trained to organize nonviolent protests. Since its formation, the King Center has trained tens of thousands of activists from all over the world in the philosophy and practice of nonviolence.

Then within two years of the King Center's grand opening, on November 2, 1983, President Ronald Reagan signed legislation designating the third Monday in January as a federal holiday honoring Martin Luther King Jr. Finally, 15 years of organizing, educating, petitioning, and political lobbying had paid off. Although it was another two years before the Martin Luther King Jr. holiday was observed for the first time on January 20, 1986, Coretta Scott King's success was not diminished by the delay. Clayborne Carson, director of the King Papers Project at Stanford University told the *Atlanta Journal-Constitution*, "I don't think people give her enough credit

Coretta Scott King continued her work as an activist on behalf of human rights throughout her life. She is shown here protesting apartheid in South Africa outside the embassy in Washington DC, November 1984.

for doing something very few people have done. If she hadn't been as dedicated and energetic as she was, the King Center wouldn't exist and the King holiday wouldn't exist."

Coretta intended the King holiday to be more than just another day off from work or school. She wanted people to use the day as an opportunity to reflect on the life and teachings of Martin Luther King Jr., and to find ways to build the "beloved community." This dream could be realized only by people working together to create necessary changes. "We have called for people to remember to celebrate, and most importantly, to act," she declared. "We like to say we celebrate the birthday and not memorialize it, as we do in April. Now we should ask people to really commemorate his life with some form of service and to give back to the community."

A Global Perspective

Even after achieving her dream of opening the King Center and creating a national King holiday, Coretta Scott King did not stop working to advance the worldwide cause of civil and human rights. In 1983 she organized the Coalition of Conscience to sponsor the 20th Anniversary March on Washington, commemorating the 1963 event at which Martin Luther King delivered his historic "I Have a Dream" speech. In 1985, Coretta and three of her children were arrested for protesting South Africa's apartheid system of racial segregation and discrimination. In 1988 she reconvened the Coalition of Conscience and led more than 55,000 people in the 25th Anniversary March on Washington. In 1988 she also served as the head of the U.S. delegation of Women for a Meaningful Summit in Athens, Greece, and in 1990 she was a co-organizer of the Soviet-American Women's Summit in Washington.

In reflecting on her life of service to the civil rights movement, Coretta Scott King said, "I had a commitment even before I met Martin. If I didn't believe in this, I wouldn't be working 18-hour days. I don't have another life. This is my life. I'd like to see the legacy [of Martin Luther King] prevail because if it does, we would have a better world. . . . I didn't learn my commitment from Martin. We just converged at a certain time." She ran the King Center for nearly 30 years, turning the leadership duties over to her son Dexter Scott King in 1995. She briefly resumed her role as the head of the Center in 2004, until her son Martin Luther King III took over as the Center's president later that year.

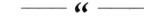

"She was a freedom fighter. She marched in Birmingham. She marched in Selma. When [Martin Luther King] was killed, she kept marching for workers' rights."
—*Rev. Jesse Jackson*

Later Years

King was a strict vegetarian who began every day with prayer, meditation, and exercise. She eventually adopted a raw-food diet and gained a reputation for drinking lots of oddly colored vegetable juice that she made herself. Her workday usually began at 7:00 a.m. and often lasted until 2:00 a.m. the next day. She was known for conducting most of her business over the telephone as she continued to travel extensively for speaking engagements.

In her later years, King continued to work for social change and world peace. She focused her activism on critical issues and concerns of disadvantaged people all over the world. She was an outspoken advocate for the cancellation of the national debts of African nations, and she brought attention to such global issues as AIDS and worldwide health security, voting rights and individual responsibility, racial justice and race relations, disarmament and peaceful conflict resolution, and reductions in military spending. She spoke out against the death penalty and called for stronger

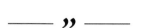

"She was always more of an activist than Martin. Although people didn't realize it, the action part was always difficult for him. He wanted to preach and reason things out. Coretta wanted to march." —Andrew Young

gun control laws. She was a staunch supporter of any cause that promoted racial and economic justice, and she encouraged individual efforts to build community through volunteerism.

King's strength and energy had been legendary, and even late in her life she was able to maintain a schedule that exhausted many of her younger assistants. But her health declined in 2005 and she suffered a series of heart attacks and strokes. By August 2005, she was severely weakened and unable to speak, although she could still sing. Despite a regimen of speech therapy and physical rehabilitation, she never fully recovered. On January 14, 2006, she made her last public appearance at the King Center's annual Salute to Greatness dinner. On January 26, 2006, she traveled to Mexico to seek treatment at a private hospital in Rosarito Beach, just south of San Diego, California. On January 30, 2006, Coretta Scott King died in her sleep at the hospital. Upon her death it was revealed that she had been battling ovarian cancer and had gone to Mexico for experimental treatment that was unavailable in the United States. The official cause of her death was listed as heart failure and ovarian cancer.

LEGACY

Coretta Scott King's lifelong dedication to advancing civil rights and her many successes in bringing about social change gave her an international reputation as a woman of great influence. She supported nonviolent freedom struggles around the world and served as an advocate for racial equality, economic justice, religious freedom, and dignity and human rights for women and children, gays and lesbians, and people with disabilities. Rev. Jesse Jackson said, "She was a freedom fighter. She marched in Birmingham. She marched in Selma. When [Martin Luther King Jr.] was killed, she kept marching for workers' rights."

King received much public recognition and numerous awards for her work, including honorary doctorate degrees from more than 60 colleges and universities. She wrote or contributed to dozens of books, edited several collections of her late husband's work, and published a nationally syndicated newspaper column. She helped found dozens of organizations including the Black Leadership Forum, the National Black Coalition for Voter Participation, and the Black Leadership Roundtable. She was also a member of the board of directors many organizations, including the National Organization for Women and the Southern Christian Leadership Conference.

King's legacy is as much a reflection of her personal character as it is of her accomplishments. She is remembered for her grace and dignity, her personal strength in times of crisis, and her equal devotion to her family and the civil rights movement. She is a woman who overcame tragedy, held her family together, and became an inspirational presence around the world. Longtime friend Andrew Young said she handled public scrutiny well and never lost her poise or showed anger, even in the face of criticism that was often harsh. Young said in *People*, "She was always more of an activist than Martin. Although people didn't realize it, the action part was always difficult for him. He wanted to preach and reason things out. Coretta wanted to march."

Speaking just after King's death, Rev. Al Sharpton talked about what made her such an effective leader. "She was a mixture of regal bearing and grace and an uncompromising freedom fighter," Rev. Sharpton said. "[People] saw her in her regality and aura and didn't realize that in her heart was a woman who believed what her husband fought for. She didn't walk behind her husband, she walked beside him. . . . She was a real activist. She had one of the most keen, aggressive social political minds that I have ever talked to. She was really committed to world peace, really committed to racial equality, really committed to civil disobedience and nonviolence. She was not just the woman [Martin Luther King Jr.] went home to. She was the one who shaped his ideas and activism and she single-handedly maintained his legacy."

"She didn't walk behind her husband, she walked beside him. . . . She was a real activist. She had one of the most keen, aggressive social political minds that I have ever talked to. . . . She was not just the woman [Martin Luther King Jr.] went home to. She was the one who shaped his ideas and activism and she single-handedly maintained his legacy." —Rev. Al Sharpton

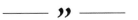

Perhaps King's own words describe her legacy best. She wrote in her autobiography, "I believe that there is a plan and a purpose for each person's life and that there are forces working in the universe to bring about good and to create a community of love and brotherhood. . . . I think what I've

———— " ————

*"I think what I've tried
to do is to empower people
to understand that they
can make a difference,"
King explained. "And by
using the method of
nonviolence as a way of life,
it becomes internalized into
your life; so everything
that you seek to do, you
use those principles."*

———— " ————

tried to do is to empower people to understand that they can make a difference. And by using the method of nonviolence as a way of life, it becomes internalized into your life; so everything that you seek to do, you use those principles. . . . I think we have cause for hope, especially if we can rekindle a new era of social activism and voter participation to achieve the reforms needed to produce genuine equality, economic opportunity for all, and peace with justice. If we keep faith with Martin's teachings and join together with an energized recommitment to create the beloved community, we will one day be celebrating his vision as a glorious reality."

WRITINGS

My Life with Martin Luther King, Jr., 1969
The Words of Martin Luther King, Jr., 1983

HONORS AND AWARDS

Annual Brotherhood Award (National Council on Negro Women): 1957
Distinguished Achievement Award (National Organization of Colored
　Women's Clubs): 1962
Citation for work in peace and freedom (Women's Strike for Peace): 1963
Louise Waterman Wise Award (American Jewish Congress Women's
　Authority): 1963
Wateler Peace Prize: 1968
Woman of Conscience Award (National Council of Women): 1968
Woman of the Year (National Association of Television and Radio
　Announcers): 1968
Dag Hammarskjold Award (World Organization of the Diplomatic
　Press): 1969
Nehru Award for International Understanding: 1969
Pacem in Terris Award (International Overseas Service Foundation): 1969
Leadership for Freedom Award (Roosevelt University): 1971
Martin Luther King Memorial Medal (College of the City of New York): 1971

Named one of the 40 Most Respected Women in the United States (*Good Housekeeping*): 1975
UAW Social Justice Award (United Auto Workers Union): 1980
Eugene V. Debs Award: 1982
Candace Award (National Coalition of 100 Black Women): 1987
Freedom Award (National Civil Rights Museum): 1991
Frontrunner Award (Sarah Lee Corporation): 1996
Humanitarian Award (Martin Luther King Jr. State Holiday Commission): 1999
Congressional Gold Medal (United States Congress): 2004

FURTHER READING

Books

Contemporary Black Biography, Vol. 3, 1992
Jakoubek, Robert. *Black Americans of Achievement: Martin Luther King, Jr.*, 2005
King, Coretta Scott. *My Life with Martin Luther King, Jr.*, 1969
Notable Black American Women, 1992
Press, Petra. *Coretta Scott King: An Unauthorized Biography*, 2000
Rhodes, Lisa Renee. *Black Americans of Achievement: Coretta Scott King*, 2005
Schraff, Anne. *Coretta Scott King: Striving for Civil Rights*, 1997
Siebold, Thomas. *People Who Made History: Martin Luther King, Jr.*, 2000
Who's Who in America, 2006

Periodicals

Atlanta Journal-Constitution, Feb. 1, 2006, p.A1; Feb. 4, 2006, p.A11; Feb. 7, 2006, pp.A1, D4, D6, D8, D14, and D19; Feb. 8, 2006, pp.A1 and D6
Current Biography Yearbook, 1969
Ebony, Jan. 1990, p.116; Jan. 2002, p.116; Aug. 2003, p.164
New York Times, Feb. 1, 2006, p.A1
People, June 22, 1998, p.46
Times (London), Feb. 1, 2006, p.60
U.S. News & World Report, Jan. 16, 1995, p.54

Online Articles

http://www.stanford.edu/group/King//about_king/encyclopedia/king_coretta_scott.htm
   (King Encyclopedia, "King, Coretta Scott (1927-2006)," undated)
http://www.achievement.org/autodoc/page/kin1int-1
   (Academy of Achievement, "Coretta Scott King," undated)

http://www.thekingcenter.org/csk/bio.html
  (TheKingCenter.com, "Mrs. Coretta Scott King, Human Rights Activist
  and Leader," undated)
http://www.time.com/time/archive/printout/0,23657,901556,00.html
  (Time.com, "Bearing Witness," Oct. 3, 1969, archived article)

Online Databases

Biography Resource Center Online, 2006, articles from *Contemporary Authors Online,* 2006, *Contemporary Black Biography,* 1992, and *Notable Black American Women,* 1992

WORLD WIDE WEB SITE

http://www.thekingcenter.org

Rachel McAdams 1976-
Canadian Actress
Star of the Hit Movies *Mean Girls*, *The Notebook*,
Wedding Crashers, and *Red Eye*

BIRTH

Rachel McAdams was born in London, Ontario, Canada, on
October 7, 1976. Her mother, Sandra, is a nurse. Her father,
Lance, is a truck driver. She has a younger brother, Daniel, and
a younger sister, Kayleen.

YOUTH

McAdams, who describes herself as a "little hick girl from Canada," grew up in the small town of St. Thomas, near London.

She loved to perform from an early age and staged productions in the backyard with her sister as her "trusty sidekick." At age seven she told her parents she wanted to be a performer. "[They] didn't discourage me, but they didn't go out and find me an agent," she said.

Naturally athletic, McAdams figure skated competitively from about age four through high school. But she found solo skating "a fairly ruthless sport in terms of time and energy." When she teamed up with a synchronized skating group, things lightened up a little. "We wore costumes and blue eye shadow up to our eyebrows and a bottle of hair spray each," she remembered with a laugh.

> "I'd always wanted to do musicals, so I signed up for the Disney camp, and I was so embarrassed," McAdams recalled. "I was with these eight-year-olds who were going to be Broadway stars, singing at the top of their lungs, dancing since they were two. I was so clumsy, I would just go home and cry."

McAdams found a more satisfying outlet for her performing desires in the theater camps that she attended from about age 12. She admits, though, that her first experiences at the camp were discouraging. "I'd always wanted to do musicals, so I signed up for the Disney camp, and I was so embarrassed," she recalled. "I was with these eight-year-olds who were going to be Broadway stars, singing at the top of their lungs, dancing since they were two. I was so clumsy, I would just go home and cry."

Luckily, she was steered to drama via the plays of William Shakespeare, the renowned 16th-century English playwright. "The [camp] director came up to me and said, 'Maybe you'd be happier in the Shakespeare group.'" McAdams said. "I said, 'I can't do Shakespeare.' So he says, 'Well, you can't sing or dance, either!'"

Despite her reservations, McAdams immediately fell in love with acting. "I did Shakespeare in this outdoor Greek amphitheater at 12 years old," she recalled. "We were playing fairies in *A Midsummer Night's Dream*. We wore our beach towels as capes, and our director would play [music by Irish singer] Enya. He'd turn on this beautiful music, it was nine in the morning, and I just remember peering out through my beach-towel cape, seeing incredible trees and the sun coming through, and thinking, 'All right, I can see doing this for a while.'"

Over the next few years McAdams worked hard at developing her acting abilities. Audiences soon took notice. In 1995, for example, she won a prestigious acting prize when her high school group performed at a regional drama festival. "For Rachel to get that award tells how even in her high school years she stood out," said Linda Maskell Pereira, her drama teacher, who co-directed the play. "This was an ensemble, and the lines were evenly distributed between 22 people. But Rachel held your attention."

EDUCATION

McAdams attended her local high school in St. Thomas, where she was a far cry from the teen queen she portrayed in the film *Mean Girls*. "High school was hard," she said. "I didn't have a group. I had me." She admitted that her insecurity sometimes drove her to be less than kind to her fellow students. The few times someone would invite her into a group, the talk often was negative and critical of others. "That I feel bad for," she said. "But it came out of this place of just wanting to belong, and I think that's so much of what gossip is. If you're the follower, you usually just want that sort of approval."

> "*[Gossiping in high school] came out of this place of just wanting to belong, and I think that's so much of what gossip is,*" McAdams said. "*If you're the follower, you usually just want that sort of approval.*"

Even in her last year of high school, social pressures remained strong for McAdams. As a senior, she joined the student council simply to make use of the council's private office at lunchtime. She was relieved to be able to avoid the lunchroom, where "you'd never sit at a table where you didn't belong, so that dreaded walk through the cafeteria was like a death march."

As her high school graduation approached, McAdams planned to major in cultural studies at York University in Toronto. But a last-minute intervention by her drama teacher, Maskell Pereira, steered her toward acting. "She literally grabbed me the day before university applications were due and said, 'Why aren't you going into theater?'" McAdams recalled. "It just ignited something that had been there and that I hadn't been brave enough to follow through with." McAdams immediately changed her application to theater studies.

When McAdams started college, one of her instructors, David Rotenberg, remembered that "she was shy, but sort of had a twinkle. By the time she got to me in the fourth year, she was landed, she had feet." His confidence in her abilities led him to cast her as the lead in the play *Lulu* by Frank Wedekind. "It was fascinating to watch the agents watch her, their eyes rolling back into their heads [during her performance]," he remembered. "They came chasing me after the first act." McAdams earned a bachelor of fine arts (BFA) degree in theater studies at York in the late 1990s.

FIRST JOBS

McAdams nabbed her first paid professional acting jobs when she was still at York. She took small roles on a number of television programs, and during spring break of her senior year, she signed on for her first feature film. In this film, an Italian-Canadian production called *My Name Is Tanino,* McAdams played a wealthy American girl on a European vacation who is romanced by an Italian film student named Tanino. The action revolves around the film student's misadventures when he comes to the United States to pursue her. Though little noticed, the 2002 film did give McAdams the opportunity to ride an airplane for the first time. "When the [flight attendants] were offering the newspaper, I was like, 'Do I have to pay you?' I just had no idea how anything worked," she recalled.

McAdams's next role was as a 15-year-old in the Canadian independent film, *Perfect Pie,* released in 2002. The role won her national recognition, including a nomination for a Genie Award, the Canadian equivalent of an Oscar. In spite of her success, McAdams still did not see herself as bound for Hollywood, the center of the American film industry. "I thought I would refuse to be part of it," she said. "I thought, 'I'm just going to do theater and be poor, and it will be really romantic.'"

But by this time McAdams had already taken her first cautious steps toward Hollywood. In 2001 she auditioned for a pilot television show based on the Nancy Drew mystery novels. "I didn't get it, and I was devastated," she said. "I thought I'd blown my only chance." Feeling she had nothing to lose, she tried out for a role in *The Hot Chick,* a comedy starring the comedian Rob Schneider. To her complete amazement, she got the part.

The Hot Chick

In *The Hot Chick* (2002), McAdams plays the title role of a gorgeous high-school cheerleader with a nasty streak. When a small-time crook, played by Schneider, steals her magical earrings, the two change personalities and physiques. The movie exploits the crude humorous possibilities that might occur if a self-absorbed teenage blonde woke up as a nerdy 30-year-old man and he woke up in a young female body. Critics generally panned the film, but acknowledged that fans of raunchy humor would love it. "*The Hot Chick* is completely ridiculous, and involves toe-curling scenes of gender confusion and inappropriate sexual advances," declared the *Toronto Sun* in a typical review. "All the more reason for the target audience to love this film."

McAdams didn't attract much attention playing second fiddle to Schneider. "[The role was] such a strange little entrance to make," she said. "I guess it could have been an exit as well." But McAdams continued to work. She returned to Canada to act in a television miniseries called "Slings and Arrows." She played the role of an actress from small-town Ontario who wins the role of Ophelia in the Shakespeare play *Hamlet,* then pursues the actor who plays the title role. Her performance won McAdams a Genie Award for best actress in 2003.

Mean Girls

McAdams then returned to the United States to take a leading role in *Mean Girls* (2004), a comedy set in a suburban high school. The movie stars Lindsay Lohan as Cady, a girl entering an American high school after years of being home-schooled in Africa by her anthropologist parents. Cady quickly discovers that, when it comes to the

"Regina is absolutely in a league of her own at the very top," McAdams confided *about her character in* **Mean Girls.** *"She and her friends practically run the school, since they dictate what's cool and what's not, the style of clothing everyone should wear, and how people should behave."*

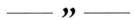

struggle for social survival, teenagers are more vicious than beasts. At the top of her school's food chain is Regina George—played by McAdams— the attractive but thoroughly nasty leader of the Plastics, a clique of shallow, popular girls. "Regina is absolutely in a league of her own at the very top," McAdams confirmed. "She and her friends practically run the school, since they dictate what's cool and what's not, the style of clothing everyone should wear, and how people should behave."

The director of *Mean Girls*, Mark S. Waters, helped McAdams tap into mean-girl instincts by giving her tapes of classic screen villains like Joan Crawford. Her best inspiration, though, turned out to be Alec Baldwin's ruthless character in the movie *Glengarry Glen Ross.* Equally rousing was

McAdams (second from right) took Hollywood by storm as the conniving teen queen Regina in Mean Girls. *Fellow "mean girls" in the film included Lindsay Lohan (left) as Cady, Amanda Seyfried (second from left) as Karen, and Lacey Chabert (right) as Gretchen.*

the punk rock band Hole. "I was jogging and listening to [Hole lead singer] Courtney Love and getting totally revved up," McAdams said. "It makes you feel angry somehow, but empowered and filled with this weird, carnal strength."

Critics and audiences loved *Mean Girls,* describing it as a definite cut above the usual teen-flick storyline. "In a wasteland of dumb movies about teenagers, *Mean Girls* is a smart and funny one," wrote reviewer Roger Ebert in the *Chicago Sun-Times.* "It even contains some wisdom." McAdams, meanwhile, won special praise for her portrayal of outrageously self-centered Regina. "[McAdams is] the funniest of the Plastics," according to *USA Today.* "[She uses] both her blond looks and comic flair to make a direct hit as a high school villainess."

The Notebook

If *Mean Girls* was a showcase for McAdams's comic sparkle, her next release, *The Notebook* (2004), revealed her dramatic depth. Based on a bestselling novel by Nicholas Sparks, the film depicts passionate lovers separated by class prejudice. McAdams plays the role of Allie, a feisty southern debutante. She falls in love with Duke (played by Ryan Gosling), a boy from the sawmill who is as unsuitable as he is irresistible. Their story is told as a series of flashbacks from the present day, as an elderly man reads chapters from a notebook to his ailing wife. "When I read the script I couldn't stop crying," she said. "It's a big, sweeping, epic love story and the biggest lead I've ever done. I'm a hopeless romantic; I'm a softie and smooshy inside. It's a very honest and pure love story and they are not told as much as they should be."

McAdams tried out for the role of Allie after it was turned down by established star Reese Witherspoon. The director, Nick Cassavetes, said that a dozen better-known and more experienced performers also were under consideration. But McAdams gave a terrific audition, and she got the part. Gosling declared that her natural spirit and empathy set her apart from the other actresses. "We needed somebody who was going to step in and say, 'I'm a girl. I know [how to play Allie]. Shut up and roll the camera,'" he said. "We needed that because the character was such a strong character. The truth is, I don't think we would have done the movie without Rachel. This is Rachel's movie. She's driving it."

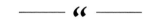

"The Notebook changed me. I grew up a little bit, and I don't think I can go back," McAdams said. *"Mean Girls was kind of my last hurrah playing a 16-year-old. I'm ready to move on."*

To help transform a small-town Ontario girl to a wealthy Southern belle, Cassavetes enrolled McAdams in etiquette classes and ballet lessons. She also attended several fancy weddings in the American South and talked with debutantes. But she created most of the character of Allie straight from her heart. "I just saw someone [who] was just really hungry for life and life experience and for love, someone who was really brave, and I have that in my life," McAdams explained. "I tend to attack things head on. I wouldn't be out here coming from a small town unless I sort of had that sense."

By coincidence, Gosling grew up in London, Ontario, only a few miles from where McAdams was raised. They even discovered they had been born in the same hospital. But the two had never met before filming. This factor, combined with the intimate nature of the movie, made it a challenge for the two actors to develop the necessary comfort level with each other. "There are so many trust issues and you're working all that stuff out

The on-screen kiss between McAdams and co-star Ryan Gosling was a big hit with movie fans.

in the beginning," McAdams explained. "It takes a lot of time." By the end of filming, though, their chemistry was clearly convincing: The two picked up several fans' awards for their on-screen romance, and when McAdams and Gosling accepted an MTV Movie Award for best on-screen smooch of 2005, they replayed their passionate kiss at the podium.

Some critics complained that *The Notebook* was too sweet and syrupy to be considered a top-notch film. But many reviewers noted that the performances turned in by McAdams and her co-stars lifted the movie above the level of a typical tear-jerker. "McAdams's expressive beauty moved thrillingly between rapture and heartbreak," noted the *Los Angeles Times* reviewer. A *Detroit News* critic heralded her as a "full-blown dramatic actress who has to deal with tragedy, conflict, and heartache, all while winning over the audience."

"When I read the script I couldn't stop crying," McAdams said. "It's a big, sweeping, epic love story and the biggest lead I've ever done. I'm a hopeless romantic; I'm a softie and smooshy inside. It's a very honest and pure love story and they are not told as much as they should be."*

As for McAdams, she was happy for the opportunity to move on from her comic teen-aged roles. "It was a drastic change, but it certainly was a welcome change," she said. "I always imagined myself doing drama instead of comedy." She said it would be hard to ever return to younger roles. "*The Notebook* changed me. I grew up a little bit, and I don't think I can go back," she said. "*Mean Girls* was kind of my last hurrah playing a 16-year-old. I'm ready to move on."

Wedding Crashers

McAdams returned to comedy for her next role, in the 2005 hit comedy *Wedding Crashers.* The film stars Owen Wilson and Vince Vaughan as zany lawyers who crash wedding receptions to pick up women. McAdams played a supporting role in the film as a bridesmaid at a wedding that they crash. When Wilson falls in love with her, it causes a rift between the buddies. McAdams said that Wilson always kept her on her toes during shooting. "He'd always do something silly right before the cameras rolled," she said. "He'd make funny faces or whisper something."

McAdams called both Wilson and Vaughan "comic geniuses." But the actor she most connected with on the shoot was Christopher Walken, who

Claire (McAdams) and John (Owen Wilson) in a scene from Wedding Crashers.

played her father. "One of the last scenes I shot was with him. We were in the flower market, and I don't know, there was this synergy," she said. The movie and her performance were generally well reviewed. A reviewer for *Maclean's* magazine singled out "a star-making performance by McAdams, who has the most radiant smile since Audrey Hepburn."

Indeed, with this role McAdams really began to stand out to critics—even though she played a secondary role in the film. "It's not easy to pigeonhole actress Rachel McAdams," wrote reviewer Marcy Medina. "There are her ever-changing hairdos, for one—from the long platinum tresses in *Mean Girls* to the flame-colored waves in *The Notebook* to the brown curls in her most recent film, *Wedding Crashers*. And so far, each character on her resume bears little resemblance to the last. The one constant, however, is her engaging screen presence that keeps moviegoers' eyes on McAdams whenever she appears."

Red Eye

Soon after the release of *Wedding Crashers,* yet another McAdams film hit American movie theatres. In this movie, *Red Eye* (2005), she proved that she could knock out audiences in another movie genre: the thriller. *Red Eye* was directed by Wes Craven, creator of teen-slasher classics like *A Nightmare on Elm Street* and *Scream*. Unlike those notoriously bloody films, though, *Red Eye* relied on subtlety and escalating suspense to keep audiences riveted to their seats.

McAdams stars as Lisa Reisert, a hotel manager on her way home from her grandmother's funeral on a late-night flight. After a preflight encounter with Jackson Rippner, a handsome stranger, Reisert finds herself seated beside him on the plane. At first the two carry on a flirtatious dialogue, but once they are in the air he reveals that he is a terrorist plotting to kill a government official scheduled to stay at her hotel. He informs her that if she doesn't help him carry out the assassination, her father will be murdered by an accomplice. "It's a pretty dire situation," McAdams said. "If she helps Jackson carry out his plot, she is as much a murderer as he is."

Most of *Red Eye* takes place in the claustrophobic airplane cabin. "The psychological mind play between these two characters in that confined space was the element I was most attracted to in the script," McAdams said. "[Not] having a lot of dialogue, having to have a lot of the work done kind of behind your eyes and hoping that it comes across: The subtleties were so significant."

People magazine called *Red Eye* "the kind of solid mainstream film making that has become all too rare in recent years." The reviewer singled out McAdams for a rave review: "As the resourceful Reisert, McAdams, whose work has grown more confident with each film since last year's *Mean Girls*, blossoms into a movie star. With a face so expressive it could probably act out the alphabet, McAdams manages to outsmile Julia Roberts and outcry Demi Moore."

The Family Stone and Future Projects

McAdams returned to a supporting role for the holiday 2005 release, *The Family Stone*. Playing the youngest in a family of five, she joined an ensemble cast including Dermot Mulroney and Luke Wilson as her brothers, Sarah Jessica Parker as Mulroney's uptight girlfriend, and Diane Keaton and Craig Nelson as her parents. In this generally well-received "meet-the-parents" comedy, McAdams and Keaton scheme together to derail Mulroney's romance. The film earned mixed reviews, as some critics found the characters and plot twists not completely believable. But McAdams still earned praised for her work as sister Amy Stone, as in this review from *Vogue* magazine: "You may leave the theater talking about rising star Rachel McAdams, who shone in two of the summer's hits, *Wedding Crashers* and *Red Eye*. Well versed in playing teenage vixens—she was Lindsay Lohan's archenemy in *Mean Girls*—this 29-year-old Canadian makes Amy Stone an enjoyably wicked piece of work, a beauty whose venom is all the more lethal because she smiles so prettily."

Without a doubt, the positive "buzz" about McAdams that started with *Mean Girls* has grown with each successive role. Critics and colleagues agree that she is well on her way to major movie stardom. "She hates being compared, but I often said to her, 'You can be Meryl Streep. You can be Sigourney Weaver or Julia Roberts,'" said David Dobkin, director of

———— " ————

*"My life comes to a
screeching halt when
I'm not making movies.
I really like to ride
my bike around town,
garden, cook, and play
Ultimate Frisbee," McAdams
said. "It's better than
going to the gym. It's
really social, you're
outside with other
people.... I'm hooked."*

———— " ————

Wedding Crashers. Wes Craven, director of *Red Eye,* called her a performer "of enormous range and great charisma . . . not to mention a fantastic beauty." In its end-of-year 2005 issue, *People* magazine designated McAdams the year's "Rising Star."

McAdams admits that she sometimes feels bowled over by her sudden and dramatic rise to stardom. "It's exciting and daunting all at the same time," she said of her success. "And I'm hesitant and overwhelmed and overjoyed." McAdams is also excited about a number of future films she is considering, noting that "opportunities are definitely coming up.... Being in a position to be able to choose [what role to play next] is very stressful, but it's also very amazing, wonderful, and such a gift."

HOME AND FAMILY

McAdams owns a house in Toronto. The city is "my home," she said. "It suits who I am and it helps me step away from the business.... When I'm in Toronto I spend time with friends and family."

HOBBIES AND OTHER INTERESTS

"My life comes to a screeching halt when I'm not making movies," McAdams said. "I really like to ride my bike around town, garden, cook, and play Ultimate Frisbee," a combination of soccer and football with a flying disk. "It's better than going to the gym," she said. "It's really social, you're outside with other people.... I'm hooked."

When McAdams is in Toronto, she also likes to play pool and hang out at Stones Place, a bar that features memorabilia from the English rock group, the Rolling Stones. She is well known for her sweet tooth. "I always get in trouble for drinking my mom's maple syrup," she said.

In spite of her home-loving ways, McAdams has a sense of adventure, too. In recent years she has taken backpacking trips through parts of Australia and Costa Rica.

SELECTED FILM CREDITS

My Name Is Tanino, 2002
The Hot Chick, 2002
Mean Girls, 2004
The Notebook, 2004
Wedding Crashers, 2005
Red Eye, 2005
The Family Stone, 2005

HONORS AND AWARDS

Best Supporting Actress in a Drama Series (Genie Awards): 2003 for
    "Slings and Arrows"
Best On-Screen Team (MTV Movie Awards): 2005, with Lacey Chabert
    and Amanda Seyfried, for *Mean Girls*
Breakthrough Female (MTV Movie Awards): 2005, for *Mean Girls*
Best Movie Actress in a Drama (Teen Choice Awards): 2005, for
    The Notebook

FURTHER READING

Books

Who's Who in America, 2006

Periodicals

Allure, Nov. 1, 2005, p.189
Backstage West, Jan. 6, 2005, p.12
Boston Herald, June 20, 2004, p.A3
Chicago Tribune, Aug. 18, 2005, p.10; Aug. 20, 2005, p.C21
Entertainment Weekly, June 18, 2004, p.52
Interview, July 2005, p.54
Los Angeles Times, May 8, 2005
Newsweek, Aug. 22, 2005, p.77
Ottawa Citizen, May 22, 2004, p.L5
People, July 12, 2004, p.114
Toronto Star, July 11, 2004, p.D8
Toronto Sun, June 20, 2004, p.S18
USA Today, June 25, 2004, p.D3; July 7, 2004, p.2

Online Databases

Biography Resource Center Online, 2004

ADDRESS

Rachel McAdams
Gersh Agency
41 Madison Avenue
33rd Floor
New York, NY 10010

WORLD WIDE WEB SITES

http://www.meangirls.com
http://www.thenotebookmovie.com
http://www.redeye-themovie.com
http://www.weddingcrashersmovie.com
http://www.thefamilystone.com

Cesar Millan 1969?-
Mexican Dog Behavior Specialist
Star of the TV Series "The Dog Whisperer"

BIRTH

Cesar Millan was born around 1969 in Culiacan, Mexico, during a hurricane that tore the roof off his family's house. His
mother, Maria Teresa Favela d'Millan, was a seamstress. His
father, Felipe Millan Guillen, was a newspaper deliveryman
and photographer. Millan has one brother and several sisters.
He was especially close to his grandfather, Teodoro Millan
Angulo, as he was growing up.

YOUTH

Millan and his family lived in Culiacan much of the time. But he spent his childhood weekends and summers on his grandparents' farm in Ixpalino, Mexico, about an hour from his house. The farm had no electricity, and he woke up before the sun rose. Mexico had many farms or ranches that were owned by the patrones, who were wealthy, while the land was worked by the campesinos, who rented the land and earned little. Millan's grandfather was a campesino. He took care of cattle for the patrones, and the family also raised chickens and other animals for their own sustenance.

When Millan was growing up, most people he knew were working class and did not have much money, so he never felt poor. His grandparents' four-room house on the farm was crowded with his siblings and cousins, but Millan thought the place was paradise and that he belonged there, close to the animals. He recalled his early connection to them in his book *Cesar's Way*: "The only place I really wanted to be was among the animals. From as early as I can remember, I loved to spend hours walking with them or just silently watching them, trying to figure out how their wild minds worked. Whether it was a cat, a chicken, a bull, or a goat, I wanted to know what the world looked like through the eyes of each animal—and I wanted to understand that animal from the inside out. I never thought of them as the same as us, but I can't remember ever thinking animals were 'less' than us, either. I was always endlessly fascinated—and delighted—by our differences."

> "The only place I really wanted to be was among the animals. From as early as I can remember, I loved to spend hours walking with them or just silently watching them, trying to figure out how their wild minds worked. . . . I never thought of them as the same as us, but I can't remember ever thinking animals were 'less' than us, either. I was always endlessly fascinated —and delighted—by our differences."

On the farm, Millan learned that in order for the dogs to live in harmony with the family—working willingly and remaining calm and submissive—the humans had to establish their role as pack leaders. His grandfather's dogs always walked beside or behind him, and his grandfather never resorted to violence, bribery, or raising his voice. His confidence and even temperament projected dominance over the pack and Millan observed this and learned to imitate him.

Millan had plenty of opportunity to spend time with dogs. He was always comfortable around them, and he found that the dogs were content when the humans exuded this confidence. He explained how this early exposure to dogs shaped his future with them: "In our family, having dogs around was like having water to drink. Canines were a constant presence in my childhood, and I can't overstate their importance to my development in becoming the man I am today. I wouldn't want to imagine a world that didn't have dogs in it. I respect dogs' dignity as proud and miraculous animals. . . . To say that I 'love' dogs doesn't even come close to describing my deep feelings and affinity for them."

Moving to the Big City

Educational opportunities were lacking in Culiacan, where the family lived. So when Cesar was about six years old, the family moved to the large coastal city of Mazatlan, where Millan's father took a job delivering newspapers. At first, the family lived in a small apartment. This new living arrangement was not suitable for dogs, as the animals were accustomed to running free and the city was crowded and the streets were busy. Most of the dogs in the resort town where the family now lived were scavengers, and people mistreated them. Millan didn't like city life, where his mom worried about him walking just to the corner and he was separated from nature and the animals on the farm. The weekends spent on the farm could not come quickly enough for him.

Once he was hired as a photographer for the government, Millan's father bought the family a nice home near the ocean. But Cesar still longed to find his place in the big city. He started following a local doctor who regularly walked his purebred Irish setter. It was the first purebred dog Millan had ever seen, and he was mesmerized. When the dog had puppies, Millan asked the doctor for one of the dogs, and the man refused. Purebred puppies were valuable, and Millan was just a kid. Two years later, the doctor granted his wish and gave him a puppy from one of the Irish setter's litters. Saluki became his constant companion.

Fitting In

While Millan made fast friends with his canine companion, he felt out of place around his peers in Mazatlan. But he tried to fit in. Using his dog pack mentality, Millan made attempts to submit to the "pack" of city kids

who were not so accepting of the boy from the country. "I hung out with them and went with them to the beach, played baseball and soccer, but deep inside I knew I was faking it. It was never like on the farm, chasing a frog here and there, catching fireflies in jars and then setting them free, or simply sitting under the stars, listening to the crickets' song. Nature had always offered me something new to learn, something to think about. Sports were just working off energy and trying to fit in."

It wasn't until his parents enrolled him in judo classes that he felt he had something special to connect to away from the farm. By the time he was 14, Millan had won six judo championships in a row, and he learned many techniques that would later serve him as a dog psychologist—single-mindedness, self-control, quieting the mind, and deep concentration. He credits his parents with finding the perfect outlet for his frustration with living in a place where he felt like a stranger. "Only when I was with Mother Nature or doing judo was I truly in my element."

EDUCATION

Growing up in Mexico, Millan attended local schools in Culiacan and Mazatlan. Despite his proficiency with dogs, he has had little formal education and is entirely self-taught.

FIRST JOBS

When Millan was a teenager, his classmates began discussing what careers they would like to have when they grew up. Millan knew he wanted a job that had something to do with dogs. He had been enthralled by the television shows "Lassie" and "Rin Tin Tin," which were filmed in English and dubbed in Spanish. He learned that dog trainers were standing offscreen, directing the dogs' actions, and he thought he had found his calling. His dream of becoming the best dog trainer in the world was born. "Saying to myself 'I'm gong to work with dogs and be the best trainer in the world' felt to me like being given a glass of water after nearly dying of thirst. If felt *natural*, easy, and it felt really *good*. Suddenly, I wasn't fighting myself anymore. I knew the path I would take on the way to my future."

To begin working toward his new career goal, Millan got a job at a local veterinarian's office at the age of 15. He started with sweeping and cleaning up after the animals, quickly moved to grooming, and then became a veterinary technician. His employers realized his gift with dogs, and he was enlisted to control dogs even the veterinarian didn't want to approach.

During Millan's time at the vet's office he was dubbed "El Perrero," or "The Dog Boy," by his peers. This was not a complimentary nickname, as Mexican dogs in the big cities were considered filthy and a nuisance. Millan was treated the same as the dogs he loved. "Did I care? No. I was on a mission."

> ———— **"** ————
>
> *"Saying to myself 'I'm gong to work with dogs and be the best trainer in the world' felt to me like being given a glass of water after nearly dying of thirst. If felt* **natural,** *easy, and it felt really* **good.** *Suddenly, I wasn't fighting myself anymore. I knew the path I would take on the way to my future."*
>
> ———— **"** ————

CAREER HIGHLIGHTS

Crossing the Border

The next step in Millan's mission was immigrating to the United States when he was about 21. To legally emigrate from Mexico, a large sum of money is needed for a visa. Raising that much money is nearly impossible for working-class Mexicans. So over a half-million Mexicans instead enter the United States illegally every year. The U.S. government has made great efforts to curb this trend, citing overcrowding and the loss of jobs for American citizens.

After three failed attempts to cross the border on his own, Millan decided to use a coyote — someone who helps Mexicans illegally cross the border into the United States. He paid the coyote the entire $100 he had with him to get him out of Mexico. The trip was harrowing. They ran to the point of exhaustion, froze in a water hole for hours, and mucked through mud. Once across the border, the coyote gave a taxi driver in the States $20 of Millan's money, and sent him on his way. "Fortunately, the taxi driver spoke Spanish, because I knew not one word of English. He drove me to San Diego and dropped me off there — dripping wet, filthy, thirsty, hungry, my boots covered with mud. I was the happiest man in the world. I was in the U.S." Millan later paid a fee to the U.S. government for his illegal crossing, and he is now a U.S. citizen.

> ——— **"** ———
>
> *"Unconsciously, I was beginning to apply the dog psychology I had learned on my grandfather's farm. I was interacting with the dogs the way they interacted with one another. This was the birth of the rehabilitation methods I still use today, although I couldn't have explained in words what I was doing at the time — neither in English nor in Spanish. Everything I did just came instinctually to me."*
>
> ——— **"** ———

Working with Dogs

Millan's first words of English were "Do you have a job application?" He had lived on the streets for over a month when he was hired by the owners of a dog grooming parlor. He has called these two women his American guardian angels, as they hired him despite his filthy appearance and his inability to speak English. Once they learned he was homeless, the angels allowed him to live in the store. "Believe me, not a day goes by that I don't remember how truly blessed I've been with the people who've been put in my path."

His next stop was Los Angeles, where Millan began working at a dog training establishment. Clients brought their dogs here to learn commands such as sit, stay, and heel. Millan did not agree with the center's methods of training, and he began to feel the urge to implement his own ideas. He felt that intimidation and fear were not effective means to train dogs and that an understanding of the animals' psychology would provide much better results.

Instead of yelling at the troubled dogs, Millan was quiet and did not touch or look directly at them when he first approached. His position as leader was established this way, as in a natural setting, where the dog that is calm and assertive becomes the leader and is followed by the other animals. "Unconsciously, I was beginning to apply the dog psychology I had

Millan enjoying time outside with his dogs.

learned on my grandfather's farm. I was interacting with the dogs the way they interacted with one another. This was the birth of the rehabilitation methods I still use today, although I couldn't have explained in words what I was doing at the time — neither in English nor in Spanish. Everything I did just came instinctually to me."

Lessons in Business

While Millan was working at the center, one of his clients hired him away to wash his fleet of limousines. This change of direction for Millan proved invaluable, as he learned the ins and outs of running a business from his new boss. Part of his compensation was the use of a minivan, and he considered this a very big deal. "I didn't have the pink slip — but for me, it symbolized the first time I truly felt I had 'made it' in America."

Once Millan had use of a vehicle, he started his own dog training business, called Pacific Point Canine Academy. His new goal was not to train movie dogs in Hollywood but to help regular dogs and their owners build better relationships. His new boss knew many people and helped spread the word about Millan's training abilities. "He'd call up his friends and say, 'I've got this great Mexican guy who's amazing with dogs. Just bring 'em over.'"

Working with the owner is an important part of dog training.

The business took off, and in 1998 Millan purchased two acres of property in a tough neighborhood of South Los Angeles to establish his business, the Dog Psychology Center. At the Center, he worked with his clients' dogs and took in orphaned dogs that were likely to be euthanized. One of his early customers was actress Jada Pinkett Smith, who became a mentor to Millan. She referred him to her friends and hired an English tutor for him. "I knew that the minute he was able to articulate what he does, he was going to fly," Pinkett Smith said. "I've always known there was no way in the world he wasn't going to accomplish what he wanted to. Cesar is a go-getter and a hard worker."

Through his broken but improving English, Millan set out to teach people how to behave with their dogs. He wanted to help people understand that they should not treat dogs like humans. "Thinking back to my natural relationship with them [dogs], I began to see how I could help dogs in the United States become happier, healthier creatures — and help their owners, too. . . . My fulfillment formula is simple: for a balanced, healthy dog, a human must share exercise, discipline, and affection, in that order!" It was then that Cesar began his daily ritual of walking the dogs from the center, off leash, on hours-long treks through the neighborhood. People commented, "It's like watching the Pied Piper go by."

A Television Series

After being featured in the *Los Angeles Times*, Millan was pursued by Hollywood producers who wanted to showcase his talents on television. He eventually sold his series, "The Dog Whisperer," to the National Geographic Channel. The weekly half-hour program debuted in 2004 and was hugely successful. In 2006, the series was expanded to hour-long episodes.

On "The Dog Whisperer," Millan rehabilitates dogs and trains people. He shows people who have had trouble with their dogs how to become the pack leader, through calm, assertive energy. He stresses with every client the need to walk their dog, provide rules and boundaries, and give rewards only when the dog is in a submissive state. The *Los Angeles Times* said the following in a review of his show: "His brand of tough love is simple. He avoids condescension or blame while gently, unequivocally informing people that they've been selfish and insensitive to their dog's needs. . . . Whether he's in front of a camera or not, Millan has the bearing of a leader. His gaze is direct, his posture commanding. He's a superb mimic and can snarl, scratch, pant and yip with the best (or worst) of them as he assumes the demeanor of an excited or fearful dog."

> *"His brand of tough love is simple. He avoids condescension or blame while gently, unequivocally informing people that they've been selfish and insensitive to their dog's needs. . . . Whether he's in front of a camera or not, Millan has the bearing of a leader. His gaze is direct, his posture commanding. He's a superb mimic and can snarl, scratch, pant, and yip with the best (or worst) of them as he assumes the demeanor of an excited or fearful dog."*
> —*the* **Los Angeles Times**

On the show, Millan has gone to the homes of the owners without prior information and has supervised remarkable transformations in both humans and dogs. He helped Buddy the beagle's owners help him overcome his fear of the garden hose and showed bulldog Matilda's family how to keep her from chasing skateboards. He spent two days at a women's correctional facility where the inmates foster troubled dogs, and he taught actress Daisy Fuentes how to become the pack leader for her English bulldog, Alfie.

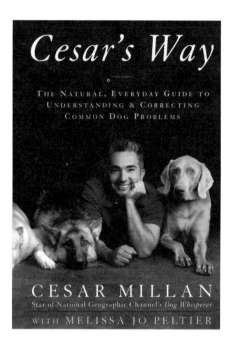

Millan has taken his training message to dog owners across the country through several different means. In addition to his work on television, he has also conducted live seminars for dogs and their owners. He wrote a book, *Cesar's Way: The Natural, Everyday Guide to Understanding and Correcting Common Dog Problems*, which was published in 2006. He has also been the author of a bi-weekly column for the web site www.pets911.com. He has called Oprah Winfrey "the number one role model for my own professional behavior" and has appeared several times on her television program, "The Oprah Winfrey Show." He has said of Winfrey, "In the human world, she is not only always in charge, she is also amazingly calm and even-tempered."

MARRIAGE AND FAMILY

Ilusion Wilson Millan was just 16 when she and Cesar began dating. He was over 21. He was told by a friend that U.S. law made it illegal for him to have a girlfriend who was so young. Afraid of being arrested and deported, Millan broke off their relationship. Ilusion sought him out when she turned 18, and they were married. Millan says he learned a lot from his wife about how to be a better husband. Having grown up in a patriarchal household, Millan acted dominant and jealous, behavior that reflected what he experienced in Mexico. That behavior created problems in his marriage: Ilusion left him and would only reconcile when he agreed to marriage counseling. "You know," he admitted, "it took a long time for me to actually let go of this machismo thing. Machismo allows you to be ignorant, stupid, dumb. You know, all the bad things. So you're not really sensitive to the person. It's all about you."

The Millans have two sons, Andre and Calvin. He does feel it is proper, in fact necessary, to show dominance in his role as a father. "Watch 'Nanny 911' or any of those shows—kids who get nothing but affection are impossible to deal with. . . . What they really need to do is run around the block and then do their homework. Just like dogs, if you don't take a dominant position over your kids, they'll take a dominant position over you."

SELECTED WRITINGS

Cesar's Way: The Natural, Everyday Guide to Understanding and Correcting Common Dog Problems, 2006 (with Melissa Jo Peltier)

SELECTED CREDITS

Videos

People Training for Dogs, 2005
Becoming a Pack Leader, 2006

Television

"The Dog Whisperer," 2004-

FURTHER READING

Periodicals

El Andar Magazine, Summer 2001, p.42
Latina, Sep. 2005, p.100
Los Angeles Times, Oct. 18, 2004, p.E1
Men's Health, May 2005, p.104
People, Dec.9, 2002, p.199
San Diego Union-Tribune, Oct. 17, 2004, p.F1

ADDRESS

Cesar Millan
Dog Psychology Center of Los Angeles
919 East 61st Street
Los Angeles, CA 90001

WORLD WIDE WEB SITES

http://www.dogpsychologycenter.com
http://www.nationalgeographic.com/channel/dogwhisperer

Steve Nash 1974-

Canadian Professional Basketball Player with the
Phoenix Suns
NBA Most Valuable Player for 2004-05

BIRTH

Steven John Nash was born on February 7, 1974, in Johan-
nesburg, South Africa. His father, John Nash, was a professional soccer player at the time of his birth. When his soccer
career ended, John Nash moved the family to Victoria, British
Columbia, Canada, where he worked as a marketing manager
at a credit union. Steve's mother, Jean Nash, worked as a spe-

cial education teacher's assistant. The family also included Steve's brother, Martin, and sister, Joann.

YOUTH

Thanks to his father's athletic background, Steve grew up loving soccer. In fact, his first word was "Goal!" and he received a soccer ball for his first birthday. Throughout his youth, Steve excelled in soccer, hockey, baseball, and lacrosse. But while his siblings stuck with soccer into adulthood (Martin followed in their father's footsteps to become a professional soccer player, and Joann served as the captain of her college team), Steve's life changed when he discovered basketball in eighth grade. He fell in love with the sport instantly and told his mother that he would grow up to play in the National Basketball Association (NBA).

In the mid-1980s, as Nash was reaching adolescence, the popularity of the NBA had spread around the world. At that time, the league featured a number of star players who were at the peak of their careers, including Michael Jordan, Isiah Thomas, Magic Johnson, Larry Bird, and John Stockton. Nash idolized these players and studied their moves endlessly. He watched training videos made by Thomas and Johnson and practiced four hours a day.

> "When I was in high school, I'd just dribble," Nash recalled. "If I was going to a friend's house, I'd just dribble. If we were going to play ball, instead of riding a bike, I'd dribble."

After a while, it seemed that Nash and his basketball were inseparable. "When I was in high school, I'd just dribble," he recalled. "If I was going to a friend's house, I'd just dribble. If we were going to play ball, instead of riding a bike, I'd dribble." Nash found a group of like-minded friends who would play pickup games at the nearby University of Victoria. "Me and my friends used to jimmy the doors [to the gym] so that when they closed up, we could get in," he admitted. "Friday night, instead of drinking beers at the beach, we'd sneak in and it'd be World War III and they had no idea. This was when we were 13."

EDUCATION

Nash started high school at Mt. Douglas Secondary School in Victoria. By this time, he was already recognized as one of the best basketball players

Nash led the Broncos to the NCAA tournament in three of his four years at Santa Clara.

in his age group in all of Canada. After two years, he transferred to St. Michaels University School, also in Victoria. St. Michaels had an outstanding basketball team, and Nash made the move in hopes of advancing his basketball career. The one drawback to the decision was that he was forced to sit out his junior season due to rules governing transfers. During his senior season in 1992, though, Nash led his team to the British Columbia senior boys' high school championship.

If Nash had lived in the United States, his next step would have been simple: he would have selected from among the dozens of universities recruiting him, and he would have received an all-expenses-paid athletic scholarship to that school. But the situation was different for Nash because he played in Canada. "After high school, Canada doesn't really have a next level," he explained. "Not enough kids, not enough tradition."

Realizing that Nash's options would be limited if he remained in Canada, his coach at St. Michaels, Ian Hyde-Lay, launched a campaign to bring his star player to the attention of American universities. During Nash's senior year, Hyde-Lay wrote dozens of letters to the coaches of Division I colleges in the United States. He told the coaches how good Nash was and invited them to come see for themselves. "I wrote to everybody and heard back from nobody," Hyde-Lay remembered. "You don't want to stereotype it, but a 6-1 white point guard from Nowhere, British Columbia, was a tough sell."

Despite averaging an impressive 21.3 points, 9.2 rebounds, and 11.3 assists per game during his senior year, Nash was almost completely ignored by American schools. "The lack of a response hurt me," he later admitted, "because I thought I was good enough that people would come knocking on my door." Finally, though, one U.S. school did come knocking—Santa Clara University, located near San Francisco, California.

College Years

When Hyde-Lay sent out the letters about Nash, he included a videotape showing the young guard in action during one of his high school games. Even though the video was grainy and hard to see, Santa Clara Assistant Coach Scott Gradin could tell right away that Nash had talent. He showed the tape to Head Coach Dick Davey. "The first [video] was not the best quality, and the [opposing] players were not very good," Davey recalled. "I remember my assistant watching it and laughing, and I asked him what was so funny. He said, 'This video of a Canadian kid who makes defenders fall over.'"

Davey asked Hyde-Lay to send a second tape. After viewing this footage, Davey traveled to Vancouver to watch Nash play in the British Columbia senior boys' high school championship tournament. "About 30 seconds into watching warm-ups, I was looking around to see if [any other college coach] was there," he remembered. "You could just see the guy was special." After the game, Davey approached Nash and offered him a full basketball scholarship to Santa Clara. Nash happily accepted the coach's offer.

As soon as he arrived at Santa Clara, Nash became a "gym rat," constantly hanging out at the team's practice facility and working on all facets of his game. Davey described Nash as "easy-going and popular" off the court, but practically "deranged" in his dedication to basketball. It did not take long for Nash's spirit and enthusiasm to rub off on his teammates. "We'd practice all day, then he'd eat dinner and come back with five teammates to play 3-on-3," Davey recalled. "He made all the other players deranged too."

> *Santa Clara Head Coach Dick Davey described Nash as "easy-going and popular" off the court, but practically "deranged" in his dedication to basketball. "We'd practice all day, then he'd eat dinner and come back with five teammates to play 3-on-3," Davey recalled. "He made all the other players deranged too."*

Nash went on to have an outstanding career at Santa Clara that helped bring the Broncos into the national spotlight. He left college in 1996. It's unclear whether he graduated or left school without completing his degree.

CAREER HIGHLIGHTS

College — The Santa Clara University Broncos

Nash had an exceptional start to his basketball career at Santa Clara University. During his freshman season with the Broncos, he led his team to a coveted spot among the 64 colleges invited to play in the National Collegiate Athletic Association (NCAA) tournament. Although Santa Clara was one of the lowest-ranked teams in the tournament, the Broncos stunned the highly rated University of Arizona Wildcats in the first round. Nash sank six free throws in the final 30 seconds of the game to seal the victory for his team.

Nash led the Broncos to the NCAA tournament in two of his next three years. During his senior season in 1995-96, Santa Clara entered the national Top 25 rankings for the first time since 1972. Along the way, the Broncos knocked off better-known and higher-ranked teams from Oregon State, Michigan State, and most memorably, the University of California-Los Angeles (UCLA).

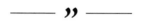

"The NBA is the major dream in my life and the grail I chase every day," Nash said before the draft. *"I am obsessed with it."*

When Santa Clara faced UCLA in the season-opening Maui Invitational tournament in Hawaii, the Bruins were the defending national champions. Far from being intimidated, however, Nash looked around the locker room before the game and told the rest of the Broncos, "I can't believe a bunch of yahoos like us are about to beat UCLA." His statement gave his teammates the confidence they needed to claim a 78-69 victory. Nash scored 19 points while also holding UCLA's star guard, Cameron Dollar, scoreless.

The Santa Clara-UCLA game was nationally televised. Afterward, *Sports Illustrated* magazine ran a feature article about Nash. The little-known point guard from a small university had suddenly emerged as a nationally known college basketball star. Nash went on to average 17 points per game during his senior year and earn his second straight Most Valuable Player award from the West Coast Conference. By the end of the season, he was widely considered to be the top college point guard in the country, and it appeared likely that he would be selected within the first 20 picks in the 1996 NBA draft. "The NBA is the major dream in my life and the grail I chase every day," Nash said before the draft. "I am obsessed with it."

NBA — The Phoenix Suns

When draft day finally arrived, Nash waited anxiously to see where he would start his professional basketball career. He ended up being selected by the Phoenix Suns with the 15th pick in the first round. Phoenix fans were not pleased with the selection, and those attending the draft actually booed when the Suns announced Nash's name. Many fans were unfamiliar with his game, since he was a Canadian who had played at a small college. In addition, the Suns already had two talented veteran point guards on the roster, Jason Kidd and Kevin Johnson, and many fans felt that the team had no need for another one. But the Suns had decided to select the best available player with the 15th pick, and management felt that player was Nash.

Nash started his professional career with the Phoenix Suns, playing behind the veteran point guards Jason Kidd and Kevin Johnson.

Playing behind two veteran point guards, Nash spent most of his first two NBA seasons on the bench. He averaged just over 10 minutes per game during his rookie season, then doubled his playing time to 20 minutes per game in his second year. Despite his limited minutes, Nash established himself as a solid outside shooter, hitting an impressive 41 percent of his three-point attempts in his second season. He also learned a great deal by watching Kidd and Johnson. He absorbed tips from the veteran stars on distributing the ball to teammates while also controlling the tempo of the game. He also learned how important it was to play good defense in the NBA.

After two years, the Suns decided to make a trade in an effort to improve the team. In June 1998 Phoenix sent Nash to the Dallas Mavericks, a team that needed a starting point guard with three-point range. The trade turned out to be the best thing that could have happened to Nash. He signed a six-year contract worth $33 million, and he joined the starting lineup of an NBA team for the first time.

Becoming a Starter for the Dallas Mavericks

Nash faced high expectations from the start of his career with the Mavericks. Unfortunately, injuries hampered his play during his first two seasons with the team. He injured his foot near the beginning of the 1998-99 season, but he did not tell the coaching staff. Favoring the foot caused him to strain his lower back, which further limited his play. Soon, it became obvious to coaches and fans alike that something was wrong. Nash still made excellent passes to his teammates—in fact, he led the Mavs in assists, averaging 5.5 per game—but he simply could not shoot the ball well. In one game, he missed his first eight shots, and after that the Dallas fans booed every time he touched the ball. "That was the low point of my career," Nash remembered. "It had a huge impact. Half the time I'm confident because of the success I've had. The other half of the time, I'm saying to myself, 'You'd better work hard!'"

> **In one game, the Dallas fans booed every time Nash touched the ball. "That was the low point of my career," Nash remembered. "It had a huge impact. Half the time I'm confident because of the success I've had. The other half of the time, I'm saying to myself, 'You'd better work hard!'"**

The injuries eventually forced Nash to sit out half of his first season in Dallas. The 1999-2000 season did not turn out much better, as a right ankle tendon strain knocked him out of action for 25 games. On the positive side, he averaged a career-high 8.9 points in the games that he was able to play. In addition, Nash combined with young stars Dirk Nowitzki and Michael Finley to lead the Mavericks to the NBA playoffs for the first time in 10 years. Dallas lost in the first round, but it was still a huge step forward for the team.

During the summer of 2000, Nash decided that he wanted to represent Canada at the Olympic Games in Sydney, Australia. Before Nash joined the Canadian national basketball team, it was not expected to make it into the Olympic tournament. But as one of only two NBA players on the Canadian team, Nash became a leader both on and off the court and helped Team Canada earn a trip to Sydney. During the Olympic tournament, Nash helped the Canadians upset several higher-ranked teams—including Yugoslavia, Russia, and Spain—before losing to France in the quarterfinals, just short of the medal round.

Nash challenges Toronto Raptors guard Alvin Williams, 2002.

Even though he did not win a medal, Nash gained a great deal from his Olympic experience. As the best player on the Canadian team, he had emerged not only as the team's playmaker, but also as one of its chief scoring threats. He averaged over 20 points per game during the Olympic tournament, and when he returned to the Mavericks at the beginning of the 2000-01 season, he was ready to raise his NBA game to the next level.

Elevating His Game

Finally healthy for the first time since the trade from Phoenix, Nash put together his best season as a pro. He nearly doubled his career scoring average to 15.6 points per game, and he also averaged a career-high 7.3 assists and 3.2 rebounds. In addition, he led the team in three-point shooting and finished fourth in the entire league in free-throw shooting percentage (.895). Observers agreed that the biggest difference in Nash's game was his increased willingness to shoot the basketball. "I needed him to shoot," said Dallas Head Coach Don Nelson. "He struggled until he got my message." Dallas made the playoffs once again, this time reaching the second round before losing to the San Antonio Spurs.

During the 2001-02 season, Nash's scoring average jumped to 17.9 points per game, and he was selected to play in the NBA All-Star Game for the first time in his career. The Mavericks made the playoffs again that year, but they lost in the second round for the second consecutive season, this time to the Sacramento Kings. Still, Nash's emergence as a star point guard made fans and teammates alike express optimism about the team's future. "We get along real well and we're winning," said his teammate Michael Finley. "Everything we worked hard for is coming together."

> **Nash's emergence as a star point guard made fans and teammates alike express optimism about the Mavericks' future. "We get along real well and we're winning," said his teammate Michael Finley. "Everything we worked hard for is coming together."**

The Mavericks came out strong to start the 2002-03 season, winning 14 games in a row. Nash played in all 82 games that year and helped Dallas post the best regular-season record in the league, at 60-22. He averaged 17.7 points and 7.3 assists per game, set career highs for free throws made and steals, and was selected to the All-Star team for the second straight year. In the playoffs, Dallas knocked off the Portland Trailblazers in the first round. Then the Mavericks beat Sacramento in the second round to reach the Western Conference finals for the first time since 1988. Unfortunately, the Mavericks lost the series to in-state rival San Antonio, 4-2.

As the 2003-04 season got underway, many analysts predicted that Dallas would contend for the NBA title. The Mavericks acquired two new players during the off-season, Antoine Walker and Antoine Jamison. Together with Nash, Finley, and Nowitzki, the new players ensured that the Mavericks could put five All-Stars on the floor at one time. Unfortunately, the changes seemed to affect team chemistry, and Dallas never came together that year. Nash had another outstanding season, averaging 14.5 points and a career-high 8.8 assists per game, but it was not enough to lead Dallas to

Nash beats Tim Duncan to a loose ball during the NBA Western Conference Finals between the Phoenix Suns and the San Antonio Spurs, 2005.

the NBA Finals. In fact, the team and its fans were stunned when Dallas lost to Sacramento in the first round of the playoffs.

Facing a Tough Decision

The Mavericks' early elimination from the playoffs led to a number of changes during the off-season. Nash was in the final year of his contract with Dallas, which meant that he had to decide whether to sign a new deal

———— **"** ————

"When you have a point
guard who can pass as
well as he can, it makes
the game a lot easier," said
center Amare Stoudamire.
"I considered him the best
point guard in the league
when he was with Dallas.
And, Steve's a great
guy as well."

———— **"** ————

with the Mavericks or become a free agent and sign with another team. Prior to the disappointing 2003-04 season, it was almost a foregone conclusion that Nash would stay with Dallas. But when the free-agent signing period began, the Phoenix Suns offered him a stunning contract—$65 million for six years—to return to the city where he had started his NBA career. Dallas made a counteroffer, but the best deal the organization could come up with was $51 million for five years. Nash found the Mavericks' offer insulting. "I thought they would come a lot closer than they did," Nash stated. "To me it was like they never really had any aspirations of keeping me."

The flamboyant owner of the Mavericks, Mark Cuban, claimed that the reality of the situation was that Nash never had any intention of remaining with Dallas. "It was Steve's choice to leave for the money," he said. "It was my choice not to pay him the money." In any case, Nash left the Dallas Mavericks after six seasons and rejoined the Phoenix Suns.

Rejoining the Phoenix Suns

In Phoenix, Nash joined one of the most talented young teams in the league. Although the Suns had been plagued by injuries and finished the previous season with a disappointing 29-53 record, many observers claimed that the team was only one player short of being a contender. Phoenix already had two of the NBA's most talented and explosive young players, center Amare Stoudamire and forward Shawn Marion. But without a skilled point guard to get them the ball, the effectiveness of these big men was limited.

With Nash on board, the situation improved immediately. "We went from not having a point guard to having a point guard," Marion recalled. "When you've got a point guard that's thinking pass first, everybody else just falls into place with that." "When you have a point guard who can pass as well as he can, it makes the game a lot easier," Stoudamire agreed. "I considered him the best point guard in the league when he was with Dallas. And, Steve's a great guy as well."

Nash was a perfect fit in Phoenix Coach Mike D'Antoni's up-tempo, fast-break offense. In order to be effective, it required a point guard who could make good decisions on the fly. Nash proved that he could do that and more in 2004-05. In fact, he had one of the best seasons ever by an NBA point guard. Although his scoring average dropped slightly to 15.5 points per game, he led the league by averaging an amazing 11.5 assists, and he led all guards by shooting over 50 percent from the field.

The addition of Nash helped the Suns stage a miraculous turnaround. By the halfway point in the season, Phoenix had already topped its win total from the previous year. The Suns went on to finish the regular season with an NBA-best 62-20 record, an amazing 33 games better than the previous year. The team's success surprised even Nash. "I certainly didn't think we'd be the best team in the league, record-wise," he admitted. By posting the best record in the league, the Suns gained home-court advantage throughout the playoffs.

Phoenix started off strong in the playoffs, sweeping the Memphis Grizzlies 4-0 in the first round. The second round saw Nash play against his former team, the Dallas Mavericks. He scored a career-high 48 points in Game 4 to help lead the Suns to a 4-2 series victory. In the Western Conference Finals, the Suns faced the powerful San Antonio Spurs. The winner of the seven-game series would play for the NBA title. Nash continued his spectacular play throughout the postseason, averaging 23.9 points, 11.3 assists, and 4.8 rebounds over 15 playoff games. But despite his strong performance, the Suns fell to the eventual NBA champion Spurs in five games.

Winning the NBA Most Valuable Player Award

Although Nash was disappointed that his team did not make it to the NBA Finals, the end of the season did bring him a major consolation prize. He narrowly defeated center Shaquille O'Neal of the Miami Heat to win the NBA's prestigious Most Valuable Player Award. Nash received 65 first-place votes and 1,066 total points, while O'Neal gathered 58 first-place votes and 1,032 points. Nash thus became the first Canadian player ever to claim MVP honors in the NBA.

———— " ————

"This is the pinnacle of a player's career, individually, in many ways," Nash said upon collecting his MVP trophy. "It's very important to me to make sure that my teammates know and the world knows this is due to my team's terrific character and camaraderie."

———— " ————

Nash proudly displays his NBA MVP trophy, 2005.

Nash knew that the award represented a significant milestone in his career, but he still felt a little uncomfortable about being singled out for his individual performance in a team sport. "This is the pinnacle of a player's career, individually, in many ways," he said upon collecting his trophy. "But the pinnacle of a player's career is also defined by winning. So 62 wins is as big a pinnacle as winning the MVP. That's the only reason I'm in this position. It's very important to me to make sure that my teammates know and the world knows this is due to my team's terrific character and camaraderie."

To show how much he valued his teammates, Nash called the rest of the Suns up to the podium when he received the MVP award. To D'Antoni, Nash's actions proved that he deserved the honor. "It should be all about winning, it shouldn't be about anything else," said the coach. "What I like about it is someone being an unselfish player and . . . putting the team first and coming out on top. That's a pretty important message. You can score 15 points and be an MVP."

Basketball fans across Canada rejoiced upon Nash's selection as MVP, and the award cemented his popularity in the United States as well. Widely regarded as the best pure passer in basketball, Nash won the trophy because his selfless play made everyone on his team better. In addition, some observers claimed that he and the Suns helped return the excitement to pro basketball. "A dash of Nash and his high-scoring Suns is just what the NBA game sorely needed," Sean Gregory wrote in *Time Canada.* "The pinball Canadian has almost singlehandedly put the fun back into the American game."

While the MVP Award brought Nash new recognition for his skills, he also receives a great deal of attention for his long, shaggy mane of hair. It has earned him countless female admirers—as well as male imitators—and the nickname "Hair Canada." Nash finds all the fuss about his hair rather amusing. "I really don't care what people's response is, this is just how my hair is," he laughed. "I don't take care of it, or comb it, or put anything in it, or style it or anything. When people comment on it, it is funny to me that it draws such attention. It makes me realize how insignificant that sort of thing is, how silly it is to get carried away by that."

MARRIAGE AND FAMILY

In June 2005, Nash married his girlfriend of three years, personal trainer Alejandra Amarilla. They have twin daughters, Bella and Lola, who were born in November 2004. Nash loves everything about being a father, even getting up in the middle of the night to feed the babies. "It's hard when you get to the gym and you're exhausted," he admitted. "But when you wake up in the middle of the night to see those little suckers, it's the greatest thing in the world."

HOBBIES AND OTHER INTERESTS

Nash is known as one of the smartest and most politically active NBA players. Off the court, it seems like he always has a book in his hands, and his curiosity about the world around him drives him to constantly seek out new learning opportunities. "I have a lot of interests," he admitted. "Books, music, current events, sports—I find things fascinating. I don't feel like I have to go back to school and become a professional student necessarily, but I like to learn."

> "I have a lot of interests," Nash admitted. "Books, music, current events, sports—I find things fascinating. I don't feel like I have to go back to school and become a professional student necessarily, but I like to learn."

Nash is not afraid to speak his mind when he believes deeply in a subject. Since the United States went to war in Iraq in 2003, he has not hidden his antiwar feelings. In fact, he created a stir at the 2003 NBA All-Star Game by wearing a T-shirt that read "No War. Shoot for Peace." "In Canada, we are very grateful and thankful for our relationship and many of the benefits the United States offers us," he acknowledged. "But I'm against war. I didn't take a stand against war to tell people how to think, or to tell them what to believe in, or to draw attention to myself. I just feel that in the present international state of affairs, it's important for people to educate themselves on what is happening so that they can make informed decisions."

Like many professional athletes, Nash tries to share his success by helping out with various charitable efforts. His main passion is helping to improve the lives of children, especially those who do not enjoy the advantages he had while growing up. Toward this end, Nash sponsors a 10,000-member basketball program for kids in British Columbia called Steve Nash Youth Basketball. "This is where I learned the game," he noted. "I wanted to say thank you. This is one way I can give back to the place that helped foster the development of my skills. I hope to encourage many more kids to love the game of basketball."

In addition to his work with the youth league, Nash operates the Steve Nash Foundation, which was founded in 2001 to support causes and events that encourage kids to live healthy lifestyles and participate in physical activities. He also purchases a block of tickets for every Suns home game and distributes them to local charities.

HONORS AND AWARDS

West Coast Conference Player of the Year: 1995, 1996
NBA All-Star: 2002, 2003, 2005
All-NBA First Team: 2005
NBA Most Valuable Player: 2005

FURTHER READING

Periodicals

Chicago Tribune, Nov. 23, 2004, p.8
Current Biography Yearbook, 2003
Maclean's, July 8, 1996, p.12; Dec. 24, 2001, p.30; Mar. 10, 2003, p.48
New York Times, Aug. 30, 2003, p.D5
Rochester Democrat and Chronicle, May 8, 2002, p.D1
San Diego Union-Tribune, Apr. 24, 2005, p.C2
San Francisco Chronicle, Dec. 7, 2002, p.C1
Sporting News, Feb. 11, 2002, p.44
Sports Illustrated, Dec. 11, 1995, p.62; Dec. 17, 2001, p.102; Feb. 7, 2005, p.50; May 23, 2005, p.36
Sports Illustrated for Kids, Dec. 2003, p.42; June 2005, p.T4
Time Canada, May 16, 2005, p.46; June 20, 2005, p.42
Toronto Sun, Dec. 15, 1995, p.S12; Jan. 30, 2005, p.S14; May 28, 2005, p.S4
Vancouver Province, Dec. 13, 2004, p.A34
Vancouver Sun, Mar. 21, 2003, p.C11; Aug. 20, 2003, p.F1; May 9, 2005, p.D1; May 12, 2005, p.E2

Further information for this profile came from an interview with Nash for "All Things Considered," broadcast on National Public Radio on February 19, 2005.

ADDRESS

Steve Nash
Phoenix Suns
201 East Jefferson Street
Phoenix, AZ 85004

WORLD WIDE WEB SITES

http://www.nba.com
http://sports.espn.go.com/nba/players

Nick Park 1958-

British Writer, Director, and Producer of
Animated Films
Oscar-Winning Creator of the Wallace and Gromit
Movies and *Chicken Run*

BIRTH

Nicholas Wulstan Park, known as Nick Park, was born on
December 6, 1958, in Preston, the capital of county Lancashire
in northwest England. He was the middle child of Roger Park,
a professional photographer, and Celia Park, a dressmaker.
Nick grew up with three brothers, Adrian, Andrew, and Adam,
and one sister, Janet.

YOUTH

Park was interested in art from a very young age. His parents and teachers encouraged him to develop his talent, so young Nick had hours of free time to just draw, doodle, and create. Being known as the class artist "was a good boost because I was absolutely rubbish at everything else," he recalled. "I didn't do well academically. I'm a very slow reader. But I liked writing stories." He found many ways to exercise his imagination. He collected old toys and machine parts and kept them in a box under his bed. "I used to call it 'my box of useful things' and I used to talk with my brothers about how one day we'd be able to build a rocket or a time machine if we kept all these bits and pieces."

Park's family also provided him with inspiration. His father was a commercial photographer who spent hours at home building things. His mother was also creative, sewing clothes for the family. Once the elder Parks created a camping trailer from a box and a set of wheels. The trailer came complete with furniture and wallpaper on the interior to make it feel cozy, and the family used it on a trip to Wales. This "do-it-yourself" inventiveness would inspire young Nick's first attempts at animation, as well as his most famous characters, Wallace and Gromit.

> *Park collected old toys and machine parts and kept them in a box under his bed. "I used to call it 'my box of useful things' and I used to talk with my brothers about how one day we'd be able to build a rocket or a time machine if we kept all these bits and pieces."*

As a youth, Park was fascinated with animated films and began experimenting with the format. His first attempt was a zoetrope, which creates the illusion of animation by spinning images on a cylinder. He submitted the zoetrope to a cereal-box contest in hopes of winning a movie camera, but failed to win anything. The disappointment didn't stop him, especially after he discovered his mother's standard 8mm movie camera had a "single frame" button. By using this button to shoot one frame of film at a time, Park created his first animated work. "Walter the Rat" was shot from a book of drawings, but the film was ruined during processing. Despite this disappointment, the aspiring animator continued making short films during his spare time. He experimented with paper cutouts, puppets, clay figures, and homemade cels (transparent pages) in his films, which he shared with family and friends.

By the time Park was in his teens, he was gaining attention for his hobby. His teachers encouraged him to screen his work at school. "When the school found out I did [films], they insisted I show them at assembly," the animator recalled. "People loved it, which was great because I loved making people laugh, but wasn't much by way of a performer." At age 15, he entered a short film, "Archie's Concrete Nightmare," in a competition for young animators sponsored by the British Broadcasting Corporation (BBC). Although he failed to win a prize, the BBC still aired the film on nationwide television. According to Park, "I received instant fame in my school at the age of 15; I thought I had reached the pinnacle of my career."

———— " ————

Park was quite young when one of his short films was broadcast on national television. "I received instant fame in my school at the age of 15; I thought I had reached the pinnacle of my career."

———— " ————

EDUCATION

After finishing secondary school, Park took a series of arts courses, fearing it would be too difficult to break into the film industry. He learned art techniques from sculpture to stained glass and then entered Sheffield Polytechnic (now part of Sheffield Hallam University), one of Britain's top art schools. When his advisors learned of his film-making hobby, they encouraged him to take classes that would support it. He majored in communication arts and completed his Bachelor of Arts (BA) degree in 1980. During his time at Sheffield he completed an animated film of "Jack and the Beanstalk," using chalk images drawn on a blackboard. The film earned him a prize in a student competition and also won him a spot in Britain's National Film and Television School (NFTS).

At the NFTS, Park spent his first year learning the basics of filmmaking: lighting, camera work, sound, and editing. After completing these classes he specialized in animation and began working on a 35mm film to help fulfill his graduation requirements. He wrote a script about an inventor who builds a rocket and travels to the moon with the help of his dog. He decided to work in Plasticine, a synthetic modeling clay that stays pliable in air but won't melt under film lights. He also decided to use stop-motion technique, a very labor-intensive and time-consuming way to make a movie.

In stop-motion technique, the filmmaker sets up a scene using models and then uses a special camera to take a picture of the scene. Then the film-maker makes a tiny adjustment to the figures and takes another picture. The filmmaker continues this way—move the object, take a picture, move the object, take a picture. Each of those pictures becomes a single frame of film, and just one second of movie film requires 24 frames. When the frames are linked together and shown continuously, the object appear to move. To show a character walking through a door, for example, might require a hundred or more frames of film. For each of those frames, Park would have to adjust the positions of the door, the character's arms and legs, and the character's facial features, in order to create the illusion of movement and expression.

Unfortunately, when Park decided to use stop-motion technique, the NFTS didn't have a camera suitable for model animation; it wasn't until his third year there that they could supply him with the right equipment. It took him another year to film the first page of his script, as he had to change each model's position for every single frame of film. He graduated from the NFTS in 1983 but stayed to work on the film. He was running low on time and money when the NFTS helped him meet some film industry contacts that offered him a way to finish it. Animators Peter Lord and David Sprox-ton came to speak at the NFTS, and they became interested in Park's work. They not only offered him a job, but the chance to finish his film.

CAREER HIGHLIGHTS

An Award-Winning Debut

In 1985, Park began working at Aardman Animation, which Lord and Sproxton had founded in 1976. He moved to Bristol, England, and used Aardman's facilities to continue filming his story of a trip to the moon. Splitting his time between his duties for Aardman and his own project, it took Park another four years to complete a film just over 20 minutes long. (At 24 frames of film per second, that meant posing and shooting around 30,000 separate scenes of his Plasticine models.) *A Grand Day Out* finally debuted in 1989 and introduced Park's signature characters, Wallace the inventor and his dog, Gromit. In *A Grand Day Out*, Wallace decides he would like to vacation on the moon, since it is made of his very favorite thing: cheese. He builds a spaceship—Gromit contributing to the con-struction by hammering, drilling, welding, and painting—and the two travel into space. During their visit to the moon, they nibble on the cheesy landscape (with crackers, of course) and meet a lonely robot before return-ing home.

Wallace and Gromit made their first appearance in the 1989 short film
A Grand Day Out.

A Grand Day Out introduced Wallace and Gromit and also established Park's signature style: intricate gadgets to provide action; amusing visual details; and incredibly expressive characters who can communicate a wealth of emotion by just moving an eyebrow. Gromit never speaks or smiles (his model doesn't even have a mouth), but viewers can easily understand his exasperation when Wallace uses him as a sawhorse or drips paint on his head. The lunar robot, which looks like a strange, coin-operated oven, uses only a pair of metal arms to express emotions from puzzlement and surprise to panic and despair. These complete characters give depth to the story, while clever visuals—Wallace's first scribbles at his drawing board are really games of tic-tac-toe; the inside of the spaceship looks like the inside of the house—create laugh-out-loud moments of enjoyment. *A Grand Day Out* won several animation awards, including best short animated film from the British Academy for Film and Television Arts (BAFTA) in 1990 and an Academy Award ("Oscar") nomination for best animated short film from the Academy of Motion Picture Arts and Sciences in 1991.

Although *A Grand Day Out* lost at the 1991 Academy Awards, Park could not be disappointed: the winner that year was another of his creations, the five-minute short *Creature Comforts.* This Plasticine stop-motion film was completed as part of his work for Aardman. In his work there he had performed animation for commercials and television shows such as *The Amazing Adventures of Morph;* he also contributed to Aardman's groundbreaking music video for Peter Gabriel's number-one hit "Sledgehammer."

Creature Comforts was part of a series of short animated films Aardman produced for British television's Channel 4. First aired in 1989, the film presents several zoo animals being interviewed about their living conditions. While the voices sound like everyday people, the visuals are full of Park's usual inventive detail. A jungle cat complains of the cold and damp; the youngest member of a polar bear family enjoys their habitat; a chicken speaks of the superiority of zoo life to the circus life of her sisters; an ape relates the boredom of captivity; and a turtle finds excitement in reading. "I found that almost anybody's conversation is funny if you put it in an animal's mouth, because you can have the animals doing things that the humans were not," Park explained. "You can have fun changing the context."

Besides winning an Oscar, *Creature Comforts* earned a BAFTA Award nomination in 1990 (losing to *A Grand Day Out*) and several animation festival prizes. In 2003, Aardman expanded the original *Creature Comforts* into a multi-part series for British television.

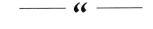

"I found that almost anybody's conversation is funny if you put it in an animal's mouth, because you can have the animals doing things that the humans were not," Park explained. "You can have fun changing the context."

Wallace & Gromit Captivate Audiences

After the success of his first films, Park had the freedom to continue creating his own animated stories. He decided that Wallace and Gromit would star in another adventure, titled *The Wrong Trousers,* but this time he wanted to improve on both the plot and the animation. "I've always thought of myself as a filmmaker first and foremost," Park commented. "With *The Wrong Trousers,* I wanted to do something much more complex and ambitious." He decided to design, light, and film the models as if they were live-action film sets. "I really wanted *The Wrong Trousers* to have the look of a mini-feature film with Hitchcockian and B-movie references thrown in." Aardman and the BBC invested almost £700,000 (over $1 million) in the 13-month shoot.

When it debuted on TV during the 1993 Christmas season, the 30-minute film captivated critics and audiences. *The Wrong Trousers* opens on Gromit's birthday, with the dog hoping for a nice present from Wallace (voiced by British actor Peter Sallis). Instead, he gets a pair of "techno-trousers" that can take him for walks. The gift leaves Wallace's piggy bank empty, so he

Park on the set of The Wrong Trousers, *with Feathers McGraw in the background, 1994.*

decides to rent out a room in their house. Unfortunately, their new boarder is the notorious criminal Feathers McGraw, a penguin who has evil plans for Wallace and the techno-trousers. Although Gromit is driven away from the house by the penguin, he comes to Wallace's rescue, saving the day after an amazing model train chase.

The Wrong Trousers demonstrated the technical improvements Park had made in design, animation, light, and sound. But it was the film's story, wit, and visual details that made it a hit. There are sly references to the pair's previous adventure: Gromit's newspaper proclaims "Moon cheese shares soar!"; replicas of their spaceship decorate the living room wall; and Feathers McGraw uses Gromit's copy of *Electronics for Dogs* to take control of the techno-trousers. There are fantastic inventions, including the device to get Wallace dressed in the morning that ends up trapping him in the techno-trousers. And there are witty visual jokes, such as the books titled *Sheep* and *Sticks* in Gromit's doghouse, or the billboard for sleeping pills that Wallace passes as he sleepwalks in the techno-trousers. The fun is underpinned by Wallace and Gromit's relationship: viewers can feel Gromit's sadness when the penguin takes his place in the home, as well as Wallace's relief when Gromit comes to rescue him. *The Wrong Trousers* was the top-rated TV program in Britain during the 1993 holiday season, and it also won audience and jury prizes at festivals around the world. In 1994 it won both the BAFTA Award and the Academy Award for best short animated film.

Audiences wanted more Wallace and Gromit, so the BBC commissioned a third adventure for broadcast on Christmas Day 1995. Park had only 18 months to write, design, and animate the duo's next adventure, so he ended up turning over much of the animation to staff at Aardman. He taught them the "style" of animating Wallace and Gromit, and found other time-saving measures. For instance, the filmmaker noted, "we pre-make all the mouth shapes, 'a', 'e', 'i', 'o', 'u' and all the other consonants, and we can replace the mouths each time and smooth it over. But even with that we have to watch that it doesn't look too mechanical." Being more of a supervisor was a challenge for Park, he revealed: "I found it quite frustrating not doing much animation myself and it was odd seeing other people handling my ideas." Nevertheless, when *A Close Shave* aired in 1995, it was unmistakably Park's creation. In this 30-minute adventure, a stray sheep leads Wallace and Gromit to discover who has been rustling local flocks and causing a yarn shortage. When Gromit is framed for the crime, it's up to Wallace to rescue his dog—as well as local yarn shop owner Wendolene Ramsbottom, who may be involved in the plot.

Like previous Wallace and Gromit films, *A Close Shave* is packed with interesting inventions, including Wallace's window-cleaning gadgets and the combination sheep-shearing/ sweater-making "Knit-O-Matic" machine stolen by the villain. It has amazing action sequences, including a car chase with a dozen sheep riding Wallace's motorcycle. And it has plenty of visual jokes for the observant viewer, such as the evil dog Preston's *Telegruff* newspaper (a take-off on the name of the famous British paper the *Telegraph*), or the copy of *Crime and Punishment* by "Fido Dogstoyevsky" (a take-off on the name of the Russian author Fyodor Dostoyevsky) that Gromit reads while in jail. This attention to detail is deliberate, the filmmaker observed: "I'm glad [when people] notice those little things, that's what I hope for. I want the films to have a personal touch to them, a kind of handmade quality." *A Close Shave* earned Park his third trophies for best animated film at both the BAFTA Awards and the Academy Awards, plus another nine awards at film festivals around the world.

Although short films rarely get seen outside of occasional television and festival appearances, Park's Wallace and Gromit films were finding many fans. Videos of the pair's adventures were translated into 20 languages and sold well throughout the world, especially in the United States and Japan. Merchandising of Wallace and Gromit took off, with products from clocks and clothing to stuffed animals available to fans. Wallace's mention of Wensleydale cheese even saved one dairy that produced it from bankruptcy. Although he wants to keep the characters associated with quality items, Park noted the merchandising is "quite thrilling, be-

Wallace and Gromit in a scene from A Close Shave. *Park accidentally left the models of Wallace and Gromit in the trunk of a New York City cab during a press trip, but they were recovered after frantic appeals in the press.*

cause I always dreamt I would create something that would be popular." When Park accidentally left models of Wallace and Gromit in a New York taxi during a press tour, it made headlines in Britain and America. Luckily, two days later the cab driver located and returned the Plasticine figures, worth $10,000.

Making a Feature-Length Film

Park and his colleagues at Aardman were interested in branching out into feature films, and with Wallace and Gromit's Oscar wins they were able to secure the financial backing. They entered a deal with the American studio DreamWorks (which produced the popular *Shrek* animated films) to co-produce Aardman's first full-length movie. Park did not want to rush Wallace and Gromit into a feature film without a solid story behind them; instead he pitched the idea of an escape movie starring chickens. His partners loved the concept, and Park and co-director Peter Lord began the long process of directing *Chicken Run*. With over 115,000 frames of film to shoot, they "split direction down the middle, because we worked on the original idea together and the storyboards [so] each knew what the other wanted," Park explained.

In the film, a group of chickens are living at the Tweedy farm. Ginger (voiced by Julia Sawalha) tries to lead her fellow chickens to freedom from Mrs. Tweedy's dreaded pie machine. Her attempts are thwarted until the appearance of Rocky (voiced by Mel Gibson), an American stunt rooster she believes can teach them to fly. Much of the story of *Chicken Run* drew on Park's own teenaged experiences working in a chicken-packing factory. One day he staffed the slaughterhouse, where "chickens were hung up by their feet and they'd peck at the

> **"**
>
> *"I'm glad [when people] notice those little things, that's what I hope for. I want the films to have a personal touch to them, a kind of handmade quality."*
>
> **"**

shackles." For a young man who grew up with pet chickens in his house, "it was absolutely horrible," Park remembered, and thus certain scenes in the film resemble classic horror films. *Chicken Run* also recalls such famous World War II prison movies as the 1963 classic *The Great Escape;* other sequences mirror such adventure films as *Raiders of the Lost Ark.*

When *Chicken Run* debuted in 2000, it charmed both audiences and critics. The Plasticine stop-motion animation and the lack of child characters or musical numbers made it different from most animated films. With its superb comic timing and eye-popping action, it was a family film that all ages could enjoy. As a result, *Chicken Run* received many awards for best animated film of the year, including awards from the National Board of Review, the Broadcast Film Critics Association, and the International Press Academy. It was also nominated for the Golden Globe for best mu-

In this scene from Chicken Run, *Ginger and Rocky are trapped in Mrs. Tweedy's dreaded pie machine.*

sical/comedy and the BAFTA Award for best British film, in both cases competing against live-action films. (The film received no Academy Award nominations, as there was no best animated feature Oscar until the following year.) *Chicken Run* was also a financial success, earning over $100 million at the U.S. box office and almost $225 million worldwide. DreamWorks was so pleased with the film that shortly before its debut they announced they would collaborate with Aardman on another four feature films.

Wallace and Gromit Return

Much to the delight of fans, when Aardman and DreamWorks announced their next project, it was to be a full-length Wallace and Gromit film. "[A full-length] film always seemed like a natural step," Park explained. "But part of the reason why we did *Chicken Run* first is because I was naturally a bit cautious. What happens in a short-film format often works because it is short. We were really waiting for the right idea to come along." Creating a feature film meant Park and co-director Steve Box had to turn over animation of the pair to the staff at Aardman. To get them familiar with the characters, "every week we have Wallace and Gromit classes where everybody has to do exercises with Wallace and Gromit, just to get into character." The animators also trained by creating a series of ten two-minute films about Wallace's wild inventions, called "Cracking Contraptions." These debuted on the BBC during Christmas 2002, and the following year *Wallace & Gromit: The Curse of the Were-Rabbit* began filming. Even with between 20 and 30 animators working on over 30 different sets, the film took three years to finish.

The Curse of the Were-Rabbit, which debuted in 2005, is a tribute to such classic horror movies as *Frankenstein, Dracula,* and *The Wolf Man.* Park called it the "world's first vegetarian horror film" because the only things in jeopardy are the town's prize vegetables. Wallace and Gromit's humane pest control business, "Anti-Pesto," is getting plenty of action as their town gets ready for the annual vegetable competition at Lady Tottington's estate. When the bunnies they trap start filling up their basement, Wallace attempts to brainwash them out of their love for vegetables. His "Mind Manipulation-O-Matic" goes wrong, however, and creates a giant rabbit that terrorizes the town. Lady Tottington's suitor, the sinister Victor, believes a gun is the best way to handle the situation, leaving it up to Gromit to save the day in another fantastic chase sequence. The film also continues the tradition of visual jokes: when Wallace becomes stuck in his dressing machine, a jar of "Middle Age Spread" is seen at the breakfast table; a bookcase with volumes titled *Swiss Cheese Family Robinson* and *Grated Expectations* hides his stash of cheese.

> "
>
> *"There is no worse situation to be in than Oscar night," Park noted. "It's not the winning or losing, just the fact that you might have to get up and say something in front of every famous face you've ever seen."*
>
> "

The film was a critical and financial success, opening in October 2005 at No. 1 in the U.S. box office. Unfortunately, that same weekend an electrical fire at an Aardman warehouse destroyed most of the original drawings, storyboards, and sets Park used in the first Wallace and Gromit films and in *Chicken Run.* Park considered himself lucky because no one was injured and current studio projects were unaffected. Still, the news coverage of the event moved him: "It sort of said, 'This is an important part of British film history.' I never knew that was how it was being valued, so that was quite nice." He was also pleasantly surprised when *Curse of the Were-Rabbit* was nominated for the best British film at the 2006 BAFTA Awards, especially after it beat out such "proper films" as *The Constant Gardener* and *Pride and Prejudice* to win the trophy. When the Academy Awards were presented the next month, it was no surprise that Wallace and Gromit walked away with the Oscar for best animated feature film, bringing Park's total to four. Despite his success in Hollywood, "there is no worse situation to be in than Oscar night. Not knowing whether you've won is completely draining," Park noted. "It's not the winning or losing, just the fact that you might have to get up and say something in front of every famous face you've ever seen."

> *"I see myself in both of them actually," Park said about his famous characters. "They're both opposites. There's a kind of tension, you know, Gromit wanting the quiet life and order and Wallace constantly going off on tangents and causing chaos and getting mad ideas."*

The worldwide success of his films sometimes amazes Park, because Wallace and Gromit seem so particularly British in their humor and setting. In creating the films, he said, "we just did what made us laugh, instinctively, and we never really thought about age groups and targeting certain people." But viewers all over the world can understand the realistic relationship — almost like that of a long-married couple — that underlies Wallace and Gromit's adventures. "I see myself in both of them actually," the filmmaker admitted. "They're both opposites. There's a kind of tension, you know, Gromit wanting the quiet life and order and Wallace constantly going off on tangents and causing chaos and getting mad ideas." In playing off this emotional tension, Park can make films that are "about the real world," the filmmaker remarked. "Things are cruel, life is cruel: people are inconsistent and they do things without realizing." Gromit is "more human than Wallace. . . . He's more aware and more emotional. He carries with him all these doubts about Wallace — you know he's been hurt in the past." It is this emphasis on character that ultimately explains Wallace and Gromit's worldwide appeal.

Park has begun experimenting with computer-generated graphics, or CG animation, working on a film tentatively called *Flushed Away* about a penthouse rat whisked down to a sewer. But Plasticine still remains his medi-

Wallace and Gromit and the Anti-Pesto SWAT Team are on the case, in a scene from Wallace & Gromit: The Curse of the Were-Rabbit.

um of choice. The chunky arms and lopsided smiles it creates are suited to his sense of humor. "I love working with models," he said. "Basically what you've got is a puppet in front of a camera. There's a certain amount of improvisation. Other techniques, like drawn animation, especially with computers, you've got the chance to keep perfecting it. Here, you've got to play it by ear a lot — go for it." It may sometimes look old-fashioned, but Park explained that "we don't mind fingerprints on the characters — they're real, made from real materials." The future will most likely include more adventures for Wallace and Gromit, the director has stated, but his first concern is to find a great story to tell. "My animation has developed over the years but my fascination for the magic of animation which began at 13 has remained unchanged."

HOME AND FAMILY

Never married, Park lives alone in a 150-year-old cottage not far from the Aardman studios in Bristol, England. Interestingly, the filmmaker has never owned a dog, not even as a child. "I never had a dog," he explained. Better behaved—and quieter—than any real-life pet, "[Gromit is] the dog I never had."

MAJOR INFLUENCES

Park cites many moviemakers as inspiration for his work, including suspense film director Alfred Hitchcock and animators Walt Disney, Tex Avery (creator of Daffy Duck and Bugs Bunny's phrase "What's Up, Doc?"), and Chuck Jones (creator of the Road Runner and Wile E. Coyote). The works of American Ray Harryhausen, however, really stand out. Harryhausen's films used stop-motion animation to depict famous myths and legends, creating such monsters as fighting skeletons, a dragon, a one-eyed Cyclops, and a Hydra, a serpent with many heads. "I have memories of one Christmas Eve, cosily watching the TV, 10 years old, and [seeing Harryhausen's 1951 short] *Hansel and Gretel*," Park recalled. "I just loved it completely for its quality and at the time I was starting to dabble in animation. . . . I didn't really know how it was done, but I just loved the feeling of it, and it just remained with me."

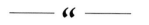

> *Park has never owned a dog, not even as a child. "I never had a dog," he explained. "[Gromit is] the dog I never had."*

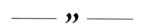

HOBBIES AND OTHER INTERESTS

Park's work-intensive films leave him little free time, but he does enjoy walks in the British countryside. He also lends his time and characters to charities. In 1995, Wallace and Gromit's "Grand Appeal" was established to raise funds for a new children's hospital in Bristol. In 1997, the charity sponsored the first "Wrong Trousers Day," asking ordinary citizens to contribute to their fund and wear crazy-looking pants; that year they raised £500,000 (over $900,000). From 2000 to 2002, similar events raised money for seven other children's hospitals and hospices in Britain. In 2003, the Wallace and Gromit's Children's Foundation was established, making "Wrong Trousers Day" an annual event across Britain. Park serves as a patron of this charity (online at http://www.wallaceandgromitfoundation.org).

MOVIES

Short Films; Writer and Director

A Grand Day Out, 1989
Creature Comforts, 1989
The Wrong Trousers, 1993 (written with Bob Baker)
A Close Shave, 1995 (written with Bob Baker)

Feature Films; Producer (with Peter Lord and David Sproxton)

Chicken Run, 2000 (director and author of story with Peter Lord)
Wallace & Gromit: The Curse of the Were-Rabbit, 2005 (director with Steve Box; author with Steve Box, Bob Baker, and Mark Burton)

HONORS AND AWARDS

BAFTA Award (British Academy of Film and Television Arts): 1990, best short animated film, for *A Grand Day Out;* 1994, best short animated film, for *The Wrong Trousers;* 1997, best short animated film, for *A Close Shave;* 2006, Alexander Korda Award for outstanding British film of the year, for *Wallace & Gromit: The Curse of the Were-Rabbit*
Academy Award (Academy of Motion Picture Arts and Sciences): 1991, best short animated film, for *Creature Comforts;* 1994, best short animated film, for *The Wrong Trousers;* 1997, best short animated film, for *A Close Shave;* 2006, best animated feature film, for *Wallace & Gromit: The Curse of the Were-Rabbit*
Commander of the British Empire: 1997
National Board of Review Award: 2001, best animated film, for *Chicken Run*
Broadcast Film Critics Association Award: 2001, best animated film, for *Chicken Run*
Golden Satellite Award (International Press Academy): 2001, best motion picture, animated or mixed media, for *Chicken Run*
British Animation Award: 2002, best European feature film, for *Chicken Run*
Annie Awards (International Animated Film Society): 2006 (four awards), best animated feature, best character design in an animated feature, best directing in an animated feature, and best writing in an animated feature, for *Wallace & Gromit: The Curse of the Were-Rabbit*

FURTHER READING

Books

Authors and Artists for Young Adults, Vol. 32, 2000

Boorman, John, and Walter Donahue, editors. *Projections 5: Filmmakers on Filmmaking,* 1996

Contemporary Theatre, Film, and Television, Vol. 33, 2001

Grant, John. *Masters of Animation,* 2001

International Dictionary of Films and Filmmakers, Volume 4: *Writers and Production Artists,* 2000

Something about the Author, Vol. 113, 2000

Periodicals

Animation Magazine, June 2000, p.10

Entertainment Weekly, June 23, 2000, p.58; Oct. 7, 2005, p.43

Film Journal International, July 2005, p.76

Guardian (London), June 2, 2000, p.8

Independent (London), Apr. 4, 1994, p.18; Mar. 10, 1996, p.2; Nov. 22, 1997, p.22

New York Times, Dec. 1, 1996, sec. 6, p.110; Apr. 30, 2000, sec. 2A, p.27; Sep. 11, 2005, sec. 2, p.48

People, July 24, 2000, p.135

Print, May/June 1997, p.86

Washington Post, Mar. 19, 1995, p.Y7

Online Articles

http://news.bbc.co.uk/1/hi/entertainment/film/4309544.stm
   (BBC News, "Gromit Film 'A Force of Britishness,'" Oct. 9, 2005)

http://www.bfi.org.uk/features/interviews/harryhausenpark.html
   (British Film Institute, "Ray Harryhausen and Nick Park," Nov. 22, 2003)

http://filmforce.ign.com/articles/655/655696p1.html
   (IGN Entertainment, "Interview: Nick Park," Oct. 4, 2005)

http://www.museum.tv/archives/etv/P/htmlP/parknick/parknick.htm
   (Museum of Broadcast Communications, "Encyclopedia of Television 1st edition: Nick Park," 1997)

http://www.premiere.com/article.asp?section_id=6&article_id=2264
   (Premiere Magazine, "Nick Park: Our Exclusive Interview," 2005)

Online Databases

Biography Resource Center Online, 2006, articles from *Authors and Artists for Young Adults,* 2000; *Contemporary Authors Online,* 2006; *Contemporary Theatre, Film, and Television,* 2001

ADDRESS

Nick Park
Aardman Animations, Ltd.
Gas Ferry Road
Bristol BS1 6UN
England

WORLD WIDE WEB SITES

http://www.aardman.com
http://www.wallaceandgromitfoundation.org

Rosa Parks 1913-2005
American Civil Rights Activist
Recipient of the Congressional Gold Medal of Honor

AN ICON OF THE CIVIL RIGHTS MOVEMENT

Perhaps every American knows the name Rosa Parks. Through-out her life, she fought through peaceful means for the rights of all people. Parks became a hero to African Americans and civil rights activists around the United States when, during a time and in a place of intense racism and segregation, she refused to give up her seat on the bus to a white man. Her simple but courageous action led to a 381-day bus boycott in Montgomery, Alabama. The boycott brought an end to bus segregation in Montgomery — and, more importantly, it sparked the modern-day civil rights movement.

Rosa Parks died of natural causes at her home in Detroit, Michigan, on October 24, 2005. She was 92. For a week, the whole country celebrated her life and mourned her death. Three separate funerals were held in three different cities—Montgomery, Alabama; Washington, DC; and Detroit, Michigan. Thousands of mourners waited for hours at each location to say good-bye. Rosa and her late husband, Raymond Parks, did not have any children. She is survived by one aunt, 13 nieces and nephews, and numerous cousins. (For additional information on Parks, see also earlier profiles in *Biography Today*, 1992, and Update in 1994 Annual Cumulation.)

EARLY YEARS

Rosa Parks was born on February 4, 1913, in Tuskegee, Alabama. She grew up in a time when discrimination was a way of life for African Americans in the United States, particularly in the South. African Americans did not have the same rights as their white counterparts.

Like most blacks in the South at the time, Parks grew up poor. Her father, James McCauley, was a carpenter. Her mother, Leona McCauley, was a schoolteacher. Rosa's parents separated when she was very young. After that, Rosa, her mother, and her younger brother, Sylvester, went to live with her grandparents in Pine Level, Alabama. Parks would often accompany her grandparents to pick crops on nearby plantations. It was not unusual

Parks recalled, "I never had more than five or six months of education a year while the white children went to school for nine months."

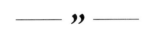

for black children to work in the fields to earn money to help support their families. In fact, some black schools closed three months earlier than the schools for white children so that the black children could work in the fields. Parks recalled, "I never had more than five or six months of education a year while the white children went to school for nine months."

Parks grew up during a period of U.S. history in which black Americans did not have the same rights and opportunities that white Americans enjoyed. This was especially apparent in the country's southern states, where racist attitudes towards black people remained strong in many white communities. In fact, all of the southern states built political and social systems that were blatantly unfair to African-American citizens. For example, southern states like Alabama embraced the system of segregation, which kept white and black people separated from one another in most aspects of everyday life. Segregation was enforced in restaurants, theaters, buses, and other public places. This was based on an 1896 Supreme Court case, *Plessy v. Ferguson*, which created the concept of "separate but equal." In nearly every instance, though, the facilities that were designated for whites were much nicer and cleaner than those that were assigned to blacks. Alabama was one of several states that supported separate schools for white and black children. This was perhaps the most destructive element of segregation, since these schools provided an inferior education that further limited opportunities for African Americans.

Many African-American people resented the unequal system in which they lived. But black communities of the American South were powerless to change things. White men occupied nearly every important political and law enforcement office across the South, and most of them did not want African Americans to gain greater political, economic, or social power. As a result, they used a variety of means to keep black families "in their place." For example, some officials forced African Americans to pass difficult written tests before they would allow them to register to vote. The poll tax was another popular tool to repress the black vote, because most black people were so poor that they could not afford the expense. Finally, whites used violence and intimidation to make sure that African Americans remained in their inferior position in society.

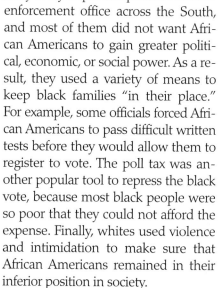

> "Back then, we didn't have any rights," Parks wrote in her autobiography. "It was just a matter of survival, . . . of existing from one day to the next. I remember going to sleep as a girl and hearing the Klan ride at night and hearing a lynching and being afraid the house would burn down."

Parks was aware of the inequalities she faced as a black child growing up in the South. She saw how blacks worked in the fields for meager wages, lived in impoverished homes, ate in segregated restaurants, attended substandard schools, and even drank from separate drinking fountains. Even as a child, she knew this was wrong. Worse yet, she saw black men being harassed and beaten by white men simply because of the color of their skin and black churches being burned by the Ku Klux Klan. "Back then, we didn't have any rights," Parks wrote in her autobiography, *Rosa Parks: My Story*. "It was just a matter of survival, . . . of existing from one day to the next. I remember going to sleep as a girl and hearing the Klan ride at night and hearing a lynching and being afraid the house would burn down."

Parks was a seamstress in 1955, at the time of the Montgomery bus boycott.

EDUCATION

Leona McCauley wanted the best for her daughter, and she particularly stressed the importance of education. When Parks was 11, her mother had saved up enough money to send her to the Montgomery Industrial School for Girls, a private school run by whites from the North. Parks lived with her aunt while attending the school, which was burned down twice by whites who were trying to close it. Rosa recalled the most important lesson she learned at school was "that I was a person with dignity and self-respect, and I should not set my sights lower than anybody else just because I was black." These sentiments reinforced what she learned from her family at home. Her grandfather kept a shotgun nearby in case any Klansmen bothered his family. He refused to call white men "Mr." and told Rosa and her brother that they should not put up with mistreatment. In her autobiography, Parks wrote, "It was passed down almost in our genes."

Parks later attended a high school run by the Alabama State Teachers College, but was forced to drop out at the age of 16 to care for her aging grandparents and her mother. She returned to high school after she was married and earned her high school diploma in 1933 at the age of 20.

TAKING PART IN THE CIVIL RIGHTS MOVEMENT

From a young age, Rosa was very involved in her church, the African Methodist Episcopal (AME) Church. Her strong faith continued throughout her life. She loved to sing and pray. In her teen years, she also started to get involved in some of the local civil rights organizations. When she was 19 years old, Rosa met a barber named Raymond Parks through a mutual friend. They both shared a passion for civil rights and found that they had much in common, including their love of God. The two married in December 1932. It was through his encouragement that she decided to return to school to earn her high school diploma.

Together, Rosa and Raymond worked to gain equal rights for all Americans. Raymond was a member of the National Committee to Save the Scottsboro Boys, an organization formed to support a group of nine young black men who had been falsely accused of raping a white woman in 1931. He and Rosa were both involved in the Montgomery Voters League, whose purpose was to encourage blacks to vote and to become politically empowered. Parks recalled that they had a difficult time getting blacks registered to vote. "Even if we succeeded in getting applications filled out," she said, "the registrars would take them and tell us we would hear by mail if we passed. Very few ever heard, of course. Whites got their certificates right away. If ever you did get registered, you had to pay poll tax."

> "Even if we succeeded in getting applications filled out," Parks said, "the registrars would take them and tell us we would hear from them by mail if we passed. Very few ever heard, of course. Whites got their certificates right away. If ever you did get registered, you had to pay poll tax."

One particular incident of racism had a deep effect on Rosa Parks. While riding on a bus, she saw a young black soldier step in front of the bus. The driver got off and beat the soldier with a metal ticket puncher until the soldier was so badly hurt that he had to go to the hospital. Parks attended the trial of the bus driver, who was fined $24 for assault and battery—but he didn't lose his job. That incident inspired her to join the Montgomery chapter of the National Association for the Advancement of Colored People (NAACP) in 1943; she was soon elected secretary. At the NAACP, she worked to set up meetings, arranged speakers, helped people to register to vote, and worked with youth groups. Parks became quite well known in the Montgomery area for her civil rights activities and was well respected by the black community. She also attended an interracial leadership workshop at the Highlander Folk School in Tennessee, which trained its students to work for civil rights. At this school, she studied side-by-side with blacks and whites from all over the country who were dedicated to fighting segregation.

THE MOMENT THAT CHANGED AMERICA

In 1955, Rosa Parks was working as a seamstress for the Montgomery Fair department store. At that time, the bus was the main source of transportation for most blacks in Montgomery, including Parks. She rode the bus to and from work. Even though as many as 75% of the bus passengers were black, it was the black passengers who were treated poorly. They were forced to sit in the back of the bus. If a white passenger boarded the bus and there were no seats in the front, the black riders were required to give up their seats for the white passenger. Also, after black passengers paid their fare at the front of the bus, many drivers made them get off the bus and board from the rear entrance. Some drivers would take off as the black passengers made their way around to the back entrance.

On that fateful day—Thursday, December 1, 1955—Rosa Parks took the bus home from work, as usual. Most days, she would check the driver before boarding. A Montgomery bus driver had evicted Parks from his bus 12 years earlier because, after paying her fare, she had walked through the bus instead of getting off the bus to board from the rear. Since then she tried to avoid his buses, but on that day in 1955 she boarded without noticing that it was the same driver. Parks took a seat in the first row of the black section. A white man boarded the bus, and because all of the seats in the white section were taken, the bus driver demanded that Parks and three other black passengers in her row move to the back. (At that time a black passenger couldn't even sit in the same row as a white, and the driver could change the boundaries of the white section to give seats to all the white passengers.) "Let me have those front seats," the driver said. "Y'all better make it light on yourselves and let me have those seats."

The other three black passengers moved, but Parks refused. She was tired of being humiliated, insulted, and treated as a second-class citizen. "People always say that I didn't give up my seat because I was tired, but that isn't true," she later declared. "I was not tired physically, or no more

Scenes from the bus boycott: Parks being fingerprinted in Montgomery (top); a sheriff's department booking photo (center); Parks being escorted up the courthouse steps by E.D. Nixon (bottom).

tired than I usually was at the end of a working day. I was not old, although some people have an image of me as being old then. I was 42. No, the only tired I was, was tired of giving in." As she said in her autobiography, "I had had enough. I wanted to be treated like a human being." When the bus driver threatened to have her arrested, she calmly told him, "You may do that." She was arrested, finger-printed, and put in jail.

Parks was not the first African American to be arrested for disobeying the bus segregation laws. In the previous year, several black women, including a 15-year-old girl, had been arrested for the same reason. The black community had talked in the past about staging a demonstration against the buses, but they were waiting for the right opportunity. When word got out that Rosa Parks had been arrested, they agreed this was the opportunity they had been waiting for. Parks was well respected in Montgomery, and black leaders felt that the community would rally around her case.

Several hours after her arrest, E.D. Nixon, president of the Alabama chapter of the NAACP, contacted the liberal white lawyer Clifford Durr for help. Those two, along with Durr's wife, Virginia, posted the $100 bond for Parks's release from jail. That night, they asked if she would be willing to challenge her arrest at her trial the following Monday. They would use her case to challenge the constitutionality of the bus segregation laws. It could be dangerous, but Parks agreed.

"People always say that I didn't give up my seat because I was tired, but that isn't true. I was not tired physically, or no more tired than I usually was at the end of a working day. I was not old, although some people have an image of me as being old then. I was 42. No, the only tired I was, was tired of giving in."

Over the weekend, leaders in the African-American community worked together to plan how to challenge the arrest. They decided to announce a bus boycott for Monday, December 5, the day of the trial. More than 35,000 flyers were distributed throughout Montgomery asking citizens to boycott the buses on the day of Parks's trial. The leaflet said, "Don't ride the buses to work, to town, to school, or anywhere on Monday." The boycott was publicized in a Montgomery newspaper and also in African-American churches that Sunday, as black preachers exhorted their congregants to stay off the buses on Monday.

Rev. Martin Luther King discusses strategies for the boycott with his advisors and organizers. Parks is seated in the front row, with fellow civil rights leader Rev. Ralph Abernathy to the left.

THE MONTGOMERY BUS BOYCOTT

At her trial, Parks was found guilty of violating the state segregation laws. She was fined $10 plus $4 in court fees. But the bus boycott worked—it was so effective that 90 per cent of blacks stayed off the buses that first day. And leaders of the boycott immediately began planning how to continue it.

That same night, a group of boycott supporters held a church rally and decided to continue the boycott. One of the preachers involved in the bus boycott was the young Reverend Martin Luther King Jr., who had only recently started preaching at the Dexter Avenue Baptist Church. He had been asked to lead the Montgomery Improvement Association, a group formed to direct the boycott. King gave a speech in front of thousands of African Americans who came to support the boycott. In his speech, King said, "There comes a time when people get tired of being trampled over by the iron feet of oppression. . . . We are here, we are here because we are tired now."

During the boycott, Parks herself spent time organizing carpools for those who chose to give up the buses. She also traveled around the country raising money to fund the boycott. It was a tremendous hardship for all involved. Some people managed to get rides to work, but many had to walk up to 20 miles each day. Boycott supporters were harassed, and both Rosa and Raymond Parks lost their jobs and were threatened.

For over a year, boycotters refused to ride the buses in Montgomery. This took a major financial toll on the bus companies, nearly bankrupting some. On February 1, 1956, the Montgomery Improvement Association, headed by Martin Luther King Jr., filed a lawsuit in the U.S. District Court stating that the Alabama segregation laws were unconstitutional. On June 2, the lower court agreed, declaring segregated seating on buses unconstitutional. The U.S. Supreme Court upheld the lower court order that Montgomery buses be integrated. Finally, on December 20, 1956, Montgomery officials were given a court order to end bus segregation. The boycott ended the next day, after 381 days. The success of the Montgomery bus boycott spurred blacks in other cities around the country to follow suit.

Some 30 years after the incident, Parks said, "At the time I was arrested, I had no idea it would turn into this. It was just a day like any other day. The only thing that made it significant was that the masses of the people joined in."

LIFE AFTER THE BOYCOTT

Life for Rosa did not get any easier during or after the boycott. She and Raymond were both fired from their jobs, and they were constantly threatened by white supremacists. Because of all the violence directed at them and other blacks in the community, Raymond suffered a nervous breakdown. In 1957, Rosa, Raymond, and Rosa's mother moved to Detroit, Michigan, where Rosa's brother lived. Rosa worked as a seamstress for several years. Then in 1965, Representative John Conyers, a member of the U.S. Congress, hired her to work in his office. Parks worked for Rep. Conyers until she retired in 1988.

In Detroit, Parks remained active in civil rights activities. She joined the NAACP and participated in peaceful demonstrations, including the 1963 March on Washington. She made public appearances with Dr. King. She

Martin Luther King Jr. gave a speech in front of thousands of African Americans who came to support the boycott: "There comes a time when people get tired of being trampled over by the iron feet of oppression. . . . We are here, we are here because we are tired now."

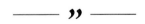

Parks receiving the Medal of Freedom from President Bill Clinton in the Oval Office of the White House, 1996.

was also involved in the Southern Christian Leadership Conference and served as a deaconess at the St. Matthew African Methodist Episcopal Church. She also spent much of her time working with youth groups and working to house the homeless in Michigan.

Raymond Parks died of cancer in 1977, but Rosa continued her work for equal rights. In 1987, she founded the Rosa and Raymond Parks Institute for Self-Development. This organization took children of different races around the country, traveling by bus, to learn about the civil rights movement.

In August 1994, a young unemployed black man broke into Parks's home and beat and robbed her. He knew who she was, but he was high on drugs and alcohol. Rather than condemn the man, Parks sympathized with him. She said, "I pray for this young man and the condition of our country that has made him this way."

For years after her refusal to give up her seat on the bus, Parks was recognized for her bravery. She received numerous awards over the years, including the Spingarn Medal, awarded in 1979 by the NAACP; the Medal of Freedom, awarded in 1996 by President Bill Clinton; the first International

Freedom Conductor Award, awarded in 1998 by the National Underground Railroad Freedom Center; and the Gold Medal of Honor, awarded in 1999 by President Clinton and the United States Congress. This is the highest governmental award possible for an American civilian. For her contribution to American ethnic diversity, Parks was one of 80 people to receive a medal of honor at the Statue of Liberty's 100th birthday celebration. Across the country, schools, streets, and libraries have been named after her. She is discussed in virtually all U.S. history books, and children around the country learn about her courageous act.

Toward the end of the 1990s, Parks made fewer and fewer public appearances. Her health was worsening, and she began to develop dementia. In April 1999, her attorneys filed a lawsuit against the rap group OutKast for using her name without consent in their 1998 song "Rosa Parks." Some of her legal representatives felt that the song exploited her, but the members of OutKast explained that they meant to honor her and thank for her civil rights work. (For more information on OutKast, see *Biography Today*, Sep. 2004.) The case was finally settled in April 2005. As part of the settlement, the group and the record label agreed to help produce a tribute album about Parks.

In December 2000, the Rosa Parks Library and Museum was opened in Montgomery, Alabama, in the exact spot where she sat on the bus. The library and museum cover 50,000 square feet and include a life-sized bronze sculpture of Parks.

On December 1, 2005, President George W. Bush signed bill HR 4145, giving Congress approval to place a statue of Rosa Parks in Statuary Hall, which is next to the Capitol Rotunda in Washington, DC. This made her the first African-American woman to be honored with a statue in the Capitol. During the signing ceremony, Bush said, "It is fitting that this American hero will now be honored with a monument inside the most visible symbol of American democracy. We hope that generations of Americans will remember what this brave woman did and be inspired to add their own contributions to the unfolding story of American freedom for all."

SAYING GOOD BYE TO ROSA PARKS

Rosa Parks died peacefully in her home in Detroit, Michigan, on October 24, 2005. Her longtime assistant, Elaine Steele, said that, "She was peaceful. She passed away in her sleep." News of Parks's death brought together many people from all over the country. Because she was such an influential figure in American history, three separate funerals were held in her honor.

On October 29, 2005, Rosa Parks's body was brought to Montgomery, Alabama. Southwest Airlines donated a commercial flight to transport her casket from Detroit to Montgomery. Lou Freeman, the first black chief pilot to fly for a major airline, donated his time, as did his crew, to bring her to Alabama. The funeral was held at the St. Paul African American Episcopal Church, where thousands of mourners, young and old alike, lined up to say good-bye. Many drove from miles away and stood in line for hours to catch a glimpse of the legendary Rosa Parks. During the service, Bobby Bright, mayor of Montgomery, told the crowd that there had been talk of giving an official pardon to Parks for her act of defiance 50 years earlier. He said that instead, he would like to "ask that Mrs. Rosa Parks pardon us. Pardon us for the way we treated her." Secretary of State Condoleezza Rice said, "I think I can quite honestly say that if it were not for Rosa Parks, I would not be standing here today. It is really the actions and courage of individuals that matter, and this woman mattered." Other speakers included Oprah Winfrey, Dorothy I. Height, president emerita of the National Council of Negro Women, and Melvin Watt, Chair of the Congressional Black Caucus. Over 20,000 people came to pay respects at her viewing.

> "I think I can quite honestly say that if it were not for Rosa Parks, I would not be standing here today," said Secretary of State Condoleezza Rice. "It is really the actions and courage of individuals that matter, and this woman mattered."

On October 30, 2005, Rosa Parks's body was brought to Washington, DC. Not only did she make history when she was alive, but she also made history after her death. She became the first woman to lie in honor in the Rotunda of the U.S. Capitol Building in Washington, DC. She was also the second African American and the 30th American in the nation's history to have this honor.

People from across the country came to say good-bye to this prominent civil rights activist. The line of mourners waiting to walk past the casket took several hours just to reach the Rotunda. As they walked by her casket, many people thanked Parks for what she did in 1955. Early the next morning, the wait was still estimated to be five hours long. Officials said that they would keep the Capitol open as long as it took.

Many dignitaries attended the memorial service at the Capitol building. Approximately 500 people crowded inside the Rotunda for the memorial

Mourners stood in line for hours to file past the casket of Rosa Parks as it rests in honor in the Rotunda of the U.S. Capitol Building in Washington, DC, October 31, 2005.

service. President George W. Bush and First Lady Laura Bush presented the presidential wreath for the center of the casket.

Parks's body was then brought to Detroit, Michigan, her final resting place. Her body lay in state at the Charles H. Wright Museum of African American History. Approximately 8,000 people stood in the rain to wait for her arrival. More than 75,000 people visited Parks at the museum.

On the day of her funeral, the first row in hundreds of Detroit buses was left empty to honor Rosa Parks's memory. Many VIPs attended the service at the Greater Grace Temple, including former President Bill Clinton, Rev. Jesse Jackson, Rev. Al Sharpton, and Louis Farrakhan. President Clinton was the first to speak. He said that Rosa Parks was worthy of honor and praise because "her single simple act of dignity and courage struck a lethal blow to the foundations of legal bigotry. . . . Let us not forget [Rosa's] simple act. In a lifetime of grace and dignity, she made us see and agree that everyone should be free." Detroit Mayor Kwame Kilpatrick said that because of Rosa Parks, "a little chubby kid on the west side of Detroit grew to believe he could be anything he wanted to be." He continued, "Thank you for sacrificing for us. Thank you for praying when we were too cool and too cute to pray for ourselves. . . . Thank you for allowing us to step on your mighty shoulders." Other speakers at the service included Senator Hillary Clinton; Bruce Gordon, head of the NAACP; Marc H. Morial, president of the National Urban League; Jennifer Granholm, Governor of Michigan; Senator John Kerry; and many more. The service was scheduled to last three hours, but it lasted more than seven hours.

After the funeral, Parks's casket was transported to Detroit's Woodlawn Cemetery. Before her body was brought into the cemetery's mausoleum, 152 doves were released, a U.S. Marine played the bagpipes, and there was a 21-gun salute.

THE LEGACY OF ROSA PARKS

"Rosa Parks has shown the awesome power of right over might in history's long journey for peace and freedom," said Rev. Jesse Jackson. "She sat down in order that we might stand up. Paradoxically, her imprisonment opened the doors for our long journey to freedom."

Although few people knew her personally at the time of her death, Rosa Parks touched the lives of many Americans. In honoring and remembering her, public figures around the United States praised her for her role in changing the country.

Coretta Scott King, widow of Martin Luther King Jr., said that "by sheer force of her will, she set in motion a revolution that continues to reverberate in nation after nation and remains an inspiration to liberation movements everywhere." Their daughter, Reverend Bernice King, said that Rosa Parks "was the catalyst of one of the most important freedom movements, not only in American history, but in the world history. . . . Indeed she became the symbol and personification of our nonviolent struggle for liberation and human dignity."

Senator Barack Obama from Illinois called Parks a national hero. "Through her courage and by her example, she helped lay the foundation for a country that could begin to live up to its creed," Obama said. "Just as important, she reminded each and every one of us of our personal responsibilities to stand up for what is right and the central truth of the American experience that our greatness as a nation derives from seemingly ordinary people doing extraordinary things." He also said that Parks was a woman who "held no public office, she wasn't a wealthy woman, didn't appear in the society pages. And yet when the history of this country is written, it is this

The District of Columbia Honor Guard showing respect for the memory of Rosa Parks.

small, quiet woman whose name will be remembered long after the names of senators and presidents have been forgotten."

Poet Rita Dove, former U.S. Poet Laureate and winner of the 1987 Pulitzer Prize for Poetry, maintained that Parks was an example for all people. "It is the modesty of Rosa Parks's example that sustains us," Dove affirmed. "It is no less than the belief in the power of the individual, that cornerstone of the American dream, that she inspires, along with the hope that all of us—even the least of us—could be that brave, that serenely human, when crunch time comes."

Perhaps Rev. Jesse Jackson best summed up the legacy of Rosa Parks. "With quiet courage and nonnegotiable dignity, Rosa Parks was an activist and a freedom fighter who transformed a nation and confirmed a notion that ordinary people can have an extraordinary effect on the world," said Jackson. "Rosa Parks has shown the awesome power of right over might in history's long journey for peace and freedom. She sat down in order that we might stand up. Paradoxically, her imprisonment opened the doors for our long journey to freedom."

HONORS AND AWARDS

Spingarn Medal (NAACP): 1979
Martin Luther King Jr. Award: 1980
Martin Luther King Jr Nonviolent Peace Prize: 1980
Eleanor Roosevelt Women of Courage Award (Wonder Woman
    Foundation): 1984
Martin Luther King Jr. Leadership Award: 1987
Medal of Freedom: 1996
International Freedom Conductor Award (National Underground Railroad
    Freedom Center): 1998
Congressional Gold Medal of Honor: 1999

WRITINGS

The Autobiography of Rosa Parks, 1990, reprinted as *Rosa Parks: My Story*,
    1992 (with Jim Haskins)
*Quiet Strength: The Faith, the Hope, and the Heart of a Woman Who Changed a
    Nation*, 1994 (with Gregory J. Reed)
Dear Mrs. Parks: A Dialogue with Today's Youth, 1996 (with Gregory J. Reed)
I Am Rosa Parks, 1997 (with Gregory J. Reed)

FURTHER READING

Books

Biography Today, 1992; 1994 (Update)
Contemporary Authors, Vol. 150, 1996
Contemporary Authors, New Revision Series, Vol. 102, 2002
Contemporary Black Biography, Vol. 35, 2002
Encyclopedia of World Biography, 1998
Hull, Mary. *Rosa Parks*, 1994 (juvenile)
Notable Black American Women, Vol. 1, 1992
Parks, Rosa, with Jim Haskins. *Rosa Parks: My Story*, 1992
Who's Who among African Americans, 2005
Who's Who in America, 2006

Periodicals

Chicago Tribune, Oct. 25, 2005, p.1
Current Biography Yearbook, 1989
Ebony, Jan. 2006, p.126
Economist, Oct. 29, 2005, Obituary

Jet, Nov. 21, 2005, p.6
New York Times, Nov. 3, 2005, p.A16
Time, June 14, 1999
Washington Post, Oct. 31, 2005, p.A1

Online Articles

http://www.cnn.com/2005/US/10/24/parks.obit
(CNN, "Civil Rights Icon Rosa Parks Dies at 92," Oct. 25, 2005)
http://www.npr.org/templates/story/story.php?storyId=4973548&source
Code=gaw
(NPR, "Civil Rights Icon Rosa Parks Dies," Oct. 25, 2005)
http://www.time.com/time/time100/heroes/profile/parks01.html
(*Time*, Heroes and Icons, "Rosa Parks: Her Simple Act of Protest
Galvanized America's Civil Rights Revolution," June 14, 1999)
http://www.washingtonpost.com/wp-dyn/content/article/2005/10/24/
AR2005102402053_pf.html
(*Washington Post*, "Bus Ride Shook a Nation's Conscience," Oct. 25,
2005)

Online Databases

Biography Resource Center Online, 2006, articles from *Contemporary Authors
Online*, 2005; *Contemporary Black Biography*, 2002; *Encyclopedia of World
Biography*, 1998; and *Who's Who among African Americans*, 2005

WORLD WIDE WEB SITES

http://www.rosaparks.org
http://teacher.scholastic.com/rosa

Danica Patrick 1982-

American Race Car Driver
First Female Driver to Lead the Indy 500

BIRTH

Danica Sue Patrick was born on March 25, 1982, in Beloit,
Wisconsin. She has one younger sister, Brooke. Patrick's parents, T. J. and Bev, met at a snowmobile race where T. J. was a
competitor and Bev was a mechanic. Danica and her sister grew
up in Roscoe, Illinois, a suburb of the city of Rockford. Her parents owned a glass installation business and a coffee shop.

YOUTH

Patrick and her family agree that when she was a youngster, she had little interest in cars or driving. "She was a girlie girl," recalled her mother. "She didn't want to get grease under her fingernails." Instead, she liked to play and dream of a career as a veterinarian, a singer, or a secretary. All of that changed at age 10, though, when Patrick went with Brooke to a go-kart race. "I didn't want to get left out, so I went ahead and tried it, too," Patrick recalled.

Go-karts are popular vehicles that children and adults can drive at many theme parks or courses especially made for the pastime. The karts are usually confined to small tracks surrounded by walls of rubber tires. But go-karting is also a popular amateur sport, with local and national circuits for people who want to compete in races.

Patrick's debut as a racer was hardly promising. Her brakes failed, which led to a bruising crash. Even worse, she got "lapped" (passed) twice within the first six laps of the race. Nevertheless, the sport took hold of her imagination. Her younger sister decided not to pursue racing, but Patrick was so captivated that she entered a local junior racing league. With the support, coaching, and encouragement of her father, she improved quickly and finished second in points at the end of the 22-race season. "I loved the way you could see yourself get better in racing," she told *Sports Illustrated.* "I might finish a second and a half ahead of everyone, but it was never good enough. I could always be better."

"You have to find your passion in life," Patrick said. "I grew up in a family where I was never told I can't do anything."

With each passing month, Patrick learned more from her father about the mechanics of go-karts and the strategies for developing physical and mental toughness. The family also invested money and time getting her to both local and national go-kart competitions. Patrick later credited this support as a major factor in her racing success. "You have to find your passion in life," she explained. "I grew up in a family where I was never told I can't do anything." Outside observers noticed her family's support as well. "All the funding that could have gone to a nice home and vacations for the family went into Danica's racing," former race car driver Lyn St. James said. "Her younger sister was there to polish the car. So not only did you have talent, drive, and determination, you had everything you need to have [to succeed]."

*Patrick stands by her car before qualifying for a June 2003
race in Monterey, California.*

Two years after her first race, the 12-year-old Patrick won her first national points championship from the World Karting Association (WKA), Yamaha Sportsman class. Meanwhile, she won both the Yamaha Sportsman and the US820 Sportsman championships while competing in a local circuit called the Great Lakes Sprint Series. In 1996, at age 14, Patrick won 39 of the 49 feature races she entered, earning WKA national points titles in both Junior and Restricted Junior classes. One year later, in her final full season of go-karting, she captured the WKA Grand National Championship, HPV class.

By this time, Patrick was routinely beating older male drivers. One key to her success was that she refused to let them intimidate her, despite her small stature and youth. During one indoor go-kart practice run in Florida, for example, a 30-year-old male driver twice rammed into her tires after she had lapped him three times in a matter of minutes. Patrick retaliated by stepping on the gas and slamming the driver into the wall. "After the race, he came up and punched her in the helmet," recalled a witness. "So she punched him right back, as if to say, 'No one messes with me.' I don't think the guy realized she was a girl because her helmet was on. I think when he saw all that brown hair fall out of it, he just about died.'"

EDUCATION

Patrick faced some tough decisions as her racing career expanded. During her years at Hononegah Community High School, for example, she tried to participate in normal activities such as volleyball, choir, and cheerleading while simultaneously competing in go-kart races around the country. As time passed, however, she decided that she could not stay in school and still pursue the racing career she wanted. She dropped out during her junior year of high school, although she later earned a GED (general equivalency diploma).

Patrick's decision to leave school early was due in part to the encouragement she received from her mentor Lyn St. James, a former Indy driver and one of only four women to compete in the Indianapolis 500. St. James saw budding talent in Patrick, who trained for about two years in her driving school. "Out of the 200 that have gone through my program, no more than 10 set themselves apart that I've gone out of my way to help behind the scenes," St. James said. "They have to be exceptional. It's not good enough to just be good. The reality is you have to be extraordinary. I saw Danica as extraordinary."

> "Out of the 200 that have gone through my program, no more than 10 set themselves apart that I've gone out of my way to help behind the scenes," said Lyn St. James, a former Indy driver who runs a driving school where Patrick trained. "They have to be exceptional. It's not good enough to just be good. The reality is you have to be extraordinary. I saw Danica as extraordinary."

CAREER HIGHLIGHTS

In 1998 the 16-year-old Patrick made the dramatic decision to try her racing luck in England, which boasted competitive racing leagues that attracted promising young drivers from around the world, "If you want to be the best lawyer, you go to Harvard," her mother later explained. "If you want to be the best driver, you go to England."

Leaving her family behind, Patrick relocated to Milton Keyes, England, and joined the extremely competitive Formula Vauxhall Series, sponsored by the United Kingdom's Vauxhall Motor Company. Most of the Vauxhall races are on demanding open roads or courses with irregular curves. In 1999—her first full season with Formula Vauxhall—Patrick finished ninth in the Formula Vauxhall Championship. The next year she earned a spot with England's Zetek Formula Ford series, considered one of the toughest proving grounds for young drivers. Patrick excelled on the circuit, and her second-place finish at the prestigious Formula Ford Festival in 2000 was the best-ever showing by an American *or* a female driver in the history of the event.

Patrick later recalled that the years she spent racing in England—first in Formula Vauxhall, later in Formula Ford—were the most difficult of her life. "I know that England changed me a bit," she admitted. "I know I became a little bit colder, a little different. . . . What doesn't kill you makes you stronger. It was tough, but it's made me what I am today. I hope people like it. If they don't, this is me. I'm very true to myself and true to my personality."

> "I know that England changed me a bit," Patrick said. "I know I became a little bit colder, a little different. . . . What doesn't kill you makes you stronger."

Patrick's performance in England gained her the respect and attention of racing giants like Bobby Rahal, a former Indianapolis 500 winner and the co-owner (with talk show host David Letterman) of the Rahal-Letterman racing team, one of the top teams in the Indy Racing League (IRL). "When you race in England as a young person, there's no quarter given there," Rahal later said. "It's a hostile environment, and it's even more hostile for a woman, or a young girl. If you're a guy, you can go out with the guys and drink beer. What's a girl supposed to do? That spoke volumes in my mind about what she was all about."

Signing with Team Rahal-Letterman

In 2001 Patrick won the Gorsline Scholarship Award for top upcoming road race driver. This accomplishment further intrigued Rahal. He recognized that she was competing on open road courses rather than banked oval tracks such as those found in the IRL, but he liked her determination and her mental toughness. In 2002 he signed her to a multi-year contract with Team Rahal-Letterman, confident that she could prepare herself to compete on the Indy Racing League (IRL) circuit.

Even with all her years of European experience, Patrick had to learn more before she entered the big leagues. She began 2002 with the Barber Dodge

Pro Series, running a limited schedule of five races. Patrick immediately showed that she belonged. In her debut in Toronto, Ontario, she qualified 11th but finished seventh in the race. Her best showing with Barber Dodge came on July 28, 2002, when she finished fourth in a race in Vancouver, British Columbia. Pleased with her accomplishments, Rahal announced that he would promote her to the Toyota Atlantic Series for her first full season in American racing.

As the 2003 racing season progressed, Patrick proved that Rahal's confidence in her was justified. She posted top-five finishes in five races and earned two podium (top three) finishes: one in Monterrey, Mexico, and one in the season finale in Miami, Florida. These finishes marked the first two times in the 30-year history of the Atlantic Series that a female driver had earned a spot on the podium.

Patrick returned to the Toyota Atlantic Series in 2004. She was the only driver that season to compete in every lap of every race. Not surprisingly, she posted another strong year. She made history as the first woman driver to win a pole position (the lead position at the beginning of a race) for a Toyota Atlantic event, and by season's end she had earned three podium visits. Overall, she compiled an impressive 10 top-five finishes in 12 races. Her third-place finish at the Toyota Atlantic Championship was the best ever for a female in the series. For a time she led the series in points, also a first for a female driver.

Joining the IndyCar Series

Despite her success, though, Patrick was shocked when Rahal announced on December 8, 2004, that she would become the third teammate on the Rahal-Letterman IRL IndyCar Series. She had made it to the top level of Indy racing. Only three other women had advanced to the famous series before Patrick: Janet Guthrie (1977), Lyn St. James (1992), and Sarah Fisher (2000). None of those three had the top-flight equipment and support at Patrick's command, however. This support, combined with her self-confidence and her attractive physical appearance, led many observers to wonder if a new star had arrived on the IRL circuit.

Team Rahal-Letterman provided Patrick with a first-class car for her rookie campaign: a pioneer No. 16 Panoz/Honda/Firestone (Panoz is the chassis, or body of the car; Honda made the engine; and the car was outfitted with Firestone tires). Patrick used the first four races of the 2005 season to become accustomed to her new ride, then found herself staring in the face of her first Indianapolis 500 — only her fifth race with the IRL, and her first at the distance of 500 miles.

Patrick during the 2005 Indy 500, where she became the
first woman to lead at Indy.

Oval-track races consist of two events. First the drivers must qualify. That means they must drive alone around the track at the highest speed they can achieve. The fastest driver gets the pole position. When all the qualifying drivers are ranked, their starting positions in the race have been determined. Only a limited number of spots are open, though, so some drivers miss the cut entirely and are relegated to the sidelines for the race.

Incredibly, Patrick claimed the fourth spot in the entire field during qualifying by posting an average speed of 227.004 miles per hour — a spectacular showing for a rookie driver. This performance increased the attention swirling around her from sports broadcasters and journalists. Although she admitted to having "3,000 knots" in her stomach, Patrick faced the media with grace and promised she would live up to her hype when the race began.

Making an Impact at Indy

On Sunday, May 29, 2005, the 89th running of the Indianapolis 500 began when an announcer said, "Lady and gentlemen, start your engines." A few moments later, the green starting flag was waved and Patrick and her fellow drivers roared forward before a crowd of more than 300,000 and a national television audience.

Patrick drove steadily during the early part of the race. She kept her fourth-place spot until she entered the pits on the 78th lap. In what she later described as a "rookie mistake," she stalled while trying to re-enter the race. The blunder dropped her to 16th place. Then, at lap 155, she spun on a turn and hit another racer. The accident damaged the front of her Panoz/Honda, forcing her to make another trip to the pit for a new nose cone. The pit crew repaired the damage in one minute, and she returned to the race.

Just four laps later, Patrick entered the pits again, to fill her tank with fuel and get new tires. She had 41 laps left to drive in the race, and Rahal decided to "roll the dice" and have her try to stay on the track and conserve fuel. He knew that the drivers ahead of Patrick in the race at that point would all need to pit for fuel at least one more time. If Patrick conserved her gas and drove smoothly, she had a shot at winning the race and making Indy 500 history.

The gamble appeared to pay off, as one by one the drivers ahead of her pulled in to pit row for fuel. Patrick kept roaring around the track at an average speed of 225 miles per hour, and at Lap 172 she claimed first place in the 200-lap race.

One big question loomed: Would Patrick have enough fuel in her car to finish the race? She had to slow her speed to conserve the remaining gas. She knew that caution flags—which require drivers to slow down so that track officials can clear accidents from the track—would help her cause, but the caution flag only came out once during the final laps of the race. In the end the racers were running full throttle, and Patrick was passed on the 194th lap by veteran British driver Dan Wheldon, who eventually won the race. Two other drivers passed Patrick as well, pushing her to a fourth-place finish.

> **"**
>
> *"[Danica Patrick] single-handedly injected the 89th running of the Indianapolis 500 with the sort of voltage it knew back in the day," declared sportswriter E.M. Swift.*
>
> **"**

Patrick was a little disappointed that she had been unable to pull off a storybook victory in her first Indianapolis 500. But her performance had changed the history of Indy racing forever. She became the first woman ever to run in the lead in the Indianapolis 500, the first woman to finish in the top five, and the first to be considered a serious contender for victory. "[Danica Patrick] single-handedly injected the 89th running of the Indianapolis 500 with the sort of voltage it knew back in the day," declared sportswriter E.M. Swift.

The New Face of Indy Racing?

In the days following the 2005 Indy 500, it was clear that Patrick had captured the imagination of the national media. Patrick appeared on the cover of *Sports Illustrated*—the first Indy car driver to be so honored since 1981. She did a full round of television appearances and was featured in *People, Us Weekly,* and *TV Guide* magazines. In addition, several companies approached her with commercial endorsement proposals. Before long, Patrick had agreed to promote a variety of products in TV commercials and print advertising in exchange for millions of dollars in fees.

Corporate America's interest in Patrick stemmed from its recognition that she was, in the words of E. M. Swift, a "5'1", 100-pound package of marketing gold." Not only was she a talented, aggressive driver, she was also beautiful, poised, and willing to sell her sport. For more than a decade, the IRL has lost fans to the more popular NASCAR series, a racing league that uses regular automobile chassis rather than the sleek, open-wheeled Indy cars. Since her 2005 debut with the IRL, however, Patrick has generated significantly higher TV ratings for Indy events.

> "I absolutely want the success more than anything," Patrick said. "My goal is not to be the first female to do things, and it's not to be a poster child or a calendar girl. It's just to win."

Patrick's presence has also been cited as an important factor in attracting new fans to IRL races. "Danica" merchandise sells briskly at events and in stores, and reporters have coined the term "Danicamania" to describe the media frenzy that surrounds her at races. "Like a Tiger Woods, Patrick not only gets props for her talent but attracts the eyes of those who care little about sports," wrote Michelle Hiskey. "She's got a fresh face, guts, and a good Midwestern story of gumption. If anyone can reverse the dipping popularity of open-wheel racing, it's she."

Racing in a Man's World

Patrick appreciates her expanding fan base and her rising popularity. But the recognition she treasures most, though, concerns her on-track performance. Patrick finished her rookie season ranked 12th in points out of a field of 36 drivers, an impressive showing for a first-year participant. At the end of the 2005 IRL season, Patrick was named IRL Indy Car Rookie of the Year.

Patrick, shown here signing autographs for racing fans, became one of the most popular drivers in the Indy Racing League (IRL) during her rookie campaign.

Are the male racers in the Indy series jealous of Patrick's share of the limelight? Most of them are very grateful that she has entered the league. Her popularity has helped spark renewed interest in open-wheeled racing and has attracted new fans, especially women. "She's going to bring everybody around," said fellow racer Helio Castroneves. "Everybody is going to benefit from [her popularity]. Hopefully, she will take advantage of it. Hopefully, we will take advantage of it. It's just great. I'm a big fan of hers."

A few fellow drivers have complained that Patrick's weight — a mere 100 pounds — gives her an unfair advantage behind the wheel. They suggest that the lighter a car is, the faster it can run. Patrick counters that the 2004 Indianapolis 500 was won by the heaviest car on the track, and that her weight has nothing to do with how her vehicles perform.

Patrick has many advantages as she looks into her future. She is young and still learning the finer points of race management. She has the best equipment to use, a winning veteran driver, Bobby Rahal, as a coach, and the respect of the men she races against. "I absolutely want the success more than anything," she clarified. "My goal is not to be the first female to do things, and it's not to be a poster child or a calendar girl. It's just to win."

MARRIAGE AND FAMILY

On November 19, 2005, Patrick married Paul Hospenthal in a quiet cere-mony in Scottsdale, Arizona. She met Hospenthal, a physical therapist, when he began treating her for a hip ailment. The couple has no plans to start a family at this time, since that would interfere with Patrick's career. When not racing, she lives in Arizona.

HOBBIES AND OTHER INTERESTS

Patrick is a serious athlete who is very careful about what she eats and how she exercises. "They've done tests on drivers, and their heart rate can stay at 180 beats per minute for like two hours, which is incredibly demand-ing," she explained. "Every time you turn the wheel side to side, you can feel everything from your neck and shoulders down to your lower back working." Patrick exercises every day to keep in shape for driving. She lifts weights several times a week, and practices yoga for balance and flexibility.

HONORS AND AWARDS

Grand National Champion, Yamaha Class (World Karting Association): 1994
Manufacturers' Cup, Yamaha Sportsman Class (World Karting Association): 1994
National Points Title, Yamaha Junior and Restricted Junior Classes (World Karting Association): 1996
Grand National Champion, Yamaha Lite and HPV Classes (World Karting Association): 1997
Gorsline Scholarship Award: 2001
IRL Rookie of the Year (Indy Racing League): 2005

FURTHER READING

Books

Ingram, Jonathan. *Danica Patrick: America's Hottest Racer,* 2005
Who's Who in America, 2006

Periodicals

Auto Week, Jan. 28, 2002, p.38
Chicago Sun-Times, May 29, 2005, p.122
Chicago Tribune, Mar. 10, 2005, p.2; July 20, 2005, p.C1
Current Biography Yearbook, 2005

Muscle and Fitness, Nov. 2003, p.31
New York Daily News, Sep. 22, 2005
New York Times, May 30, 2005, p.A3; May 31, 2005, p.D1; June 3, 2005, p.D1; June 12, 2005, p.8
People, June 6, 2005, p.126
Sports Illustrated, Sep. 2, 2002, p.14; June 6, 2005, p.54; June 20, 2005, p.87; Dec.12, 2005, p.96
Sports Illustrated for Kids, Aug. 2005, p.13
Time, June 13, 2005, p.6

Online Databases

Biography Resource Center Online, 2006

ADDRESS

Danica Patrick
Rahal Letterman Racing
4601 Lyman Drive
Columbus, OH 43026

WORLD WIDE WEB SITES

http://www.danicaracing.com
http://www.indyracingleague.com
http://www.rahal.com/drivers/patrick/index.jsp

Jorge Ramos 1958-
Mexican Journalist
Anchorman for Univision's Spanish-Language News
Broadcasts

BIRTH

Jorge Ramos was born on March 16, 1958, in a lower middle-class neighborhood of Mexico City, Mexico. His father, also named Jorge, was an architect, and his mother, Lourdes, looked after the family. The eldest in a family of five children, Ramos has three brothers, Alejandro, Eduardo, and Gerardo. He also has one sister, Lourdes, who works as a television journalist in Mexico.

YOUTH

Ramos was raised in a tight-knit family. "My mother was the one who lent emotional support and my father the one who imposed discipline, though those who really got to know him knew that deep down my father was a softie," recalled Ramos. Although his father was an architect, he struggled to find work during long stretches because the nation's building construction industry was so weak. As a result, the family had to be very careful about spending money. In his autobiographical memoir *No Borders: A Journalist's Search for Home,* Ramos recalled that his parents could only afford to take the family out to a nice restaurant once or twice a year. "We lived right on the border of the middle class," was how he described their situation.

Despite his descriptions of tight economic times, Ramos also has many fond childhood memories. He and his siblings were surrounded by a large and supportive family, and he came to know both sets of grandparents. He also liked to roam the neighborhood, looking for swimming invitations from neighbors who owned swimming pools. When his neighbors went swimming, he recalled in *No Borders,* "my brothers and I would climb up on the wall surrounding their property so they would see us, hoping they would feel some pity and thereby extend an invitation to go swimming. It was healthy envy."

———— **"** ————

"My mother was the one who lent emotional support and my father the one who imposed discipline, though those who really got to know him knew that deep down my father was a softie," recalled Ramos.

———— **"** ————

Like many other Mexican boys, Ramos also loved soccer. In fact, he became so skilled at the sport that his neighborhood friends nicknamed him "Borjita Ramos," after a famous player on the Mexican national team. According to Ramos, soccer was "what divided the world; on the one hand were those who knew how to play, and on the other . . . everyone else."

Ramos's dexterity abandoned him when it came time to learn practical skills, though. "Hammering nails or fixing a simple problem with an electric appliance was a virtually impossible task for me to do," he recalled. "I am the exact opposite of a handyman." When it became clear that he would not grow up to be an engineer, as his father had initially hoped, Ramos made a special effort to develop other skills. He decided, for example, that writing and debating skills "would allow me to compensate for my lack of understanding of the machines that surround me." He also became a talented classical guitar player. He trained for eight years, and at the age of 12 he appeared on television in a guitar competition.

EDUCATION

From kindergarten through high school, Ramos was sent away from home to attend Catholic schools run by Benedictine priests. His first school was the Colegio Tepeyac (later renamed the Centro Escolar del Lago) on the outskirts of Mexico City. "I never had any academic problems," he recalled. "I didn't need to study much to get good grades." He also became such a poised public speaker from an early age that he bragged that he could talk his way through any class presentation.

> —— " ——
>
> *"That night, at home in the kitchen, I told my mother [about my spinal condition], and I began to cry like never before," Ramos recalled in his memoir. "So many years, so much hard work, and so many plans, all in vain."*
>
> —— " ——

Not surprisingly, Ramos's favorite part of school was recess, when he could play soccer and basketball with his friends. But he deeply disliked the Benedictine priests who ran the school. "[They] used their position of authority and their supposed heavenly contacts to try and fill our heads, using blood, shouts, punishment, and fear, with their reactionary ideas," he charged. He later claimed that the priests instilled an unhealthy fear of hell and the devil in him and some of his other classmates. Ramos also came to feel that the priests favored unnecessarily cruel punishments against students who broke their rules.

As he matured and grew more confident, Ramos rejected the organized religion of the priests, declaring that he "wanted nothing to do with the god that they represented." In its place, he developed his own personal form of spirituality and strived to live an honest and decent life. As Ramos explained in *No Borders*, his experience in Catholic school turned him into "an agnostic who wanted to be a believer."

Attending an Olympic Training School

When he was 14, Ramos entered a very different kind of school, the Centro Deportivo Olimpico Mexicano. This school works to prepare student athletes who have the potential to make the Mexican Olympic team. Ramos had always dreamed of representing his country in the Olympics as a runner or a high jumper. Though he did not demonstrate exceptional talent in either event as a teen, he wrote such a convincing letter to a member of the Olympic Committee that he was given a place at the school.

Once enrolled, Ramos began training for the high jump, but a seemingly minor back injury forced him to switch to running the hurdles. Strong showings in several national competitions gave him hope that he might qualify for the Olympic team in 1976 or 1980. But the back injury kept getting worse, and medical tests revealed that one of the vertebrae in his spinal column had not completely formed. When the doctors told him that the condition would prevent him from ever fulfilling his Olympic dream, Ramos was crushed. "That night, at home in the kitchen, I told my mother, and I began to cry like never before," he recalled in his memoir. "So many years, so much hard work, and so many plans, all in vain." He reluctantly obeyed the doctors and stopped training for the Olympics. Ever since then, though, he has remained a dedicated runner and recreational soccer player, and fortunately his spinal condition improved over time.

Deterred from his dreams of a career as an athlete, Ramos entered Universidad Iberoamericano (Latin American University) in Mexico City in 1977. It was the first school he attended for which he did not have a scholarship to pay his way, so he juggled his classroom responsibilities with a part-time job at a travel agency. He also decided to pursue studies in communication and psychology. He did not know quite what he would do following such studies, but he knew that he loved to study ideas and philosophy and to discuss such issues with his growing circle of friends. "Journalism did not interest me then," he admitted in *No Borders*. "'I don't like to chase after people,' I told my friends who had already started to fall under the journalistic spell. 'I prefer to make news, not cover it.' It wouldn't be long before I would have to eat my words." He graduated in 1981, earning a bachelor's degree with honors in communication.

"Journalism did not interest me then," Ramos said about his early years in college. "'I don't like to chase after people,' I told my friends who had already started to fall under the journalistic spell. 'I prefer to make news, not cover it.' It wouldn't be long before I would have to eat my words."

Ramos during an interview with Cuban leader Fidel Castro in 1991 in Guadalajara, Mexico. According to Ramos, "When I asked him about the lack of democracy in Cuba, his bodyguards took me aside and pushed me away."

Ramos later returned to school. He took journalism classes at the University of California at Los Angeles (UCLA) from 1983 to 1984, earning a professional designation in journalism. He also attended the University of Miami from 1993 to 1995, earning a master's degree in international studies.

FIRST JOBS

Ramos's first experiments with journalism stemmed from a basic need for money for tuition and living expenses. When he took a part-time job in the newsroom of a local radio station so that he could afford groceries, he was surprised to find that the work actually appealed to him. As he gained more experience, he gradually became convinced that he wanted to explore a career in television journalism. His big break came on March 30, 1981, when an assassination attempt was made on U.S. President Ronald Reagan. The radio station wanted to send someone to Washington, DC, to cover the story, and Ramos was the only journalist in the office who had both a reasonable command of English and a passport and visa that allowed him to travel.

Partly on the strength of the experience he gained covering the Reagan shooting, Ramos was able to make the leap to television when he returned to Mexico City a few weeks later. He accepted a position as an investigative journalist for the Mexican television station Televisa later that year. He quickly became disillusioned with the job, however. Televisa and the Mexican government both heavily censored his reports on official corruption and abuses of power.

In Mexico, the Partido Revolucionario Institucional (PRI) exerted the kind of political control that is unknown in the United States. Candidates for local office were hand-picked by the party, and the party demanded loyalty and obedience from all media sources, including television. The directors of one Mexican news show named "60 Minutes"—not to be confused with the news show of the same name in the United States—instructed Ramos to delete elements of a story he had submitted that were critical of the PRI. When he made only minor changes, the directors of the show ordered someone else to re-write it and then pressured Ramos to present the censored story on the air.

The experience was too much for a young man who was becoming deeply committed to ideas of press freedom and independence. Ramos resigned his position, writing that "what was asked of me goes against my honesty, principles, and professionalism." He also declared that the directors' actions amounted to "an assault on the most simple and clear idea of what journalism is: a search for truth."

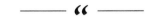

"Mexico in the early 1980s was suffocating me," Ramos wrote. "If I had remained in Mexico, I would probably have been a poor, censored, frustrated journalist, or maybe a psychologist or university professor speaking out eternally and pathetically against those who censored me."

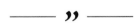

Ramos decided that he would have to relocate to the United States to pursue his dreams of independent journalism. "Mexico in the early 1980s was suffocating me," he later stated in his memoirs. "If I had remained in Mexico, I would probably have been a poor, censored, frustrated journalist, or maybe a psychologist or university professor speaking out eternally and pathetically against those who censored me."

In January 1983 Ramos left Mexico. He moved to California, where he took courses in television and journalism at the University of California-Los

Angeles (UCLA). He rented a small room in a rambling house near the UCLA campus and bought a hot plate to prepare his meals in his closet, since he had no kitchen. "For months I ate rice and noodles in a closet," he recalled. Later he found a job as a waiter for $15 a day. He later described being a waiter as the hardest job in his life, but he kept it because he received a free meal with every shift. Ramos did not complete his studies at UCLA, but he later returned to school and earned a master's degree in international studies from the University of Miami.

CAREER HIGHLIGHTS

Starting Over in American TV

Almost a year to the day after arriving in the United States, Ramos began working for KMEX-Canal 34, a Spanish-language television station in Los Angeles. His initial salary of $28,000 felt like an enormous sum. As he gained experience, Ramos worked at refining his skills as a reporter. He polished his interviewing skills and toned down his heavy native accent so that he would be acceptable to the multicultural Spanish-speaking audience in the L.A. area. Ramos also strived to develop his own unique on-air style, adopting a natural, relaxed quality in front of the camera. This sense of ease, combined with his handsome face and piercing blue eyes, made him very popular with viewers.

Ramos covered a number of interesting stories in his first year on the job. He reported on the 1984 Olympics, held in Los Angeles. He also traveled back to Mexico to report on the terrible earthquake that struck the city in September of 1985. "Canal [channel] 34 was a wonderful school," recalled Ramos in *No Borders.* During his first year at Canal 34, Ramos also tried his hand at a new form of TV reporting: the live news program. Ramos later recalled his first efforts on the live morning news program, "Primera Edición" ("First Edition"), as a "disaster on air. We didn't know how to change cameras, and we were only able to read a few stories without making a mistake."

Yet for all the mistakes, Ramos's charm won out. The show became such a popular hit that it drew the attention of two executives from the Spanish International Network (SIN), the largest Spanish-language broadcaster in the world. They contacted Ramos and asked him if he would move to SIN offices in Miami, Florida, to host a morning variety and news program called "Mundo Latino" (Latin World). Ramos happily accepted, and in early 1986 — just two years after arriving in the United States — he began his rise to the upper echelons of the television news industry.

Filing Reports around the World

Ramos further honed his television broadcasting abilities on "Mundo Latino," a program that was broadcast in a dozen countries around the world. "The morning program put me to the test in unimaginable ways," he declared. "Even though that was not what I really wanted to be doing, it gave me the experience and confidence I needed to survive on a live television program."

Ramos's move to Miami also taught him a great deal about the politics of Spanish-language journalism in the United States. Within a short time of his arrival, he became acutely aware of the grim contest being waged between the city's Cuban-American and Mexican-American leaders for leadership of Miami's Hispanic community. That contest grew heated in the summer and fall of 1986 when a news personality linked to Mexico's PRI government nearly seized control of SIN's news division before being defeated. When that dispute was settled, Ramos—who had avoided taking sides in the struggle—was appointed co-anchor (along with Maria Elena Salinas) of "Noticiero SIN," the network's nightly news show. Suddenly, Ramos had become the face of the largest Spanish-language news source in the world.

— " —

"The morning program put me to the test in unimaginable ways," Ramos declared. "Even though that was not what I really wanted to be doing, it gave me the experience and confidence I needed to survive on a live television program."

— " —

As might be expected for someone so young, Ramos experienced some early bumps in the road as an anchor. "I was an erratic newsreader," he admitted. "I had a baby face and zero credibility." Despite his youth, however, he soon earned high marks for various reports on important issues facing Hispanics and Latinos in the Western hemisphere. He conducted interviews with important heads of state, ranging from the presidents of Guatemala and the Honduras to U.S. President George H.W. Bush (he has since interviewed every American president). Ramos also delivered first-hand reports from dangerous war zones around the world.

On several occasions these assignments placed Ramos in mortal danger. In 1989, for example, he and his crew were shot at by government soldiers while covering the civil war in El Salvador. Two years later, while reporting

Ramos posing in 1994 with U.S. President Bill Clinton.

on the first Persian Gulf War in the Middle East, a military transport plane in which he was riding nearly crashed. Another life-threatening moment came in 2001, when he slipped into Afghanistan to cover the U.S. war against the Taliban, the fundamentalist Muslim government of Afghanistan that had been linked to the terrorist attacks against the United States on September 11, 2001. Ramos thought that he was traveling with guerrillas opposed to the Taliban, but one of the men revealed that he was a follower of terrorist mastermind Osama bin Laden. The guerrilla brought up his rifle to shoot Ramos, but the journalist escaped when he offered the rifleman a cash bribe.

A Famous Face

Today, Ramos and Salinas are regarded as fixtures on "Noticiero Univision" (which was renamed from "Noticiero SIN" after a change in ownership). During his tenure on the program, the show has expanded to 13 Latin American countries, and it is estimated that broadcasts of the news program now reach over one million viewers each night. In American cities with heavy Hispanic populations, the ratings for "Noticiero Univision" even surpass those of the nightly news programs for the major American networks, ABC, CBS, and NBC.

Like other famous American anchormen of the last 20 years—Dan Rather, Tom Brokaw, and Peter Jennings—Ramos also has become something of a celebrity in his own right. The research firm *Hispanic Trends* called him one of the "most influential Latinos" living in the United States in 2000; *Latino Leaders* magazine listed him as one of the "Ten Most Admired Latinos" in 2004; and *Time* named him as one of the 25 most influential Hispanics in America in 2005. He also has won numerous regional and national awards for news broadcasting, including Columbia University's Maria Moors Cabot Award in 2001.

During his long reign as anchorman of "Noticiero Univision," Ramos has also been a news story himself on a few occasions. In 1991, for example, his tough questioning of Cuban dictator Fidel Castro prompted Castro's bodyguards to roughly shove the journalist aside. A few years later, Ramos also posed tough questions to Venezuelan president Hugo Chavez, another Latin American leader who has suppressed press freedoms in his country. Perhaps his most memorable moment on television, however, occurred in December 2000. That month, Mexicans ended years of PRI rule and elected Vicente Fox as president. Ramos covered the story like a professional, but at one point the network cameras caught him breaking away to dance in the streets of Mexico City with other joyful countrymen.

"I'm tired and sick of trying to explain the story in two minutes, of trying to give sense to a story about a war or a kid dying or an earthquake in two minutes," Ramos said.

Beyond the News

Though he has made his career on TV news, Ramos has frequently proclaimed that anyone who gets their news only from television is not well-informed. According to Ramos, many complex stories can not be adequately explained in just a few minutes of television coverage. "I'm tired and sick of trying to explain the story in two minutes, of trying to give sense to a story about a war or a kid dying or an earthquake in two minutes," he has complained.

This frustration led Ramos to explore the written word as a way of conveying the complexities of the stories he covers. In 1997 he published *Detras de la mascara* (Behind the Mask), in which he described his impressions of people he has interviewed during his career. Two years later, he published *Lo que vi: experiences de un periodista alrededor del mundo* (What I Saw: Ex-

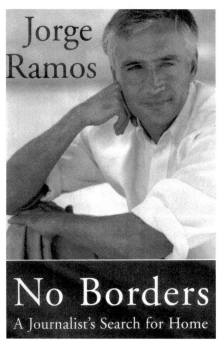

No Borders

A Journalist's Search for Home

Ramos discussed his experiences as an immigrant in great detail in his autobiographical memoir, No Borders.

periences of a Reporter Around the World). This memoir recounted Ramos's career in journalism, including some of his most exciting and frightening experiences.

In 2000 Ramos published *La Otra Cara de America,* which compared the immigration experiences of modern Latinos to the United States with those of earlier waves of U.S. immigration. Two years after its initial publication, this book became the first of Ramos's works to be translated into English, as *The Other Face of America: Chronicles of the Immigrants Shaping Our Future.* Since then he has explored immigration issues in two other books. In 2004 he published *Ola Latina (Latino Wave: How Hispanics Will Elect the Next American President),* which explores the growing political power of the Hispanic community in the United States. One year later he released *Morir en el Intento (Dying to Cross: The Worst Immigrant Tragedy in American History),* an account of a deadly incident in which 19 Mexican immigrants suffocated in the back of a truck being used to smuggle them across the U.S. border. In each of these books, Ramos focused on the complex social, psychological, and political issues that immigrants face as they try to build lives in the United States. These subjects resonated very strongly with Ramos, who is openly sentimental about his love for his home country, yet committed to the life he has built for himself in America.

Ramos discussed these warring emotions in great depth in 2002 in *Atravesando fronteras: un periodista en busca de su lugar en el mundo (No Borders: A Journalist's Search for Home),* his most popular book. This memoir traces his life from his early childhood through his years of spectacular career success. Upon its release, Ramos explained that he wrote it partly for his children. "I wanted to let them know who their father is and what I went through in the first 44 years of my life," he said. But he also wrote the book for English-speaking Americans who need to recognize "that immigrants are here to work and make this a better country and that we are not criminals and that we are not terrorists."

Ramos has also used other platforms to speak out on Hispanic issues in recent years. He writes a weekly newspaper column that appears in 40 papers in the United States and Latin America, and he is a frequent guest on U.S. television programs that discuss Hispanic issues. In 2002 he created a TV book club called "Despierta Leyendo" ("Wake Up Reading"), which appears monthly on Univision. The book recommendations he makes on this program have been credited with boosting numerous titles to the top of the Spanish-language bestseller lists.

Ramos's popularity and his willingness to speak out on political issues has led some observers to wonder whether he might some day run for political office, either in the United States or Mexico. He doesn't rule out the possibility. As of 2006, however, Ramos appears quite content to remain Hispanic TV's top newsman.

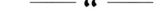

Ramos said that Americans need to recognize "Immigrants are here to work and make this a better country and that we are not criminals and that we are not terrorists."

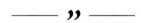

MARRIAGE AND FAMILY

Ramos has one daughter, Paola, from a late 1980s relationship with Gina Montaner, a Spanish television producer. Their relationship ended in 1989, when Montaner took Paola back to her native Spain. Though he described his separation from his daughter as "one of the most painful experiences" in his life, Ramos has continued to spend a lot of time with his daughter. In 1991 Ramos met his future wife, Lisa, and they were married on August 24, 1992. Their son, Nicolás, was born in 1998.

Though Ramos calls Miami home, he travels constantly, and he admits that there "are long periods of time . . . when I am absent and distant." Despite the demands of writing and broadcasting stories from around the world, he treasures his time with his extended family. "Wherever Nicolás and Paola are, together, that is home," he wrote in *No Borders*.

HOBBIES AND OTHER INTERESTS

Many of Ramos's favorite hobbies involve sports. He plays soccer on the Univision company team. He also jogs to keep himself in shape, and in

1997 he ran in the New York City Marathon. Ramos also keeps his hand in a variety of other activities, from playing basketball with his daughter to solo ocean kayaking. Beyond his love of sports, Ramos commits himself to several hours of reading and writing every day.

SELECTED WRITINGS

Detras de la mascara (Behind the Mask), 1997

Lo que vi: experiences de un periodista alrededor del mundo (What I Saw: Experiences of a Reporter Around the World), 1999

La Otra Cara de America, published in English as *The Other Face of America: Chronicles of the Immigrants Shaping Our Future,* 2002

Atravesando fronteras: un periodista en busca de su lugar en el mundo, published in English as *No Borders: A Journalist's Search for Home,* 2002

Ola Latina, published in English as *Latino Wave: How Hispanics Will Elect the Next American President,* 2004

Morir en el Intento, published in English as *Dying to Cross: The Worst Immigrant Tragedy in American History,* 2005

HONORS AND AWARDS

Emmy Award: 1998 (2 awards), Outstanding Instant Coverage of a News Story; 2005, Spanish Emmy Award for "extraordinary contributions to Spanish-language television in the United States"

Maria Moors Cabot Award (Columbia University): 2001

Ruben Salazar Award (National Council of La Raza): 2002, for his positive portrayal of Latinos

Ron Brown Award (National Child Labor Committee): 2002, for "helping young people overcome prejudice and discrimination"

David Brinkley Award for Journalistic Excellence (Barry University): 2003

Journalist of the Year (Latin Business Club of America): 2004

FURTHER READING

Books

Contemporary Hispanic Biography, Vol. 2, 2002

Ramos, Jorge. *No Borders: A Journalist's Search for Home,* 2002

Who's Who in America, 2006

Periodicals

Current Biography Yearbook, 2004

Greensboro (NC) News & Record, Oct. 24, 2003, p.D1

Hispanic Magazine, Jan. 2001, p.62
Houston Chronicle, Oct. 16, 2002, p.1
Miami Herald, Oct. 8, 2000, p.M2
Publishers Weekly, Oct. 13, 2002; May 31, 2004, p.66
Television Week, May 30, 2005, p.26
Time, Aug. 22, 2005, p.53
Washington Post, Feb. 18, 2002, p.C2; Feb. 2, 2003, p.T10

Online Articles

http://www.hispaniconline.com/magazine/2001/jan_feb/CoverStory
 (*Hispanic Magazine,* "Jorge Ramos: Making News," Jan.-Feb. 2001)

Online Databases

Biography Resource Center Online, 2006, article from *Contemporary Hispanic Biography,* 2002

ADDRESS

Jorge Ramos
Univision Television Network
9405 NW 41st Street
Miami, FL 33178

WORLD WIDE WEB SITES

http://www.jorgeramos.com
http://www.univision.net

Ben Roethlisberger 1982-

American Professional Football Player with the
Pittsburgh Steelers
Youngest Quarterback Ever to Win the Super Bowl

BIRTH

Ben Roethlisberger (pronounced ROTH-liss-bur-ger) was born
on March 2, 1982, in Lima, Ohio. He was the only child of Ken
Roethlisberger, an auto executive, and Ida Roethlisberger. They
divorced when Ben was only two years old; six years later, his
mother was killed in an automobile accident. By that time his
father had re-married, and he and his wife Brenda provided

Ben with a loving environment to overcome this tragedy. They also gave Ben a younger sister, Carlee.

YOUTH

Roethlisberger grew up in Findlay, Ohio, a blue-collar town 90 miles northwest of the state capital of Columbus. Overcoming the loss of his mother, who died when he was only about eight years old, was a painful challenge for young Ben. "You go through a lot of things, especially at that young of [an] age," he recalled. "That's why I think my dad and I are so close. It was always him and I. That's the thing I was truly blessed with, to have someone like my dad there for me and with me through it all." Ken Roethlisberger also instilled in his son the values of hard work and humility, which he demonstrated on the sports field. Young Ben seemed to have a natural aptitude for athletics, excelling even while in grade school. He played sports from a young age, mostly basketball and football.

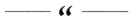

"You go through a lot of things, especially at that young of [an] age," Roethlisberger said about his mother's death. *"That's why I think my dad and I are so close. It was always him and I. That's the thing I was truly blessed with, to have someone like my dad there for me and with me through it all."*

EDUCATION

Roethlisberger attended Findlay High School, playing both basketball and football. As a freshman and sophomore, he played quarterback for the school's junior varsity team. As a junior, he moved up to the varsity football team, playing wide receiver. He was tall but thin, so he gave way to the starting quarterback—the coach's son, who was a senior. According to the coach, "there was no controversy about it at the time. For Ben, it was all about basketball back then. He was never even going to play college football." Because of the position switch, Roethlisberger didn't get much interest in his quarterbacking talents from major college programs. Between his junior and senior years, he attended a camp at Miami University in Oxford, Ohio. Miami's coach, Terry Hoeppner, was impressed with his skills but wasn't ready to extend him a scholarship offer. "I didn't want to be the genius to offer this guy who never played quarterback a scholarship," the coach said. When the senior threw six touchdowns in his first high school game, Hoeppner recalled, "I said, 'That's good enough for me.'"

Roethlisberger went on to have an outstanding senior year as Findlay's quarterback. He led the team to a 10-2 record that year, taking them to the second round of the Ohio state playoffs. The ten wins included a last-minute victory in which his team trailed by four points with only 33 seconds left. He set state records by throwing for 4,041 yards and 54 touchdowns. For his senior year performance in 1999, he was named the state's Division I Offensive Player of the Year. By that time major college programs, including Ohio State University, had come calling. Roethlisberger was concerned about playing time, however, and he thought at Miami University of Ohio, a member of the Mid-American Conference (MAC), he might have a chance to be a four-year starter. He connected with Coach Hoeppner, whom he now considers a "second father" to him. In December he signed a letter of intent to attend Miami; he spent the rest of his senior year captaining Findlay's basketball and baseball teams. He played point guard for the basketball team and shortstop for the baseball team, and was named to all-league and all-district teams in both sports. He also set Findlay's scoring record in basketball, shooting 1,095 points during his three-year varsity career.

After graduating from Findlay High, Roethlisberger entered Miami University in the fall of 2000. He majored in physical education as he concentrated on improving his football skills. After attending Miami for four years, Roethlisberger decided to leave school for the National Football League. Only four credit hours shy of his degree, he plans to finish his university schooling sometime in the future.

CAREER HIGHLIGHTS

College — The Miami (Ohio) University RedHawks

At Miami, Roethlisberger sat out his first year while senior quarterback Mike Bath led the RedHawks. By taking this "redshirt" season, he could practice with the team without using any of his four years of athletic eligibility. In 2001 he won the starting quarterback position and opened the season with two losses against Michigan and Iowa, two teams from the powerful Big Ten Conference. At home against cross-state rival Cincinnati, however, Roethlisberger completed 20 of 25 passes for 264 yards and two touchdowns in a 21-14 victory. He led the team on a seven-game winning streak before finishing the year 7-5. This included a last-second victory over Akron that inspired the quarterback's nickname. The 70-yard "Hail Mary" touchdown pass that won the game was called "Big Ben," and the name soon stuck to the 6'5" quarterback. Roethlisberger set several Miami single-season records in 2001, with 241 completions for 3,105 yards and 25

In 2003, Roethlisberger's last season with Miami of Ohio, the RedHawks won 13 straight games, including their first MAC Championship. Here, Big Ben (left) sets up for a pass as teammate Mike Smith (right) fakes a handoff.

touchdowns. As a result, he was named Mid-American Conference Freshman of the Year and a member of All-MAC second team. In addition, he was named to the Freshman All-America Team by the Football Writers' Association of America.

Roethlisberger has said that it was his second season in which he started feeling comfortable with Miami's offensive system. He also bulked up physically, going from 210 pounds to 240. In 2002, he led the team to another winning season, as the RedHawks again finished 7-5. He completed 271 of 428 passing attempts for 3,238 yards and 22 touchdowns, posting new school records in each of those categories. He made honorable mention on the NFL Draft Report's All-American team and was second-team All-MAC behind Marshall's Byron Leftwich, a future NFL star for the Jacksonville Jaguars.

Nevertheless, Roethlisberger wanted more than anything to win a championship at Miami. He faced the pressure of being ranked as one of the top 25 players in the nation—the *Sporting News* named him their top quarterback—and he responded. He started the 2003 season with an opening loss against Iowa, in which he threw for 250 yards but also four interceptions. But after that, the quarterback led his team to a dream season. The RedHawks won 13 straight games, including their first MAC Championship game, a decisive 49-27 victory over Bowling Green. With a 49-28 victory over Louisville in the GMAC Bowl, Miami finished the 2003 season with a No. 14 ranking in the Associated Press (AP) national poll, their highest ranking since 1975. Roethlisberger rewrote Miami's single-season records yet again, completing 342 of 495 passes (69.1%) for 4,486 yards and 37 touchdowns, as well as gaining 4,597 yards in total offense. His Miami offense also set MAC records for season scoring (553 points) and total offense (7,016 yards). He was named one of the ten semifinalists for the Davey O'Brien Award, given each year to the top college quarterback of the year, and finished ninth in the voting for the Heisman Trophy, awarded to the best player in college football.

> **"**
>
> *"I'd say I got my feet wet, but I got my whole leg wet,"* Roethlisberger said about his first game as a rookie. *"It's tough, you come out and your first game is against probably one of, if not the best, defense in the NFL."*
>
> **"**

Having accomplished a conference title, bowl-game victory, and a final ranking in the Top 15, Roethlisberger decided to leave Miami even though he had one year of eligibility left. After three years as a starter, he owned most of the school's career passing records, including 1,304 passing attempts, 65.5% pass completion percentage, 84 touchdowns, and 10,829 total passing yards. The mobile quarterback, who ran for seven touchdowns during his college career, also held the school's record for total offense, with 11,075 yards. He entered the 2004 NFL Draft as the Mid-American Conference Offensive Player of the Year, a third-team selection on the Associated Press's All-America list, and an NFL Draft Report first-team All-American. The Pittsburgh Steelers selected him in the first round, making him the 11th player drafted overall. He signed a six-year contract that paid him $14 million, plus an $8 million roster bonus.

NFL — The Pittsburgh Steelers

When the Steelers drafted Roethlisberger in 2004, they had intended to give him time to learn their offensive system. Professional football is a much faster and more complex game than college football, and quarterback is the most demanding position. Roethlisberger was to be the third quarterback on Pittsburgh's roster, but a season-ending injury to backup Charlie Batch during training camp moved him up the depth chart. Then, during the second game of the season, against the Baltimore Ravens, starting

Roethlisberger holds up a Pittsburgh Steelers jersey after being selected 11th overall in the first round of the 2004 NFL draft.

quarterback Tommy Maddox went down with an elbow injury. Roethlisberger entered his first NFL game with his team losing in the third quarter, 20-0. Although he threw two touchdowns, he also gave up two interceptions, including one returned for a Baltimore touchdown. Pittsburgh lost the game 30-13, but the rookie quarterback was unfazed by the loss. "I'd say I got my feet wet, but I got my whole leg wet," Roethlisberger said. "It's tough, you come out and your first game is against probably one of, if not the best, defense in the NFL."

Maddox's injury was severe enough to keep him out of the lineup, so the next week Roethlisberger made his first NFL start against the Miami Dolphins. Facing wet weather, Steelers head coach Bill Cowher kept the game plan simple; Roethlisberger only made 22 passing attempts, completing 12 of them with one touchdown and one interception. Pittsburgh's defense held Miami to a single field goal and the rookie quarterback led the offense on a game-clinching touchdown drive in fourth quarter as the Steelers won 13-3. The next week against the Cincinnati Bengals, Roethlisberger completed 17 of 25 passes with no interceptions, leading the offense to the go-ahead touchdown in the fourth quarter in the Steelers' 28-17 victory. In Big Ben's third start, his mobility helped him elude the

Cleveland Browns' defense. He not only went 16-for-21 for 231 yards and one touchdown, he rushed for another Pittsburgh score en route to a 34-23 victory.

NFL fans and teams were noticing Roethlisberger's fast start. His ability to stand in the pocket and deliver the ball quickly, yet scramble away from trouble when necessary, led some to compare him to Hall-of-Famer Dan Marino of the Miami Dolphins, the NFL's all-time passing leader. In his next two games, Roethlisberger went 39-of-49 in a comeback 24-20 victory over the Dallas Cowboys and a decisive 34-20 win over the defending Super Bowl champs, the New England Patriots. The latter performance led Cowher to name Roethlisberger Pittsburgh's permanent starting quarterback. The following week the rookie threw two touchdowns in a 27-3 win over the previously unbeaten Philadelphia Eagles, stretching his record as starter to 6-0 and earning him honors as AFC Offensive Rookie of the Month. Roethlisberger didn't light up the scoreboard in his next three games, but even though his production was low, Pittsburgh's league-leading defense made up for it and the Steelers extended their winning streak to 9-0. The nine wins also tied Roethlisberger for most wins by an NFL rookie. As he continued winning, the city of Pittsburgh went wild for Big Ben, with local eateries naming sandwiches after him and sales of his No. 7 jersey skyrocketing.

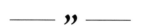

> "I told someone, 'If I'm dreaming, I don't want to wake up because I want to keep this going.' What's so special about this team is everyone is selfless."

If Roethlisberger had any doubters, they were silenced by his performance in week 13 of the season against the Jacksonville Jaguars. Down by two points with less than two minutes left, the quarterback led his team to score the game-winning field goal. He finished 14-for-17 for 221 yards, two touchdowns, and a near-perfect passer rating of 158. (In the NFL, this rating is calculated using completion percentage and yards, touchdowns, and interceptions per attempt, with 158.3 being a perfect score.) His poise helped rally the Steelers over the New York Giants in week 15, and his toughness helped Pittsburgh clinch home-field advantage throughout the playoffs the following week, when he played despite enduring a rough hit to the ribs while throwing a touchdown pass against Baltimore. Roethlisberger left that game in the fourth quarter, and Tommy Maddox started Pittsburgh's final game of the season, a victory over the Buffalo Bills. Although he didn't play in this last game, Roethlisberger was thrilled with

Roethlisberger drops back to pass during a game against the Jacksonville Jaguars in December 2004.

Pittsburgh's 15-1 season: "I told someone, 'If I'm dreaming, I don't want to wake up because I want to keep this going.' What's so special about this team is everyone is selfless."

A Rookie in the Playoffs

There was no question Roethlisberger would lead the Steelers into the playoffs, especially since he had two weeks to heal before their first game, against the New York Jets. At first, the rookie seemed affected by the pressure: he gave up an interception that was returned by the Jets for a touchdown. After leading the Steelers to tie the score, a second Roethlisberger interception gave the Jets the chance to win the game with a field goal. A Jets miss led to overtime, and Big Ben took his team from their own 13-yard line to kick their own game-winner. Despite the 20-17 victory, the quarterback knew he hadn't performed his best. "I did everything I could to lose the game," he said. "I've got to play better. That was terrible. The game we played today is not going to cut it."

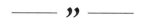

> "When there are doubters, it always fuels the fire a little bit," Roethlisberger commented. "When people say you can't do something, if you are a competitor, that drives you. I think there probably is a little chip on my shoulder. But that's not the whole drive. Wanting to be the best and wanting to win, they push me, too."

The Steelers had home field for the AFC title game the following week, a rematch against New England. Roethlisberger hoped to become the first rookie quarterback to lead his team to the Super Bowl, but the defending champs had a game plan that put pressure on Big Ben. He threw three interceptions, including one returned for a touchdown that gave the Patriots a 24-3 lead. Although Roethlisberger later threw two touchdowns, it wasn't enough and the Steelers lost the game 41-27. The young quarterback tried to be philosophical after the loss: "It wasn't a great game on my part, but I learned an awful lot this season. We had a great season, but there are a lot of people — some in that locker room — that now think [it's a disappointment]."

Roethlisberger's talent, determination, and modesty had made him the toast of Pittsburgh during his first NFL season. Although his sub-par performance in the playoffs brought him some criticism, there was no denying the quarterback had enjoyed an incredible rookie season. His 13 wins as a starter set a record for most wins by a rookie quarterback and also made him the first NFL quarterback ever to achieve a 13-0 regular season record. He broke Dan Marino's records for highest rookie quarterback passer rating (98.1) and highest rookie quarterback completion percentage (66.4%), both of which were also Pittsburgh team records. The Associated Press named him their Offensive Rookie of the Year, while the *Sporting News* accorded him Rookie of the Year honors. When the NFL voted on their Rookie of the Year Award, Roethlisberger was their unanimous selection. His success also earned him some $4.5 million in endorsement deals his first year.

A Super Season

When Pittsburgh opened the 2005 season, Roethlisberger was determined to take his team to the next level. Part of it was to prove himself against naysayers who gave most of the credit for the Steelers' great season to their outstanding running backs and No. 1 ranked defense: "When there are doubters, it always fuels the fire a little bit," the athlete commented. "When people say you can't do something, if you are a competitor, that drives you. I think there probably is a little chip on my shoulder. But that's not the whole drive. Wanting to be the best and wanting to win, they push me, too." Still, he recognized it would be difficult to duplicate the team's success of 2004. "The bottom line is that I can have a better season [statistically] and we could still win fewer games than we did a year ago. What matters is that we win the ones that count."

In the Steelers' season opener against the Tennessee Titans, Roethlisberger made his statistics count: 9-of-11 for 211 yards and two touchdowns, for a perfect passer rating of 158.3. Combined with a record-breaking day by running back Willie Parker, the Steelers won 34-7. The quarterback shook off a sore knee to lead Pittsburgh to a 27-7 win over the Houston Texans to extend his regular season victory streak to 15. In a rematch against Super Bowl champ New England, however, Roethlisberger experienced his first regular-season loss as a starter, although he did complete an 85-yard touchdown pass to Hines Ward. Big Ben returned the team to their winning ways in their next game against the San Diego Chargers, but suffered a knee injury on the game-winning drive. Roethlisberger sat out the next game, a loss to Jacksonville, but returned to throw two touchdowns the following week in a 27-13 victory over Cincinnati. He then threw two more scores in a close 20-19 victory over Baltimore, but reinjured his knee during the game.

Roethlisberger's injury, a slight tear in the cartilage that stabilizes the knee, was enough to require arthroscopic surgery. He missed three more games, during which Pittsburgh raised their record to 7-3. He returned for a Monday night game against the undefeated Indianapolis Colts, but suffered two interceptions and three sacks as the Colts defense smothered Pittsburgh, 26-7. With a loss to division rival Cincinnati the next week, the 7-5 Steelers were in danger of missing the playoffs. Roethlisberger set to work: despite a sprained thumb on his throwing hand, he led the Steelers to four straight victories. Over the four games he completed 60% of his passes, threw only two interceptions (neither led to opponent scores), and rushed for the game's only touchdown in an 18-3 victory over the Chicago Bears. The Steelers finished the season 11-5, earning the last AFC spot in the playoffs.

Receiver Hines Ward called Big Ben "the catalyst of our whole offense. The quarterback has to have confidence, or how else will the rest of the 10 guys follow him? He's going out there confident and having trust in his teammates to make plays."

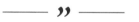

Winning On and Off the Field

The Steelers had a tough road to the Super Bowl: being seeded sixth in the AFC meant they would have to play all their games on the road. Their first game was against Cincinnati, with whom they had split two games during the regular season. Bengals quarterback Carson Palmer went out with an injury on the first play, but Cincinnati still led 10-0 after the first quarter. Roethlisberger brought the team back to win 31-17, going 14-of-19 for 208 yards with three touchdowns. The next week brought a rematch with Indianapolis; although Roethlisberger threw two touchdowns, Pittsburgh fans will forever remember it for "The Tackle." The Steelers had the ball near the Indianapolis goal line with 80 seconds left in the game and a three-point lead. They only had to hang on to the ball to win the game, but usually sure-handed running back Jerome Bettis fumbled. Colts defensive back Nick Harper picked up the ball and looked like he would run it back for the winning touchdown. Instead, Roethlisberger ran back, twisted his body, and made a one-handed tackle of Harper. The defense then limited the Colts to a field goal attempt, which was no good. The Steelers won 21-18, becoming the first No. 6 seed to go to a conference championship.

Playing against the Denver Broncos at their home stadium in the AFC title game, Roethlisberger directed the Steelers offense to a quick lead, including a 101-second touchdown drive just before halftime that made it 24-3. He finished the game 21-of-29 for 275 yards, two touchdowns, and no intercep-

Roethlisberger (# 7) and Nick Harper (# 25) of the Indianapolis Colts, in the play that became known to Pittsburgh fans as "The Tackle." Big Ben prevented a touchdown, and the Steelers won 21-18.

tions. He also scored the game's last touchdown on a four-yard run, making the final score 34-17. Pittsburgh was going to the Super Bowl, the first team ever to beat the top three seeds in the playoffs. Although Roethlisberger was the first to credit the play of his teammates, receiver Hines Ward noted that Big Ben was "the catalyst of our whole offense. The quarterback has to have confidence, or how else will the rest of the 10 guys follow him? He's going out there confident and having trust in his teammates to make plays."

At the age of 23, Roethlisberger was about to lead his team in one of the most high-pressure situations in all of sports: the Super Bowl, where the Steelers would face the Seattle Seahawks. At first, the Steeler offense looked shaky against Seattle: they failed to make a first down until the second quarter, then on the same drive Roethlisberger threw an interception. On Pittsburgh's next possession, however, the quarterback converted a crucial third down-and-28 with a pass to the game's eventual Most Valuable Player, Hines Ward. Roethlisberger capped the drive with a one-yard touchdown run that barely crossed the goal line. That gave Pittsburgh the lead, 7-3, and the Steelers never looked back. Although he threw a second interception that led to a Seahawks touchdown, the team held on to win 21-10.

Roethlisberger's passer rating of 22.6 — he was 9-of-23 for 123 yards, no touchdowns, and two interceptions — was the lowest ever by a winning Super Bowl quarterback. But what the statistics didn't show were the little things he did to help his team: escaping sacks, scrambling for first downs to keep drives alive, and throwing a key block on the trick pass play from Antwaan Randle El to Ward that scored Pittsburgh's last touchdown. As usual, Big Ben was forthright in assessing his game: "When you think about the Super Bowl, you imagine yourself coming out and playing your best football, and it wasn't that way." He credited his teammates for the victory, noting: "They're not my supporting cast — I'm their supporting cast." Despite a less-than-ideal performance, however, Roethlisberger had become the youngest quarterback ever to lead his team to a Super Bowl victory. "A lot of people say you can't do it, they doubt you, they disbelieve, and it shows anything can be done."

> "When you think about the Super Bowl, you imagine yourself coming out and playing your best football, and it wasn't that way," Roethlisberger said about his performance. He credited his teammates for the victory: "They're not my supporting cast — I'm their supporting cast."

With all his success on the football field, Roethlisberger is determined to give back to the community off the field. He has gotten involved in charities on both the national and local level. After the horrific tsunami that hit Asia in December 2004, Roethlisberger donated his first playoff game paycheck, worth $18,000, to the relief effort. He has also donated his time, appearing at fundraisers and visiting children in the hospital. "Young people with special needs and without special needs need to have someone give them hope," he said. "If my position with the Steelers makes me a role model to young people, I want to demonstrate to others that everybody deserves respect and compassion." While victories on the football field excite the fans, Roethlisberger would rather touch people's lives by inspiring them to help others. "When I'm done playing football," he noted, "I would like people to say, 'Not only was Ben a good quarterback, most of all he was a good guy who thought of others before himself.' I consider myself a passionate person and I want to share that."

HOME AND FAMILY

Roethlisberger owns a townhouse near the Pittsburgh Steelers' practice facilities. He is single, but lives with his dog Zeus, a Rottweiler. He keeps in close contact with his parents, who attend all Steelers games and stay with him on home-game weekends.

HOBBIES AND OTHER INTERESTS

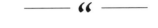

Roethlisberger still enjoys basketball and has also taken up golf and fishing. He is a movie fan, citing action movies like *Gladiator* and *Bad Boys* as his favorites. He also enjoys playing video games and watching pro wrestling. During the off-season, he likes to spend time riding his motorcycles. In June 2006 his hobby caused controversy when he was injured in a collision with an automobile. Roethlisberger was not wearing a helmet (which is legal in Pennsylvania) and fractured his nose, upper and lower jaws, and facial bones. His injuries, which also included two lost teeth and a mild

"When I'm done playing football," Roethlisberger noted, "I would like people to say, 'Not only was Ben a good quarterback, most of all he was a good guy who thought of others before himself.' I consider myself a passionate person and I want to share that."

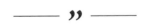

concussion, required seven hours of surgery to repair. Doctors felt confident that he could recover in time for the 2006 regular football season, so Big Ben was lucky. According to the National Highway Traffic Safety Administration, an unhelmeted motorcycle rider in a crash is 40 percent more likely to suffer a fatal head injury and 15 percent more likely to suffer a nonfatal injury than a rider wearing a helmet.

HONORS AND AWARDS

Named First Team Freshman All-American (Football Writers Association of America): 2001
Named First Team All-American (NFL Draft Report): 2003

Pepsi Rookie of the Year Award (National Football League): 2004
NFL Rookie of the Year Award (*Sporting News*): 2004
NFL Offensive Rookie of the Year Award (Associated Press): 2004

FURTHER READING

Books

Roethlisberger: Pittsburgh's Own Big Ben, 2004

Periodicals

Detroit Free Press, Feb. 6, 2006, Sports section, p.4
Exceptional Parent, Sep. 2005, p.16
Forbes, July 4, 2005, p.138
New York Times, Sep. 9, 2005, p.D3; Nov. 28, 2005, p.D1; Jan. 22, 2006, sec. 8, p.1
Philadelphia Daily News, Feb. 6, 2006, p.108
Pittsburgh Post-Gazette, Jan. 29, 2006; June 14, 2006
San Jose Mercury-News, Feb. 3, 2006, p.C1
Sporting News, Sep. 15, 2003, p.14; Nov. 22, 2004, p.16
Sports Illustrated, Oct. 25, 2004, p.31; Nov. 8, 2004, p.54; Sep. 5, 2005, p.92
Sports Illustrated for Kids, Sep. 1, 2005, p.30
Time, Jan. 10, 2005, p.58
USA Today, Jan.12, 2005, p.C1; Feb. 3, 2006, p.E1

Online Articles

http://www.nfl.com/gamecenter/recap/NFL_20040919_PIT@BAL
    (NFL.com, "Ravens Run Past Steelers, 30-13," Sep. 19, 2004)
http://www.nfl.com/gamecenter/recap/NFL_20050102_PIT@BUF
    (NFL.com, "Steelers' Backups Bop Bills 29-24," Jan. 2, 2005)
http://www.nfl.com/gamecenter/recap/NFL_20050115_NYJ@PIT
    (NFL.com, "Struggling Steelers Stave off Jets in OT," Jan. 15, 2005)
http://www.nfl.com/gamecenter/recap/NFL_20050123_NE@PIT
    (NFL.com, "Patriots Rout Steelers in AFC Title Game," Jan. 23, 2005)
http://www.nfl.com/gamecenter/recap/NFL_20060122_PIT@DEN
    (NFL.com, "Steelers Super Bowl Bound with 34-17 Win," Jan. 22, 2006)
http://www.superbowl.com/gamecenter/recap/NFL_20060205_SEA@PIT
    (NFL.com, "Steelers Capture Super Bowl XL Title, 21-10," Feb. 5, 2006)

Online Databases

Biography Resource Center Online, 2005

ADDRESS

Ben Roethlisberger
Pittsburgh Steelers
P.O. Box 6763
Pittsburgh, PA 15212

WORLD WIDE WEB SITES

http://www.steelers.com
http://www.bigben7.com
http://www.nfl.com
http://www.nflplayers.com

Lil' Romeo 1989-

American Rap Musician and Actor
Creator of the Rap Albums *Lil' Romeo*, *Game Time*, and
Romeoland
Star of the Television Show "Romeo!"

BIRTH

Lil' Romeo was born Percy Romeo Miller on August 19, 1989,
in New Orleans, Louisiana. His father, Percy Miller II, is the
successful businessman, actor, and rap musician known as
Master P. His mother, Sonya Miller, serves as vice president of
Master P's record company, No Limit, and related businesses.
Lil' Romeo is the oldest of their six children.

318

YOUTH

Lil' Romeo's parents, who met in high school, once lived in the crime-ridden Calliope housing project in New Orleans. But they always knew that they wanted a better life for themselves and their family. "We didn't consider the ghetto home," Master P recalled. "We both wanted to make it out. We both refused to let the ghetto be a burden to us. We were just there for the time being, but we both dreamed of better things."

Just months after Lil' Romeo was born, Master P inherited $10,000 from his grandfather. He wanted to be sure that he invested the money wisely. First, he moved with his wife and young son to Richmond, California, to be near his mother. Once there, he and Sonya used the money to open the No Limit record store, which sold rap and hip-hop music at cheap prices. Within six months, the store was earning almost $10,000 per month.

After launching the successful record store, the Miller family moved back to Louisiana, where Master P used his connections in the music industry to start his own record company. Master P recorded several rap albums himself, and his No Limit label also released albums by other hip-hop and rap artists. The record company became yet another successful business venture for the Miller family. Within ten years, Lil' Romeo's parents had not only escaped the ghetto, but had become extremely wealthy. In fact, by the early 2000s, several sources listed Master P among the richest men in the United States, with a fortune estimated at $500 million.

> "*True wealth is not just about money,*" *Master P explained. "It ain't about the music; it ain't about the movies. It's about family. It's about making a way out for them.*"

Thanks to his father's success, Lil' Romeo enjoyed a privileged childhood. But his parents taught him to appreciate what they have. "True wealth is not just about money," Master P explained. "It ain't about the music; it ain't about the movies. It's about family. It's about making a way out for them." Lil' Romeo's parents often took him back to their old neighborhood so that he would understand where he came from. They also tried to set a good example for him by supporting charities that help the less fortunate.

Lil' Romeo with his father, Master P.

Following in His Father's Footsteps

Lil' Romeo learned to rap at an early age by listening to his father. Master P started his music career when Lil' Romeo was just a toddler. He formed the rap group Tru with his two brothers, Vyshonn (known as Silkk the Shocker) and Corey (initially known as C-Murder, he changed his name to C-Miller after a second-degree murder conviction in 2003). Lil' Romeo and his cousins often snuck into the studio when their fathers were recording. When Lil' Romeo was just three years old, he sang in the introduction to one of his dad's songs.

As he grew older, Lil' Romeo began recording his own rap songs. "Me and my cousin used to go in the studio while my dad was on tour and make our own songs," he recalled. "One day, my dad came home from a tour and the producer was playing our songs." Master P asked the producer who was singing, and he was surprised to learn that it was Lil' Romeo. Master P asked his son if he was serious about singing. When Lil' Romeo said that he was indeed serious, his dad decided to help him get started in the music industry.

EDUCATION

Lil' Romeo is a straight-A student at Winward High School in Los Angeles, California. His favorite subject is math. Even though his successful music and acting careers keep him busy, he always makes time to study. When he is away on a concert tour or movie location, he hires a private tutor to help him keep up with his homework. "I do well in school because it's important to have your education," he stated.

Lil' Romeo learned the value of education from his parents. His father always encouraged him and his siblings to read by telling them it would help build the muscles in their brains. Master P also warned Lil' Romeo that he would put an end to his music career if he did not do well in school. "I always have to bring back an all-A report card," Lil' Romeo noted.

CAREER HIGHLIGHTS

Breaking into the Rap Scene

When Lil' Romeo began rapping as a child, Master P recognized his son's talent right away. His experience in the recording industry told him that Lil' Romeo had the potential to be a star. Lil' Romeo's songs were unlike most rap songs on the airwaves at that time, which tended to be full of violence, anger, and profanity. In contrast, Lil' Romeo's songs featured innocent lyrics and youthful subject matter that could appeal to people of all ages. The first rap song he wrote was called "Your ABCs"; he recorded it when he was only five or six years old. "I make music for the kids," Lil' Romeo said. "Grownups come to shows with their kids; that's a good thing. But I make music for everybody — kids, grownups, teenagers, everybody."

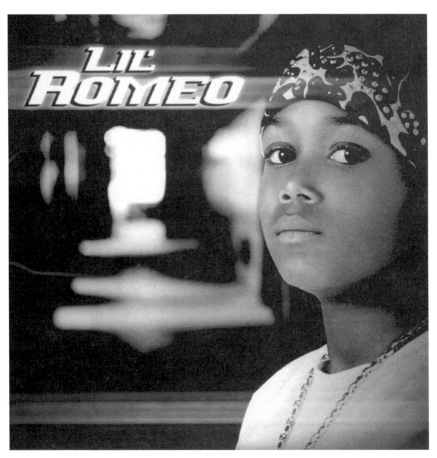

Lil' Romeo's first release.

From the beginning of his career, Lil' Romeo has written all of his own songs. "I always write them or I won't feel like it's my song," he explained. "I write all my songs and then my dad comes in and tells me what I need to change." Lil' Romeo also depends on input from his cousins. "I know it's a hot track when my cousins like it and start bouncing to the music," he noted. "If nobody bounces to the music, it's not [the] beat for me."

Lil' Romeo released his first album, entitled *Lil' Romeo,* in 2001. The first single from the album, "My Baby," made it to the No. 2 position on the Hot R&B/Hip-Hop Singles chart only six weeks after its release. At the age of 11, Lil' Romeo became the youngest artist ever to reach that position on the nation's music charts—breaking a record that had been held for decades by pop star Michael Jackson.

Lil' Romeo's debut album made him widely known among rap fans of all ages. His appeal stemmed not only from his musical talent, but also from his youthful good looks and outgoing personality. Violet Brown, director of urban music for Wherehouse Entertainment, said that the young artist "has it all—looks, personality, intellect, and talent," adding that *Lil' Romeo* "is an album parents can feel good about buying for their kids."

Lil' Romeo released his second album, *Game Time*, in 2003. It included such songs as "True Love," "Too Long," and "Clap Your Hands." Many of the songs on this album used pieces from older songs by such artists as Luther Vandross, Teena Marie, and KC and the Sunshine Band.

Lil' Romeo's third album, *Romeoland*, was released in 2004. As the rapper moved into his teen years, he began to explore more mature subjects in his music. "On every album I try to talk about something different," he explained. "On my first album I focused mostly on myself. I was letting my fans get to know the real me. On my second release, I rapped a lot about my fans. I wanted to show how much I appreciated them. On this new one, I talk a whole lot about girls."

Discovering Other Talents

Lil' Romeo's fame as a rap artist led to numerous guest appearances on television awards shows, talk shows, holiday specials, and game shows. He even played himself in a cartoon on the Disney channel. Lil' Romeo soon found that he enjoyed acting and had an appealing presence onscreen.

> *"I know it's a hot track when my cousins like it and start bouncing to the music,"* Romeo noted. *"If nobody bounces to the music, it's not [the] beat for me."*

In the early 2000s Lil' Romeo branched out into an acting career. He starred in several television shows and feature films, many of them with his dad. Since 2003, for instance, Lil' Romeo and Master P have starred in the Nickelodeon family TV series "Romeo!" Although fictional, the show is based on the Miller family and shares many similarities with their real lives. Master P's character is a successful music executive whose name is Percy Miller. Percy is a single father with three kids of his own and a white foster son. Lil' Romeo plays the part of one of the sons, and his character's name is Romeo. The show follows the trials and tribulations of the family.

Both Lil' Romeo and his father enjoy working on the show, largely because it allows them to spend time together. "It's rare to see fathers and sons working together," Master P acknowledged. "You always hear about black

Members of the cast of the Nick show "Romeo!"

fathers not taking care of their kids. We spend a lot of time together doing this show. It's important to be with your kids. This show definitely involves family."

Also in 2003, Lil' Romeo played the role of Benny in the movie *Honey*. It tells the story of an aspiring hip-hop dancer and choreographer, played by Jessica Alba, who works in the inner city. She reaches out to Benny and helps him during his struggle with drugs. Mekhi Phifer and Missy Elliott were also featured in the film.

Lil' Romeo has also teamed up with his dad once in a movie called *Uncle P*. In this film, Master P again plays a role similar to his real life — a multimillionaire businessman and rapper named P. Miller who lives in New York. His sister, is a single mother living in California, becomes ill. So he agrees to move in with her to help take care of the kids. Although he has no experience with raising kids, he quickly learns the necessary skills. Along the way, he realizes that family happiness is more important that material success. Lil' Romeo plays the part of a rebellious teen who needs a father figure in his life. The movie is not yet released.

Taking Care of Business

Lil' Romeo has also collaborated with his father in several business ventures. In 2002, for example, they worked together to create two lines of clothing: the P. Miller Shorties and P. Miller Signature. The P. Miller Shorties line features streetwear that appeals to children, while the P. Miller Signature collection is aimed at young men. Both are affordable for a person with an average income.

Master P wants Lil' Romeo to be involved in his business ventures so that his son will have something to fall back on when his music career ends. "He's a natural talent, but I look at reality," Master P stated. "[The music industry] is a cutthroat business. But by me opening up other avenues and us owning this, we have independence."

Master P hopes that Lil' Romeo will learn enough to take over the business someday. "I want him to be able to take the business and run it successfully one day," he noted. "Just to have him educated and business-minded enough to know that your talent is what sells the music, but your business is what keeps it financially independent. I want to give him enthusiasm, and occasionally put him in the position where he can make decisions so he won't be afraid to make decisions once he has to run the business."

"It's rare to see fathers and sons working together," Master P acknowledged. "You always hear about black fathers not taking care of their kids. We spend a lot of time together doing this show. It's important to be with your kids. This show definitely involves family."

Giving Back to the Community

Lil' Romeo's parents remember what it was like to be poor, and they both feel that they were lucky to escape that life. They taught their children about the importance of giving back to the community and helping people less fortunate than themselves, and Lil' Romeo took the lesson to heart.

In 2002, for instance, Lil' Romeo played in a charity basketball game that raised over $80,000 for leukemia, cancer, and AIDS research. Just a few weeks later, Lil' Romeo and Master P participated in an event dubbed "Game Time" at a video game arcade in New York City. About 180 needy or homeless children were invited to meet the famous rap artists while enjoying free food, drinks, and video games. During the holiday season, Lil' Romeo and Master P visit children's hospitals to deliver Christmas gifts to patients. "We've been very blessed, so it means a lot to visit these kids in the hospital and help them smile," Master P said.

Lil' Romeo also uses his celebrity to influence other kids to study hard and stay in school. In an effort to promote the importance of reading, he participated in Scholastic's Read for 2003. He joined many other celebrities to record messages that encouraged children, parents, and teachers to recognize the power of reading.

In August 2005, Lil' Romeo and his family were deeply affected when Hurricane Katrina devastated their hometown of New Orleans and large areas of the Gulf Coast of the United States. They had numerous relatives living in the disaster zone, and a home they owned in New Orleans was destroyed. The Miller family quickly came to the aid of hurricane victims. They formed Team Rescue, a relief organization that placed hundreds of evacuees in apartments around the country for three months. Master P also participated in a hurricane relief telethon on Black Entertainment Television.

> "There is a business side to this, but I wouldn't be doing this if I wasn't having fun," Lil' Romeo explained. "This is a lot of hard work for a kid. But I'm having fun because my parents keep me well grounded. This is just a hobby for me."

Staying Grounded

Despite the pressures that come with fame, Lil' Romeo enjoys his multifaceted career. "There is a business side to this, but I wouldn't be doing this if I wasn't having fun," he explained. "This is a lot of hard work for a kid. But I'm having fun because my parents keep me well grounded. This is just a hobby for me."

Lil' Romeo considers himself a normal teenager, and his parents try to make sure that it stays that way. "We dress average. We act average. We have rules in the house," Master P stated. "We have to wash the dishes, clean the house. We sit around and watch TV like everyone else. We try to stay as close as possible to regular." Since he thinks of himself as a regular person, just like his fans, Lil' Romeo always obliges people who ask for his autograph. "My dad taught me to always sign autographs and told me not to change because I was famous," he explained.

HOBBIES AND OTHER INTERESTS

Lil' Romeo's favorite hobby is playing basketball. "I always want to play basketball," he said. "That's my No. 1 outlet. I've been loving basketball since the age of two. Always basketball. You'll see me in the NBA real soon." Lil' Romeo plays on an Amateur Athletic Union (AAU) basketball team called the Texas No Limit Ballers. Master P, who is a skilled player in his own right, serves as the coach. At one point, Lil' Romeo was ranked nationally among the top 50 players in his age group. Among his favorite NBA players are Allen Iverson, Kobe Bryant, Shaquille O'Neal, Vince Carter, and Michael Jordan.

Basketball is Lil' Romeo's favorite hobby.

Like most kids his age, Lil' Romeo also enjoys hanging out with family and friends, playing video games, and listening to music. "I listen to everything—pop, R&B, rock," he noted. "I listen to good music." Some of his favorite artists include Bow Wow, Nelly, Britney Spears, *NSYNC, and of course Master P.

HOME AND FAMILY

Lil' Romeo lives in Los Angeles, California. He remains very close to his family, which he considers the most important thing in his life. "Family always gonna be there," he explained. "The material things, they come and go."

SELECTED CREDITS

Albums

Lil' Romeo, 2001
Game Time, 2003
Romeoland, 2004

Films

Shorty, 2002
Pieces to the Puzzle, 2002
Honey, 2003

Television

"Romeo!," 2003-

HONORS AND AWARDS

Billboard Music Awards: 2001, Rap Artist of the Year and Rap Single of the
    Year, for "My Baby"

FURTHER READING

Books

Who's Who among African Americans, 2005

Periodicals

Baton Rouge Advocate, Apr. 7, 2005, p.A15
Billboard, June 9, 2001, p.24
Cleveland Plain Dealer, Apr. 5, 2002, p.10
Ebony, June 2002, p.56
Florida Today, July 27, 2001, People, p.1
Girls' Life, Dec. 2004, p.42
Jet, Feb. 3, 2003, p.58
Norfolk Virginian-Pilot, July 17, 2002, p.C1
Orlando Sentinel, Aug. 4, 2004, p.D5
People, Feb. 10, 2003, p.59

Online Articles

http://www.cbsnews.com
    (CBSNews.com, "Lil' Romeo: Hip-Hop Sensation," Dec. 24, 2003)
http://www.mtv.com
    (MTV.com, "Dave Matthews Band, Master P, Morgan Freeman Are also
    among Those Offering Help," Sep. 2, 2005)
http://www.usatoday.com
    (*USA Today*, "Desperate Message Triggers Calls from across USA," Aug.
    31, 2005; "Stars Roll up Sleeves for Hurricane Relief," Sep. 14, 2005)

Online Databases

Biography Resource Center Online, 2005, article from *Who's Who among African Americans,* 2005

ADDRESSES

Lil' Romeo
Koch Records
740 Broadway, 7th Floor
New York, NY 10003

Lil' Romeo
Nickelodeon Studios
231 W. Olive Ave.
Burbank, CA 91502

WORLD WIDE WEB SITES

http://www.nickelodeon.com
http://www.kidzworld.com/site/p829.htm

Adam Sandler 1966-

American Actor and Comedian
Star of the Hit Films *Billy Madison, Happy Gilmore,
The Wedding Singer, The Waterboy, 50 First Dates,*
and *The Longest Yard*

BIRTH

Adam Richard Sandler was born on September 9, 1966, in
Brooklyn, New York. His father, Stan Sandler, was an electrical
engineer, and his mother, Judy Sandler, was a nursery school
teacher. He was the youngest of four children in his family. He
has an older brother, Scott, and two older sisters, Elizabeth and
Valerie.

YOUTH

When Adam was a boy, the Sandler family moved from Brooklyn to the quiet, leafy town of Manchester, New Hampshire. He grew up in a loving, supportive environment. According to his brother, Adam was "perpetually performing" from an early age. Both of his parents encouraged the side of him that loved to entertain. His mother often asked him to sing her favorite song, "Maria," from the musical *West Side Story*. When he was seven, she arranged for him to perform the song "Candy Man" for residents of a local nursing home.

Sandler's father was a jovial man who loved to laugh. He exposed his son to the slapstick comedy of such funnymen as Jerry Lewis, Mel Brooks, Abbott and Costello, and Rodney Dangerfield. From the time he was a little boy, Sandler would tell jokes and do impressions to amuse his parents and siblings. "He's always been funny," said his mother. "We knew he would be an entertainer. The only one who minded was Grandma Anna. She'd ask him, 'Why can't you be a funny doctor?'"

Sandler continued performing music as he got older. When he was 12, he sang the Ringo Starr tune "You're 16" at his sister's wedding. "The first time I was ever on stage was at my sister's wedding," he recalled. "My mother threw me up there." His first song received polite applause, so he tried for an encore. "Things started to go downhill," he remembered. "'One was enough,' they said." Sandler went on to sing "House of the Rising Sun" in a seventh-grade talent show, despite the fact that his voice was changing and cracked throughout the performance. During his teen years, he played the guitar in several bands that he formed with his friends.

> "
>
> *"One time, my mother was yelling, 'Why don't you ever try?'" Sandler remembered. "I had a tape recorder in my hand. When she stopped shouting, I played it back to her. She laughed for half an hour. That was my life: doing something wrong, getting yelled at, and making the person laugh. Then it would be all right."*
>
> "

Sandler also continued to watch and enjoy comedy as he entered his teen years. He was a big fan of the late-night, sketch-comedy series "Saturday Night Live" from the time it made its television debut in 1975. "My big thing was trying to stay up to watch it," he recalled. "In the schoolyard the cooler kids were talking about it and I wanted to be part of that conversation." The release of the 1980 comedy *Caddyshack* proved to be a turning point in his life. He and his brother watched the movie over and over again and memorized all of the dialogue. "I have seen *Caddyshack* 300 times," he admitted. "It's the reason I got into comedy."

As Sandler focused more and more on being funny, he lost his focus on school and started getting into trouble. But he also found that comedy could occasionally help him get out of a jam. "One time, my mother was yelling, 'Why don't you ever try?'" he remembered. "I had a tape recorder in my hand. When she stopped shouting, I played it back to her. She laughed for half an hour. That was my life: doing something wrong, getting yelled at, and making the person laugh. Then it would be all right."

"You've seen his movies?" said one of his teachers, Isabel Pellerin. "That's the way he was here. I can't believe he's making all that money for doing things he was punished for here. I thought he would grow up. Instead, he grew rich."

EDUCATION

Shortly after his family moved to Manchester, Sandler started first grade at Webster Elementary School. For the first week or so, he became so homesick that he left school every day at recess. His mother always made him a sandwich and then walked him back to school. Once he adjusted to his new surroundings, he stayed in school all day and became a good student.

By the time he entered Hillside Junior High, however, Sandler found that he enjoyed fooling around more than studying. He became a class clown, willing to do outrageous things to make his classmates laugh. "Until sixth grade, I did really well in school," he said. "All of a sudden I said, . . . 'I can't take it anymore. I can't read and be so serious in class anymore.' I don't know why, but I just started goofing off. Instead of being book smart, I decided to have fun."

As a student at Manchester Central High School, Sandler was a member of the drama club, served on the student council, and played sports. But he made the biggest impression on his teachers and fellow students by always getting in trouble. "You've seen his movies?" said one of his teachers, Isabel Pellerin. "That's the way he was here. I can't believe he's making all that money for doing things he was punished for here. I thought he would grow up. Instead, he grew rich." "Teachers would ask him to leave the class," recalled his principal, Bob Schiavone, "but they were laughing while they asked. He was hilarious." Despite his antics, Sandler earned respectable grades and graduated from high school in 1984.

As his high school years neared an end, Sandler considered his career options. "I had no idea what I wanted to do with my life," he remembered. "So I asked my brother what I should major in—he said acting, and that's how it started. I didn't know what else to do. But I love my brother, and I always thought he was smarter than me, so I thought I'd do what he said." Sandler applied to New York University (NYU) and, to his surprise, was one of only 300 students nationwide to be accepted into its highly competitive theater program, the Lee Strasberg Institute.

NYU's drama program trained actors to draw from their personal experiences in order to convey realistic emotions on stage. Sandler had trouble taking the classes seriously, though, prompting one professor to tell him that he would never make it as a professional actor. "I was a comedian in the Lee Strasberg acting program," he recalled. "Everyone else was pretty intense, whipping out the names of playwrights. We were all supposed to go on stage and dig out our emotions. At that time, I couldn't even look another person in the eye. I'm thinking, once I dig out my emotions, where do they go?"

Nevertheless, Sandler enjoyed his time at NYU. He formed close friendships with a number of like-minded students—including Tim Herlihy, Judd Apatow, Jack Giarraputo, and Frank Coraci—who later helped write, produce, and direct some of his movies. While still in college, Sandler also began to prepare for his future career. He took a year off to perform stand-up comedy in Los Angeles, and he also got his start on "Saturday Night Live" at about the same time. Sandler graduated from NYU in 1991 with a Bachelor of Fine Arts (BFA) degree.

CAREER HIGHLIGHTS

Performing Stand-Up Comedy

Sandler first performed stand-up comedy during the summer before he enrolled at NYU. While visiting his brother at Boston University, the 17-year-old took part in an open-mike night at a Boston club called Stitches. Sandler was reluctant to go on stage at first, but his brother talked him into it. "If he hadn't said to do it, I wouldn't have thought it was a normal thing to do," he acknowledged. "I would have said, 'Mom and Dad are going to get mad at me.' But because he told me to do it and I knew that my parents respected his brain, [I figured] it must be okay."

*Sandler with Kevin Nealon on the Weekend Update set on
"Saturday Night Live," where Sandler got his first big break.*

Even though Sandler's first attempt at stand-up comedy was not very
funny, he immediately felt drawn to the stage. "It was the first time in my
life where I said, 'All right, I think I can,'" he noted. "I became kind of obsessed with getting good at comedy. Growing up I wasn't that great at
anything." For the rest of that summer, and throughout his college years,
he took advantage of every opportunity to perform his stand-up routines
in clubs and other venues. Although he found performing before an audi-

ence difficult and sometimes humiliating, it was all worthwhile when he made the audience laugh. "My friends were always around to say, 'Hey Sandler, you're funnier than that,' and that's what kept me going," he recalled. "They were always telling me I was a funny guy, and it took at least four years working in the comedy clubs until I believed it."

Sandler's comedy routines, as well as his confidence, improved steadily over time. He became the headliner at a popular New York club called Comic Strip Live, and he made contacts that helped him find other work. A friend introduced him to comedian Bill Cosby, for instance, which led to an audition for the hit family TV series "The Cosby Show." In 1987 Sandler appeared on four episodes of the program as a friend of Cosby's teenage son, Theo Huxtable. In 1990 Sandler took time off from college and moved to Los Angeles to test himself in comedy clubs there. He appeared at The Improv, a famous club where performers were sometimes "discovered" for movie careers. The year in Los Angeles helped Sandler develop a distinctive comedy style. "His act was not what I would call A-1 material," recalled Improv owner Bud Friedman. "It was more about his attitude, his little-boy quality, his vulnerability."

Joining the Cast of "Saturday Night Live"

By the time Sandler returned to New York to complete his college degree, he had emerged as one of the most talked-about stand-up comedians working on the club circuit. In 1990 he was invited to audition for Lorne Michaels, the creator of "Saturday Night Live." As a longtime fan of the show, Sandler jumped at the opportunity. Michaels hired him to join the show's writing staff—a group of comedians who came up with ideas and created characters for the comedy skits that appeared on the air. The cast of the show at that time included Chris Rock, David Spade, and Chris Farley.

The first sketch written by Sandler appeared on the air on December 8, 1990. He recalled how nervous he felt as he waited backstage: "Sitting with [guest host] Tom Hanks ten seconds before the lights come up on my first skit on the air, I said, 'I might faint. There is a good chance I'm going to faint.' Hanks looks over, real concerned, and says, 'Well, don't.'"

In 1991 Sandler was promoted to "featured player," meaning that he appeared in occasional skits but was not part of the regular cast. He finally became a full-fledged cast member during the 1993-1994 season. During his time on "Saturday Night Live," Sandler created several characters that became pop culture icons. One of his most famous characters was Opera Man, who would dress up in robes and provide a singing summary of current news stories. He also created Cajun Man, who spoke with such a thick accent that no one could understand him, and did impressions of numerous rock stars, like Eddie Vedder, Axl Rose, and Bruce Springsteen.

Sandler made his final appearance on "Saturday Night Live" on May 13, 1995. It remains unclear whether he quit to pursue a movie career or was fired so that the show — which was widely criticized during his tenure for not being very funny — could go in another direction. "I loved being on that show, I loved getting to do my stuff every Saturday night, do something new, and see these bands and these celebrity hosts. It was great," Sandler stated. But he also admitted that, after five years on the show, he started to feel like he was repeating himself. "I didn't want to do that," he said. "I wanted to get into growing as much as I can."

———— **"** ————

"There's just something really safe and likeable about seeing this guy up there," said comedian David Spade. "Even if you're only five years old, you poke your friend and say, 'At least I'm not as dumb as that idiot!'"

———— **"** ————

Making Comedy Albums

In 1993, during his time on "Saturday Night Live," Sandler released his first comedy album, *They're All Gonna Laugh at You.* Full of rude humor and foul language, it became a huge hit. It sold three million copies and was even nominated for a Grammy Award as Best Comedy Album.

In 1996, shortly after leaving "Saturday Night Live," Sandler released a second album, *What the Hell Happened to Me?* In addition to numerous comedy routines, this album featured "The Hanukkah Song," which became one of the most-requested songs of the holiday season. Drawn from his own experience growing up as one of the few Jewish kids in Manchester, the humorous song lists the names of celebrities who celebrate the holiday.

Sandler continued making occasional comedy albums as his movie career took off, releasing *What's Your Name?* in 1997 and *Stan and Judy's Kid* the following year. He released his fifth album, *Shhh . . . Don't Tell,* in 2004. Sandler viewed the albums as an opportunity to cut loose with profanity and dirty jokes that he could not include in his movies. Although the albums carry strict warning labels to keep them out of reach of children, together they have sold more than five million copies.

Becoming a Movie Star

In addition to making comedy albums, Sandler also had small roles in several movies during his years on "Saturday Night Live." He made his big-screen debut in *Shakes the Clown,* a 1991 comedy about the strange world of adults who make a living by appearing as clowns at children's parties. Sandler played Dink, the sad clown. The movie disappeared quickly from theaters, but later earned a cult following on video. He also appeared in *The Coneheads,* a poorly received 1993 comedy adapted from a popular "Saturday Night Live" skit. He played a larger role in *Airheads,* a 1994 comedy about three heavy-metal musicians who inadvertently take over a radio station.

As his time on "Saturday Night Live" drew to a close, Sandler began writing a movie script with his college friend Tim Herlihy. This effort turned into the 1995 comedy *Billy Madison.* Sandler starred as Billy, a good-natured but very lazy young man who is forced to repeat his entire education — kindergarten through high school — in six months in order to collect a large inheritance. In *Billy Madison,* Sandler created the "loveable loser" persona that he returned to often in his later films. "He's like a big lug who can't get things right," explained his childhood hero, Rodney Dangerfield. "At the end of the movie, when he gets things right, the audience loves him. When he wins, he wins for everybody."

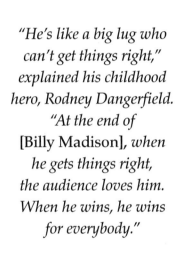

"He's like a big lug who can't get things right," explained his childhood hero, Rodney Dangerfield. "At the end of [Billy Madison], when he gets things right, the audience loves him. When he wins, he wins for everybody."

Although critics panned the movie, it did well at the box office and became a cult hit on video. Indeed, the movie also initiated what has since become the typical response to the opening of Adam Sandler movies: while many critics disparage his movies, his audiences love them, seeing them in theaters and then watching them repeatedly on video.

Sandler and Herlihy collaborated again the following year to write and produce *Happy Gilmore.* Sandler played the title character, a former hockey star with a violent temper. When he accidentally discovers that he can use his wicked slap shot to drive a golf ball, Happy enters a golf tournament in hopes of winning enough money to pay the overdue taxes on his grand-

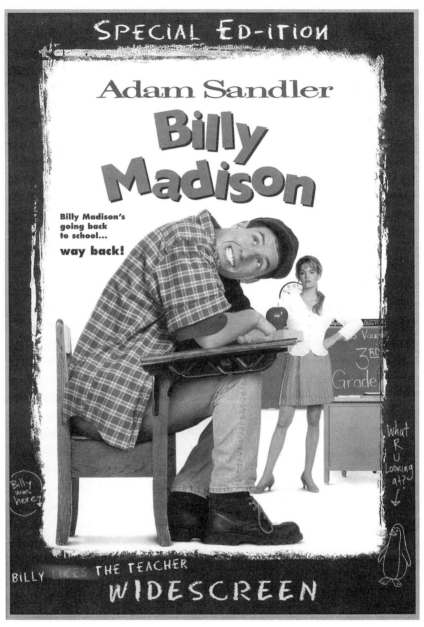

Billy Madison *was the first movie that Sandler co-wrote, and his first big movie success.*

mother's house. He causes trouble in the stodgy world of golf with his outbursts and fighting. Shot on a $12 million budget, *Happy Gilmore* earned a respectable $40 million at the box office. Although many critics dismissed it, a few found it amusing. "It's sort of like a Gen-X *Caddyshack*," Michael Sauter wrote in *Entertainment Weekly*, "with some good, punchy slapstick and delightfully sick twists."

The success of these two early films helped turn Sandler into a box-office draw. Audiences enjoyed his brand of humor, but the print media generally presented him in a negative way, criticizing both his acting and his writing abilities. "When I first read a bad thing about me," he recalled, "I was like, 'Oh, that doesn't feel very good, why should I read this anymore?'" Around this time, Sandler stopped giving interviews to newspapers and magazines. He focused all of his promotional appearances on TV and radio talk shows, where he felt that his words were less likely to be taken out of context. "The press really didn't give him any respect," said his friend and fellow comedian Chris Rock. "Everybody dissed him, and it's like, 'Now you want me to talk to you?' If I were him, I wouldn't talk either."

Playing the Romantic Lead

The first role that earned Sandler critical praise came in the 1998 romantic comedy *The Wedding Singer*. He played Robbie Hart, a sweet-natured man forced to give up his dream of becoming a rock star and settle for singing at weddings and bar mitzvahs at a local banquet hall. After being left at the altar by his fiancée, he falls in love with a waitress, played by Drew Barrymore, who is engaged to a cad. Although the film did include some slapstick moments, the romantic leading man role was a departure for Sandler. It won him new fans among young women — which helped *The Wedding Singer* make an impressive $80 million at the box office — and also earned favorable reviews from critics. "A spirited, funny, and warm saga, the picture serves up Sandler and Drew Barrymore in a new way that enhances their most winning qualities," Leonard Klady wrote in *Variety*. "The candy-colored movie generates a fair amount of good will, especially when Sandler is singing," Jami Bernard added in the *New York Daily News*.

Many reviewers commented on the chemistry between Sandler and Barrymore, and indeed, his costar was pretty effusive in her praise. "Adam is amazing — he's one of the most incredible men in the world," Barrymore enthused. "He makes you laugh by combining humor and intellect, which to me is the most important combination I think a human being can attain. Someone who can do that makes you happy; they're like medicine. I worship comedians."

Scenes from some of Sandler's hit movies: The Wedding Singer *(top),* Happy Gilmore *(middle), and* Big Daddy *(bottom).*

Later in 1998, Sandler returned to his previous formula for success in *The Waterboy*. He played Bobby Boucher, a good-hearted dunce who works as the waterboy for a college football team. But the players use him as a tackling dummy, and he is fired by the coach. Angry, Bobby moves to another team, where his out-of-control rages turn him into a star offensive tackle. Despite poor reviews, *The Waterboy* became a huge hit. It earned a non-summer record of $39.4 million in its opening weekend and went on to take in an amazing $161 million during its theatrical run. "I had the best time making this—I got to hang out with my buddies, throw a football around, and I had a lot of fun tackling people," he said. "It was fun pretending I was tough. In real life I'm nothing. I have no fighting skills. If you wanted to hit me, I wouldn't do anything about it. I'd just cry like a baby. In fact," he joked, "I'm gonna go find my mom now."

Until this point, many of Sandler's comedies had followed a similar path —except, perhaps, for *The Wedding Singer*. As Richard Corliss explained in *Time* magazine, "[The typical Sandler comedy] is about a nerdy sociopath who learns to channel his rage into an acceptable format: winning a spelling bee, playing golf, or tackling football players 'You don't have what they call the social skills,' he is told in *The Waterboy*; that is Sandler's gimmick and, for many, his charm. The plot is a competition for which our hero is unqualified but which he always wins, over some smarmy exemplar of the status quo and in a climax tinged with sentiment and demagoguery."

> *"I had the best time making* [The Waterboy]— *I got to hang out with my buddies, throw a football around, and I had a lot of fun tackling people," Sandler said. "It was fun pretending I was tough. In real life I'm nothing. I have no fighting skills. If you wanted to hit me, I wouldn't do anything about it. I'd just cry like a baby."*

But with his next movie, Sandler began to move away from that path. In *Big Daddy* (1999), he played Sonny Koufax, an immature underachiever whose girlfriend dumps him because he won't grow up. So when his roommate's son shows up, needing a home, Sonny agrees to take care of him—just so he can convince his girlfriend that he can be responsible. Instead, Sonny ends up teaching the boy all sorts of bad habits—like how to pee in public, put sticks in the paths of inline skaters to watch them fall, and smash canned goods at the supermarket to get a discount on damaged goods. As their relationship grows, though, Sandler managed to infuse both humor and sweetness into the story. "There's a good amount of toilet humor but it's overshadowed by the sheer quirkiness of the script. It's just plain fun to watch a goofy man-child interact with a child," wrote reviewer Tom Grabon. "*Big Daddy* is easily the most heartfelt of Sandler's films." As before, the film received generally poor reviews but performed well at the box office, earning an amazing $163 million.

Sandler's next big hit came in 2002, when he appeared in *Mr. Deeds*. Based on an old Frank Capra film called *Mr. Deeds Goes to Town*, it tells the story of an unassuming man who suddenly inherits a fortune. Sandler starred as Longfellow Deeds, a happily dysfunctional pizza delivery boy who inherits $40 billion and has to figure out how to spend it. He travels to New York, where unscrupulous people try to take advantage of him, but he manages to evade their schemes through utter cluelessness. Although many critics, like Owen Gleiberman of *Entertainment Weekly*, complained that Sandler was "running on empty, repeating what he's already done way too often," the movie nevertheless earned $126 million at the box office.

> "*50 First Dates* is an almost perfect Valentine's movie," wrote critic Eleanor Ringel Gillespie. "And who would have ever guessed the goofy little girl from **E.T.—The Extra-Terrestrial** and the goofy guy from **Billy Madison** could strike such delicious sparks."

Also in 2002, Sandler stretched his acting ability by playing a dramatic role in *Punch-Drunk Love*, directed by Paul Thomas Anderson. Sandler starred as Barry Egan, a painfully shy and insecure salesman who collects airline reward miles in hopes of someday escaping from his mundane life. When he meets a beautiful but mysterious woman, he must break out of his shell to win her over. Unlike Sandler's previous efforts, the film earned a great deal of critical acclaim but only generated $17.8 million at the box office. Gleiberman described *Punch-Drunk Love* as a "deeply rich and strange new romantic comedy" and called Sandler "utterly winning to watch."

Expanding His Range

Sandler scored yet another box-office smash in 2003 with *Anger Management*, which earned $134 million. He played Dave Buznick, a wimpy guy who cannot muster the courage to kiss his girlfriend or stand up for himself

Sandler and Barrymore in a scene from the romantic comedy 50 First Dates.

at work. When he is mistakenly accused of assaulting an airline flight attendant, Dave is ordered to undergo anger management counseling in order to stay out of jail. He winds up working with a radical therapist (played by Jack Nicholson) whose unconventional methods make Dave truly angry. "Every Sandler movie is a course in anger management: in the care and feeding of rage, first suppressed, then geysering into an explosion of smashed crockery and punched-out supporting players," Richard Corliss noted in *Time*. "[But] even a longtime Adamphobe has to admit that Sandler is an agreeable presence here, and that the film . . . should make audiences happy."

In 2004 Sandler once again teamed up with Drew Barrymore in the romantic comedy *50 First Dates*. He played Henry Roth, a ladies' man who falls in love with a woman (Barrymore) who has no short-term memory. Roth wins her over one day, only to have her forget him by the next. Audiences flocked to see the movie, helping it to earn $120 million. Critical response was much more positive than for earlier films, and reviewers generally found it silly and sweet. "Sandler, confronted with a girl who can't remember him, is forced to become the ultimate romantic, a man who woos with every breath," Gleiberman noted in *Entertainment Weekly*. "The movie is sort of an experiment for Sandler," Roger Ebert wrote in the *Bergen County Record*. "He reveals the warm side of his personality and leaves behind the hostility, anger, and gross-out humor. To be sure, there's projectile vomiting on a vast scale in an opening scene, but it's performed by a walrus, not one of the human characters. . . . This is a kinder and gentler Sandler." That view was echoed in the *Atlanta Journal-Constitution* by Eleanor Ringel Gillespie. "*50 First Dates* is an almost perfect Valentine's movie. Like the stars' last collaboration, *The Wedding Singer*, it's charmingly romantic and funny (think chick flick). And like so many of Sandler's lowest-common-denominator comedies, it's suffused with slapstick and gross-out gags (think very guy Sandler fan). *50 First Dates* comes down to chemistry. And who would have ever guessed the goofy little girl from *E.T.* — *The Extra-Terrestrial* and the goofy guy from *Billy Madison* could strike such delicious sparks."

——— **"** ———

"With so much comedy provided by other characters [in The Longest Yard*], Sandler opts for a mature approach not often seen in his films. He absorbs punishment from sadistic guards and is roughed up," wrote Rick Cantu. "It's all part of a skillful blend of action and comic relief, a remake that scores big."*

——— **"** ———

Later in 2004, Sandler took on another serious role in *Spanglish,* directed by James L. Brooks. He played John Clasky, a successful Los Angeles chef struggling to raise two children with his neurotic wife (Tea Leoni). They hire a Mexican housekeeper (Paz Vega), who cannot speak English, a decision that ends up transforming their marriage and their family. Critics generally found that the story lacked focus, but they praised the actors' performances.

In 2005 Sandler appeared in *The Longest Yard,* a remake of a popular 1974 prison movie that starred Burt Reynolds. Sandler played a washed-up professional football player who gets sent to prison for smashing up his rich girlfriend's car. While there, he puts together a ragtag team of inmates to face the guards in a football game. "Led by Adam Sandler, a surprisingly effective quarterback for the convicts, the new version takes its audience on a fast-paced joyride of adult humor and body-slamming action," Rick Cantu wrote in the *Austin American-Statesman.* "With so much comedy provided by other characters, Sandler opts for a mature approach not often seen in his films. He absorbs punishment from sadistic guards and is roughed up by [former Dallas Cowboys wide receiver Michael Irvin] in a one-on-one game of basketball. It's all part of a skillful blend of action and comic relief, a remake that scores big."

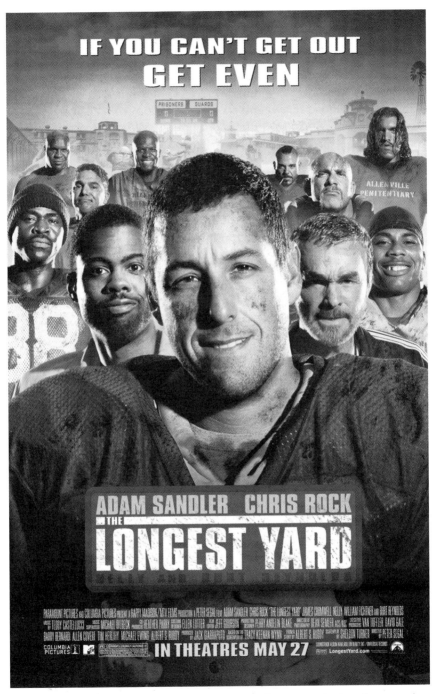

Sandler teamed up with Chris Rock in The Longest Yard.

Public Opinion

In addition to starring in movies, Sandler runs his own film-production company, Happy Madison Productions. The staff of his company, known as Team Sandler, consists mainly of his good friends from college. "Making a movie is a long process," he noted. "I want to be around people I can have fun with." Sandler exercises a great deal of creative control over his own movies — writing, producing, and choosing the director and supporting cast for many of them. "He's in charge of every detail of his comedy," said Henry Winkler, his co-star in *The Waterboy.* "He hears it in his head and guides whatever scene, whether he is in it or not, to his vision." Sandler also develops scripts for other comedians through Happy Madison Productions. The company has produced several movies for Rob Schneider, for instance, including *Deuce Bigalow: Male Gigolo* and *The Hot Chick.*

> *"He's a genius," said Amy Pascal, vice chairman of Sony Pictures. "He understands something none of the rest of us do — what makes people laugh, and what touches people's hearts."*

While Sandler is one of Hollywood's biggest stars and earns more than $20 million per picture, he is also very unpopular among some segments of the movie-going public, who find his acting wooden and his humor juvenile. Just as there are people who will go to see any Sandler movie, there are others who refuse to see any movie with him in it. "Just as the population is split between Republicans and Democrats, Coke and Pepsi drinkers, and SUV lovers and haters, so is it apparently divided over the appeal of Adam Sandler," Todd McCarthy explained in *Variety.*

Film critics may dismiss Sandler's work, but audiences still flock to theaters whenever he releases a new movie. They know what they will get from the star, and they know that it will be entertaining. "It's unfair to put Adam's comedies into the larger world of film," said "Saturday Night Live" creator Lorne Michaels. "It is like comparing candy to the whole world of food. Everyone knows what a Snickers is and why you like it. To deconstruct it, to point out that it only has peanuts and chocolate, is to take all the fun out of eating it."

Given the remarkable success of his films, it is clear that Sandler has millions of dedicated fans who enjoy his silly humor, crazy antics, and typical storylines about an unlikely hero who manages to prevail despite himself. "There's just something really safe and likeable about seeing this guy up there," said comedian David Spade. "Even if you're only five years old, you poke your friend and say, 'At least I'm not as dumb as that idiot!'"

Sandler may play dumb characters in his movies. But within Hollywood, he receives a great deal of respect for his ability to understand his audience and fill the seats of movie theaters. "He's a genius," said Amy Pascal, vice chairman of Sony Pictures. "He understands something none of the rest of us do — what makes people laugh, and what touches people's hearts."

MARRIAGE AND FAMILY

Sandler married actress-model Jackie Titone on June 22, 2003. The wedding took place at sunset on a friend's oceanfront estate in Malibu, California. The otherwise traditional Jewish ceremony included Sandler's two bulldogs, Meatball and Matzoball, who wore tuxedos and carried the couple's wedding rings. "Jackie's the finest woman I've ever met," he stated. "She's got it all — brains, looks, a sense of humor, and most unbelievable of all, she likes me for me."

SELECTED CREDITS

Films

Shakes the Clown, 1991
The Coneheads, 1993
Airheads, 1994
Billy Madison, 1995 (also screenwriter)
Happy Gilmore, 1996 (also screenwriter)
Bulletproof, 1996
The Wedding Singer, 1998
The Waterboy, 1998 (also screenwriter)
Big Daddy, 1999 (also screenwriter)
Little Nicky, 2000 (also screenwriter)
Punch-Drunk Love, 2002
Eight Crazy Nights, 2002 (also screenwriter)
Mr. Deeds, 2002
Anger Management, 2003
50 First Dates, 2004
Spanglish, 2004
The Longest Yard, 2005

Television

"Saturday Night Live," 1990-95

Recordings

They're All Gonna Laugh at You!, 1993
What the Hell Happened to Me?, 1996
What's Your Name?, 1997
The Wedding Singer: Original Motion Picture Soundtrack, 1998
Stan and Judy's Kid, 1999
Shhh . . . Don't Tell, 2004

HONORS AND AWARDS

MTV Movie Awards: 1996, for best fight in *Happy Gilmore* (with Bob
    Barker); 1998, for best kiss in *The Wedding Singer* (with Drew
    Barrymore); 1999, for best comedic performance in *The Waterboy*; 2000,
    for best comedic performance in *Big Daddy*; 2004, for best on-screen
    team in *50 First Dates* (with Drew Barrymore)
Blockbuster Entertainment Awards: 1999, for favorite actor/comedy in *The
    Wedding Singer* and *The Waterboy*; 2000, for favorite actor/comedy in *Big
    Daddy*
Kids' Choice Award as Favorite Actor: 1999, for *The Waterboy* and *The
    Wedding Singer*; 2000, for *Big Daddy*; 2003, for *Mr. Deeds*; 2005, for *50
    First Dates*
People's Choice Awards: 2000, for favorite movie star/comedy; 2005, for fa-
    vorite on-screen chemistry in *50 First Dates* (with Drew Barrymore)
Teen Choice Award as Best Comedian: 2001, 2002, 2004, 2005

FURTHER READING

Books

Contemporary Musicians, Vol. 19, 1997
Crawford, Bill. *Adam Sandler: America's Comedian*, 2000
Epstein, Dwayne. *People in the News: Adam Sandler*, 2004
Newsmakers, Issue 2, 1999
Seidman, David. *Adam Sandler*, 2001

Periodicals

Biography, Apr. 2003, p.16
Current Biography Yearbook, 1998
Entertainment Weekly, Feb. 17, 1995, p.26; June 18, 1999, p.24; Oct. 18, 2002,
    p.87; Apr. 18, 2003, p.44; June 3, 2005, p.60
Interview, Dec. 1994, p.104

Los Angeles Times, Nov. 5, 2000, Calendar, p.8
People, Nov. 30, 1998, p.73
Premiere, Dec. 2004/Jan. 2005, p.110
Time, Nov. 23, 1998, p.102; Oct. 21, 2002, p.70
USA Today, Apr. 8, 1994, p.D5; Feb. 13, 1998, p.D18
Washington Post, Nov. 13, 1998, p.D1

Online Databases

Biography Resource Center Online, 2005, articles from *Contemporary Authors Online,* 2003, and *Contemporary Musicians,* 1997

ADDRESS

Adam Sandler
Happy Madison Productions, Inc.
10202 West Washington Blvd.
Culver City, CA 90232

WORLD WIDE WEB SITE

http://www.adamsandler.com

Russell Simmons 1957-

American Entrepreneur and Business Leader
Co-Founder of Def Jam Records, CEO of Rush
Communications, Chairman of Hip-Hop Summit
Action Network, Creator and Producer of "Def
Comedy Jam" and "Def Poetry Jam"

BIRTH

Russell Wendell Simmons, known as "Rush," was born on
October 4, 1957, in Queens, one of the five boroughs in New
York City. His father, Daniel, was a teacher and administrator
for New York Public School District 29. His mother, Evelyn,
was a painter who also worked as the recreation director for
the New York City Department of Parks. Simmons's parents

both graduated from Howard University, where they met. A middle child, Simmons has two brothers: Danny is four years older and Joey (known as Run of the rap group Run-D.M.C.) is seven years younger.

YOUTH

Simmons grew up surrounded by artistic people. "There are no retiring people in the Simmons family — we are all creative, strong-willed, dynamic people." He describes his parents as highly educated, creative, and opinionated. During the 1960s, Simmons's father was politically active in civil rights issues and often participated in demonstrations, sometimes taking Russell along. His father also wrote poetry, some of which later appeared in Run-D.M.C. raps. Simmons remembers his mother as sophisticated, worldly, and very supportive of her sons' artistic interests. His older brother Danny was a painter, and younger brother Joey studied music and began writing his own songs at a young age. Meanwhile, Simmons was developing his own interest in music. "As a teen, my musical taste was forming, and it reflected my overall attitude toward life. I liked gutsy, cool music, nothing too pop. . . . The music I liked was very ghetto and gritty."

"As a teen, my musical taste was forming, and it reflected my overall attitude toward life. I liked gutsy, cool music, nothing too pop. . . . The music I liked was very ghetto and gritty."

Drugs and Gangs

In 1965 the Simmons family moved to Hollis, a working-class neighborhood in Queens. They lived in a small house on a neat suburban street of well-kept homes. But just a few blocks away was one of the busiest drug-dealing corners in Queens. When Simmons was a teenager, he got caught up in the drug world and began selling marijuana. He explained that his decision to sell drugs wasn't based on desperation or need, but rather on peer pressure and greed. "People were making money all around me," he said. "So from my silly teenage perspective, selling [made sense]. . . . It was a way to get the things I wanted — things that in retrospect were ridiculous and unnecessary."

Around this same time, Simmons was also involved with a gang called the Seven Immortals. "We didn't have guns and we didn't kill people as gangs do today. . . . We were really young and not that fearsome." They spent most of their time hanging out, not doing much more than riding the subway and trying to intimidate people. Things got a little rougher when some of the gang members began to vandalize stores and rob people. Simmons began to realize that there was no real purpose to being in a gang. He was finally convinced to leave it after another gang member was killed. "My gang career ended not long after the murder of a Seven Immortals member named Big Bear. . . . I guess it hit me that I already had a strong family, so why was I risking my safety like this?" Simmons left the gang, but continued to sell drugs.

A Close Call

Simmons has identified a pivotal moment of his youth in his autobiography *Life and Def*. In the book, he described a close call that made a big impact on him. While selling drugs, he was robbed by a neighborhood thief named Red. Simmons was pressured by the other drug dealers in the area, who expected him to do something about the theft. The next time he saw Red, Simmons and several others chased him and cornered him. "Somebody handed me a gun," he recalled. "It was the first (and only) time I've held a gun with the intention to shoot." When Red broke free and was running away, Simmons fired a shot and barely missed. "It's a feeling I've never forgotten. . . . In my heart I knew missing Red was the best thing I ever did." Simmons was 16 at the time.

> "We didn't have guns and we didn't kill people as gangs do today," Simmons said. "My gang career ended not long after the murder of a Seven Immortals member named Big Bear. . . . I guess it hit me that I already had a strong family, so why was I risking my safety like this?"

Simmons does not glamorize this time in his life. He has made no apologies for his past, but he does regret that it might send the wrong message to young people. "I can't emphasize enough how reckless I was and how badly my life could have ended up," he stressed. "The sad thing is how many of my Hollis Crew peers were killed by the drug lifestyle. Some got hit in the head by thieves one time too many. Some got shot. Some died of AIDS in jail. The common denominator was drugs—they were killed pursuing a high or selling a high, by an addict or by their own addiction."

EDUCATION

Simmons's parents arranged for him to attend elementary school at P.S. 135, an integrated school in a white area of Queens, instead of P.S. 134, the neighborhood school in Hollis. For junior high he attended J.H. 109, a predominantly white school. Simmons cites these years as extremely important in forming his perspective on people, diversity, commonality, and the world in general. "Getting me into integrated schools was one of the best things my parents ever did for me, but not because the schooling was automatically superior. Even at that age I was an observer of people . . . a lifelong sociologist," he said. "I saw immediately there are no differences between whites and blacks in terms of what they want out of life. Everybody wants to be liked. . . . Being able to see beyond the obvious when it comes to black and white would be key not just to my career but to my life."

Simmons attended August Martin High School in Queens, graduating in 1975. During his senior year, his father got him a job at an Orange Julius in Greenwich Village. Although Simmons didn't like working there, he says, "Getting out of Hollis was good. It allowed me to see a wider world. The Village . . . would influence very much my vision of selling hip-hop later. It, along with SoHo, would be one of the places I would live in the future where I'd see not the differences in people, but the kinship among everyone. The attitudes that connected them is where the opportunity to sell to them existed." The job didn't last long, but it has been to this day the only regular, nine-to-five job Simmons has ever had.

"The first time I heard a rapper was in 1977. It was Kurtis Blow at the Charles Gallery on 125th Street. That changed my life," Simmons recalled. "I wanted to be in this business. Just like that I saw how I could turn my life in another, better way. . . . Just like that, I decided I no longer wanted to be involved in something like drug dealing that risked my life."

Discovering Rap

After high school, Simmons attended City College of New York in Harlem. He studied sociology and explored different parts of the city, meeting people who would shape the rest of his life. He was still selling drugs during this time, but that changed once he discovered rap music. "The first time I heard a rapper was in 1977. It was Kurtis Blow at the Charles Gallery on 125th Street. That changed my life," Simmons recalled. "I wanted to be in this business. Just like that I saw how I could turn my life in another, better way. . . . Just like that, I decided I no longer wanted to be involved in something like drug dealing that risked my life."

Simmons began following the progress of rappers who performed on street corners and in city parks, noticing the growing crowds that would gather to hear them. He met Rudy Toppin, who gave him the nickname Rush and started him in show promotion. To Simmons's surprise, he realized the toll that drug dealing had taken on his life. "Once out of that game, I felt better about myself and related to the world differently. I was more relaxed, happier, and not as edgy." Simmons eventually left college to begin promoting music shows full time.

CAREER HIGHLIGHTS

Starting Out

Simmons began promoting rap parties and concerts throughout Harlem and Queens with rapper Kurtis Blow (also known as Curtis Walker). The two had become close friends, and they worked together on show promotion. Simmons also represented Kurtis and other performers through Rush Artist Management, his newly formed company. He was committed to helping performers become successful, and he worked very hard to create opportunities for rappers.

In the early days, it was sometimes difficult to convince club owners to allow rappers to perform. At that time, disco was the most popular club music format, and most owners were reluctant to try something new. They didn't want to take a risk with rap, a relatively new style of music, because they didn't think club audiences would be interested. In order to put on a concert, Simmons would usually have to pay the night's costs up front, out of his own money. He counted on making the money back on ticket sales for the event. This strategy worked most of the time, and any profits were used to fund the next show.

One night no one came to the show, and so there were no profits. Simmons lost all of his money. He was completely broke, and went home looking for support. His father wouldn't help him because he wanted Simmons to go back to college and stop wasting his time on rap concerts. However, his mother had always believed that her sons should pursue their own goals. She gave him $2,000 from her personal savings. "It was that money that kept me afloat until Kurtis Blow broke and I entered the record business. That act of love and faith, which is what kept me in business at a key time, is my favorite memory of her."

The First Big Break

In 1979 Kurtis Blow's first single "Christmas Rappin'" became a hit. This was one of the first rap singles to receive widespread radio play. Although

*Simmons's work with Run-D.M.C., shown here in 1988,
was one of his first big successes.*

it was a Christmas song, it became so popular that radio stations continued to play it well into the summer. The song's popularity spread to other parts of the country and even crossed over to Europe. Simmons and Kurtis were invited to tour several European cities. This was a phenomenal first for a rap artist.

"I remember when 'Christmas Rappin' was a hit," Simmons reminisced. "I got a chance to get on a plane and go to Amsterdam, which, for me, was an amazing experience. I had never been on a plane at all. I went to Amsterdam in 1979 with Kurtis Blow and we were treated like—well, we thought we were kings. . . . These people watched us perform, and here we were in this big world with our own music." What impressed Simmons the most about that trip was being called "Mr. Simmons" by everyone he met on the tour. It was the first time anyone had ever addressed him that way. He recalled, "That was the best payment. It reminded me that I deserved it, that I was doing something worthwhile. I haven't gotten anything better than that since."

The success of "Christmas Rappin'" caused a stir in the rap world. Rush Artist Management, the company Simmons formed to manage and develop artists, was signing new talent every week. At that time, there were no other artist managers who were interested in rap. Simmons was busy producing records, booking shows, and helping artists develop both their music and their image. He was also traveling with Kurtis Blow, sometimes doing multiple shows in the same day. These shows brought the hip-hop sound to audiences that had never heard this type of music before.

> ───── " ─────
>
> "I remember when 'Christmas Rappin' was a hit," Simmons reminisced. "I got a chance to get on a plane and go to Amsterdam, which, for me, was an amazing experience. I had never been on a plane at all. I went to Amsterdam in 1979 with Kurtis Blow and we were treated like—well, we thought we were kings."
>
> ───── " ─────

It was an exciting time. Simmons and Kurtis were causing a revolution in the music world. At first, many people didn't know what to expect from Kurtis, who was often booked as an opening act for more famous funk or R&B performers. "We'd be up there setting up turntables on the stage and people in the crowd would mutter, 'We paid money to see a band.' But night after night people would be up dancing on their seats by the end of the set," Simmons recalled. "Davey D would just go out there and tear [it] up on the turntables, and then Kurtis would come on and rock the house."

Creating Run-D.M.C.

During the same time that Simmons was managing Kurtis Blow, he was also working with his younger brother Joey to form Run-D.M.C., which would become one of the most important and influential acts in rap history. Joey had already gained a reputation as DJ Run, and Simmons paired him with Darryl McDaniel, better known as D.M.C. The trio was completed by Jam Master Jay, also known as Jay Mizell. Simmons created a total image for Run-D.M.C., dressing them in their trademark leather suits, hats, and sneakers, and encouraging them to stay true to their musical in-

A still from the movie Tougher Than Leather. *Back row (left to right): Jam Master Jay, Run, executive producer and director Rick Rubin, executive producer Russell Simmons. Front row (left to right): producer Vincent Giodano and Darryl DMC McDaniels.*

stincts. He also produced their records, calling the track "Sucker MCs" the "single most creative thing" he's ever done.

Run-D.M.C.'s self-titled first album was a hit before it was even released: five tracks had already been released as singles and had become very popular before the album as a whole was available. With Simmons's help, Run-D.M.C. had created a totally new sound. The unique sound of tracks like "It's Like That" and "Sucker MCs" was unlike anything being played on radio stations at that time. These tracks had no traditional musical elements such as melody or bass line. The songs consisted mostly of driving drum beats, hand claps, LP scratches, and shouted rhymes.

Most record company executives and radio station programmers didn't know what to do with this new form of music. But Simmons knew that Run-D.M.C.'s sound was true to the street style of the people who gathered to hear rappers perform in city parks. He just needed to get the record into the hands of those people. The group signed a contract with Profile, an independent music label, to distribute the record. It quickly became the first gold rap album.

Once the tracks were finally being played on the radio, no one could believe how quickly Run-D.M.C. became popular. MTV began airing the video for "Rock Box," one of the tracks on this first album. This increased the group's exposure and resulted in many concert bookings and tours. Another historic milestone was reached when the song "My Adidas" became a hit. The group received a one million dollar sponsorship contract from Adidas, the first agreement of its kind between an athletic-wear company and a non-athlete.

In 1984, many of Simmons's performers were featured on the Fresh Fest tour. This tour included Run-D.M.C., Whodini, Kurtis Blow, the Fat Boys, and various breakdancers and DJs. Simmons described this as "the tour that put the boot to the ground for rap" and credited it with cementing Run-D.M.C.'s reputation as entertainers. During this tour, Simmons saw the power of bringing ghetto culture to audiences everywhere. "Run-D.M.C. didn't have to present a watered-down version of how they were or write a sellout hit to get MTV to change their programming. They simply had to be themselves, and fans responded."

> During the Fresh Fest tour, Simmons saw the power of bringing ghetto culture to audiences everywhere. "Run-D.M.C. didn't have to present a watered-down version of how they were or write a sellout hit to get MTV to change their programming. They simply had to be themselves, and fans responded."

Def Jam Records

Around the same time in 1984, Simmons met Rick Rubin, a white student at New York University who also wanted to promote rap music. Rubin had just formed a fledgling record label called Def Jam and was working to expand it. The two pooled their resources, and with $8,000 they founded Def Jam Records. The company operated out of Rubin's dorm room: Simmons managed the business and promoted artists, while Rubin scouted for new talent, produced records, and developed a broader musical approach for rappers. Rubin's knowledge of rock and punk helped rap artists like Run-D.M.C. develop a harder, edgier sound that incorporated elements of rock and punk styles.

Within two years, Def Jam had earned a reputation for supporting artists and allowing performers to express their individual style in unique ways. Simmons explains, "We had this vision that these artists were long term, that they had images that had to be protected. . . . We weren't going to change their music so it would sell more. We weren't going to sell them out or allow them to sell themselves out. We wanted to remind them to keep their integrity and promote that. We wanted to make sure that their images, their visual images, were out in the street, not just their music."

This strategy paid off. Def Jam grew to include many successful artists, including the 15-year-old L.L. Cool J and the first big white rap group, the Beastie Boys. Def Jam soon caught the attention of major record companies that were previously uninterested in rap. Columbia Records offered to promote, market, and distribute Def Jam's new recordings for a share of the profits. With financial backing and support from Columbia, 1986 was a landmark year for Def Jam. Albums like L.L. Cool J's *Bigger and Deffer* and the Beastie Boys' *License to Ill* sold many millions of copies. Run-D.M.C.'s *Raising Hell* produced rap's first top-five pop hit, a collaborative remake of Aerosmith's "Walk This Way." This track became the first rap video to get major airplay on MTV, and the collaboration with rock superstars Aerosmith introduced rap to an entirely new audience.

These successes continued to broaden the exposure and appeal of rap music. The Beastie Boys were instrumental in bringing rap music to suburban white audiences. L.L. Cool J's "I Need Love," considered to be the first rap love ballad, drew in more adult listeners as well as those with softer tastes in music. These releases were not calculated business decisions designed to increase record sales. On the contrary, Def Jam was simply supporting the rappers' individual artistic styles and growth.

The mid-1980s saw tremendous growth in the rap scene. Def Jam continued to sign contracts with new artists, including Public Enemy, Oran "Juice" Jones, and D.J. Jazzy Jeff and the Fresh Prince (who later developed a successful acting career as Will Smith). Simmons began exploring how the rap culture could expand into new media. He formed Def Pictures and produced *Krush Groove* (1985) in cooperation with Warner Brothers studios. *Krush Groove* was a rap musical based loosely on Simmons's own life. A somewhat surprising underground hit, the film grossed $20 million with its original release. He had less success with the 1988 film *Tougher Than Leather*, which critics called "'vile, vicious, despicable, stupid, sexist, racist, and horrendously made." Rick Rubin left Def Jam in 1988, and Simmons went on to develop more outlets for rap culture.

Defining Hip-Hop

The explosive growth of rap in the 1980s proved that there was a global market for the music. Rappers connected with audiences far beyond anyone's expectations. All different people from different backgrounds were identifying with rappers. There was a new culture emerging from what was at first simply a new form of music. This culture was known as hip-hop, and Simmons became one of its biggest promoters.

> "When you are in a hip-hop environment, you know it; it has a feel that is tangible and cannot be mistaken for anything else," Simmons explained. "Hip-hop represents the greatest union of young people with the most diversity — all races and religions — that people have felt in America."

Hip-hop is often defined as modern, mainstream, young, urban American culture. It is primarily a music form but it also encompasses fashion, movies, television, advertising, dancing, language, and attitude. "When you are in a hip-hop environment, you know it; it has a feel that is tangible and cannot be mistaken for anything else," Simmons explained. "Hip-hop represents the greatest union of young people with the most diversity — all races and religions — that people have felt in America."

For the 1990s, Simmons adopted the goal "to present urban culture in its most true form to the people who love it, and to those who live it." He is widely credited with breaking down barriers between rap and mainstream pop music. "Black culture or urban culture is for all people who buy into it and not just for black people. Whether it's film or TV or records or advertising or clothing, I don't accept the box that [people] put me in."

Television and Movies

By 1990, Simmons had created Rush Communications to oversee Def Jam Records, Def Jam Pictures, and a new television production company. He had an idea for a weekly television comedy show that would feature African-American comedians. "Across the country, there [are] lots of discos

*Simmons's "Def Poetry Jam" was a big hit on Broadway
and later published in book form.*

and rap music clubs that become comedy clubs for one night out of the week. And those nights are always sold out. That told me there was an interest . . . and I jumped to service that market." "Def Comedy Jam" debuted in 1992 on the HBO cable television network. The show became so popular that for several years, it was the most-watched Friday night television program in the late-night time slot.

Business continued to expand into different areas. In 1993, Simmons entered the publishing industry with *Oneworld* magazine. Also around this time, he sold the distribution rights for Def Jam recordings to Polygram for $33 million. The deal allowed him to retain complete control over Def Jam musical products, but freed more of his time to develop a growing list of new projects. His Phat Farm men's clothing line premiered in 1994, with the Baby Phat women's clothing line soon to follow. (In 2004, Simmons sold the Phat Farm/Baby Phat clothing lines for an estimated $140 million.)

Also in the 1990s, Simmons renewed his focus on television and movies. In 1995, he appeared in *The Show*, a film documenting the rise and popularity of hip-hop culture. He formed the Rush Media Company, a marketing and advertising agency that created an award-winning ad campaign for Coca-Cola in 1996. Def Pictures released several major movies, including *The Nutty Professor* (1996) starring Eddie Murphy and *Gridlock'd* (1997) starring Tupac Shakur. A syndicated television show called "Oneworld's Music Beat with Russell Simmons" began production in 1998.

Poetry and Politics

As the 1990s ended, Simmons's focus shifted once again. His attention was captured by spoken words, both for art's sake and to raise awareness of political issues. Starting from the belief that all significant change in the world is ultimately brought about by young people, Simmons found ways to give a new voice to the hip-hop community. "I feel this is our best generation, and our best opportunity to make a difference," he explained. "I plan to dedicate the rest of my life to doing what I can — through my businesses and other initiatives — to help empower people."

Part of that empowerment process included giving young thinkers an outlet for their ideas in the form of "Def Poetry Jam." The first "Def Poetry Jam" was created as a television special for HBO. The show highlighted the re-emerging interest in poetry among young people and featured spoken-word performers along with poets. Simmons considered "Def Poetry Jam" a natural progression of Def Jam Records. "These young poets come out of the same spirit as hip-hop, but without music they're challenged to say something even more profound, something that stands on its own without a hot beat to back it up." The show developed into a series for HBO, a multi-city tour, and live theater performances on Broadway in New York City. "Def Poetry Jam" was widely acclaimed and won two prestigious awards, the 2002 Peabody Award and the 2003 Tony Award for Best Theatrical Event.

Another part of that empowerment process was political action. Simmons created the non-profit Hip-Hop Summit Action Network in 2001. The Network organizes Hip-Hop Summits, which are large meetings held in cities throughout the country. The Hip-Hop Summits get young people thinking, talking, and working on issues that are relevant to the hip-hop community. Past topics have included conflict resolution among hip-hop artists and accountability for hip-hop's political, social, and economic impact.

Defending Hip-Hop

In 2000, hip-hop surpassed country music as the third-largest music category in the U.S. By 2001, one out of every ten records sold in the U.S. was hip-hop. As the community of hip-hop fans grows, so does its number of critics. Hip-hop has attracted heavy criticism for what many describe as thug imagery and lyrics that glorify violence and mistreatment of women. As one of the most well-known promoters of hip-hop culture, Simmons is also one of its most determined defenders.

"My life has largely been about promoting the anger, style, aggression, and attitude of urban America to a worldwide audience. It is [the] contrast between street knowledge and traditional values that frightens mainstream people about hip-hop and other forms of street expression."

"Rap is an expression of the attitudes of the performers and their audience. I don't censor my artists. I let them speak," Simmons argued. This is important to Simmons because many hip-hop fans are growing up in the same environments that the artists portray in their lyrics and videos. "Almost all the records that people perceive as gangster records are about people frustrated, who don't perceive themselves as having any other opportunity and it's a description of their lifestyle more than it is an endorsement of it. And so that's something that, you know, people who listen closely to the music can tell. And people from the outside, all they can hear is the language. Well, real language is OK by me, and descriptions of real situations and a real reflection of our society, a part of our society, is important to me," Simmons explained. "My life has largely been about promoting the anger, style, aggression, and attitude of urban America to a worldwide audience. It is [the] contrast between street knowledge and traditional values that frightens mainstream people about hip-hop and other forms of street expression."

The Godfather of Hip-Hop

Simmons has been called the king of rap and the godfather of hip-hop. Sean "P Diddy" Combs describes him as an inspiration, telling *Ebony* magazine that "If it weren't for Russell Simmons, I wouldn't be in the game. He gave the blueprint for hip-hop. . . . He knows how to break down color barriers without compromising who he is." Simmons credits much of his own success to his ability to connect with people regardless of background, race, or culture. "My audience is not limited by race. My core audience, my hip-hop audience, is black and white, Asian and Hispanic. . . anyone who totally identifies with and lives in the culture. . . . That is the central philosophy that has driven my career."

> *"[Simmons] gave the blueprint for hip-hop. . . . He knows how to break down color barriers without compromising who he is,"* said Sean "Diddy" Combs.

Another important factor in Simmons's successful career has been his refusal to be limited in any way. "All of the businesses that I've gotten in, I got in because I didn't know I couldn't." He has cited real estate developer Donald Trump as his mentor, saying that Trump taught him a lot about achieving success in business. "Trump has been very influential in helping me expand my vision. Sometimes I talk to Donald two or three times a day."

Although Simmons maintains six business offices (three in New York City and three in Los Angeles), he does most of his work at home. He is never without his two cell phones, which ring constantly. His work day usually begins sometime in the afternoon and normally lasts well into the night. He visits an average of 15 different clubs a week, scouting for new talent and observing the hip-hop scene. He tries to stay as close to the hip-hop community as he can.

Simmons's future plans are focused on his social and charitable projects. "I'm hopeful that I can be a better participant in relieving some of that suffering I have seen. I find that as you get older you just realize that there are more people in the universe than just yourself. I think we're all connected. . . . Tolerance is what it's all about."

MARRIAGE AND FAMILY

Simmons is married to former supermodel Kimora Lee. They met at a fashion show in which Kimora was modelling. They were married on the Caribbean island of St. Bart's in 1998. The wedding ceremony was performed by Simmons's brother Run (Joey), who is a minister. Rev. Run amended the wedding vows to have the couple promise to stay together "for richer, for richer." Simmons and Kimora have two daughters: Ming Lee, born in 2000, and Aoki Lee, born in 2002. The couple maintains an apartment in Greenwich Village, a house in Saddle River, New Jersey, and a house in the Hamptons on Long Island, New York.

HOBBIES AND OTHER INTERESTS

Simmons practices yoga and meditates every day. He says that studying the spiritual teachings of yoga have had a profound influence on the way he approaches his work: "For any business to be successful in the long run, it

Simmons with his wife, Kimora Lee Simmons, and their two children, Aoki Lee and Ming Lee, 2004.

has to be conscious of the fact that giving is, and will always be, the foundation of your success. All the religious teachings say the same thing . . . that you reap what you sow. Reading the yoga sutras caused these basic ideas to resonate within me. I use the science and the practice of yoga and the reading of various texts to remind me of these basic truths on a regular basis."

Simmons follows a vegan diet, meaning that he does not consume any foods containing meat or other animal products such as eggs or cheese, and is known as an animal welfare activist. He has partnered with non-profit organizations such as PETA (People for the Ethical Treatment of Animals) and the SPCA (Society for the Prevention of Cruelty to Animals) on various projects intended to raise awareness of animal welfare issues.

Simmons founded the Rush Philanthropic Arts foundation to support arts programs for young people throughout the U.S. The Foundation is run by his brother Danny and holds major fundraising events every year.

SELECTED WRITINGS

Life and Def, 2001 (with Nelson George)

HONORS AND AWARDS

Moet & Chandon Humanitarian Award (Moet & Chandon Champagne): 1998

Lifetime Achievement Award (*The Source*): 1999

Black Enterprise Company of the Year (*Black Enterprise* magazine): 2002, for Rush Communications

Peabody Award (University of Georgia): 2002, for "Russell Simmons's Def Poetry Jam"

Tony Award (American Theatre Wing): 2003, Best Theatrical Event, for "Russell Simmons's Def Poetry Jam"

FURTHER READING

Books

Business Leader Profiles for Students, Vol. 2, 2002
Contemporary Black Biography, Vol. 30, 2001
Contemporary Musicians, Vol. 7, 1992; Vol. 47, 2004
George, Nelson. *Hip Hop America,* 1998
Gueraseva, Stacy. *Def Jam, Inc.,* 2005
Ogg, Alex. *The Men Behind Def Jam,* 2002
Simmons, Russell, and Nelson George. *Life and Def,* 2001
Who's Who among African Americans, 2005
Who's Who in America, 2006

Periodicals

Billboard, Nov. 4, 1995, p.32
Black Enterprise, Dec. 1997, p.66; Dec. 1999, p.78
Black Issues Book Review, Sep. 2001, p.43
CosmoGirl!, Feb. 2005, p.84
Current Biography Yearbook, 1998
Ebony, Jan. 2001, p.116; July 2003, p.168
Essence, Sep. 2004, p.50
Fast Company, Nov. 2003, p.76
Fortune, May 17, 2004, p.41
Inc., April 1, 2004
Nation, Jan. 13, 2003, p.21

Newsweek, July 28, 2003, p.40
People, July 1, 2002, p.97
Rolling Stone, Nov. 15, 1990, p.106
Time, May 4, 1992, p.69

Online Articles

http://www.businessweek.com/bwdaily/dnflash/jan2004/nf20040113_4406
_db074.htm
(Business Week Online, "Tapping the Spirit of Success: Entrepreneur
Russell Simmons Thanks Yoga's Philosophy for Giving Him the
Principles to Operate His Ever-Growing Hip-Hop Empire," Jan. 13,
2004)
http://www.inc.com/magazine/20040401/25simmons.html
(Inc.com, "America's 25 Most Fascinating Entrepreneurs: Russell
Simmons, Rush Communications," April 2004)
http://www.pbs.org/wgbh/theymadeamerica/whomade/simmons_hi.html
(PBS, "Who Made America: Russell Simmons, Cross-Marketing
Culture," undated)

Online Databases

Biography Resource Center, 2005, articles from *Business Leader Profiles for
Students,* 2002, *Contemporary Black Biography,* 2001, *Contemporary
Musicians,* 2004, *Who's Who among African Americans,* 2005

ADDRESS

Russell Simmons
Rush Philanthropic Arts Foundation
512 Seventh Avenue, 43rd Floor
New York, NY 10018

WORLD WIDE WEB SITES

http://www.defjam.com
http://www.hsan.org
http://www.rushphilanthropic.org

Jamie Lynn Spears 1991-

American Actress
Star of the Hit Nickelodeon TV Series "Zoey 101"

EARLY YEARS

Jamie Lynn Marie Spears was born on April 4, 1991, in McComb, Mississippi, a town that is only a few miles from her family's home in Kentwood, Louisiana. Her father, Jamie, worked as a building contactor, and her mother, Lynne, was an elementary school teacher. Jamie Lynn has an older sister, Britney, and an older brother, Bryan.

When Jamie Lynn was born, Britney was 10 years old and already an aspiring singer and actress. (For more information on Britney see *Biography Today*, Jan. 2001.) Their parents encouraged their oldest daughter to pursue her dreams and were willing to make big sacrifices to see Britney succeed in the entertainment business. A few months after Jamie Lynn was born, she moved to New York City with her sister and her mother Lynne to further Britney's singing and acting career, while father Jamie and brother Bryan remained in Kentwood. In New York City, Britney attended the Professional Performing Arts School for three summers, appeared in television commercials, and acted in off-Broadway plays. In 1992 Britney landed a role on "The Mickey Mouse Club," which filmed in Orlando, Florida, and the entire family moved there for two years until the series was cancelled. They moved back to Kentwood in 1993.

When Jamie Lynn was only six years old, Britney signed a recording contract with Jive Records and had to leave home to record her first album, *Baby One More Time,* which was completed in 1999. It turned out to be an overwhelming success, and Jamie Lynn got to see her sister become a superstar. She also accompanied her sister on several concert and television appearances. It was difficult to see her big sister leave home at such an early age. Jamie Lynn loved being the baby of the family, but it was hard too. "The best thing is they all spoil me," she said recently. "Then it kind of sucks 'cause I don't have anybody at home.

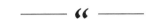

> *Jamie Lynn loved being the baby of the family, but it was hard too. "The best thing is they all spoil me," she said recently. "Then it kind of sucks 'cause I don't have anybody at home. I'm the only kid."*

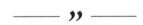

I'm the only kid." Jamie Lynn tried acting herself, trying out for several school plays. "My only part in a school play was as an extra orphan in *Annie* at age nine," she recalled. "I was never the lead. I was pretty shy." However, she realized that she wanted to act and sing, and her parents encouraged her to audition for local plays and television commercials.

MAJOR ACCOMPLISHMENTS

In 2002 Spears got her first job in the entertainment business. She made a brief appearance in *Crossroads,* a film that starred her older sister, Britney. "It was cool doing it with Britney because she could really help me—although, I didn't get to say anything in the movie!" Jamie Lynn said in a re-

Jamie Lynn and the cast of "All That."

cent interview. "But it was fun being in front of the camera. And it'd be fun to work with my sister again." She also appeared in the MTV documentary "Driven," which focused on Britney's climb to the top of the music charts. During the show, Jamie Lynn performed a rap number with her brother, Bryan.

When Nickelodeon executives saw her sing and dance, they invited her to audition for their hit show "All That," a comedy sketch show performed by kids for kids. It was quite an opportunity for Jamie Lynn, because "All That" is the same show that launched the careers of other young stars, including Amanda Bynes and Kenan Thompson. In her audition, Jamie Lynn did a funny impression of an 84-year-old bouncer named Thelma Stump, who throws people out of windows and attacks them with leaf blowers — a character she based on her own grandmother.

Joining the Cast of "All That"

Nick executives loved what they saw, and in 2002 they invited Jamie Lynn to join the cast of "All That." "Based on her audition, I would have added her to the cast of 'All That' even if she had not been a Spears," asserted the producer of the show, Dan Schneider. "I see the same drive in her as in Britney," claims Virgil Fabian, the director of "All That" who had also directed Britney on "The Mickey Mouse Club" in the early 1990s. Britney also saw a special quality in her sister. "Of course I'm biased, but I definitely think Jamie Lynn has the 'It' quality," Britney asserted. "She shines, and I'm proud of her."

Jamie Lynn was thrilled to join the hit show, but she was also nervous. "At first I was too scared to act in front of these people, so I was real shy," she remembered. "But then, they were actually really nice. I thought they were going to be these serious people. But they were a lot of fun." It wasn't long before Jamie joined right into the silliness of the show—she was tossed into trash bins and doused with water and egg yolks, and she performed funny impressions in front of a studio audience. Her castmates were impressed with her attitude. "I was expecting someone who was going to be a little kiddish, kind of immature," said Shane Lyons, a fellow cast member on "All That." "But what we got was someone who could relate and talk and just mess around with us on our level." Fellow cast member Chelsea Brummet agreed. "Jamie has the maturity level of, like, a 15-year-old, which is awesome." Others thought that because her sister is a superstar, Jamie Lynn might be stuck up. "I thought she'd have a limo and bodyguards," revealed castmate Lisa Foiles, "but she's totally cool."

> **❝**
>
> *Some cast members on "All That" thought that because her sister is a superstar, Jamie Lynn might be stuck up. "I thought she'd have a limo and bodyguards," revealed castmate Lisa Foiles, "but she's totally cool."*
>
> **❞**

"Zoey 101"

Jamie Lynn became a success with her role on "All That." After two years on the popular show, she met with the producer, Dan Schneider, who offered her her own series on Nick. "It was a total blessing," she remembered. "When they told me, I started screaming and called all my friends. I was even more excited than with 'All That' because it was my very own show."

Schneider created "Zoey 101" especially for Jamie Lynn. Her character, Zoey Brooks, is a 13-year-old girl who is one of the first females to enroll in an all-male school, the Pacific Coast Academy. "She's a lot like me," said Jamie Lynn. "It's a lot of fun. I get to go to work and be myself all day." Jamie Lynn has pointed out both similarities and differences between her and the character of Zoey. "I could never try out for the all-boys basketball team like she did!" she said in an interview. "She's probably more assertive than I am. Like, she does a lot of things I'd never think of doing, like going to a boarding school. I just could never be away from home for that long— I'm so close with my family."

Jamie Lynn also got to work with her sister, Britney, to record the theme song of the show. Britney co-wrote the song and coached her sister in the studio. "She totally helped me out in the studio," Jamie Lynn recalled. "She'd say, 'Stop being nervous, you have a great voice.'" When people have compared her to her famous older sister, Jamie Lynn is flattered. "It's hard," she admitted in an interview. "But Britney is pretty great, so it's the biggest compliment I could get. I never look at it as a bad thing." Britney's celebrity has taught her younger sister a few valuable lessons. "I've learned to stay close with my family as she has and that it's really hard work in show business," Jamie Lynn revealed. "I've also learned to not listen to all of the gossip. I guess people don't really realize that less than half that stuff is really true."

> *Jamie Lynn has pointed out both similarities and differences between her and the character of Zoey. "I could never try out for the all-boys basketball team like she did!" she said in an interview. "She's probably more assertive than I am. Like, she does a lot of things I'd never think of doing, like going to a boarding school. I just could never be away from home for that long—I'm so close with my family."*

"Zoey 101" quickly became one of the most popular shows on Nickelodeon. To capitalize on the show's success, Nick released a soundtrack of "Zoey 101," a book series, and a clothing line. At the Nickelodeon's Kids Choice Awards in 2006, Jamie Lynn won the award for Favorite TV Actress. She has been featured on the covers of several magazines, including *American Cheerleader* and *Seventeen.* Although she is now recognized as a star in her own right, Jamie Lynn has tried to stay grounded. "I wouldn't say I'm a celebrity, but the best thing is just being able to go to work every day and do something I love," she said. "I'm just one of those people that doesn't want to be noticed or anything."

Jamie Lynn does lend her celebrity to raise money for worthy causes. She filmed a public service announcement to help raise funds for the victims of the tsunami in Indonesia, has been active in raising money for the victims

"Zoey 101" has been so successful that it produced a book series, a DVD collection, a CD music mix soundtrack, and even a clothing line.

of Hurricane Katrina, and has volunteered with the American Red Cross. Despite her busy schedule, Jamie Lynn has said that she will always find time to volunteer and help raise money for people in need. "I think that, out of everything I do, helping other people is the most important thing you can do," she asserted. "There's always time for that!"

Education

Jamie Lynn attends Parklane Academy in McComb, Mississippi. She is outgoing and athletic, playing on both the softball and basketball teams. She is also on her school's cheerleading squad, which was invited to participate in the 2006 National All-Star Cheerleading Championship. Although she is recognized as a celebrity, her schoolmates do not treat her any differently.

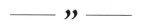

> "I have a lot of guy friends, but I don't want a boyfriend or anything," Jamie Lynn claimed. "I'm not allowed to go on a date until I'm 16 anyway."

"I've grown up with these people all my life, so they don't really treat me different," she claimed. "I've taken some of my friends on the set. They get to be extras, so they like it a lot." She has described herself as a serious student. "I'm the more outgoing one between me and my sister Britney, but I like to get my school stuff done because I want good grades. Or try, at least!"

Jamie Lynn loves growing up in Kentwood. "I know everybody," she declared. "There's nobody in that town I don't know; it's just fun to know everybody and all my friends live, like, five minutes from me." Jamie Lynn is away in Los Angeles a couple of months out of the year filming "Zoey 101" and also has to travel for business. "I like it a lot but, when you're away from home, you're always going to get a little homesick," she said in an interview. "At the most, I'm away for about three months at a time. The good part is that my friends come out and visit for a week, which is awesome." Those friends don't include a boyfriend, at least not yet. "I have a lot of guy friends, but I don't want a boyfriend or anything," she claimed. "I'm not allowed to go on a date until I'm 16 anyway."

Future Plans

Jamie Lynn has talked about starting a singing career, like her sister, Britney. For the past few years, she has concentrated on her acting career and her hit series "Zoey 101," as well as her classes, cheerleading, and soft-ball. "I'm just focusing on 'Zoey' right now, but I'd like to do movies later," she commented in a recent interview. "I've always said I want to do scary movies, but then I read scripts for funny movies, and I think, 'Oh, I have to do this!' So you never know!"

TELEVISION CREDITS

"All That," 2002-2004
"Zoey 101," 2004-

HONORS AND AWARDS

Kids Choice Award (Nickelodeon): 2006, for Favorite TV Actress

FURTHER READING

Periodicals

Girls' Life, Apr.-May 2005, p.40
New York Post, Apr. 7, 2005, p.86
New York Times, Aug. 7, 2005, p.AR26
Newsweek, Jan. 24, 2005, pp.24, 75
People, Mar. 3, 2003, p.106

ADDRESS

Jamie Lynn Spears
Nickelodeon Studios
231 W. Olive Ave.
Burbank, CA 91502

WORLD WIDE WEB SITES

http://www.jamielynnspears.com
http://www.nick.com

Jon Stewart 1962-

American Comedian and Actor
Host of "The Daily Show with Jon Stewart"

BIRTH

Jonathan Stewart (some sources say "Stuart") Leibowitz was
born on November 28, 1962, in Lawrence, New Jersey. He
shortened his name to Jon Stewart in the mid-1980s, when he
became a comedian. His father, Donald Leibowitz, was a
physicist who worked for RCA. His mother, Marian, worked
as an educational consultant and special-education teacher.
He has one older brother, Larry.

YOUTH

Even as a youngster, Stewart enjoyed making people laugh. But he admits that his constant joking probably got a little tiresome for those around him. "Some people can paint," he said. "I can't. Some people can sing. I can't. Some people make a joke of everything. I've done that since I was four or five years old. I don't remember a time when people didn't think I was a wiseass. I hope I've gotten more artful over time, because when I was younger, I was just obnoxious."

Stewart grew up in one of the few Jewish families in his neighborhood. His background often made him the target of name-calling and bullying. "They will find what is unique about you and destroy you for it," he observed. "So if you're Jewish and most people aren't, OK, let's go with that. But it just as easily could have been because I was short."

When Stewart was still a pre-teen, he was stunned when his parents informed him that they were getting a divorce. The situation became even more painful when his father made little effort to maintain a relationship with his sons afterward. From that point forward, Stewart was raised by his mother, whom he has described as "passionate about education and current events." Her passion about these issues was a big factor in his own evolving interest in politics and current affairs.

> *"Some people can paint,"*
> *Stewart said. "I can't.*
> *Some people can sing.*
> *I can't. Some people*
> *make a joke of everything.*
> *I've done that since*
> *I was four or five years*
> *old. I don't remember*
> *a time when people*
> *didn't think I was a*
> *wiseass. I hope I've*
> *gotten more artful over*
> *time, because when*
> *I was younger, I was*
> *just obnoxious."*

Despite his difficult adolescence, Stewart has expressed great affection for his home state of New Jersey. "There are a lot of jokes about Jersey, but it really is a great place," he said. "It's a very diverse state. It's very diverse ethnically, religiously. There's different food, culture. To put it in perspective, Jersey is the perfect scarecrow. People see the turnpike and think, 'Oh, what a mess.' But five minutes from there, you'll find a great lake or great scenery. I like that people think it's a mess, then there's less people there and it's better for me."

EDUCATION

Stewart attended public schools in Lawrence. After graduating from high school around 1980, he enrolled at Virginia's College of William and Mary. He promptly joined a fraternity, but he resigned his membership after six months. He felt disgusted by the group's hazing practices, and he refused to pretend to be friends with frat brothers he did not even like. Stewart spent the next few years playing soccer, studying, and — by his own admission — partying too much. In 1984 he earned a bachelor's degree in psychology, then promptly returned to New Jersey. "I had no idea what I was doing [at college]," he admitted. "And then I got out and I still had no idea."

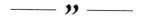

> *"It was grueling and hilarious," Stewart said of his early stand-up days. "I remember walking home at three in the morning going, If it doesn't get any better than this, it's still better than I ever thought it'd be."*

FIRST JOBS

Stewart spent the next couple years moving from job to job, trying to find his place in the world. He staged puppet shows for disabled kids, worked as a contract administrator for a local college, conducted field research for a state study on encephalitis, and worked as a bartender. He enjoyed this carefree lifestyle on a day-to-day basis, but after a while he became restless. "I started thinking, 'This is it for the next 70 years?'" he recalled. "So I told my mom I was going to New York to do comedy. I never discussed it with the — what's the other one called? — dad."

Stewart landed in New York City in 1986. Looking back, he expressed pride in his decision to leave his safe existence behind and take a chance. "I might have become a bitter guy at the end of the bar, complaining about how I could've been somebody," he said. "But I sold my car and moved up to New York with no job because I wanted something different. I yearned, and I went for it."

CAREER HIGHLIGHTS

Diving into Stand-Up Comedy

Stewart found work in New York City as a bartender, then set about trying to establish himself in the ultra-competitive world of stand-up comedy.

One of the first things he did was to drop his last name and introduce himself as "Jon Stewart." After achieving stardom, Stewart said that he took this step because comedy club emcees and owners kept mispronouncing and misspelling his family name. But he has also hinted that he dropped the Leibowitz name in part because of his nonexistent relationship with his father.

Stewart endured some rough nights on stage during those early years. "The first night I ever went on stage, about three minutes into my stand-up act, some guy yelled, 'You suck.' And he hasn't stopped hounding me since," he joked. But with each passing night, Stewart became a little more sure of himself. "I never had any talent or affinity

Stewart got his start doing stand-up routines at various comedy clubs.

for any other artistic thing," he explained. "I went through a period of time where I said, 'I'm going to be a cartoonist. I'm going to be a novelist. I'm going to be a trumpet player.' A few weeks into each, it became apparent that it was not my calling. When I was on stage, the clouds didn't part and someone didn't call from above, 'Yes, you are a comedian,' but it was something I felt comfortable with."

By the late 1980s Stewart was known as one of the funniest comics in the city. Although he did not focus on the political humor that later became his ticket to fame, his act was full of wry and cutting observations about human nature and the American way of life. "It was grueling and hilarious," he said of his early stand-up days. "I remember walking home at three in the morning going, If it doesn't get any better than this, it's still better than I ever thought it'd be." He also was popular with other comedians, even though they were competing for spots in New York's top clubs. "I, like almost every other female in the comedy community, had a crush on him," recalled comedian Janeane Garofalo. "He's just one of those guys everybody likes."

Stewart in his office.

Stewart's comic skills eventually attracted attention from promoters and entertainment executives across the country. He was invited to appear on several HBO comedy specials and on "Late Night with David Letterman." In the early 1990s he was selected to host "Short Attention Span Theater" on the Comedy Channel (now Comedy Central). From there he moved on to MTV, where in 1993 he was given his own half-hour talk show. When "The Jon Stewart Show" was canceled one year later, Paramount Studios promptly approached him about doing a syndicated one-hour talk show.

This show, also called "The Jon Stewart Show," won praise from a number of critics. They described Stewart's casual, conversational approach as a refreshing change of pace from the heavily scripted shows airing elsewhere on late-night TV. "[Stewart] seems like Letterman's younger, hipper brother," declared *People.*

Stewart's show struggled to find an audience, though. In addition, the comedian found that he was no longer having fun. "About four months into it, I thought, Wow, this unbelievable opportunity will be taken away from me, and when someone asks, Did you even enjoy it? I'm going to say no." Years later, Stewart described the show "as a watershed, and I don't mean comedically. I mean emotionally. I was playing scared. I was playing not to lose."

Joining "The Daily Show"

In 1995 "The Jon Stewart Show" was cancelled after months of poor ratings and mixed critical reviews. The cancellation did not derail Stewart's career, though. Instead, he kept busy on a variety of cable television shows (including a recurring role on HBO's popular "Larry Sanders Show"). He also took supporting roles in a handful of films. He even wrote a book called *Naked Pictures of Famous People,* a 1998 collection of essays that took comic aim at everyone from Adolf Hitler to Martha Stewart.

In 1998 Stewart received a phone call from Comedy Central executives, who had been trying to get the comedian back on the network for several years. They asked him if he wanted to take over as host of "The Daily Show" in place of Craig Kilborn, who was leaving for another late night program. Stewart quickly accepted the offer, and in January 1999 he stepped on stage for the first time as host of "The Daily Show with Jon Stewart."

During Kilborn's years as host, the show's humor had focused on celebrities and weird news stories, and many of the jokes had a malicious edge to them. It did not take long for Stewart to decide that the show needed to change its tone and focus. "It was a conscious decision to move to relevance — to make the show something people care about," he said. "I did what I wanted to do, with like-minded people who'd bring passion, competence, and creativity to it."

Stewart freely admits that some members of the staff resisted the show's increasing focus on politics, current events, and the news media. In fact, a number of the writers continued to churn out mean-spirited material targeting ordinary Americans and harmless celebrities who found themselves in the news. "I can't tell you my first year here was particularly pleasant," he said. "I can't say there weren't days of knock-down, drag-'em-out yelling." But these writers gradually drifted away, and they were replaced by people who felt excited about the prospect of turning their comic ammunition on leading politicians and journalists.

By 2000 the content of "The Daily Show with Jon Stewart" was much more to Stewart's liking. Assisted by a group of fake news correspondents, Stewart offered audiences a nightly dose of comic news coverage that seemed to become more clever and insightful with each broadcast. The show's coverage of the 2000 presidential election, which it dubbed "Indecision 2000," was particularly funny and perceptive. These broadcasts, which relentlessly poked fun at the campaigns of both Republican nominee George W. Bush and Democratic nominee Al Gore, brought thousands of new viewers to the show.

Stewart on the set of "The Daily Show."

Becoming a "Fake News" Phenomenon

Over the next few years, Stewart and his colleagues perfected their fake-news act. Blending Stewart's anchorman monologues with fake feature stories and real interviews with politicians, journalists, and celebrities, the show's trademark mix of humorous political commentary attracted bigger audiences and earned greater critical praise with each passing month. By 2001 *Esquire* magazine was describing "The Daily Show" as "the smartest, most innovative show on TV."

Reviewers agreed that Stewart was the glue that kept the show together. "Stewart's on-air persona is that of the outraged individual who, comparing official pronouncements with his own basic common sense, simply cannot believe what he — and all of us — are expected to swallow," wrote Susan J. Douglas in *The Nation*. According to *Rolling Stone* writer John Calapinto, this outrage is fed not only by Stewart's desire to get laughs, but also by his own take on world events. "Two minutes in Stewart's company shows you that he's scary smart," wrote Calapinto. "Stewart actually thinks about stuff. Serious stuff, and thinks about it critically and deeply."

By 2003 Stewart and his show had become a genuine force in American politics. "You simply can't understand American politics in the new millennium without 'The Daily Show,'" declared journalist Bill Moyers. With this in mind, in September 2003 U.S. Senator John Edwards decided to announce his candidacy for the 2004 Democratic presidential nomination on

Stewart's show. Stewart responded by joking that the announcement did not count because it came on a fake news show.

Stewart downplayed his show's growing influence, insisting that he and the other writers and performers were just having fun. "There's a difference between making a point and having an agenda," he said. "We don't have an agenda to change the political system. We have a more selfish agenda, to entertain ourselves. We feel a frustration with the way politics are handled and the way politics are handled within the media."

Creating Controversy on "Crossfire"

Despite Stewart's protests, Washington-based politicians and journalists agree that his show has become quite influential. This influence became clearer in 2004, when Stewart appeared on CNN's "Crossfire," a program in which liberal and conservative political analysts argue over the issues of the day. "Crossfire" hosts Paul Begala and Tucker Carlson clearly expected the interview with Stewart to consist of little more than light-hearted joking. Instead, Stewart used his appearance to raise concerns about the media in general and "Crossfire" in particular. Stewart criticized the program as "partisan hackery" that did not make a serious attempt to examine important issues. Carlson angrily told the comedian to tell some jokes, but Stewart continued to condemn "Crossfire" and similar news shows.

"There's a difference between making a point and having an agenda," Stewart said. "We don't have an agenda to change the political system. We have a more selfish agenda, to entertain ourselves. We feel a frustration with the way politics are handled and the way politics are handled within the media."

"The reason everyone on 'Crossfire' freaked out is that I didn't play the role I was supposed to play," Stewart later said. "I was expected to do some funny jokes, then go have a beer with everyone. By stepping outside of my role, I stunned them. Imagine going on 'Crossfire' and expressing an opinion that causes a problem. Apparently the only people you cannot put in the crossfire are the hosts of 'Crossfire.' . . . What I ultimately said was, 'Tomorrow I'll go back to being funny, and you guys will still blow.' . . . It was as if they thought I was suddenly taking myself too seriously. What do you think 'The Daily Show' is about? Just because we're comedic doesn't mean we don't care about this stuff. We do."

A few months later CNN announced the cancellation of "Crossfire." At that time, the network president, Jonathan Klein, admitted that Stewart's comments had been on target. "It's time for us to do a better job of informing our audience in an engaging way, as opposed to head-butting and screaming," he said.

Writing *America (The Book)*

By the end of 2004 "The Daily Show" and its host had won numerous awards, including several Emmy and Peabody awards. The program also attracted more than a million viewers every night — triple the number of viewers it had when Kilborn was the host. In addition, research studies have indicated that people who watch the show are better informed about current events and American politics than people who rely on other news sources. "We don't make things up," explained Stewart. "We just distill it to, hopefully, its most humorous nugget. And in that sense it seems faked and skewed just because we don't have to be subjective or pretend to be objective. We can just put it out there."

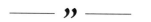

> *"We don't make things up," explained Stewart. "We just distill it to, hopefully, its most humorous nugget. And in that sense it seems faked and skewed just because we don't have to be subjective or pretend to be objective. We can just put it out there."*

Stewart and his fellow "Daily Show" writers have also branched out into writing books. In late 2004 they released *America (The Book): A Citizen's Guide to Democracy Inaction.* Organized like a weird textbook, it uses biting humor to comment on the country's history and the current state of its government institutions and news media. An immediate bestseller, it was widely praised by reviewers. *People* called it "a hilarious book with a distinct liberal bias. . . . Rude, crude, and utterly delightful." *Fortune's* Brian O'Keefe described it as "truly laugh-out-loud funny. How do I know? When it first arrived on my desk, I opened it to a random page and immediately laughed out loud."

America (The Book) made such a huge splash that *Publishers Weekly* named it the book of the year for 2004. "Beneath the eye-catching and at times goofy graphics, the dirty jokes and the playful ingenuousness, shines a serious critique of the two-party system, the corporations that finance it, and the 'spineless cowards in the press' who 'aggressively print allegation and rumor independent of accuracy or fairness,'" declared the magazine.

THE DAILY SHOW WITH JON STEWART PRESENTS

AMERICA

(THE BOOK)
★ ★ ★

A Citizen's Guide to Democracy Inaction

With a Foreword by Thomas Jefferson

Meanwhile, Stewart and his "Daily Show" colleagues continue to make fun of American politicians and political parties in all sorts of clever ways. "The Daily Show" holds both Democrats and Republicans up for ridicule, but most observers agree that it takes special delight in attacking the Bush administration. Stewart admits that he thinks Bush is a poor president who often misleads the American people. But he insists that his show is not a public relations arm of the rival Democratic Party, and he points out numerous occasions when he and his colleagues have made Democratic lawmakers look bad.

In many ways, though, the biggest target of "The Daily Show" is the American news media. In Stewart's view, most American news organizations no longer make much of an effort to force politicians to tell the truth or behave ethically. "Politicians are doing what politicians do," Stewart said. "I liken it to when you go to the zoo, and the monkeys are sitting in there ... throwing their s—. And you just gotta go, 'Well, they're monkeys.' But you can yell at the media and go, 'You know, your job is to tell them when they're being bad monkeys.'... The TV networks have an opportunity to bring noise or clarity. So much of what the government and corporations do is bring noise because they don't welcome scrutiny. They don't necessarily want you to know what they're up to. So if you're working in a medium that has an opportunity to bring clarity and you instead choose to create more distraction, that's theater — which is what these news channels have become."

In 2004 "Daily Show" fans rejoiced when Stewart signed a new contract that will keep him behind the anchor desk on the show through the 2008 presidential election. Stewart admits that he is happy with the agreement, which pays him about $2 million a year. But he insists that he will not stay on "The Daily Show" forever, because he has other projects he would like to pursue. "I want to breed a race of ninjas," he joked.

MARRIAGE AND FAMILY

In 2000 Stewart married Tracy McShane, a veterinary technician, after a long courtship. They live in Manhattan with their son, Nathan Thomas. "We usually have a nice dinner, play with the dog, watch whatever's on, do a crossword puzzle together, and go to bed," Stewart said. "I hate to say it: I feel content. And driven at the same time. Hopefully, that's a combination that will work for a while."

HOBBIES AND OTHER INTERESTS

Stewart enjoys reading on a wide range of subjects, including American history and current events. He is also a big sports fan.

SELECTED CREDITS

Television

"Short Attention Span Theater," 1991-92
"You Wrote It, You Watch It," 1992
"The Jon Stewart Show," 1993-95
"The Daily Show with Jon Stewart," 1999-

Films

Playing by Heart, 1998
The Faculty, 1998
Barenaked in America, 1999
Big Daddy, 1999
Jay and Silent Bob Strike Back, 2001
Death to Smoochie, 2002

Writings

Naked Pictures of Famous People, 1998
America (The Book): A Citizen's Guide to Democracy Inaction, 2004 (with the
    writers of "The Daily Show with Jon Stewart")

HONORS AND AWARDS

George F. Peabody Award: 2001, for "Indecision 2000" coverage on "The
    Daily Show with Jon Stewart"; 2005, for "Indecision 2004" coverage on
    "The Daily Show with Jon Stewart"
Emmy Award: 2003 and 2004, for best writing for a comedy series, for
    "The Daily Show with Jon Stewart"; 2004, for best variety, musical, or
    comedy show, for "The Daily Show with Jon Stewart"
Book of the Year (*Publishers Weekly*): 2004, for *America (The Book)*
Best News and Information Program (Television Critics Association): 2004,
    for "The Daily Show with Jon Stewart"
100 Most Influential People (*Time*): 2005

FURTHER READING

Books

Authors and Artists for Young Adults, Vol. 57, 2004
Who's Who in America, 2005

Periodicals

Cosmopolitan, Jan. 1, 1999
Current Biography Yearbook, 2004
Entertainment Weekly, Oct. 31, 2003, p.30; Sep. 17, 2004, p.10
Esquire, July 2001, p.62
Fortune, Sep. 20, 2004, p.60
Los Angeles Times, Nov. 30, 1994, p.F1
Nation, May 5, 2003, p.24

New York Times, Mar. 13, 1994, Section 2, p.34; Oct. 3, 2004, Section 7, p.20
New Yorker, Feb. 11, 2002, p.28
Newsweek, July 31, 2000, p.60; Dec. 29, 2003, p.70
O Magazine, June 2005, p.186
People, Apr. 4, 1994, p.99; Dec. 27, 2004, p.63
Publishers Weekly, Sep. 28, 1998, p.73; Sep. 6, 2004, p.58; Dec. 6, 2004, p.31
Rolling Stone, Jan. 26, 1995, p.26; Oct. 28, 2004, p.58
Washington Post, Apr. 16, 1995, p.G8; May 2, 2002, p.C1; Oct. 23, 2004, p.A1

Online Articles

http://www.cbsnews.com/stories
(*CBS News,* "60 Minutes: Jon Stewart Roasts Real News," Dec. 21, 2004)
http://www.pbs.org/now/
(*NOW with Bill Moyers,* "Bill Moyers Interviews Jon Stewart," July 11, 2003)

Online Databases

Biography Resource Center Online, 2005, articles from *Authors and Artists for Young Adults,* 2004, and *Contemporary Authors Online,* 2004

ADDRESS

Jon Stewart
"The Daily Show with Jon Stewart"
Comedy Central Viewer Services
1775 Broadway, 10th Floor
New York, NY 10019

WORLD WIDE WEB SITE

http://www.comedycentral.com/shows/the_daily_show

Joss Stone 1987-

British Soul Singer
Creator of the Popular Albums *The Soul Sessions* and
Mind, Body, & Soul

BIRTH

Joss Stone was born as Joscelyn Eve Stoker on April 11, 1987, in the town of Dover, Kent, England. She adopted her stage name at 14, when she signed her first recording contract. Joss was the third of four children born to Richard Stoker, who ran a dried-fruit business, and Wendy Stoker, who managed vacation cottages. She has an older brother, Daniel; an older sister, Lucy; and a younger brother, Harry.

YOUTH

Joss grew up in rural Devon, in the English countryside. Although her parents were not musical, they greatly enjoyed listening to music and exposed their children to a range of musical styles. Her father tended to favor rock and roll, and he was an avid fan of the Beatles. Her mother leaned more toward folk and soul music, and her favorites included Melissa Etheridge and the Motown sound. "My parents used to play a lot of music around the house," she recalled. "Some of it was soul, some of it wasn't."

Thanks to her parents' influence, Joss enjoyed all sorts of music as a girl. Her interest turned toward soul at the age of 12, when she heard a greatest hits album by Aretha Franklin, the Motown recording artist known as the "Queen of Soul." "In a way, soul found me," she explained. "I kind of clicked into soul more than anything else because of the vocals. You've got to have good vocals to sing soul music." Joss always liked to sing, but she never took any formal voice lessons. "I learned to sing by listening to Aretha Franklin," she noted. "She was my teacher."

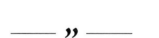

"In a way, soul found me," Stone explained. "I kind of clicked into soul more than anything else because of the vocals. You've got to have good vocals to sing soul music."

When Joss was 13, she overcame her natural shyness to audition for "Star for a Night," a talent program that was televised in England by the BBC (the U.S. version of the show is "American Idol"). She earned a spot on the show by singing Aretha Franklin's soul classic "(You Make Me Feel Like a) Natural Woman" at the audition. Most of the teenagers who performed on the program sang pop songs in the manner of Britney Spears, and members of the audience expected Joss to follow suit. Instead, she blew away the competition by turning in a mature, soulful performance of Donna Summer's "On the Radio."

Joss's brilliant performance on "Star for a Night" earned her a contract with a talent agent. A few months later, she and her mother flew to New York City so that Joss could audition for Steve Greenberg, the head of S-Curve Records. Since Joss had not even prepared a "demo" tape yet, Greenberg downloaded some karaoke tracks from the Internet and asked her to sing along with such classics as "Midnight Train to Georgia" and "(Sittin' on the) Dock of the Bay." "When I first heard her sing, I really couldn't believe that this big, soulful, nuanced, precious, wonderful, knowing voice was coming out of this 14-year-old girl," Greenberg recalled. "I was half-convinced there was a hidden tape recorder somewhere." He immediately signed her to a recording contract with S-Curve.

EDUCATION

Joss attended the Uffculme Comprehensive School near Cullumpton, England. She struggled in school because she suffers from a mild form of dyslexia, a condition in which the brain mixes up the order and direction of letters and numbers. "Always, on my school report card, I'd get 'Must try hard-

Stone with her mentor and collaborator, Betty Wright.

er,' or 'Joscelyn has a problem with remembering,'" she noted. Joss sang in the school choir and performed in some student plays. But she found academics so frustrating that she was desperate to quit school, and signing a record deal gave her that opportunity. She ended her education in 2002, at the age of 15, after taking the necessary exams to earn a General Certificate of Secondary Education (GCSE), the equivalent of an American high school diploma.

CAREER HIGHLIGHTS

Working on *The Soul Sessions*

After signing with S-Curve Records, Stone was eager to begin working on an album. She expected to follow the usual process for new artists: write some songs, then put together a band and record them. But Greenberg had another idea. He felt that the best way to showcase Stone's unique voice would be to have her team up with well-known musicians and record some soul classics of the 1970s. "He had the idea of doing an EP [extended play] with these soul legends," Stone recalled. "Then it turned into this whole album thing."

Greenberg sent Stone to Miami, Florida, to work with Betty Wright, a Grammy Award-winning gospel and soul singer and record producer. Like Stone, Wright had launched her singing career during her teen years, and she went on to record a number of hit songs during the 1970s. Wright was pleased to work with the young British singer, whose voice she described as "a gift from heaven." "She's really like an oxymoron—she's young but she's old," Wright said of Stone. "She could go pop but she's definitely soulful. She has a soulful base." Wright became a mentor to Stone and pushed her to develop her talents. "She has a pair of drumsticks that she carries around with her—all the time," Stone noted. "So every time I'd do something wrong, she'd get her sticks out and threaten me with them. It's really funny. She's crazy like that."

Wright used her connections in the music industry to assemble a top-notch band for Stone's album. It featured legendary soul musicians from the 1960s and 1970s, like guitarist Willie "Little Beaver" Hale and pianist Benny Latimore. Wright and Stone then selected vintage soul and R&B songs that had enjoyed some success in their time, but had not become top hits, and therefore might seem new to today's audiences. "I didn't write those songs, but I can relate to every one of them," Stone stated. "It's soul music. I have to feel it, in order to sing it with a little bit of soul." Finally, Wright arranged for Stone to perform duets with such well-known artists as Mick Jagger, Donna Summer, Chaka Khan, and Melissa Ethridge.

> *When I first heard her sing, I really couldn't believe that this big, soulful, nuanced, precious, wonderful, knowing voice was coming out of this 14-year-old girl," recalled Steve Greenberg. "I was half-convinced there was a hidden tape recorder somewhere."*

Stone released the result of these efforts, an album of covers entitled *The Soul Sessions,* in 2003. The album featured 70 musicians, yet it was recorded in only four days. "It was weird because they've worked with so many great, great singers," she recalled of the recording sessions. "I kind of walked in, just like this little girl, and started singing. I felt a bit weird about the whole thing because, 'Should I be here?' But it was cool because they made me feel really comfortable."

Executives at S-Curve Records did not expect *The Soul Sessions* to be a major release. They only hoped that its songs would receive some radio airplay in order to generate interest in the other album Stone was working on, which would feature her own songs. To the surprise of many, however, *The Soul Sessions* created a sensation. It sold over two million copies and appeared on *Billboard* magazine's list of the Top 40 albums in the United

States. One of the most popular singles was "Fell in Love with a Boy," a remake of the White Stripes' song "Fell in Love with a Girl." The video for the song debuted on MTV in early 2004, bringing Stone's music to a wider audience.

Releasing *Mind, Body, & Soul*

The success of *The Soul Sessions* brought Stone a great deal of public attention. The 16-year-old was the subject of numerous interviews, and she appeared as a guest on many talk and variety shows, including "The Oprah Winfrey Show" and "The Tonight Show with Jay Leno." For Stone, one of the best things about her newfound fame was getting the opportunity to meet some of her musical inspirations. She enjoyed performing a duet with Smokey Robinson on the "Motown Records 45th Anniversary" television special, for instance, and she was thrilled to sing with Gladys Knight on "VH1 Divas." "To meet, let alone sing, with Gladys," she enthused. "The power and control in that voice! I learnt so much that day, just from being in her presence." Stone also became the opening act for a concert tour by the rock star Sting.

In the meantime, Stone continued working on what she considered her "real debut album," *Mind, Body, & Soul.* Unlike *The Soul Sessions,* which consists exclusively of cover versions of previously recorded songs, Stone wrote or co-wrote 80 percent of the material for this album. As a result, it features a more funky, R&B-inspired sound than her earlier record.

Mind, Body, & Soul was released in September 2004 to rave reviews. Renee Graham of the *Boston Globe* called it "one of the year's best albums" and said that "Stone again proves she has talent to burn and soul to spare." Many reviewers commented on Stone's powerful voice and its ability to convey a range of emotions. *Interview* magazine critic Dimitri Ehrlich said that her voice "can sting like aged bourbon or melt like strap molasses." "She can croon it sad, deep and throaty, belt it out juke-joint style, or get down and funky for the bump and grind crowd," Lorraine Ali added in *Newsweek.* "And most of all, the girl has attitude."

Mind, Body, & Soul debuted at the top of the album charts in the United Kingdom, making Stone the youngest female artist to accomplish this feat. It also reached No. 11 on the *Billboard* album charts in the United States and was certified platinum, meaning that it sold over one million copies. Hit singles from the album included "Right to be Wrong" and "You Had Me." Another song, "Wicked Time," featuring Mick Jagger, appeared on the soundtrack of the 2004 movie *Alfie.*

Riding the success of her two albums, Stone won two British music industry awards in 2005, for Best British Female Artist and Best Urban Act. She was also nominated for three Grammy Awards that year, for Best New Artist, Best Pop Vocal Album, Best Female Pop Vocal Performance. Although Stone did not win a Grammy, she turned in one of the best performances of the televised award special. She teamed with folk singer Melissa Etheridge to sing "Cry Baby/Piece of My Heart," a tribute to the late singer Janis Joplin. Their duet was later released as a single that appeared in *Billboard*'s Top 40.

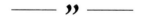

> "*Everyone keeps saying it's surprising that I sing like a 50-year-old black woman. [But] that comment makes no sense to me. Music doesn't look like anything,*" Stone stated. "*People need to get over it. My whole point is, people shouldn't listen with their eyes. . . . Soul comes from everywhere: black, white, pink, purple, it doesn't matter.*"

Showcasing Her Natural Talent

Throughout Stone's rise to stardom, the media has often made mention of the fact that she is not a "typical" soul singer. But Stone rejects this premise. "Everyone keeps saying it's surprising that I sing like a 50-year-old black woman. [But] that comment makes no sense to me. Music doesn't look like anything," she stated. "People need to get over it. My whole point is, people shouldn't listen with their eyes. . . . Soul comes from everywhere: black, white, pink, purple, it doesn't matter."

At the start of her career, Stone considered singing pop songs like so many of her peers. But she soon realized that soul music allowed her to better express her interests and utilize her talent. "Pop music doesn't annoy me, I just don't want to do it," she explained. Stone also differentiates herself from other teenaged singing sensations in her usual attire—she prefers jeans and hoodie sweatshirts to the short skirts and tight tops usually seen

on today's pop stars. Stone's habit of performing in bare feet has generated rumors about her wanting to be "closer to the earth," but she claims that "the real reason is that I don't want to fall over" on stage wearing high-heeled shoes.

Stone has experienced some problems with her vocal cords. After a hectic period of touring in 2004, she developed nodules due to strain. "I do worry my voice is going to stop working one day," she admitted. "I wish certain people would realize that I need time off occasionally and that if I keep on at this pace it could really damage me." Still, Stone remained busy in 2005. She performed at the London Live 8 charity concert, which raised money to help eliminate poverty worldwide. She also opened a series of concerts for the Rolling Stones. Seeking to expand her musical horizons, Stone collaborated with Dave Grohl of the Foo Fighters to write a rock song. She also signed a contract to become the new commercial spokesperson for

The Gap clothing stores, taking the place of actress Sarah Jessica Parker in print and television advertisements.

With her mature music and constant media presence, it seems hard to believe that Stone is still a teenager. "People say I'm an old soul," she acknowledged. "I guess you could say I'm wise beyond my years, but I don't know where the wisdom comes from. I just trust my instincts."

HOME AND FAMILY

Stone, who is single, lives in England. Her mother acts as her manager and travels with her during concert tours, personal appearances, and recording sessions. Stone bought a home of her own near Devon, England, shortly after she turned 18. She has a pet poodle named Dusty Springfield, after the British singer who was known as the "White Lady of Soul" in the 1960s and 1970s. "I'm fully aware that it's kind of Paris Hilton to carry around the little dog," Stone acknowledged. "But man, oh man! She is the cutest thing in the world."

RECORDINGS

The Soul Sessions, 2003
Mind, Body, & Soul, 2004

HONORS AND AWARDS

British Music Awards: 2005, for Best British Female Artist and Best Urban Act

FURTHER READING

Books

Contemporary Musicians, Vol. 52, 2005

Periodicals

Boston Globe, Sep. 28, 2004, p.E1
Daily Telegraph (London), Sep. 18, 2004, p.4
Entertainment Weekly, June 24, 2005, p.108
Interview, Aug. 2004, p.98
Newsweek, Sep. 20, 2004, p.55
Observer (London), Jan. 19, 2004, p.18
People Weekly, Oct. 4, 2004, p.49; Nov. 8, 2004, p.115

Teen People, Dec. 2004, p.52
Times (London), Sep. 4, 2004, p.22
Vogue, Sep. 2004, p.582
YM, Oct. 2004, p.102

Online Articles

http://www.mtv.com/news
    (MTV.com, "You Hear It First: Joss Stone," undated)

Online Databases

Biography Resource Center Online, 2005, article from *Contemporary Musicians,* 2005

Further information for this profile came from an interview with Stone that aired on National Public Radio on September 13, 2003.

ADDRESS

Joss Stone
EMI USA
6255 West Sunset Blvd.
Hollywood, CA 90028

WORLD WIDE WEB SITES

http://www.jossstone.co.uk
http://www.bbc.co.uk/devon/entertainment/music/index.shtml
http://www.bbc.co.uk/devon/entertainment/music/joss_stone/

Hannah Teter 1987-

American Professional Snowboarder
Winner of a Gold Medal in the 2006 Winter Olympics

BIRTH

Hannah Teter was born on January 27, 1987, in Belmont,
Vermont. Belmont is a tiny town with a population of approximately 328 people. Her father, Jeff Teter, is a construction fore-
man for the town of Mount Holly, Vermont. Her mother,
Patricia (Pat) Teter, is an emergency-room nurse and midwife,
a health-care specialist who provides health care for women,
especially during pregnancy and childbirth. Pat also heads the

town's volunteer rescue squad. According to Teter, her parents were hippies and met at a music festival in Colorado.

Hannah is the youngest of five children and the only girl in the family. Jeff and Pat Teter took all of their kids' names from the Bible. Amen is the oldest brother and works as Teter's manager. Abe and Elijah are members of the United States National Snowboard team and compete on the World Cup circuit. Joshua, the youngest brother, was born with a slight mental handicap. He is developmentally delayed and slightly autistic. Of the five Teter children, only Amen was born in a hospital. The other four were born at home.

YOUTH

Before Teter was born, her parents grew watermelons and cantaloupes on a small family farm in Missouri. They did not have much money, but they were happy. But one year, the summer was extremely hot and the family's well ran dry, so they moved to Vermont to start a new life. Jeff Teter described the move as a spiritual quest.

While Teter was growing up, she was always trying to keep up with her older brothers. The Teters are a close-knit family, so her brothers let her tag along. And she was able to keep up with them. Pat Teter recalled, "She was always right behind them. If they wanted to climb a 50-foot tree, she would be right up there with them, even though she was like four years old. I'd hear her yelling from the treetops, 'Mom! Mom! Look at me! I can make the tree go back and forth!'"

When Abe was 12 years old, he really wanted a trampoline. So he made and sold pies in their neighborhood for $5 each, until he earned enough money to buy one. The Teter kids spent a lot of time bouncing on that trampoline. When Hannah was just four years old, her brothers bounced her off the trampoline and onto a car. As Amen described the incident, "If you bounce right before someone else bounces, it makes them bounce three times as high. So little Hannah would be like four years old out there, bouncing, and one time, they double-bounced her. So you have this little four-year-old girl shot like 15 feet in the air off the trampoline and landing on the roof of the car." Even after that, Teter was not afraid to bounce on the trampoline with her brothers.

The Teter children grew up among skiers and snowboarders. Pat Teter worked at Okemo Mountain Resort, so they were able to ride the ski lifts for free. And Belmont is about an hour away from Stratton, which is the home of the U.S. Open Snowboarding Championships. Teter started snowboarding at the age of eight, following in her brothers' footsteps: "I started watching my four brothers, and especially Elijah, who was boarding when I was really young." Her brothers seemed to be having a lot of fun on their snowboards, so she decided to give it a try. "I was just loving watching them ride, and that's why I started," she recalled. "I wanted to have that kind of fun. And at the same time I was learning a ton of stuff from them, and then I began to go in the small contests that they did."

"I started watching my four brothers, and especially Elijah, who was boarding when I was really young," Teter recalled. "I was just loving watching them ride, and that's why I started. I wanted to have that kind of fun. And at the same time I was learning a ton of stuff from them, and then I began to go in the small contests that they did."

EDUCATION

By the time Teter reached high school, she was competing regularly. Her competition schedule required her to travel, sometimes in the middle of the week during the school year. When her public high school told her that she was not allowed to miss more than ten days of school, she decided to transfer to Okemo Mountain School, a snowboard academy in Ludlow, Vermont. At Okemo, students snowboard in the morning and take classes in the afternoon. This school also allowed her to miss class time to compete. Teter graduated from Okemo in 2005.

Teter plans to go to college some day. She would like to go to the University of Hawaii because she thinks Hawaii is "the coolest place ever."

CAREER HIGHLIGHTS

Joining Amateur Competitions

Teter began participating in amateur snowboard competitions in 1998. Before long, she was winning these competitions. In 2001, she won the boardercross event at the United States Ski and Snowboard Association (USSA) National Championships. (The USSA is the governing body for U.S. Olympic skiing and snowboarding.) In a boardercross race, groups of four to six snowboarders race down a giant slalom course that has banked turns, jumps, and other features. The first two or three to finish the course move up to the next round.

Teter competing in the semi-finals of the USSA Snowboarding Grand Prix in California, 2004.

In 2002, Teter won the halfpipe event at the Fédération Internationale de Ski (FIS) Junior World Championships. (The FIS is the governing body for international skiing and snowboarding.) The halfpipe competition is the most popular freestyle event, in which the snowboarders perform tricks in a very large snow trough. Riders glide back and forth across a giant U-shaped tube of snow. They gather speed on the downward slope, then perform high-flying aerial tricks at the top of the upward slope. A team of judges evaluates each rider's amplitude (height above the top of the pipe), smoothness (success in linking tricks together), and degree of difficulty, awarding a numerical score. All competitors make qualifying runs, after which the top scorers advance to the finals. The finals consist of more runs, and the top riders earn spots on the podium.

Moving Up to the Professional Level

Later in 2002, Teter began competing at the professional level. At the time, she was at least five years younger than most of her competitors. During her first season as a professional, she won the halfpipe event at two USSA Grand Prix contests and placed second at a Vans Triple Crown competition. At the U.S. Open Snowboarding Championships that year, she placed third in the superpipe event (a larger halfpipe) and slopestyle event (where a succession of riders goes through a series of obstacles, performing tricks along the way). With these two events, she won the overall title and claimed the prize, a brand new Jeep Wrangler. She didn't even have her driver's license yet. "I was in shock," she recalled. "When I got home that night, I was like, 'Whoa, did I just win a car?'"

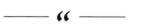

> *When Teter won the U.S. Open Snowboarding Championships and won a brand new Jeep Wrangler, she didn't even have her driver's license yet.* "I was in shock," she recalled. "When I got home that night, I was like, 'Whoa, did I just win a car?'"

When she was just 16 years old, Teter became the first woman to land a frontside 900 in competition. This move involves turning two and a half times on the snowboard while up in the air. She has continued to try new and daring moves on her snowboard.

In 2004, the North American Snowsports Journalist Association awarded Teter the Competitor of the Year Award. This was the first time a snowboarder had won this award. Also that year, she was a finalist for the ESPY Awards for Best Female Action Sport Athlete.

Throughout the 2004 and 2005 seasons, Teter continued to win or place in all of her competitions, including the Winter X Games, the Grand Prix, World Cup competitions, and the Vans Triple Crown. In 2005, Teter was ranked second among American halfpipe snowboarders. In first place was Gretchen Bleiler, a snowboarder and part-time model. Bleiler is five years older than Teter. Both competitors earned spots on the U.S. Olympic team to compete in the 2006 Winter Olympics in Turin, Italy. (For more information on Gretchen Bleiler, see *Biography Today Sports*, Vol. 13.)

First Descent

In 2005, filmmakers Kevin Harrison and Kemp Curley directed a film titled *First Descent: The Story of the Snowboarding Revolution.* As the name implies, the movie is all about the sport of snowboarding. The term "first descent" is actually a snowboarding expression. It is used to describe snowboarding down a mountain that no one else has been down before. The thrill of a first descent is that no one is sure what will happen if they snowboard down that mountain.

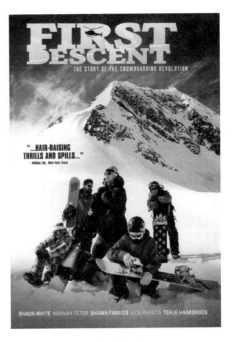

Teter appeared with other top snowboarders in the movie First Descent.

In this nonfiction film, famous snowboarders spend two weeks in Alaska doing what they do best — snowboarding. Between the snowboarding scenes, the movie features profiles of the participating snowboarders, including Teter and fellow 2006 Olympic gold medalist Shaun White. (For more information on Shaun White, see *Biography Today Sports*, Vol. 14.)

The 2006 Winter Olympics

Snowboarding was first introduced as an Olympic sport during the 1998 Winter Olympics in Nagano, Japan. At the time, snowboarding was growing in popularity, particularly among younger enthusiasts. By 2006, the National Sporting Goods Association estimated that the United States had more recreational snowboarders (6.6 million) than skiers (5.9 million).

During the 2006 Winter Olympics, the United States men's and women's teams dominated the snowboarding events. On February 12, Shaun White won the gold medal and Danny Kass won the silver medal for the United States. The women's competition was the next day, and Teter and Bleiler were to compete in the halfpipe.

Teter competing in the halfpipe finals at the 2006 Winter Olympics.

In the halfpipe competition, the snowboard competitors complete two runs, about an hour apart. Only the best run counts. After the first run, Teter was the leader. She did not need to go all out for the second run, but it wasn't her style to hold back. She did even better on the second run, making her the clear gold medal winner. Bleiler won the silver medal.

Before that second run, Teter and Bleiler, who have become good friends, decided to do a couple of practice runs to calm their nerves. The two snuck away and found an area with fresh snow. It turns out that it was a restricted area, but they couldn't resist. According to Teter, "We had about a half hour 'til finals and we went all the way up to the top of the mountain. It was good. We just kind of relaxed on the lifts and soaked up the sun and really just felt good." Bleiler added, "We didn't realize the entire mountain was blocked off. We had to cut under some ropes—sorry, but we did—and we found some powder. So we get some powder in, and we come down, and she got the gold medal and I got a silver medal. Voila. That's snowboarding."

It was always Teter's dream to compete in the Olympics, and her dream came true. With her family there to cheer her on, she gave her best performance and won the gold. Although Teter competed to win, she didn't focus on the outcome. "It's all about fun, because it's just a crazy path I get to lead right now," she said. "I'm focused on the inner self and getting along with everyone. It's about loving one another. It's not about beating people. It's about doing what you like to do."

U.S. snowboarding coach Bud Keene said of Teter, "Hannah has sparked a revolution. At 15, she was going bigger than anyone has ever gone. The others said, 'Whoa, who is this kid?'"

> "
>
> *Teter competes to win, but she doesn't focus on the outcome. "It's all about fun, because it's just a crazy path I get to lead right now," she said. "I'm focused on the inner self and getting along with everyone. It's about loving one another. It's not about beating people. It's about doing what you like to do."*
>
> "

Life after the Olympics

When asked how winning a gold medal would affect her life, Teter said, "I don't think I'm going to change. Maybe I'll smile a little more. Get my teeth whitened. I might actually be able to buy a boat so I can go wakeboarding." Teter is expected to compete in the 2010 Olympics, too. After all the hard work she put into winning the gold medal, she said, "Now I just want to go to the beach and relax. I will see you in Hawaii."

Teter has not had much of a chance to relax. Since winning gold medals, she and White are the most sought after U.S. Olympians. Teter has received frequent requests to make guest appearances on television shows and at special events. For example, she made granola with Martha Stewart on TV; was a guest on the "Late Night with David Letterman" show; and she and Bleiler even got to wave the green flag to signal the start of the Daytona 500, a major stock car race held in Daytona, Florida.

Despite the hectic pace, Teter seemed to be enjoying herself. "It's gotten busier," she said, "Way busier. I've gotten to meet a whole bunch of people and travel to a whole bunch of places. It's been fun. It's been different." She continued, "I went to the Olympics thinking, 'This is cool; it's the biggest event in snowboarding.' Everybody from around the world gets to see you. Doing well, I didn't know the opportunities it brought in. I hadn't thought that far. This is all new and crazy."

Having Fun

"I'm just having fun. That's my main priority — just to keep having fun, keep everything positive. That's when I do my best — when I'm having a good time."

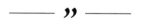

Despite all the publicity, Teter has remained level-headed. She said, "I'm just having fun. That's my main priority — just to keep having fun, keep everything positive. That's when I do my best — when I'm having a good time." According to Amen, Teter's oldest brother and manager, that's the essence of snowboarding. "It's having fun. It's going out with your friends and enjoying yourself. It's actually amazing you can go out and make a career out of it." It's a lifestyle that his sister is enjoying, according to Amen: "I'm definitely biased, but she is just this free-spirited young girl who doesn't have any qualms about saying, 'This is fun.'"

When asked about the key to her success, Teter replied, "There are a lot of combinations of things that have added up to bless me with this lifestyle. It doesn't come easy to be a pro snowboarder. It takes a lot of hard work, time, dedication, love, passion, support, and most of all, it takes failure and learning to better yourself from it."

Teter would like to be a role model for young kids, especially girls, who want to pursue snowboarding as a sport. "I just want to be a positive figure," she claimed. "My dream has always been to be the good role model and just put out good energy and motivation and inspiration for girls who are just like me." When asked what advice she would give to someone who wants to achieve a goal, she replied, "Focus your mindset, know what you want, love what you have, and give it all you've got!"

HOME AND FAMILY

Teter owns a home in South Lake Tahoe, California. Abe and Elijah live there with her, so she spends a lot of time with them. She also spends a lot of time with Amen, who is her manager. "It is the biggest blessing in the world to travel with three of my brothers," she said. "I couldn't ask for more. They help me out when I'm feeling stressed or overwhelmed with things. They cheer me on when I'm about to drop into the pipe in a contest. They just give me a strong sense of comfort so I'm always at peak performance levels." Teter also gets lots of love and support from her parents. She depends on all of them and often talks about "the fam thing."

Religion is a big part of Teter's life. The Teter family home in Vermont is near a Benedictine monastery, and Teter often goes there to meditate. She said, "I go there and kind of forget about everything — my life, my stresses, my world. They are soooo cool, they are soooo fun, and they're just super smart and jolly, you know?" Teter's parents wanted their children to make their own decisions about their faith. "We have our faith, but our mom let us all go in different directions and see what we figured out," Teter said. She described her own beliefs like this: "I'm focused on the inner self. The love — just the people of the world, and trying to get along with everyone. That's kind of what I figured out. It's about lovin' one another."

MAJOR INFLUENCES

Teter has credited her brothers with introducing her to snowboarding. She learned many of her moves by watching them and then came up with her own style. She said of her brothers, "They were my foundation. Then you grow in your own direction. You become your own tree."

Family is very important to Teter, and she talks about them all the time. "Family is the foundation of everything," she said. "This is a family thing. I got my no-fear attitude from my brothers from back when we used to bounce on the trampoline or go to the skate park."

> "I just want to be a positive figure," Teter claimed. "My dream has always been to be the good role model and just put out good energy and motivation and inspiration for girls who are just like me."

HOBBIES AND OTHER INTERESTS

When Teter is not snowboarding, she likes to practice yoga. She also likes to skateboard, hoola hoop, jump off rope swings, and bounce on the trampoline. She used to play soccer, but she had to give that up when she started to focus on snowboarding.

The whole Teter family loves maple syrup. Teter always carries a lucky bottle of syrup with her when she competes. When the Teter kids were growing up, they would make their own syrup. "The family would go in the woods together and collect the sap out of the buckets we hung on the trees," Teter recalled. "Then we would bring it back to the sugar shack in our yard and hang out with my dad while he boiled it down. Once it was done, we'd get a bowl of snow and pour the syrup on it. It's a super-good treat. We still do it every year."

Teter loves syrup so much that she decided to use it as a way to help others. She is selling her family's syrup, which she named Hannah's Gold, to earn money for World Vision, a Christian relief organization that helps children and their communities. "I've always wanted to give back after receiving so much," she said. "Snowboarding has given me the opportunity to make this dream come true. This one-of-a kind Grade A Maple Syrup is being dedicated to the desperately poor children of Africa. Through my partnership with World Vision, this project will be helping those in greatest need."

MOVIES

First Descent: The Story of the Snowboarding Revolution, 2005

HONORS AND AWARDS

Competitor of the Year Award (North American Snowsports Journalist
  Association): 2004
World Snowboard Championship: 2004, Bronze Medal
Olympic Games, Halfpipe Snowboard: 2006, Gold Medal
ESPY Awards: 2006, for Best Women's Action Sports Athlete

FURTHER READING

Periodicals

Boston Globe, Mar. 16, 2006, p.C12
Boston Herald, Feb. 11, 2006, p.O47
Daily Variety, Dec. 2, 2005, p.6
Houston Chronicle, Feb. 14, 2006, p.1
San Francisco Chronicle, Feb. 9, 2006, p.O6
Sports Illustrated, Feb. 27, 2006, p.35
Sports Illustrated for Kids, Feb. 1, 2004, p.56
Time, Feb. 27, 2006, p.60
Time for Kids, Mar. 3, 2006, p.8
Your Magazine, Jan. 2004, p.12

ADDRESS

Hannah Teter
U.S. Ski and Snowboard Association
P.O. Box 100
1500 Kearns Blvd.
Park City, UT 84060-0100

WORLD WIDE WEB SITES

http://usolympicteam.com
http://www.ussnowboarding.com
http://www.vermontel.net/~teter

Brenda Villa 1980-
American Water Polo Player
Two-Time Olympic Medal Winner

BIRTH

Brenda Villa (pronounced VEE-yah) was born on April 18, 1980, in East Los Angeles, California. Her parents, Ines and Rosario Villa, were both apparel workers. Brenda is the middle child in her family with an older brother Edgar, and a younger brother, Uriel.

YOUTH

Shortly before Brenda was born, the Villas immigrated from their native Mexico to Commerce, California — a predominantly Latino neighborhood on the east side of Los Angeles. Throughout her childhood, the Villas lived across the street from the Commerce Aquatorium. This nationally renowned swim center, built in 1961, offered free pool access and swimming lessons to the local community. Over the years, the Commerce Aquatorium produced a number of Olympic swimmers. In the early 1970s the center started hosting water polo leagues.

The sport of water polo got its start in England during the 19th century. It is most similar to the British sport of rugby, except that it is played in the water. A game of water polo is divided into four periods of seven minutes each, but periods often last longer due to penalties and time-outs, so an average game lasts around 45 minutes. Water polo teams consist of seven players, including a goalkeeper. Each team tries to score goals by throwing the ball into the opponent's net. A team can only control the ball for a maximum of 35 seconds at a time, however, before it either scores a goal or turns over possession to the other team.

Water polo is a physically demanding sport. In addition to swimming back and forth across the pool, players must be able to throw a ball while remaining afloat and fending off opposing players. Games of water polo often involve rough play, with grabbing, kicking, scratching, and punching taking place between competitors. Penalties are handled like those in ice hockey, with the offending player sent to a penalty area for a certain amount of time, and the opposition allowed to continue with a player advantage.

By the mid-1980s, the Commerce Aquatorium had achieved recognition as one of the top water polo training grounds in the United States. Brenda first became interested in the sport at age six, when her brother Edgar joined a local boys' team. As soon as she saw her brother play, Brenda starting begging her mother to let her play, too. But Rosario Villa could not swim, and she feared for her little daughter's safety in a pool full of thrashing swimmers. After two years of hearing Brenda ask to try water polo, though, her mother finally gave in.

Since there were no girls' water polo teams at that time, Brenda joined a boys' team. Playing with the boys helped her become aggressive and mentally tough. "You have to anticipate more because the boys are quicker and stronger," she explained. "I mean, you could see there was a disadvantage when I was guarding a guy that was six-foot-two and 200 pounds and could, like, bench-press me. So I figured out how to take any advantage they had and equalize it or take it away from them."

Despite her obvious talent for the sport, Brenda endured both verbal and physical harassment as a girl playing on boys' teams. "I hear comments like, 'Why are you playing a man's sport?'" she acknowledged. "But I don't get mad. Instead of getting into arguments or fights with boys, you score goals on them." From the beginning of her water polo career, the one boy Brenda wanted to impress was her older brother. "He's not one to give out compliments," she noted. "Whenever I did something, I wanted his approval. It was a way to motivate myself."

EDUCATION

Brenda attended Bell Gardens High School in Los Angeles. She played on the boys' water polo team because the school did not have a girls' team. During her freshman season in 1995, Brenda was her team's third-leading scorer with 44 goals. As a sophomore she scored 57 goals to help Bell Gardens win the California Division III High School Championship. Her brother Edgar, who was a senior that year, was named the Division III Player of the Year and went on to play water polo at Citrus College.

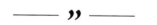

> "I hear comments like, 'Why are you playing a man's sport?'" Villa acknowledged. "But I don't get mad. Instead of getting into arguments or fights with boys, you score goals on them."

As a junior in 1997 Brenda scored 48 goals to lead her high school team to a second consecutive state championship. During her senior year, *Water Polo* magazine named her as the top young female player in the world. Villa also made the All-California Interscholastic Federation Team three times during her high school career. By the time she graduated with honors in 1998, Villa was widely viewed as the top female water polo recruit in the country.

After considering a number of offers, Villa accepted an athletic scholarship to Stanford University. She decided to "red-shirt" the 1999 and 2000 collegiate seasons, meaning that she could practice with the team but not compete. She made this decision in order retain her college eligibility while also training for the 2000 Olympic Games. "When I was 17 [water polo] was announced as an Olympic sport," she recalled. "I could actually say that I was training for something." Villa started playing women's water polo for Stanford in 2001, and she remained the top player on the Cardinal team for the next two seasons. She graduated from Stanford with a bachelor's degree in political science in 2003.

Villa's strong swimming skills help her with underwater plays.

CAREER HIGHLIGHTS

Earning a Silver Medal at the 2000 Olympics

When she was just 16 years old, Villa became a member of the U.S. National Women's Water Polo Team — which represents the country in international competitions like the Olympic Games. She was the first Hispanic woman ever to make the team. Villa played the position of "driver," which is an offensive position that involves passing or shooting the ball from the sides of the pool. Although she was shorter and stockier than most high-level water polo players, she was very well-rounded. "You look at her and you'd never think she's an Olympic athlete," U.S. Olympic Water Polo Coach Guy Baker acknowledged. "Brenda's one of our best swimmers, and she has tremendous endurance. She can go and go. The truth is, Brenda's just an athletic marvel." Villa particularly excelled as a playmaker — creating scoring chances for her team by either distributing the ball to open teammates or driving toward the goal herself.

For most of her high school years, Villa traveled to San Diego once a month for a three-day training camp with the national team. She also played in a number of major international competitions. She was the leading scorer on the U.S. team at the 1996 Women's World Cup, for instance, and she was the only high school player on the American team that competed in the 1998 Women's Water Polo World Championships.

After graduating from high school, Villa delayed the start of her college water polo career in order to concentrate on preparing for the 2000 Olympic Games in Sydney, Australia. The Sydney Games marked the debut of women's water polo as an Olympic sport. Men's water polo had been contested in the Olympics for more than a century, but the women's game was added only after many protests and a threatened lawsuit. Despite her youth, Villa played a critical role in earning the U.S. team a spot in the Olympic tournament, scoring the game-winning goal against Hungary in a "do or die" qualification game.

———— **"** ————

"You look at her and you'd never think she's an Olympic athlete," acknowledged U.S. Olympic Water Polo Coach Guy Baker. *"Brenda's one of our best swimmers, and she has tremendous endurance. She can go and go. The truth is, Brenda's just an athletic marvel."*

———— **"** ————

In Sydney, the U.S. team made it through a tough pool to advance to the gold-medal match against the top-ranked Australian team. Villa scored the first goal of the game, but the Aussies came roaring back. With the American team trailing 3-2 near the end of the game, Villa scored the tying goal with 13.1 seconds left in the fourth period. It looked like the two teams would go to overtime, but then the referee called a controversial penalty on Villa. Australia, with a player advantage, ended up scoring the game-winning goal with just 1.3 seconds left on the clock. Australia thus captured the first-ever gold medal awarded in women's water polo, and Villa and her teammates were forced to settle for silver.

Playing College Water Polo at Stanford University

After sitting out for two seasons, Villa finally began playing water polo for Stanford in 2001. She immediately proved to be worth the wait. Villa scored 69 goals that year to help lead her team to a 27-1 record. She scored in 25 games, and she scored two or more goals in 22 games, including a season-high six goals against the University of Southern California (USC).

While attending Stanford University, Villa led her team to three consecutive NCAA championships.

Stanford advanced to the NCAA championship, where Villa's two goals were not quite enough to lift her team to victory. Stanford lost a heart-breaker to the University of California-Los Angeles (UCLA) by a score of 5-4. Villa won the prestigious NCAA Division I Player of the Year Award from the American Water Polo Coaches Association. She was also named a First Team All-American and Stanford's Female Athlete of the Year.

In 2002 Stanford had a perfect season, posting a 25-0 record and defeating UCLA for the national title. Villa led her team with 60 goals on the year, including five during the NCAA tournament. She was named NCAA Player of the Year and a First Team All-American for the second consecutive year. In addition, the Stanford Athletic Board honored her with the Block "S" Outstanding Female Sophomore Award. Finally, Villa received the Pete J. Cutino Award, which is presented annually to the top collegiate female water polo player in the nation by the Olympic Club.

In 2003 Stanford posted a 20-2 record and reached the national championship game for a third consecutive year. Once again, the Cardinal faced UCLA and lost a heartbreaker, 4-3. Villa scored 43 goals on the year to bring her career total to 172, which made her Stanford's all-time second-leading scorer. She earned NCAA Player of the Year and First Team All-American honors for the third straight year.

Stanford Coach John Tanner provided his views on why Villa was such a dominant collegiate player. "She has always had this incredible sense of the game, an almost unreal ability to anticipate what's going to happen," he explained. "She puts herself in a position where the ball can find her. She's able to see the game from a low angle in the water and she also seems to have a feel for what's going on as if she were standing above the play. That's extremely rare, a real gift. She has perspective to the point where it looks as if she was born to play water polo."

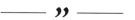

> "[She has] an almost unreal ability to anticipate what's going to happen," explained coach John Tanner. "She puts herself in a position where the ball can find her. She's able to see the game from a low angle in the water and she also seems to have a feel for what's going on as if she were standing above the play. That's extremely rare, a real gift. She has perspective to the point where it looks as if she was born to play water polo."

Winning a Bronze Medal at the 2004 Olympics

Throughout her college water polo career, Villa continued playing internationally with the U.S. National Women's Water Polo Team. Shortly after competing in the 2001 NCAA Championships, for instance, Villa traveled to Greece, where she helped the U.S. team win the Thetis Cup tournament. She also played with the national team at the 2001 World Championships in Fukuoka, Japan, where the team placed fourth.

In 2002, during her college off-season, Villa helped lead the U.S. National Team to the Women's World Cup championship in Perth, Australia. The following year, she scored 13 goals to lead the American team to victory at the 2003 World Championships in Barcelona, Spain. Villa and her teammates became the first non-European team ever to be crowned world champions in women's water polo.

The U.S. team's successful showing created high expectations for the 2004 Olympic Games in Athens, Greece. The highly regarded Americans had seven returning players from the silver-medal team of 2000. But they ended up playing in a tough bracket, which included the Eastern European powers Russia and Hungary. The U.S. team still managed to advance to the semifinals, where they suffered a heartbreaking loss to Italy, 6-5. The

Villa with her 2004 Olympic teammates, proudly displaying their medals.

Americans had held a 4-2 advantage at one point, and Italy scored the winning goal with just two seconds left in the game.

The semifinal loss cost the American team a chance to play for the gold medal. (Italy went on to win the gold medal over Greece.) Instead, the U.S. team faced Australia to determine who would go home with the bronze. "We left Sydney with bittersweet memories [in 2000]," Villa recalled. "We didn't want to go from [Athens] without anything." The determined Americans came out strong and took a 4-0 lead after two periods, but the Aussies rallied to tie the score with just over five minutes remaining in the game. Luckily, Ellen Estes of the United States scored the game winner with 2:20 left to give her team the bronze. "We wanted to be on that podium," Villa said afterward. "We wanted gold, but at least we were on the podium getting something."

Villa was the leading scorer for the American team during the Olympic tournament, and she was named to the Olympic All-Star team. Coach Guy Baker praised Villa's contributions in Athens, describing her as the "quarterback" of the U.S. team. "Over the last six months, she's [been] one of the better players in the world," he stated. "She's stronger, she swims better and faster. Her vision's great and she creates opportunities." Villa agreed that her role had expanded since her first Olympic experience. "I'm probably better-rounded," she noted. "I kind of have a leadership role in the water. I sort of do whatever I see needs doing. I try to communicate a lot." While she was not the official team captain, Villa emerged as its vocal leader. "She's our voice. She's the energy," said Baker. "And that's great. We feed off that."

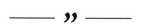

> "How many [young people] have had the opportunity to have traveled all over the world like I have?" Villa said. "The friendships I've built through playing the sport have been tremendous. What I like most about playing water polo is its tremendous competitiveness and also the camaraderie you have with your teammates."

Promoting Her Sport

Since the 2004 Olympics, Villa has divided her time between the U.S. National Team and Club Orizante in Catania, Italy. In her spare time, she returns to the Commerce Aquatorium, where she helps younger players develop their skills. Her younger brother, Uriel, is the latest member of the family to take up the sport of water polo at the facility. Villa is not sure yet whether she will try to compete in the 2008 Olympic Games in Beijing, China. She is considering going back to college for a graduate degree in public policy. "I'd like to go into some aspect of politics," she explained. "Not run for office or anything like that. But be one of those behind-the-scene people."

In 2005 *USA Today* listed Villa among its top Latina athletic role models, along with Olympic softball player Lisa Fernandez and professional golfer Lorena Ochoa. Given the small number of Hispanic players involved in water polo, Villa feels a responsibility to set an example. "I feel like water polo is a pretty expensive sport — it's not as accessible to train for as soccer or other Latin sports," she stated. "So I try to give back as much as they've given me."

Villa says that she will always appreciate the opportunities that water polo gave her. "How many [young people] have had the opportunity to have traveled all over the world like I have?" she said. "The friendships I've built through playing the sport have been tremendous. What I like most about playing water polo is its tremendous competitiveness and also the camaraderie you have with your teammates." She hopes to influence young people to take up the sport as well. "I want little girls to grow up saying, 'I want to be a water polo player,' she stated. "This sport has been so good to me, I feel I should return the favor."

HOME AND FAMILY

Villa is single and lives in a studio apartment in Long Beach, California. She returns to Commerce often to visit family and friends.

HOBBIES AND OTHER INTERESTS

In her "down time," Villa likes to relax by watching sports and reality shows on television. She also enjoys reading mystery novels.

HONORS AND AWARDS

Best Young Female Player in the World (*Water Polo*): 1998
Olympic Women's Water Polo: 2000, silver medal; 2004, bronze medal
NCAA Division I Player of the Year (American Water Polo Coaches
    Association): 2001, 2002, 2003
NCAA Women's Water Polo First Team All-American: 2001, 2002, 2003
Pete J. Cutino Award (Olympic Club): 2002
NCAA Women's Water Polo National Championship: 2002, with Stanford
    University Cardinal
Women's Water Polo World Cup: 2002
Women's Water Polo World Championship: 2003

FURTHER READING

Books

Menard, Valerie. *Latinos at Work: Careers in Sports,* 2002

Periodicals

Boston Globe, Aug. 27, 2004, p.E3
Charlotte Observer, Aug. 27, 2004, p.C7
Long Beach Press-Telegram, Dec. 3, 2003
Los Angeles Magazine, June 1, 2004, p.48
Los Angeles Times, Oct. 16, 1994, p.25; Sep. 25, 1997, p.10
New York Times, Aug. 25, 2004, p.D5
Oakland Tribune, Aug. 16, 2004
San Francisco Chronicle, May 7, 2003, p.C2
USA Today, June 23, 2004, p.C7; Mar. 29, 2005, p.C4

Online Articles

http://www.stanfordalumni.org
   (*Stanford Magazine*, "Seniors Enter International Waters," July-Aug. 2003)

ADDRESS

Brenda Villa
U.S. National Women's Water Polo Team
11360 Valley Forge
Los Alamitos, CA 90720

WORLD WIDE WEB SITES

http://gostanford.collegesports.com
http://www.usawaterpolo.org

Tyler James Williams 1992-

American Actor
Star of the Hit Television Show "Everybody
Hates Chris"

EARLY YEARS

Tyler James Williams was born on October 9, 1992, in New
York, New York. His father, Le'Roy Williams, is a sergeant for
the New York City Police Department. His mother, Angela
Williams, is a Christian singer, songwriter, and founder of Little
Light Publishing Company. Tyler is the oldest of three boys. His
younger brothers, Tyrel and Tylen, are also actors.

Williams has been acting practically his entire life. He began acting when he was only four years old. "I never decided to become an actor," he said. "It just came to me. I just performed for my mother, doing impersonations of people when I was little. People were impressed with what they saw me doing, and we contacted an agent and that was that."

Starting at age four, Williams began acting on "Sesame Street," the educational children's television show that has been on the air since 1969. "Sesame Street" uses short, fast-paced segments to teach preschool-aged children beginning number and reading skills. The show includes both people and muppets, the beloved puppets created by Jim Henson, including Big Bird, Cookie Monster, Elmo, and Kermit the Frog. Williams made regular appearances on "Sesame Street" between 1996 and 2002.

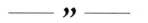

> "I never decided to become an actor," Williams said. "It just came to me. I just performed for my mother, doing impersonations of people when I was little. People were impressed with what they saw me doing, and we contacted an agent and that was that."

In 1999, Williams joined the cast of "Little Bill," an animated television series that aired on Nickelodeon. The show was created by comedian and actor Bill Cosby for preschool-aged children. Williams provided the voice for the character Bobby.

Williams appeared in several television commercials and print advertisements for such products as Fruit by the Foot (a chewy fruit snack) and Corvette (a high performance sports car). He also performed several times on NBC's popular late-night, comedy-variety show, "Saturday Night Live." His parts on "Saturday Night Live" were relatively small, so he spent a lot of time waiting on the set. But while he was waiting, he watched the other actors practicing their parts. "I got to watch them try and make scenes funnier, and how they worked on their timing," he confided. "That kind of helped me when I auditioned for 'Everybody Hates Chris.'"

MAJOR ACCOMPLISHMENTS

Auditioning for a New Show

In 2005, comedian and actor Chris Rock and his business partner Ali LeRoi had an idea for a show. They wanted to create a comedy series that chronicled Rock's life as a black teenager attending a mostly white school. When

Williams appearing with comedian Chris Rock, co-creator and executive producer of "Everybody Hates Chris."

Rock was 13 years old, his family had moved from a housing project to an apartment in the Bedford-Stuyvesant neighborhood in Brooklyn, New York. Bed-Stuy, as it's known, is a predominantly African-American community. His parents wanted him to get a good education, and they decided to send Rock to a junior high school that was three bus routes away from their home.

Rock and LeRoi decided to call the show "Everybody Hates Chris" and held auditions in California. According to LeRoi, "We started looking for someone in L.A., and what we found was that we were encountering the usual suspects. They're Hollywood kids who have been in the business for a few years. We were looking for someone who was a little raw and a little edgier. And we got [an audition] tape from New York with this kid on it." The kid on that tape was Williams. Rock and LeRoi knew right away that Williams was the right person to play the main character. LeRoi said, "The thing that sold us was his face. He has an incredibly expressive face, and it's older than his years. . . . At this particular point, there's no Hollywood in him."

Williams flew to Los Angeles for two more auditions and was given the part. Rock and LeRoi were very pleased with his performances. According to Rock, "He was the funniest kid we could find after thousands of auditions. Let me tell you, after doing all those auditions, there are lots of un-funny kids out there who need to work on their comedy."

When Williams read the script for "Everybody Hates Chris," he thought it was a good fit for him. He felt that he connected with the character. One thing that he did not like about the script was that some of his lines included swear words and crude language. "I told them up front I wasn't going to say any of those words," he recalled. When he was reading his lines, Williams looked at how the word was used. "If it is appropriate, if it can help the character or help someone else, I'll use it," he said. "Or I try to come up with a word that is just as funny." His mom, Angela, was proud of her son. "Every time he went in and auditioned, he substituted the word," she commented. "We're Christians, and there are certain things we just don't do." Rock did not pressure Williams to use those words, but he did ask him to think about it. But Angela said that her son still did not curse. "He nailed the script," she said. "He did what he was supposed to do, but he stayed true to who he was. I was just really so proud of him."

> "Kids like Tyler come around only once in a generation," Chris Rock said. "I thank God every day for this little kid being on our show because some kids have it, some kids don't. It's not about being a little adult; it's about being a kid portraying a kid, and I think that America gets it when he does it."

"Everybody Hates Chris"

"Everybody Hates Chris" debuted in September 2005 on UPN (now part of the new CW network). For the first episode, almost eight million viewers tuned in—the highest number of viewers for any show on UPN. Williams played the part of the young Chris Rock perfectly, and the show has continued to do well in the TV ratings.

Set in 1982, "Everybody Loves Chris" is narrated by Chris Rock. Williams's television father is played by former National Football League (NFL) player Terry Crews; his mother is played by actress Tichina Arnold. Like Rock's own parents, the parents on the show are loving and supportive, and they want the best for their children. Money is tight for the family, but they manage to make it work.

Williams's character faces many obstacles in school, as one of the few African-American students there. The show presents some of the difficul-

ties Rock faced in real life in a humorous light. As Rock later admitted, "I went through all this stuff. It wasn't funny at the time, but tragedy plus time equals comedy, as they say. I'm over it. Hey, I won. That's how I look at it."

"Everybody Hates Chris" does not focus only on Rock's school experiences. It is a family show, and much of the show is about his family life — his relationship with his parents and his siblings. Many have called it a refreshing look at life for a stable American family. "I just wanted to show a normal happy family," Rock explained. "There aren't a lot of poor people on TV, and it's kind of interesting to see a poor family trying to make it."

Rock is often on the set during filming of the show, and he has had great things to say about working with Williams. "Kids like Tyler come around only once in a generation. I thank God every day for this little kid being on our show because some kids have it, some kids don't. . . . It's not about being a little adult; it's about being a kid portraying a kid, and I think that America gets it when he does it."

Williams is equally eager to praise Rock. "It's fun working with him," he said. "He gives us jokes to come up with for the show, and we get to ad-lib sometimes." Williams respects Rock as an actor, comedian, and family man. He said that Rock is "an awesome comedian. He's also a husband and a daddy. One time we were doing an interview together and Chris stopped it because his little girl called. I think that was the best thing in the world."

Recent Activities

As "Everybody Hates Chris" grew in popularity, Williams began to get offers for other television shows and movies. He has made guest appear-

425

ances on many popular talk shows, including "The Oprah Winfrey Show." He also had minor roles in two recent movies. He had a small part in *Two for the Money* (2005), an adult movie about sports, gambling, and crime. He had another small part, a voiceover role, in *The Ant Bully* (2006), an animated kids' movie about a boy who tortures some ants by destroying their colony with a watergun and then is reduced to their size. Even with his busy TV schedule, Williams would still consider additional movie roles, especially when "Everybody Hates Chris" has a break in its production schedule. "Offers are coming in, and there might be an acting job during the hiatus," he said.

Sometimes Williams misses New York. "I miss some of my friends, but other friends, I can do without 'em a little bit," he admitted. "Besides, I'm sort of too busy to really spend much time thinking about that part of my life."

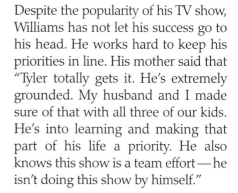

Despite the popularity of his TV show, Williams has not let his success go to his head. He works hard to keep his priorities in line. His mother said that "Tyler totally gets it. He's extremely grounded. My husband and I made sure of that with all three of our kids. He's into learning and making that part of his life a priority. He also knows this show is a team effort — he isn't doing this show by himself."

Education

Williams's parents have always stressed the importance of education. However, because Williams spends so much of his time filming "Everybody Hates Chris," he does not attend a regular school. He and the other child actors on the show have a tutor on the set. They attend classes five days a week for three hours each of those days. His favorite subjects are science and history. His least favorite subject is English. He said, "Diagramming sentences gives me a headache."

According to American child-labor laws, children cannot work more than nine-and-a-half hours a day, and three of those hours must be spent doing school work. This makes it hard for the producers of "Everybody Hates Chris." They have to come up with creative ways to minimize each child's time in front of the camera. One way around this is to minimize the number of scenes in which all of them are together. That way they can stagger the filming time. However, since Williams is the main character and needs to be present in most of the scenes, it's a challenge. It's been difficult to limit his work time, but they have managed to work it out.

HOME AND FAMILY

Williams lives with his parents, brothers, and their silky terrier named Benny "Ruff-neck" Williams. Their family home is in New York. But because "Everybody Hates Chris" is filmed in California, Williams, his brothers, and their mother spend most of their time in Los Angeles. Williams's father has stayed behind in New York because of his job. He has been with the New York Police Department for over 18 years. Williams admires his dad. "He's a sergeant, and he works out of a precinct. I'm pretty proud of him." The family flies back and forth a lot to spend time together.

Williams with his parents, Le'Roy and Angela Williams, at the 2006 NAACP Image Awards.

Sometimes Williams misses New York. "I miss some of my friends, but other friends, I can do without 'em a little bit," he admitted. "Besides, I'm sort of too busy to really spend much time thinking about that part of my life."

HOBBIES AND OTHER INTERESTS

Williams loves to watch basketball. His favorite professional basketball team is the Miami Heat. He also used to like playing football. He said. "But I can't do that much anymore. It's in my contract—so I won't get hurt."

SELECTED CREDITS

Television Series

"Sesame Street," 1996-2002
"Little Bill," 1999
"Everybody Hates Chris," 2005-

Movies

Two for the Money, 2005
The Ant Bully, 2006

FURTHER READING

Books

Contemporary Theatre, Film, and Television, Vol. 68, 2006

Periodicals

Bergen County (NJ) Record, July 31, 2005, p.E1
Ebony, Jan. 2006, p.26; Mar. 2006, p.123
Jet, Oct. 10, 2005, p.60
Parade Magazine, Feb. 12, 2006, p.20
People, Oct, 17, 2005, p.134
TelevisionWeek, June 27, 2005, p.11

Online Articles

http://www.hollywoodreporter.com
   (*TheHollywoodReporter.com,* "Laugh Track," Nov. 16, 2005)

Online Databases

Biography Resource Center Online, 2006, article from *Contemporary Theatre, Film, and Television,* 2006

ADDRESS

Tyler James Williams
CW Television Network
3300 W. Olive Ave.
Burbank, CA 91505

WORLD WIDE WEB SITES

http://tylerjameswilliams.com
http://www.cwtv.com

Gretchen Wilson 1973-

American Country Music Singer and Songwriter
Creator of the Hit CDs *Here for the Party* and
All Jacked Up

BIRTH

Gretchen Wilson was born on June 26, 1973, in Granite City,
Illinois. Her mother, Christine Heuer, was only 16 years old at
the time of Gretchen's birth. Her father, who left the family
when Gretchen was two years old, was a traveling musician.
Divorced twice by age 20, Christine Heuer supported her family by working as a bartender. Gretchen has a younger brother,
Josh, who sells souvenirs at her concerts.

YOUTH

Wilson spent most of her childhood constantly moving from one rented mobile home to another in rural Bond County, Illinois, about 40 miles east of St. Louis, Missouri. Her family crisscrossed the county's cornfields and pig farms, living in a string of trailer parks on the outskirts of numerous small towns. "We couldn't make the rent, so we'd move," Wilson explained. She mainly grew up in the area around Pocahontas, Illinois (population about 800), which she has described as "the kind of place where everybody knows everybody's business. It's the kind of place you can't get away with anything."

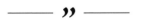

"I thought everybody was redneck when I was a kid,"
Wilson explained.
"I thought everybody had a single mom who worked two jobs and had peanut butter and jelly three nights a week for supper."

Wilson began singing at an early age. She performed regularly at family gatherings and even entertained shoppers at a local Kmart store. She has said that her singing talent comes from her father, whom she has not publicly named. "His family," she recalled, "had a little traveling band. I think it was a gospel band." Wilson has no early memories of her father, who left when she was two years old. She met him for the first time at age 12. "I think he felt he'd done the wrong thing," she has said of their time spent apart. "I think he felt my mom would do better without him, so he stepped back." Wilson has forgiven her father for his absence from her childhood, and the two are now friends. "I've been pretty understanding," she explained, "knowing they were both kids [when I was born]. I don't hold a grudge against him."

Meanwhile, Wilson's mother, Christine Heuer, juggled bartending jobs and raised her two children alone. "I thought everybody was redneck when I was a kid," Wilson explained. "I thought everybody had a single mom who worked two jobs and had peanut butter and jelly three nights a week for supper." Because of her mother's busy schedule, Gretchen usually took care of her brother, Josh. Commenting on her relationship with her mother, Wilson remarked, "There was tension between me and my mom because we were so close in age. We were almost like sisters. By about 12, I felt like the grownup in the house."

In times of stress, Wilson drew comfort from listening to music. She recalled that as a young girl, "music sometimes felt like it was the only thing that kept me going when things got incredibly tough." She has expressed the hope that her music can help others, as the music of Patsy Cline and Loretta Lynn helped her as an adolescent. "When I was a kid, I'd sit there with my headphones on crying my eyes out to sad songs [I'd] taped off the radio. Somehow it made me feel better to know that someone else had the same kind of heartbreak I had," Wilson stated. "I remember listening to [Patsy Cline] when I was 12 and how she made me understand what heartache felt in a way I don't think many 12-year-olds can even begin to feel. She was the one who made me want to sing." George Jones and Merle Haggard were two other favorites, along with several hard rock bands, especially AC/DC and .38 Special.

EDUCATION

Because her family moved so often, Wilson attended about 20 different schools. She dropped out of school after the eighth grade and went to work with her mother in a bar. "When you're a kid, you think you know it all," she said. "I thought, 'Why do I need a high-school diploma?' I figured I was going to be a singer." She added, "Looking back, it was a stupid way to think." Wilson has expressed regret about dropping out of school and has talked about returning to school for a GED, a certificate of high school equivalency. Despite her lack of formal education, Wilson is considered an intelligent and skillful businesswoman. As her road manager David Haskell commented in the *Los Angeles Times*, "Gretchen may only have an eighth-grade education, but she's got a PhD in street smarts."

FIRST JOBS

At age 14, Wilson started working at a tavern known locally as "Big O's" in Pierron, five miles outside Pocahontas. She cooked while her mother tended bar. "This place was mostly friends and family—it was like daycare," Wilson remarked. "I don't think anybody thought I was in danger there. My mom was there, and everybody knew everybody. If anybody caused any trouble, we'd just call his wife and have him dragged out of there. It was always a big family of people."

The owner of the bar, Mark "Big O" Obermark, agreed to let Wilson sing for tips. She usually sang along to tape recordings of her favorite country singers, Loretta Lynn and Patsy Cline. She'd leave a jar out for the bar patrons to fill with tips. "I started out with nine songs, and I'd sing them over and over again all night. I was playing to happy-hour, middle-aged crowds, and they thought I was cute. Before it was over with, I was booking four nights a week for $125 a night."

Within a year, Wilson was promoted to bar manager, an illegal but not un-common practice in rural areas. Since her new job sometimes required her to kick out unruly patrons, she had to be prepared, if necessary, to use the loaded, 12-gauge shotgun that hung in the bar. When she turned 16, she rented a microphone, amplifier, and tape player from a nearby music store and took her singing act to neighboring bars. Wilson performed karaoke-style at local bars while living with her uncle, Vernon "Verne" Heuer, who introduced her to the southern-rock groups Lynyrd Skynyrd and the Charlie Daniels Band. By the age of 20, Wilson was singing with two local bands, Sam A. Lama & the Ding Dongs, which covered songs of the "golden oldies" era, and Midnight Flyer, which often performed in suburban St. Louis. She also learned to play drums and electric, acoustic, and rhythm guitar. Wilson soon landed a gig fronting the rock-'n'-roll cover band Baywolfe, which became one of the busiest rock groups in the St. Louis region during the mid-1990s.

> "
>
> *"I certainly think Nashville had this mold that everybody was supposed to fit into. . . . When I was getting a deal, everybody wanted [the women] to be Shania Twain and Faith Hill. And I definitely didn't fit into that mold."*
>
> "

CAREER HIGHLIGHTS

In 1996, Wilson moved to Nashville, Tennessee, the country music capital of the United States. She had $500 in her pocket and big hopes of signing a contract with a major recording company. For the next several years, she auditioned her singing talent for many recording executives, who politely rejected her for a variety of reasons. "They thought my hair was too dated, that I was too heavy, too old," she recalled. Others responded to her audition with the comment, "I'm sorry, but that's just too country," after which Wilson wondered, "How can you be too country for country?" As she later said, "I certainly think Nashville had this mold that everybody was supposed to fit into. . . . When I was getting a deal, everybody wanted [the women] to be Shania Twain and Faith Hill. And I definitely didn't fit into that mold."

In the meantime, Wilson found work as a cocktail waitress and bartender. She continued to work after she and her steady boyfriend, Mike Penner, had a baby daughter, Grace. With no record deal in sight, she considered putting aside her dream of a big singing career. "I always said if I didn't have a deal by 30, I would quit," she has claimed.

Wilson with Big Kenny and John Rich, who helped her get started in the music business in Nashville.

Connecting with MuzikMafia

In 1998, Wilson began singing on a regular basis with the house band at a blues club where she was working. During one of her performances the following year, Wilson impressed John Rich and "Big" Kenny Alphin, better known now as the duo Big & Rich. According to one account, Rich asked Big Kenny, "Was that as good as I thought it was? Did I just hear that?" "I think so," his friend replied. After she finished singing, Rich tried to talk to her, but she thought he was just looking for a date. "John followed me up to my little cubby hole upstairs with his trench coat and cowboy hat, and I think his exact words were, 'Hey, how come you ain't got a record deal yet?'" Wilson wasn't overwhelmed. "I looked at him in disgust [and] threw him a business card and a little homemade demo and said, 'I'm busy. I'm working right now.'"

Rich began telephoning Wilson repeatedly, but she didn't trust him, and she refused to return his calls. She eventually changed her mind and accepted his offer to join the MuzikMafia network, an informal group of musicians, singers, songwriters, and artists who showcased their talents in a Nashville bar each week. These artists rejected the cookie-cutter approach to musical talent so prevalent in Nashville's recording industry. Rich introduced Wilson to his friends in the local songwriting community, who helped her polish her style and develop some experience. Through these contacts, she began recording "demo" tapes—recordings of other songwriters' music and lyrics that are used to sell a song to a particular performer. She finally had enough material to audition in what's called a "showcase" for the record company executives.

But Rich also encouraged Wilson to try writing her own songs. One night, they were watching country music videos featuring glamorous female singers. Wilson told Rich how much she disliked their diva image, declaring "I guess I'm a redneck woman." Her comment inspired him to jot down some lyrics. In less than an hour, Rich and Wilson wrote what would become her hit single "Redneck Woman."

In 2003, Wilson auditioned "Redneck Woman" for John Grady, the new president of Sony Music Nashville. Before she performed the song, according to Wilson, "[I decided] not to be who they wanted me to be, but to be who I am, like it or not. Before, I was trying to be polite. I was trying to sing songs I thought they'd like, and I was a little concerned about that. But it comes down to confidence, who you are as an artist." Grady immediately sensed the song's hit potential and signed Wilson to a recording contract. He was equally impressed by her stage presence, acknowledging that "it was the first time I was physically [moved] by a singer in a long time." Sony decided to release "Redneck Woman" as a single in early spring 2004. To express their pride in Wilson, the MuzikMafia named her the first Godmother of the Mafia in 2005.

"Redneck Woman"

With the release of "Redneck Woman," Wilson became the music success story of 2004. Anchored by its "Hell, yeah" refrain, the song became a rallying cry for the "redneck" way of life. "Redneck" has often been used as an insult to describe poor, ignorant country people. But Wilson turned that around and used it in a positive way. "To me, being a redneck woman means being a strong woman," she said. "It's about holding your head up no matter what is happening. I know the term used to have other meanings, but to me it's just another way of saying country." Her lyrics celebrated living an ordinary life, shopping for sale items at Wal-Mart and drinking beer instead of champagne: "I'm a redneck woman / I ain't no high class broad / I'm just a product of my raising / I say hey y'all and yee-haw / And I keep my Christmas lights on / On my front porch all year long / And I know all the words to every Charlie Daniels song."

Wilson's song also started a musical movement in Nashville by mixing traditional country music with elements of hard rock and hip-hop. "She has revitalized Nashville," declared Grady, president of Sony Music. Jon Bream of the Minneapolis *Star Tribune* wrote, "Wilson offers an uncompromising blend of Skynyrd, Strait, and cojones that will rock you like NASCAR, but comfort you like Oprah." Marc Oswald, one of Wilson's managers, commented on another unique aspect of her style: "She reminded everyone that they should be in the music business, not the image business. It has woken a lot of people up." Industry executives and reviewers alike have attested to her unique connection with her audience. Wilson seemed "closer to the audience than any performing musician out there today," said Grady. "She has no problem relating, and they have no problem identifying back with her. It's about empowerment."

"Redneck Woman" was released as a single in April 2004. When the song rose to No. 1 in May, Wilson became the first solo female singer to top the *Billboard* Hot Country Songs chart in over two years. She also had the fastest-rising debut single on country music charts since LeAnn Rimes released "Blue" in 1996. Fans clearly responded to the authenticity of "Redneck Woman," which reflected Wilson's hard-living background and her personal philosophy of "being honest and true to yourself." "I talk all the time about my idols being Loretta Lynn and Tanya Tucker and Patsy Cline and people like that. And I knew when I listened to a Loretta Lynn record that I was going to hear stories that were real. I hung on every word that came out of her mouth because I knew that she had lived that."

—— " ——

"To me, being a redneck woman means being a strong woman," Wilson said. "It's about holding your head up no matter what is happening. I know the term used to have other meanings, but to me it's just another way of saying country."

—— " ——

Here for the Party

Wilson's first album, *Here for the Party,* was originally scheduled for release in July 2004, but the success of "Redneck Woman" caused Sony to push the date forward to May 2004. The album debuted at No. 2 on the *Billboard* 200 pop chart and No. 1 on the *Billboard* Top Country Albums chart, where it remained for nine consecutive weeks. It sold 227,000 copies in its opening week, breaking the sales record for a country music

album. *Here for the Party* became the bestselling country album of the year and the fifth bestselling album overall for 2004 with just under three million copies sold by year's end. These sales figures made Wilson the top-selling debut artist of any genre in 2004. Meanwhile, videos from *Here for the Party* appeared regularly on Country Music Television (CMT), most notably "When I Think about Cheatin'" and "Redneck Woman." The latter video features cameo appearances by Tanya Tucker, Big & Rich, Kid Rock, and Hank Williams Jr.

Here for the Party became an instant hit with audiences and critics. One ex-planation for the record's popularity was offered by radio executive Jessie Scott in an interview on National Public Radio. "Gretchen Wilson is maybe single-handedly bringing some soul back to country," Scott said. "And the reason why I say that is so much of what's come down over the course of the last several years has been so pop that it's soulless and it's homogenized. And this is fresh and free and wonderful, and, you know, the message is great, too."

Wilson's phenomenal breakthrough continued into the summer and fall of 2004. A hit at dance clubs, the single "Here for the Party" nearly matched the success of "Redneck Woman" on both the pop and country charts. Wilson also began touring at major arenas around the country. She opened for the Brooks & Dunn and Montgomery Gentry tour in the summer of 2004. By August, Wilson began to notice big changes in her life. "I have probably made and spent a quarter of a million dollars in the last four months," she marveled. "That's more money than I could ever think about four months ago. All of a sudden, I have a corporation. I have people that work for me that I don't even know."

The music industry and country music fans showered Wilson with recognition at annual award ceremonies. In 2004, she won the Country Music Association's Horizon Award, which is given to the top new artist of the year; she also won an American Music Award for best new artist. In 2005, she won a Grammy Award for best female country vocal performance on "Redneck Woman." During this show, Wilson participated in a special tribute performance of Lynryd Skynryd's rock anthem "Free Bird" with Tim McGraw, Keith Urban, and current Lynryd Skynryd singer Johnny Van Zant. She also won two awards for best videos at the 2005 Country Music Television Awards.

All Jacked Up

With her phenomenal rise to fame behind her, Wilson turned her attention to her next album. "Fans obviously loved her 'what you see is what you get' approach to the debut project, so it only makes sense to give them more of what they want," advised Jon Anthony, program director of XM Satellite Radio's country music station. Wilson began working on her second album, although some industry experts cautioned that it was too soon for a follow-up record. According to Grady, the second album "is more about her. . . . The first record defined her but from songwriting to song selection to musician selecting to producing to sequencing, she has played a far larger role in this one." During the summer of 2005, Wilson was the opening act on Kenny Chesney's "A Place in the Sun" tour, during which she performed several songs from her then-unreleased second album.

Wilson released her second album, *All Jacked Up*, in September 2005. The record debuted at No. 1 on both the *Billboard* 200 and Top Country Albums charts, selling more than 264,000 copies during its first week. Wilson reinforced her rough-edged image with such songs as "Politically Uncorrect,"

"One Bud Wiser," "Skoal Ring," and "All Jacked Up," but she also included songs written by other artists to show another side of her talent. She performed the new ballad "I Don't Feel Like Loving You Today," written by Matraca Berg and Jim Collins, which she has cited as her favorite song on the album. She also included a hidden track, a cover of the Billie Holiday song "Good Morning, Heartache," which many critics considered an exciting demonstration of the range of her talent.

All Jacked Up was a more modest success than Wilson's debut album. Still, she was recognized with several awards at the annual awards ceremonies. In 2005, she won the Country Music Association Award for female vocalist of the year and the American Music Award for favorite female country artist. She also earned nominations for the 2006 Grammy Awards, the Country Music Televisions Awards, and the Academy of Country Music Awards, but she lost to the competition on all counts.

CONTROVERSY AND BACKLASH

Despite her popularity among fans and industry professionals, Wilson's candid subject matter, explicit song lyrics, and tough-woman persona have met with criticism. In 2005, her song "Skoal Ring" became controversial. Skoal is a brand of chewing tobacco, and a Skoal ring is a round mark left in the back pocket of those who regularly carry a can of snuff in their jeans pocket. In concert, Wilson began holding up a can of Skoal because many fans thought the song referred to a "skull ring." These performances drew notice from Tennessee's attorney general, who objected to what he called the "promotion of smokeless products, particularly as it related to the youth who attend [her] concerts and listen to [her] music." He asked her to "avoid glamorizing and normalizing the use of smokeless tobacco products" by discontinuing her practice of raising a can of Skoal smokeless tobacco during her concerts. Wilson complied with the attorney general's request. "I don't want kids out there to go buy Skoal and start dipping because Gretchen Wilson does it," she maintained. "I'm a mother, and I wouldn't push tobacco or alcohol at a child." She does chew tobacco, or "dip," a habit she started as a way to help her stop smoking cigarettes. "I traded one evil for another," she confessed. "To be honest, I've realized now that quitting smoking was easier than quitting dipping. But I will eventually be free of nicotine. I know it."

"I'm just a simple, ordinary woman. I think that's a lot of the reason why people have really connected with me. I am just like them."

The lyrics of other songs have also been considered objectionable by some listeners, to which Wilson has consistently responded, "I don't apologize for the lyrics." She has often cited Loretta Lynn as a major influence on her career because "she spoke her mind, which isn't as common as you might think in the music business. Loretta put things into songs that no woman had ever said at that time." Wilson has said that success has not changed her. During a 2006 interview with "60 Minutes" correspondent Ed Bradley, she remarked, "I'm just a simple, ordinary woman. I think that's a lot of the reason why people have really connected with me. I am just like them."

Despite such controversy, Wilson has continued to impress her fans. In 2006, She was the headline act for the "Redneck Revolution" tour, traveling with Johnny and Donnie VanZant, formerly of Lynyrd Skynyrd and .38 Special, and Blaine Larsen. She described being the headline act on a tour

Wilson performing onstage in New York City, 2005.

as "a whole lot more pressure, a whole lot more excitement. You get all the stage, you get all the drama, you get to step on stage every night knowing that those people came to see you and not the act after you." Commenting on the high energy level of her concerts, she said, "My show is a little more like a rock show, probably, compared to other females in country music. I've got pyro and an incredible AC/DC light show going on, and we're blowing stuff up, and it's loud and crazy and it's definitely rock 'n' roll." As for her fans, Wilson said, "They're unbelievable. They're on their feet from the moment the intro tape starts until the curtain comes down, and they sing along with every word to songs that haven't even been released. It's amazing."

HOME AND FAMILY

Shortly after she arrived in Nashville, Wilson began a relationship with Mike Penner, a nightclub owner. In 2001 they had a daughter, Grace. The couple never married and parted ways in 2005. Wilson makes her home with her daughter, Grace, and her mother, Christine Heuer. They live in a 4,000-square-foot house on a 17-acre estate outside Nashville, complete with a six-stall barn and nine animals.

HOBBIES AND OTHER INTERESTS

Wilson's hobbies include fishing, driving a four-wheeler, and spending time with her daughter. She has also expressed an interest in charitable activities. For example, on September 10, 2005, she performed at the Mississippi Coliseum in Jackson, Mississippi, as part of a concert to benefit victims of Hurricane Katrina. MTV, VH1, and CMT broadcast the Hurricane Katrina Relief concert, and proceeds were donated to CMT's "One Country," a new campaign that raises money for natural disaster relief. Money from this fund is disbursed among the American Red Cross, America's Second Harvest, Habitat for Humanity, the USA Boys & Girls Clubs, and Hands on America.

RECORDINGS

Here for the Party, 2004
All Jacked Up, 2005
Gretchen Wilson: Undressed (DVD), 2006

HONORS AND AWARDS

Horizon Award (Country Music Association): 2004
American Music Award: 2004, Favorite Breakthrough New Artist; 2005, Favorite Female Country Artist
Grammy Award (The Recording Academy): 2005, Best Female Country Vocal Performance, for "Redneck Woman"
Country Music Television Awards: 2005 (two awards), Best Breakthrough Video for "Redneck Woman" and Best Female Video for "When I Think about Cheatin'"
Academy of Country Music Awards: 2005 (two awards), Top Female Vocalist and Top New Artist
Country Music Association Award: 2005, Female Vocalist of the Year

FURTHER READING

Books

Contemporary Musicians, Vol. 52, 2005

Periodicals

Billboard, Sep. 24, 2005, p.50
Boston Globe, May 30, 2004, p.N1
Chicago Tribune, May 7, 2004, Tempo section, p.1
Entertainment Weekly, May 14, 2004, p.38; Oct. 29, 2004, p.14; Apr. 22, 2005, p.20
Los Angeles Times, Jan. 22, 2006, p.E1
New York Times, May 30, 2004, section 2, p.25
St. Louis Post-Dispatch, May 9, 2004, p.F1; May 27, 2004, p.23; Sep. 25, 2005, p.F1
USA Today, June 17, 2004, p.D1; Sep. 28, 2005, p.D6

Online Articles

http://www.allmusic.com
(All Music Guide, "Gretchen Wilson," undated)
http://www.npr.org
(National Public Radio, All Things Considered, "'Redneck Woman' Rules Country Charts," May 31, 2004)

Online Databases

Biography Resource Center Online, 2006, article from *Contemporary Musicians,* 2005

ADDRESS

Gretchen Wilson
Sony Music Nashville
1400 18th Ave., South
Nashville, TN 37212

WORLD WIDE WEB SITES

http://www.gretchenwilson.com
http://www.gretchenontour.com
http://www.muzikmafia.com

Photo and Illustration Credits

Carol Bellamy/Photos: U.N. Photo/Stephenie Hollyman (p. 11); Nancy R. Schiff/Hulton Archive/Getty Images (p. 14); Shah Marai/AFP/Getty Images (p. 16); AP Images (p. 18).

Miri Ben-Ari/Photos: Adam Weiss/copyright © 2003 Universal Music Group (p. 22); Frank Micelotta/Getty Images (p. 25). CD cover: THE HIP-HOP VIOLINIST copyright © 2003 Universal Music Group.

Black Eyed Peas/Photos: Christian Lantry/copyright © 2003 Universal Music Group (p. 31); Scott Gries/Getty Images (p. 36); Albert Watson/copyright © 2003 Universal Music Group (p. 43). CD covers: ELEPHUNK and MONKEY BUSINESS copyright © 2003 Universal Music Group.

Bono/Photos: NewsCom.com (p. 46); Tim Mosenfelder/ImageDirect/Getty Images (p. 50); Anton Corbijn/copyright © 2006 Universal Music Group (p. 58); AP Images (p. 60). CD covers: HOW TO DISMANTLE AN ATOMIC BOMB (Interscope) copyright © 2006 Universal Music Group; THE JOSHUA TREE (Island) copyright © 2006 Universal Music; WAR (Island) copyright © 2006 Universal Music Group. Front cover: Jo Hale/Getty Images.

Kelsie Buckley/Photos: AP Images (pp. 68, 71, 73).

Dale Chihuly/Photos: Dale Chihuly photo/Russell Johnson (p. 76); Chihuly and team in hotshop, Seattle, Wash. photo/Russell Johnson (p. 80); *Shell Pink Basket Set with Oxblood Wraps*, 1995, 9 x 22 x 22", photo/Dick Busher (p. 83); *White Seaform with Black Lip Wraps*, 1990, 14 x 25 x 19", photo/Teresa N. Rishel (p. 85); *Macchia Forest*, 2002 photo/Teresa N. Rishel (p. 87); *Gilded Silver and Aquamarine Chandelier*, 2000, 96 x 102", photo/Jan Cook (p. 88).

Neda DeMayo/Photos: Mark Muntean (p. 92); Frank Staub (pp. 95, 100); Andrea Maki (p. 98).

Dakota Fanning/Photos: Susy Wood/Paramount Pictures (p. 103); Lorey Sebastian/copyright © 2001 New Line Cinema (p. 106); Melinda Sue Gordon/copyright © 2003 Universal Studios and DreamWorks LLC (p. 109, top); copyright © 2003 Metro-Goldwyn-Mayer Pictures, Inc. (p. 109, middle); Joe Lederer/TM & copyright © DreamWorks LLC (p. 109, bottom).

Green Day/Photos: Eva Mueller (front cover, p. 113); Ken Schles/Time Life Pictures/Getty Images (p. 115); NBC Universal Photo/Paul Drinkwater (p. 121); Marina Chavez (p. 126). CD covers: DOOKIE and AMERICAN IDIOT copyright © 1998-2006 Warner/Elektra/ Atlantic Corporation.

Freddie Highmore/Photos: Warner Bros. Pictures (pp. 130, 134, 136); Miramax Films (p. 132).

Russel Honoré/Photos: AP Images (p. 139); Justin Sullivan/Getty Images (p. 143); NOAA/ Getty Images (p. 144); Paul J. Richards/AFP/Getty Images (p. 146); Nicholas Kamm/AFP/ Getty Images (p. 148).

Tim Howard/Photos: Matthew Peters/Manchester United/Getty Images (p. 152); Chris Trotman/Getty Images (p. 156); John Peters/Manchester United/Getty Images (p. 158); Simon Bellis/Reuters/Landov (p. 160).

Cynthia Kadohata/Photos: AP Images (p. 164); George Miyamoto (p. 168). Covers: KIRA-KIRA (Atheneum/Simon & Schuster) copyright © 2004 by Cynthia Kadohata. Jacket photograph copyright © 2004 by Julia Kuskin; WEEDFLOWER (Atheneum/ Simon & Schuster) copyright © 2006 by Cynthia Kadohata. Jacket photographs and photo-illustration copyright © 2006 by Kamil Vojnar.

Coretta Scott King/Photos: NewsCom.com (p. 176); John Vacha/FPG/Getty Images (p. 178); AP Images (front cover, pp. 181, 184, 187, 192); courtesy Ronald Reagan Library (p. 191). Cover: MY LIFE WITH MARTIN LUTHER KING, JR. (Henry Holt and Company) copyright © 1969 by Coretta Scott King. Revised edition copyright © 1993 by Coretta Scott King.

Rachel McAdams/Photos: copyright © 2005 Richard Cartwright/New Line Productions (pp. 199, 208); Michael Gibson/TM & copyright © 2004 by Paramount Pictures (p. 204). DVD cover: THE NOTEBOOK copyright © 2004 New Line Productions, Inc. Copyright © 2005 New Line Home Entertainment, Inc.

Cesar Millan/Photos: copyright © National Geographic Channel (pp. 213, 216, 219); Nicholas Ellingsworth/copyright © MPH Entertainment (p. 220). Cover: CESAR'S WAY (Harmony/Crown) copyright © 2006 by Cesar Millan and Melissa Jo Peltier. Jacket copyright © 2006 by Harmony Books.

Steve Nash/Photos: Jeff Gross/Getty Images (p. 224); Otto Greule, Jr./Getty Images (p. 226); AP Images (pp. 229, 231, 236); Robert Galbraith/Reuters/Landov (p. 233).

Nick Park/Photos: courtesy DreamWorks Distribution LLC (pp. 240, 244); copyright © Richard Keith Wolff/Retna (p. 246); AP Images (p. 248); courtesy of DreamWorks Pictures (front cover, p. 250); courtesy DreamWorks Animation SKG. Copyright © and TM Aardman Animations Ltd. (p. 253).

Rosa Parks/Photos: William Philpott/Getty Images (front cover, p. 258); Don Craven/ Time Life Pictures/Getty Images (pp. 261, 266); AP Images (p. 264); William J. Clinton Presidential Library (p. 268); Mandel Ngan/AFP/Getty Images (p. 271); Staff Sgt. Earle B. Wilson, Jr./Photo courtesy of U.S. Army (p. 273).

Danica Patrick/Photos: Donald Miralle/Getty Images (p. 276); AP Images (p. 278); Frank Polich/Reuters/Landov (p. 282); Brent Smith/Reuters/Landov (p. 285). Front cover: NewsCom.com.

Jorge Ramos/Photos: Rayo/HarperCollins Publishers (p. 288); Univision (p. 292); William J. Clinton Presidential Library (p. 296). Cover: NO BORDERS (Rayo/Harper Collins Publishers) copyright © 2002 by Jorge Ramos. Translation copyright © 2002 by Patricia Duncan.

Ben Roethlisberger/Photos: AP Images (pp. 302, 305, 307, 313); Grant Halverson/Getty Images (p. 309). Front cover: David Drapkin/Getty Images.

Lil' Romeo/Photos: Nickelodeon/David Ellingsen (p. 318, 324); Tim Alexander/copyright © 2003 Universal Music Group (p. 320); Mike Heffner/Getty Images (p. 327). CD cover: LIL' ROMEO (p) & copyright © 2001 Soulja Music Entertainment/Priority Records LLC.

Cumulative General Index

This cumulative index includes names, occupations, nationalities, and ethnic and minority origins that pertain to all individuals profiled in *Biography Today* since the debut of the series in 1992.

Places of Birth Index

The following index lists the places of birth for the individuals profiled in *Biography Today*. Places of birth are entered under state, province, and/or country.

Alabama
Aaron, Hank – *Mobile* . . . . Sport V.1
Allen, Tori – *Auburn* . . . . Sport V.9
Barkley, Charles – *Leeds* . . . . Apr 92
Benjamin, Regina – *Mobile* . . . . Science V.9
Flowers, Vonetta – *Birmingham* . . Sport V.8
Fuller, Millard – *Lanett* . . . . Apr 03
Hamm, Mia – *Selma* . . . . Sport V.2
Hurston, Zora Neale
   – *Notasulga* . . . . Author V.6
Jackson, Bo – *Bessemer* . . . . Jan 92
Jemison, Mae – *Decatur* . . . . Oct 92
Johnson, Angela – *Tuskegee* . . . . Author V.6
Johnson, Lonnie – *Mobile* . . . . . Science V.4
King, Coretta Scott – *Heiberger* . . . . . Sep 06
Lee, Harper – *Monroeville* . . . . . . Author V.9
Lewis, Carl – *Birmingham* . . . . Sep 96
Lewis, John – *Pike County* . . . . Jan 03
Parks, Rosa – *Tuskegee* . . . . . Apr 92; Apr 06
Rice, Condoleezza – *Birmingham* . . . Apr 02
Satcher, David – *Anniston* . . . . Sep 98
Wallace, Ben – *White Hall* . . . . Jan 05
Whitestone, Heather – *Dothan* . . . . . Apr 95
Wiles, Deborah – *Mobile* . . . . . . Author V.18
Wilson, Edward O.
   – *Birmingham* . . . . Science V.8

Alaska
Brooks, Vincent – *Anchorage* . . . . Sep 03
Schilling, Curt – *Anchorage* . . . . Sep 05

Algeria
Boulmerka, Hassiba
   – *Constantine* . . . . Sport V.1

Angola
Savimbi, Jonas – *Munhango* . . . WorLdr V.2

Arizona
Bennington, Chester – *Phoenix* . . . . . . Jan 04
Branch, Michelle – *Flagstaff* . . . . PerfArt V.3
Chavez, Cesar – *Yuma* . . . . Sep 93
Chavez, Julz – *Yuma* . . . . Sep 02
Farmer, Nancy – *Phoenix* . . . . . . Author V.6

Moreno, Arturo R. – *Tucson* . . . Business V.1
Morrison, Sam – *Flagstaff* . . . . Sep 97
Murray, Ty – *Phoenix* . . . . Sport V.7
Strug, Kerri – *Tucson* . . . . Sep 96

Arkansas
Bates, Daisy – *Huttig* . . . . Apr 00
Clinton, Bill – *Hope* . . . . Jul 92
Clinton, Chelsea – *Little Rock* . . . . . . Apr 96
Grisham, John – *Jonesboro* . . . . . Author V.1
Holmes, Priest – *Fort Smith* . . . . Apr 05
Johnson, John – *Arkansas City* . . . . . . Jan 97
Pippen, Scottie – *Hamburg* . . . . Oct 92

Australia
Beachley, Layne – *Sydney* . . . . Sport V.9
Freeman, Cathy – *Mackay,*
   Queensland . . . . Jan 01
Irwin, Steve – *Victoria* . . . . Science V.7
Norman, Greg – *Mt. Isa, Queensland* Jan 94
Travers, P.L. – *Maryborough,*
   Queensland . . . . Author V.2
Webb, Karrie – *Ayr, Queensland* . . Sport V.5

Austria
Bemelmans, Ludwig – *Meran* . . Author V.16

Belgium
Clijsters, Kim – *Bilzen* . . . . Apr 04

Bosnia-Herzogovina
Filipovic, Zlata – *Sarajevo* . . . . Sep 94

Brazil
da Silva, Fabiola – *Sao Paulo* . . . . . Sport V.9
Mendes, Chico – *Xapuri, Acre* . . WorLdr V.1
Pelé – *Tres Coracoes,*
   Minas Gerais . . . . Sport V.1

Bulgaria
Christo – *Gabrovo* . . . . Sep 96

Burma
Aung San Suu Kyi – *Rangoon* . . . . . . Apr 96
Ka Hsaw Wa – *Rangoon* . . . . WorLdr V.3

California
Abdul, Paula – *Van Nuys* . . . . Jan 92
Adams, Ansel – *San Francisco* . . . . Artist V.1

Birthday Index

517

BIRTHDAY INDEX

Biography Today

General Series

Biography Today **General Series** includes a unique combination of current biographical profiles that teachers and librarians — and the readers themselves — tell us are most appealing. The **General Series** is available as a 3-issue subscription; hardcover annual cumulation; or subscription plus cumulation.

Within the **General Series**, your readers will find a variety of sketches about:

- Authors
- Musicians
- Political leaders
- Sports figures
- Movie actresses & actors
- Cartoonists
- Scientists
- Astronauts
- TV personalities
- and the movers & shakers in many other fields!

"*Biography Today* will be useful in elementary and middle school libraries and in public library children's collections where there is a need for biographies of current personalities. High schools serving reluctant readers may also want to consider a subscription."
— *Booklist,* American Library Association

"Highly recommended for the young adult audience. Readers will delight in the accessible, energetic, tell-all style; teachers, librarians, and parents will welcome the clever format [and] intelligent and informative text. It should prove especially useful in motivating 'reluctant' readers or literate nonreaders."
— *MultiCultural Review*

"Written in a friendly, almost chatty tone, the profiles offer quick, objective information. While coverage of current figures makes *Biography Today* a useful reference tool, an appealing format and wide scope make it a fun resource to browse." — *School Library Journal*

"The best source for current information at a level kids can understand."
— Kelly Bryant, School Librarian, Carlton, OR

"Easy for kids to read. We love it! Don't want to be without it."
— Lynn McWhirter, School Librarian, Rockford, IL

ONE-YEAR SUBSCRIPTION

- 3 softcover issues, 6" x 9"
- Published in January, April, and September
- 1-year subscription, list price $62. **School and library price $60**
- 150 pages per issue
- 10 profiles per issue
- Contact sources for additional information
- Cumulative Names Index

HARDBOUND ANNUAL CUMULATION

- Sturdy 6" x 9" hardbound volume
- Published in December
- List price $69. **School and library price $62 per volume**
- 450 pages per volume
- 30 profiles — includes all profiles found in softcover issues for that calendar year
- Cumulative General Index, Places of Birth Index, and Bithday Index

SUBSCRIPTION AND CUMULATION COMBINATION

- $99 for 3 softcover issues plus the hardbound volume

For Cumulative General, Places of Birth, and Birthday Indexes, please see www.biographytoday.com.

1992

Paula Abdul
Andre Agassi
Kirstie Alley
Terry Anderson
Roseanne Arnold
Isaac Asimov
James Baker
Charles Barkley
Larry Bird
Judy Blume
Berke Breathed
Garth Brooks
Barbara Bush
George Bush
Fidel Castro
Bill Clinton
Bill Cosby
Diana, Princess of Wales
Shannen Doherty
Elizabeth Dole
David Duke
Gloria Estefan
Mikhail Gorbachev
Steffi Graf
Wayne Gretzky
Matt Groening
Alex Haley
Hammer
Martin Handford
Stephen Hawking
Hulk Hogan
Saddam Hussein
Lee Iacocca
Bo Jackson
Mae Jemison
Peter Jennings
Steven Jobs
John Paul II
Magic Johnson
Michael Jordon
Jackie Joyner-Kersee
Spike Lee
Mario Lemieux
Madeleine L'Engle
Jay Leno
Yo-Yo Ma
Nelson Mandela
Wynton Marsalis
Thurgood Marshall
Ann Martin
Barbara McClintock
Emily Arnold McCully
Antonia Novello

Sandra Day O'Connor
Rosa Parks
Jane Pauley
H. Ross Perot
Luke Perry
Scottie Pippen
Colin Powell
Jason Priestley
Queen Latifah
Yitzhak Rabin
Sally Ride
Pete Rose
Nolan Ryan
H. Norman
    Schwarzkopf
Jerry Seinfeld
Dr. Seuss
Gloria Steinem
Clarence Thomas
Chris Van Allsburg
Cynthia Voigt
Bill Watterson
Robin Williams
Oprah Winfrey
Kristi Yamaguchi
Boris Yeltsin

1993

Maya Angelou
Arthur Ashe
Avi
Kathleen Battle
Candice Bergen
Boutros Boutros-Ghali
Chris Burke
Dana Carvey
Cesar Chavez
Henry Cisneros
Hillary Rodham Clinton
Jacques Cousteau
Cindy Crawford
Macaulay Culkin
Lois Duncan
Marian Wright Edelman
Cecil Fielder
Bill Gates
Sara Gilbert
Dizzy Gillespie
Al Gore
Cathy Guisewite
Jasmine Guy
Anita Hill
Ice-T
Darci Kistler

k.d. lang
Dan Marino
Rigoberta Menchu
Walter Dean Myers
Martina Navratilova
Phyllis Reynolds Naylor
Rudolf Nureyev
Shaquille O'Neal
Janet Reno
Jerry Rice
Mary Robinson
Winona Ryder
Jerry Spinelli
Denzel Washington
Keenen Ivory Wayans
Dave Winfield

1994

Tim Allen
Marian Anderson
Mario Andretti
Ned Andrews
Yasir Arafat
Bruce Babbitt
Mayim Bialik
Bonnie Blair
Ed Bradley
John Candy
Mary Chapin Carpenter
Benjamin Chavis
Connie Chung
Beverly Cleary
Kurt Cobain
F.W. de Klerk
Rita Dove
Linda Ellerbee
Sergei Fedorov
Zlata Filipovic
Daisy Fuentes
Ruth Bader Ginsburg
Whoopi Goldberg
Tonya Harding
Melissa Joan Hart
Geoff Hooper
Whitney Houston
Dan Jansen
Nancy Kerrigan
Alexi Lalas
Charlotte Lopez
Wilma Mankiller
Shannon Miller
Toni Morrison
Richard Nixon
Greg Norman
Severo Ochoa

River Phoenix
Elizabeth Pine
Jonas Salk
Richard Scarry
Emmitt Smith
Will Smith
Steven Spielberg
Patrick Stewart
R.L. Stine
Lewis Thomas
Barbara Walters
Charlie Ward
Steve Young
Kim Zmeskal

1995

Troy Aikman
Jean-Bertrand Aristide
Oksana Baiul
Halle Berry
Benazir Bhutto
Jonathan Brandis
Warren E. Burger
Ken Burns
Candace Cameron
Jimmy Carter
Agnes de Mille
Placido Domingo
Janet Evans
Patrick Ewing
Newt Gingrich
John Goodman
Amy Grant
Jesse Jackson
James Earl Jones
Julie Krone
David Letterman
Rush Limbaugh
Heather Locklear
Reba McEntire
Joe Montana
Cosmas Ndeti
Hakeem Olajuwon
Ashley Olsen
Mary-Kate Olsen
Jennifer Parkinson
Linus Pauling
Itzhak Perlman
Cokie Roberts
Wilma Rudolph
Salt 'N' Pepa
Barry Sanders
William Shatner
Elizabeth George
    Speare

Dr. Benjamin Spock
Jonathan Taylor
  Thomas
Vicki Van Meter
Heather Whitestone
Pedro Zamora

1996

Aung San Suu Kyi
Boyz II Men
Brandy
Ron Brown
Mariah Carey
Jim Carrey
Larry Champagne III
Christo
Chelsea Clinton
Coolio
Bob Dole
David Duchovny
Debbi Fields
Chris Galeczka
Jerry Garcia
Jennie Garth
Wendy Guey
Tom Hanks
Alison Hargreaves
Sir Edmund Hillary
Judith Jamison
Barbara Jordan
Annie Leibovitz
Carl Lewis
Jim Lovell
Mickey Mantle
Lynn Margulis
Iqbal Masih
Mark Messier
Larisa Oleynik
Christopher Pike
David Robinson
Dennis Rodman
Selena
Monica Seles
Don Shula
Kerri Strug
Tiffani-Amber Thiessen
Dave Thomas
Jaleel White

1997

Madeleine Albright
Marcus Allen
Gillian Anderson
Rachel Blanchard
Zachery Ty Bryan
Adam Ezra Cohen
Claire Danes
Celine Dion
Jean Driscoll
Louis Farrakhan
Ella Fitzgerald
Harrison Ford
Bryant Gumbel
John Johnson
Michael Johnson
Maya Lin
George Lucas
John Madden
Bill Monroe
Alanis Morissette
Sam Morrison
Rosie O'Donnell
Muammar el-Qaddafi
Christopher Reeve
Pete Sampras
Pat Schroeder
Rebecca Sealfon
Tupac Shakur
Tabitha Soren
Herbert Tarvin
Merlin Tuttle
Mara Wilson

1998

Bella Abzug
Kofi Annan
Neve Campbell
Sean Combs (Puff
  Daddy)
Dalai Lama (Tenzin
  Gyatso)
Diana, Princess of Wales
Leonardo DiCaprio
Walter E. Diemer
Ruth Handler
Hanson
Livan Hernandez
Jewel
Jimmy Johnson
Tara Lipinski
Jody-Anne Maxwell
Dominique Moceanu
Alexandra Nechita

Brad Pitt
LeAnn Rimes
Emily Rosa
David Satcher
Betty Shabazz
Kordell Stewart
Shinichi Suzuki
Mother Teresa
Mike Vernon
Reggie White
Kate Winslet

1999

Ben Affleck
Jennifer Aniston
Maurice Ashley
Kobe Bryant
Bessie Delany
Sadie Delany
Sharon Draper
Sarah Michelle Gellar
John Glenn
Savion Glover
Jeff Gordon
David Hampton
Lauryn Hill
King Hussein
Lynn Johnston
Shari Lewis
Oseola McCarty
Mark McGwire
Slobodan Milosevic
Natalie Portman
J.K. Rowling
Frank Sinatra
Gene Siskel
Sammy Sosa
John Stanford
Natalia Toro
Shania Twain
Mitsuko Uchida
Jesse Ventura
Venus Williams

2000

Christina Aguilera
K.A. Applegate
Lance Armstrong
Backstreet Boys
Daisy Bates
Harry Blackmun
George W. Bush
Carson Daly
Ron Dayne
Henry Louis Gates, Jr.
Doris Haddock
  (Granny D)
Jennifer Love Hewitt
Chamique Holdsclaw
Katie Holmes
Charlayne Hunter-Gault
Johanna Johnson
Craig Kielburger
John Lasseter
Peyton Manning
Ricky Martin
John McCain
Walter Payton
Freddie Prinze, Jr.
Viviana Risca
Briana Scurry
George Thampy
CeCe Winans

2001

Jessica Alba
Christiane Amanpour
Drew Barrymore
Jeff Bezos
Destiny's Child
Dale Earnhardt
Carly Fiorina
Aretha Franklin
Cathy Freeman
Tony Hawk
Faith Hill
Kim Dae-jung
Madeleine L'Engle
Mariangela Lisanti
Frankie Muniz
*N Sync
Ellen Ochoa
Jeff Probst
Julia Roberts
Carl T. Rowan
Britney Spears
Chris Tucker
Lloyd D. Ward
Alan Webb
Chris Weinke

2002

Aaliyah
Osama bin Laden
Mary J. Blige
Aubyn Burnside
Aaron Carter
Julz Chavez
Dick Cheney
Hilary Duff
Billy Gilman
Rudolph Giuliani
Brian Griese
Jennifer Lopez
Dave Mirra
Dineh Mohajer
Leanne Nakamura
Daniel Radcliffe
Condoleezza Rice
Marla Runyan
Ruth Simmons
Mattie Stepanek
J.R.R. Tolkien
Barry Watson
Tyrone Willingham
Elijah Wood

2003

Yolanda Adams
Olivia Bennett
Mildred Benson
Alexis Bledel
Barry Bonds
Vincent Brooks
Laura Bush
Amanda Bynes
Kelly Clarkson
Vin Diesel
Eminem
Michele Forman
Vicente Fox
Millard Fuller
Josh Hartnett
Dolores Huerta
Sarah Hughes
Enrique Iglesias
Jeanette Lee
John Lewis
Nicklas Lidstrom

Clint Mathis
Donovan McNabb
Nelly
Andy Roddick
Gwen Stefani
Emma Watson
Meg Whitman
Reese Witherspoon
Yao Ming

2004

Natalie Babbitt
David Beckham
Francie Berger
Tony Blair
Orlando Bloom
Kim Clijsters
Celia Cruz
Matel Dawson, Jr.
The Donnas
Tim Duncan
Shirin Ebadi
Carla Hayden
Ashton Kutcher
Lisa Leslie
Linkin Park
Lindsay Lohan
Irene D. Long
John Mayer
Mandy Moore
Thich Nhat Hanh
OutKast
Raven
Ronald Reagan
Keanu Reeves
Ricardo Sanchez
Brian Urlacher
Alexa Vega
Michelle Wie
Will Wright

2005

Kristen Bell
Jack Black
Sergey Brin & Larry
 Page
Adam Brody
Chris Carrabba
Johnny Depp
Eve
Jennie Finch
James Forman
Wally Funk
Cornelia Funke

Bethany Hamilton
Anne Hathaway
Priest Holmes
T.D. Jakes
John Paul II
Toby Keith
Alison Krauss
Wangari Maathai
Karen Mitchell-
 Raptakis
Queen Noor
Violet Palmer
Gloria Rodriguez
Carlos Santana
Antonin Scalia
Curtis Schilling
Maria Sharapova
Ashlee Simpson
Donald Trump
Ben Wallace

2006

Carol Bellamy
Miri Ben-Ari
Black Eyed Peas
Bono
Kelsie Buckley
Dale Chihuly
Neda DeMayo
Dakota Fanning
Green Day
Freddie Highmore
Russel Honoré
Tim Howard
Cynthia Kadohata
Coretta Scott King
Rachel McAdams
Cesar Millan
Steve Nash
Nick Park
Rosa Parks
Danica Patrick
Jorge Ramos
Ben Roethlisberger
Lil' Romeo
Adam Sandler
Russell Simmons
Jamie Lynn Spears
Jon Stewart
Joss Stone
Hannah Teter
Brenda Villa
Tyler James Williams
Gretchen Wilson

Order Annual Sets of *Biography Today* and Save Up to 20% Off the Regular Price!

Now, you can save time and money by purchasing *Biography Today* in Annual Sets! Save up to 20% off the regular price and get every single biography we publish in a year. Billed upon publication of the first volume, subsequent volumes are shipped throughout the year upon publication. Keep your *Biography Today* library current and complete with Annual Sets!

Place a standing order for annual sets and receive an additional 10% off!

Regular price $239
2006 or 2005 Annual Set $192
You Save $47

Biography Today 2006 Annual Set

7 volumes. 0-7808-0940-8. Annual set, $192. Includes:

2006 subscription (3 softcover issues);
2006 Hardbound Annual; Authors, Vol. 18;
Scientists & Inventors, Vol. 11; Sports, Vol. 14

Biography Today 2005 Annual Set

7 volumes. 0-7808-0782-0. Annual set, $192. Includes:

2005 subscription (3 softcover issues);
2005 Hardbound Annual; Authors, Vol. 17;
Scientists & Inventors, Vol. 10; Sports, Vol. 13

Regular price $335
2004 or 2003 Annual Set $268
You Save $67

Biography Today 2004 Annual Set

8 volumes. 0-7808-0731-6. Annual set, $268. Includes:

2004 Hardbound Annual; Authors, Vols. 15 and 16;
Business Leaders, Vol. 1; Performing Artists, Vol. 3;
Scientists & Inventors, Vol. 9; Sports, Vols. 11 and 12

Biography Today 2003 Annual Set

8 volumes. 0-7808-0730-8. Annual set, $268. Includes:

2003 Hardbound Annual; Authors, Vols. 13 and 14;
Performing Artists, Vols. 1 and 2;
Scientists & Inventors, Vol. 8; Sports, Vols. 9 and 10

Regular price $297
2002 Annual Set $237
You Save $60

Biography Today 2002 Annual Set

7 volumes. 0-7808-0729-4. Annual set, $237. Includes:

2002 Hardbound Annual; Authors, Vols. 11 and 12;
Scientists & Inventors, Vols. 6 and 7; Sports, Vols. 7 and 8